Fabrication for Theatre and Entertainment

Fabrication for Theatre and Entertainment: Metals is a reference guide covering the characteristics of metal most relevant to the entertainment industry, layout methods for fabricators, and the tooling and machinery used to fabricate with those products.

This volume provides information that is specific to the types of projects encountered in the entertainment field and offers guidance to entertainment fabricators to ensure a repeatable accurate finished product. The book aims to introduce as many options as possible to help readers decide what the best tools and techniques are to tackle their most frequent challenges or, when faced with a new challenge, to help decide which tool or technique might be the best solution.

Fabrication for Theatre and Entertainment: Metals is intended as a reference for technical designers, technical directors, shop managers, and prop or scenic fabricators working in various parts of the entertainment industry such as film, television, theatre, themed entertainment, exhibits, and immersive installation art.

To access full-color versions of the artwork, visit www.routledge.com/9781032593210.

Michael O'Nele is the faculty Technical Director and an Associate Professor of Theatre at the University of Memphis, Department of Theatre & Dance. He believes that the art of technical direction is to transform imagination into reality, and that technology should be embraced as an artistic tool that provides theatre with new means of expression.

Fabrication for Theatre and Entertainment
Series Editor: Michael O'Nele

Fabrication for Theatre and Entertainment is a complete reference series for the process of fabricating with a range of materials and products for scenic and properties construction for theatre and entertainment arts.

The series covers lumber products, metals, polymers and non-traditional materials as well as layout methods for fabricators, and the tooling and machinery used to fabricate with lumber products including CNC applications unique to the industry. While there are references that demonstrate common scenic construction methods using lumber, this series includes a spectrum of materials and techniques used across a broader sample of entertainment genres. Readers will be introduced to a wide range of tools and techniques, which will allow them to tackle both common issues and new challenges creatively and effectively.

The series is intended as a resource for technical designers, technical directors, shop managers, master carpenters, and prop or scenic fabricators working in various parts of the entertainment industry, including film, television, theatre, themed entertainment, exhibits, and immersive installation art.

Fabrication for Theatre and Entertainment
Wood and Fiber Products
Michael O'Nele

Fabrication for Theatre and Entertainment
Metals
Michael O'Nele

Fabrication for Theatre and Entertainment

Metals

Michael O'Nele

NEW YORK AND LONDON

Designed cover image: Michael O'Nele

First published 2026
by Routledge
605 Third Avenue, New York, NY 10158

and by Routledge
4 Park Square, Milton Park, Abingdon, Oxon, OX14 4RN

Routledge is an imprint of the Taylor & Francis Group, an informa business

© 2026 Michael O'Nele

The right of Michael O'Nele to be identified as author of this work has been asserted in accordance with sections 77 and 78 of the Copyright, Designs and Patents Act 1988.

All rights reserved. No part of this book may be reprinted or reproduced or utilised in any form or by any electronic, mechanical, or other means, now known or hereafter invented, including photocopying and recording, or in any information storage or retrieval system, without permission in writing from the publishers.

For Product Safety Concerns and Information please contact our EU representative GPSR@taylorandfrancis.com. Taylor & Francis Verlag GmbH, Kaufingerstraße 24, 80331 München, Germany.

Trademark notice: Product or corporate names may be trademarks or registered trademarks, and are used only for identification and explanation without intent to infringe.

ISBN: 978-1-032-59322-7 (hbk)
ISBN: 978-1-032-59321-0 (pbk)
ISBN: 978-1-003-45417-5 (ebk)

DOI: 10.4324/9781003454175

Typeset in TimesTen
by KnowledgeWorks Global Ltd.

Access the Support Material: www.routledge.com/9781032593210

A huge thank you to all the mentors in my life who have helped me grow in my career and to my family who supported me through my life. I would not be where I am without them.

Contents

Acknowledgments ix
Online Resources xi

Introduction 1

1. **Measuring and Layout Tools for Metal Working** 3
2. **Metal Alloys** 13
3. **Steel Shapes and Applications** 25
4. **Aluminum Shapes and Applications** 49
5. **Hand Tools and Manual Machines** 63
6. **Power Tools** 93
7. **Machinery** 105
8. **Welding and Related Processes** 125
9. **Fastening** 163
10. **Blades, Bits, and Consumables** 177
11. **Techniques** 191
12. **Machining** 241
13. **Employee Safety** 271
14. **Physical Safety** 283
15. **Reference Sources** 291

Index 295

Acknowledgments

Special thanks to McNichols, HyComb USA, and Wilsonart for supplying product samples; to Adirondack Studios and Matt Jackson; to Nate Schreffler at ATOMIC; to Jake Lacher and Will Roche at Accurate Staging; to Derek Pendergrass at Meow Wolf for their support and the tours; to Erica Causi, Jake Lacher, and David Nofsinger for their contributions; finally to my students who have kept me on my toes all these years.

Online Resources

For those readers who may wish to access full-size, color versions of the images included in this volume, they are available at www.routledge.com/9781032593210.

Especially valuable are larger images of welding tips from Chapter 8, the demonstrations of techniques from Chapter 11, and the machining processes shown in Chapter 12.

Introduction

PURPOSE

This book is written primarily for use by carpenters, technical designers and shop managers in the entertainment industry. I have tried to include information that is relevant to film, television, theatre, themed entertainment, exhibits and immersive installation art. It is also my intent that the information is relevant to a great deal of the maker world since many of the tools and techniques used are similar or the same. While metal working may intimidate some fabricators unfamiliar with the process, starting with metal fabrication may be more attainable than the reader assumes. Most shops' first expansion into metal will be mild steel. This is because it can be done with a few basic power tools and a compact welder. A saw is the primary tool to cut long materials into usable pieces. An angle grinder can cut, notch, grind and finish. A compact, branded, wire-feed welder with shielding gas is a fairly low-cost piece of machinery that will last many, many years. Choosing one that can be upgraded with a spool gun at a later date expands the shop's future capabilities for working with aluminum.

Unlike the first volume in this series, this volume includes more focus on technique. Because there are many texts for wood fabrication in entertainment, the first volume focuses on expanding that knowledge in order to help shops, fabricators and managers grow their pool of solutions. There is not (to the author's knowledge) a volume focused on metal fabrication for entertainment that is still in print. There are many texts for welding, sheet metal fabrication and large steel structures, but there is no current book that distills this information in a way that is specific to the entertainment world. The author has endeavored to identify the materials, tools and techniques that are most relevant to the entertainment industry. The goal of this book is to help those interested in metal fabrication gain the knowledge they will need and aid educational and/or apprenticeship programs in the training of fabricators using methods common to various areas of the entertainment industry.

Why make the leap into metal fabrication? Metal has many unique properties that make it an excellent choice of material for many entertainment, scenic and props projects. The variety of alloys, shapes and other properties dramatically increases the ways project managers and makers can achieve a final product.

- Metal offers higher strength per size of member than wood and most other materials.
- The visual impacts of using metal include building open structures more easily, and the surface texture can be very smooth, subtly textured or have a perforated pattern while maintaining strength.
- There are so many section shapes that someone new to fabrication could be somewhat overwhelmed compared to lumber; this demonstrates just how many solutions are possible. Metal also offers unique solutions like grating, textured sheets, punched sheets and wire mesh.
- Metal is available in significantly longer lengths than lumber; up to lengths 24' for tube and 21' for pipe. Some shapes may be custom ordered up to 40' long.
- Many metal sections can be shaped relatively easily and hold a new form without compromising strength.
- The durability of metal, especially steel, is much higher than that of wood in most situations. Any unit that may be subject to rough handling will last much longer when made from metal. This is why almost all of the hardware used in the entertainment

DOI: 10.4324/9781003454175-1

industry is steel, and large buildings use steel for infrastructure. Durability is also the main reason metal is used for stage machines and mechanisms.
- Metals are much easier to reuse or recycle; shops can usually recoup a bit of money when metal is recycled.
- Hollow shapes can be used to house and/or hide hoses and cables while protecting them.
- Aluminum is especially good for outdoor exposure because it oxidizes quickly and becomes essentially self-sealing; the oxidation on aluminum doesn't wear off like the rust on steel. Steel works quite well outdoors too, as long as it is painted well. Both offer higher dimensional stability through temperature and humidity changes than lumber products.
- Paint cannot mimic polished metal (or chrome), although it can mimic distressed metal and wood quite well.

Many of the metal types and/or sizes mentioned herein are not applicable to large scenery, but are useful for their adjuncts. For example, a small aluminum square bar can be an excellent material for props and crafts, such as a complex chandelier that needs a curved structure with sharp edges or a decorative chain that may be used as stops for a trunk lid. Other materials that have a fairly narrow application have been excluded. For example, steel cable, for which there are very good existing references, is extensively used for rigging but rarely for other applications.

The information contained in this volume is based on the author's experience. He has made every effort to ensure the accuracy of this information. The author and publisher take no responsibility for the misapplication of the information contained herein. It is left to the reader to determine how applicable the techniques presented are to their individual process and how to implement them safely.

ABOUT THE AUTHOR

As a life-long maker of things, I intend this book to be about building and the tools used to do so. It also includes some information about painting and finishing of metals because the chemistry, prep and application can be quite different than wood applications. I hope it is a useful reference that can be used to compare and contrast the materials and machines fabricators use across the entertainment industry. It includes technical data and application information for tools and machinery from quality starter level (or compact and portable for those with small shops) to industrial versions that may be required for large facilities. It is hard to know what would help a shop/business grow if one is unaware of the options AND how they might solve problems. My hope is that the information included here will make that task easier.

As a professor of theatre for over 25 years and a theatrical Technical Director, I have spent a great deal of time with tools learning their ins and outs, as well as their pros and cons. Many of my students have graduated into other parts of the industry, from working on cruise ships to commercial scenic shops and even into immersive experiences. The skills learned in theatre have broad application, and I try to teach in a manner that helps students see that they are scalable. Rarely do we truly master a skill; there is almost always room to get better or to find an adjacent application for that knowledge. Over the years my interests have expanded, and I have found that many other experiences relate to my work in theatre. I have learned to be a blacksmith and use that shaping knowledge to make decorative hardware for scenery. I learned molding and casting in theatre and have expanded that knowledge into foundry work, where I have learned to cast aluminum, bronze and iron using almost the same techniques I would use to cast plaster. I now spend a good bit of time working as a historic preservationist for the Cumbres and Toltec Scenic Railroad, restoring buildings and rail cars. Many of the machining skills I have learned came from my peers in the historic preservation world. I work with everything from wood to plastics to metals as well as simple mechanisms to motors and hydraulics. As an educator, I want to introduce anyone new to being a creative fabricator to all that is possible and encourage them to keep exploring and expanding their skills. There are such an amazing variety of jobs in the entertainment world, from displays to things like car shows, themed entertainment and cruise ships, to local community theatre, and all of them are shorthanded and need creative makers to join them. If you loved LEGO® as a child and don't want to be an engineer (and even if you do!), the entertainment industry may be just the place for you. I want to show one small part of how these folks solve problems and make amazing products.

Chapter 1

Measuring and Layout Tools for Metal Working

While many tools for measuring and layout are used for a variety of materials, there are some that are particular to working with metal. As well, metal can be much harder to mark on than wood. This section is intended to help the reader determine which methods are best suited to a given project and/or material. For most projects, the techniques used will simply be adaptations of those used on other materials, such as wood. Only when the fabricator steps into machining does the methodology of measuring and layout really change from working with other materials. This is because machining often requires tolerances as fine as thousandths of an inch or tenths of a millimeter. These high tolerances will mostly be applied to measuring in that regard because marking at that level of precision is somewhat irrelevant except when marking end points. This chapter will introduce the reader to shared tools, metal-specific tools, and the adaptations that may be made when working with metal. The list of tools is not as extensive as those for working with wood products because the characteristics of metal are quite similar across varieties.

MEASURING

- Tape measure—Tape measures (or tape rules) are the "go to" tool for fabrication with almost any material because they are compact, easy to use, and relatively accurate. The addition of a magnetic tip makes working with steel even easier.
- Magnetic bench rule—These are quite handy because, unlike a desk rule, they do not slide around on a steel surface. They can also be used on a steel fence for quick measuring while cutting. The flexibility of the rule requires the user to ensure they are set in a straight line for accuracy.
- Steel desk/straight rule—These are excellent because they can be used for measuring and marking lines. A cork or rubber backing can be helpful to prevent movement on metal surfaces and helps keep ink off the edge, if used. Thicker straightedges that sit flush to the surface will be preferred if marking with a scribe; this prevents the tip of the scribe from drifting under a raised edge.
- Machinist rule—These are typically stainless steel, 6″ long and used for accurate measurements, though not as precise as calipers. They are usually divided down to either 32nds or 64ths of an inch, or .5 or 1 mm. These often have a sliding T-shaped clip that can be used as a hook rule, depth gauge or to mark a measurement.
- Saddle—These are L-shaped rules, usually made from aluminum, that wrap over the edge of the material along their long axis; these have a rule on both faces. They are excellent for working with square and rectangular sections, but their L-shape makes them equally useful on small round sections.
- Taper gauge—Similar to a step block, these vary in thickness (or width) with no steps and are usually marked in 1/10″ increments. They are primarily used for setting or measuring gaps before welding.
- Fillet gauge—These are typically sets of folding or stacking steel leaves that are used for checking the rough size of a fillet weld. They have different indicators for multiple weld types.
- Radius gauge—These gauges are sets of plates that usually have three comparative points for determining or marking small radii: 90° (for fillets), 180° concave, and 180° convex.
- Thickness gauge—These simple tools have a series of slots machined to match common sheet metal and wire gauges. Simply slide various slots over the material until one fits snugly to determine thickness

4 • FABRICATION FOR THEATRE AND ENTERTAINMENT

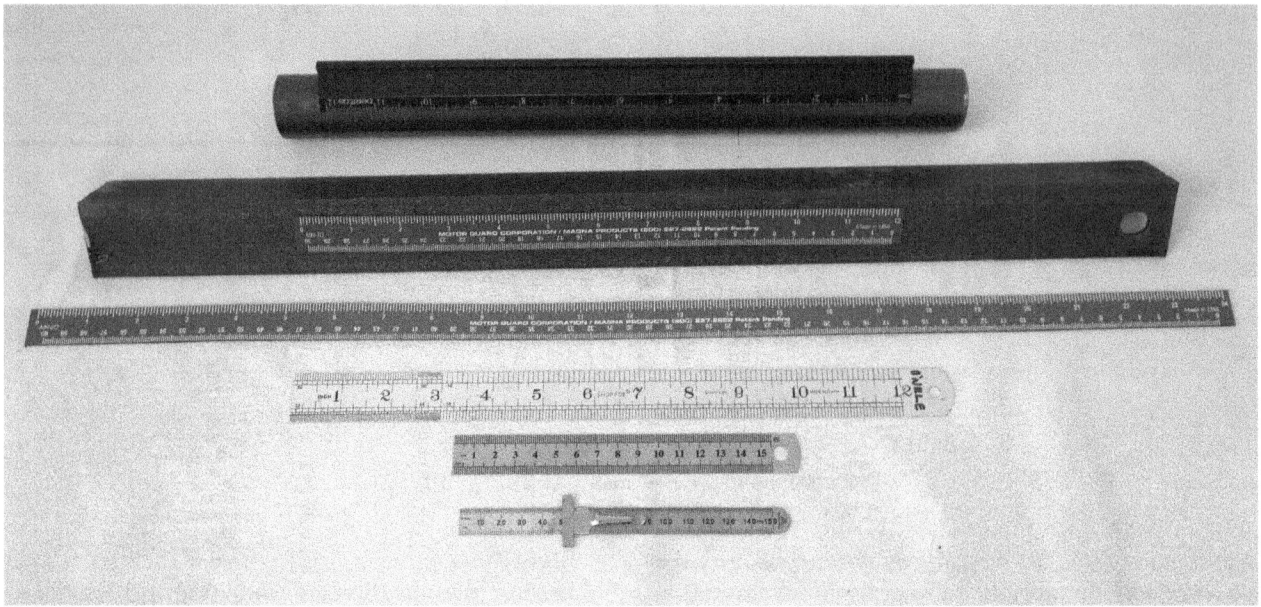

Figure 1.1 From top to bottom—a saddle rule on 1 1/4" round tube, a pair of magnetic rules, reversible desk rules marked in inch and metric scales, and a machinist rule.

Figure 1.2 From top to bottom—sheet metal and wire thickness gauges, radius gauges, and a fillet gauge.

(gauge). Most provide decimal equivalents. They are also often referred to as go/no-go gauges, but that term is particular to gauges that test crimped fittings such as for rigging or plumbing.
- Surface gauge—These are fairly simple tools that consist of a heavy machined base, an elevation rod, and clamp to hold a scribe. When set to a required height, the precision base can be slid along another machined surface to mark a height across the face of a perpendicular member.

Figure 1.3 A pair of antique surface gauges. Each was made by an apprentice machinist.

- Depth gauge—These are similar to a vernier caliper, except that they are designed to measure the depth of a groove or hole. Sliding calipers can be used to measure depth, but the broader base of these makes them more stable.

Figure 1.4 A simple depth gauge being used to check the thickness of a chain cog on a reference block. Though a machinist square would fit the bore, the wide base of the depth gauge ensures the measurement is taken perpendicular to the face.

- Vernier (sliding) caliper—These are one of the most common tools in a machinist's arsenal and are available in three varieties: ruled, dial, and digital. All versions are for accurate measurement of inside or outside measurements and depth. When tight tolerances are needed, calipers are the "go to" tool. These are available in a range of capacities from 6" up to 24". Low-cost versions will have reduced accuracy and durability but may be sufficient for many applications in the entertainment industry. Dial and digital calipers should always be re-zeroed while closed before taking a measurement.

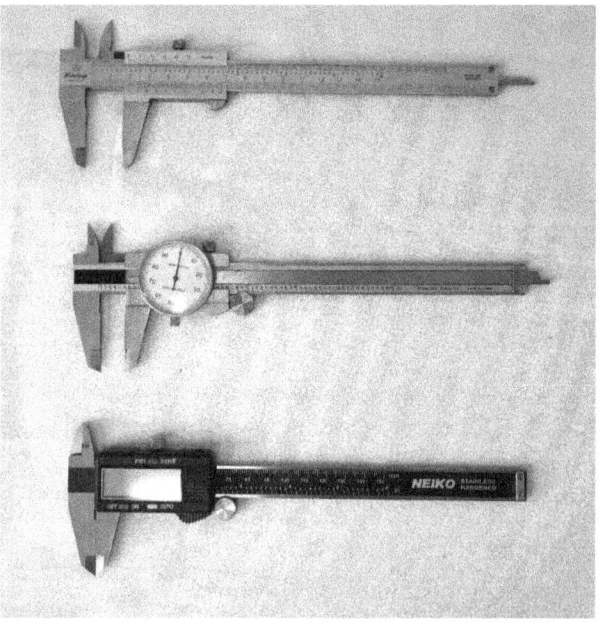

Figure 1.5 From top to bottom—ruled calipers with .001"/.1 mm increments, dial calipers (inch), and digital calipers (inch or mm).

- Dial indicator—Designed to measure either depth or movement (lash), these may be used to find run out in equipment such as mill and lathe hand wheels or to find distance from a fixed point. Specialty holders allow them to be used in various scenarios. They are mostly used in machining and mechanical applications. An example of one use is shown in Figure 12.30a. It may also be helpful to know that these may or may not have a spring return to zero. Those with a spring return are best suited to measuring distance.
- Spring caliper—These are simple but useful for comparing the size of one object to another. They are indispensable for setting a rough diameter on a lathe or width of cut on a mill. Both inside and outside measuring styles are available. For many shops, these are accurate enough for final size.
- Divider—These are designed for comparison of linear measurements without the use of a measuring tape and many have hardened points allowing them to be used as a scribe also. Jenny (or odd-leg or hermaphrodite) calipers are a hybrid divider/caliper used to transfer an offset using an edge as the reference or marking the center of a circle. These should have an adjustable scribe so it can remain perpendicular to the surface at a useable length.

6 • FABRICATION FOR THEATRE AND ENTERTAINMENT

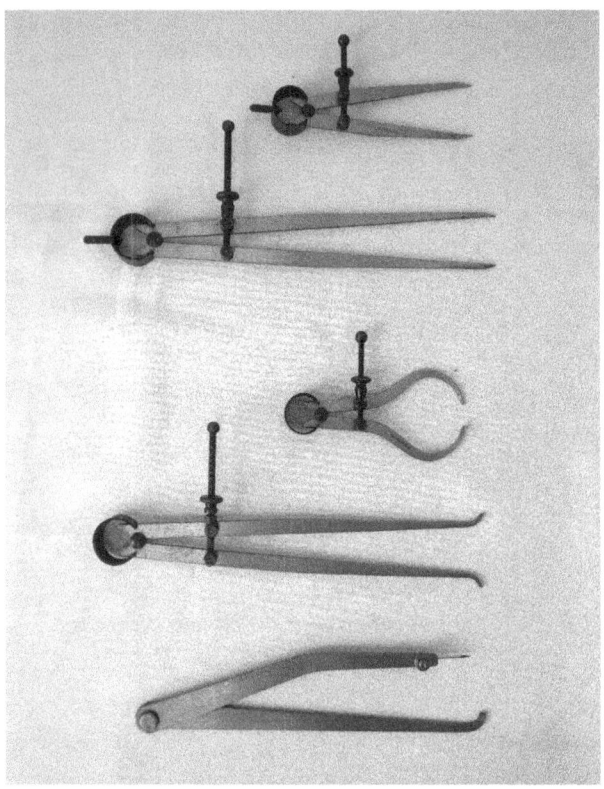

Figure 1.6 From top to bottom—small and large dividers, an outside caliper, an inside caliper, and a jenny caliper.

- Micrometer—These are designed for very precise measurement of thickness and use a dial screw to move out from zero, then back down to the material thickness. They are typically used in machining because they are a more accurate means of determining thickness than sliding calipers.

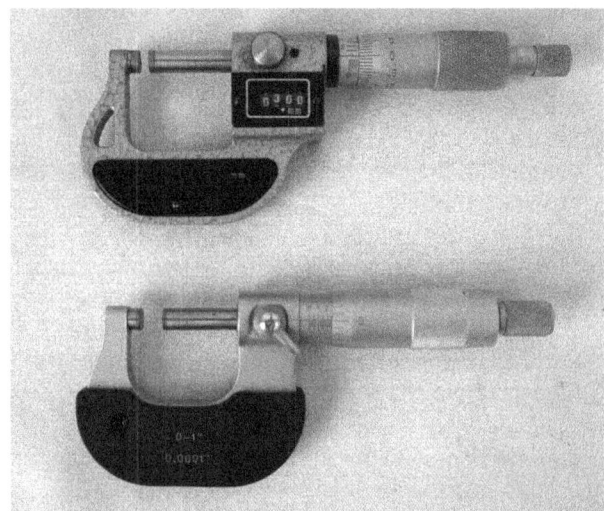

Figure 1.7 A metric micrometer (top) and imperial micrometer (bottom) with .0001" increments.

MARKING AND LAYOUT TOOLS

- Paint marker—These are best reserved for labeling the surfaces of parts that will not be seen on the finished product as they are quite permanent and will often show through other paint, either via bleed or simply that they leave a raised area. Their benefit is permanence: ink markers can rub off too easily on metal surfaces.
- Metallic Sharpie—A rare occasion when one brand stands out; so far no other company makes metallic markers that are quite so easy to use. The advantage of these gold and silver pens is that they stand out on steel far better than a black marker and are easier to clean off than paint marker.
- Soap stone—Soap stone is neither precise nor permanent, but it stands out for one main reason: it is extremely heat resistant. Other marking methods will quickly burn off if applied near a weld; soap stone is often used for guidelines for cutting with a torch because of its heat resistance. It is available both as rectangular and round sticks; metal holders that prevent breakage are available for each as well.
- Ink marker—These are one of the most common marking tools in shops. Fine point markers make a

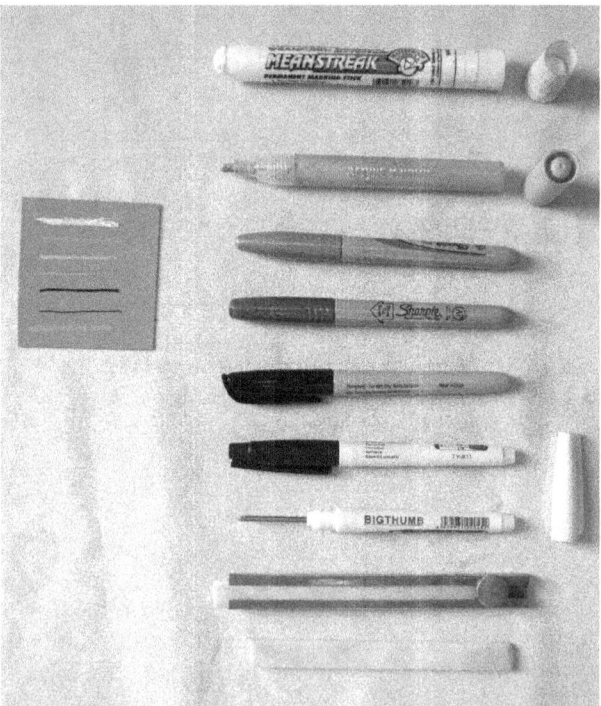

Figure 1.8 Metal marking from top to bottom—an oil crayon paint marker, acrylic paint marker, metallic Sharpies, oil/dirt resistant marker, deep reach markers, and soap stone. The sample at left shows the type of mark each makes, except the soap stone which does not mark well on a painted surface.

fairly broad line, so they are not for precision marking. Oil- and dust-resistant versions are best for the metal shop. Deep reach versions work well to mark hole placements when the accuracy of a transfer punch is not required.
- Silver pencil—These use a waxy metallic "lead" that shows up well on steel (not aluminum) and work especially well on slightly rusted surfaces where an ink marker can clog.

Figure 1.9 A rough layout of leaves on rusty sheet metal using a silver pencil.

- Marking fluid—This ink-like fluid is available in aerosol cans or brush-on formula (dauber in canister) in either red or blue. It is used with a scribe and improves contrast (i.e. making layout lines more visible). It can also be applied around the edges of a template for either layout or cutting. Most formulas do not need to be cleaned off before welding, making precision placement of components easier. If needed, the marking fluid can be cleared away by acetone or lacquer thinner. A similar effect can be achieved by applying a light coating of spray-paint, though this will interfere with welding and may impact the finished product. An example of marking fluid in use can be seen in Figure 11.37a.

- Coping template—These are clam-shell guides that provide tracing paths for coping 90°, or cutting 45°, and 22.5° joints in tubing or pipe. Each is sized for a narrow range of pipe or tube diameters for accurate layout.

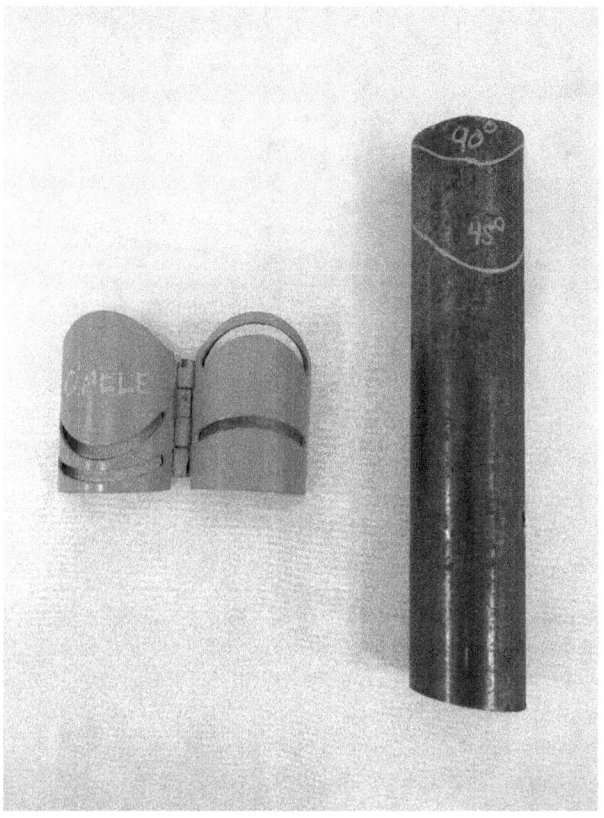

Figure 1.10 A coping template for 2″ diameter sections as well as a sample of pipe showing the layout lines the template will create.

- Scribe—For precision marking of metal, scribes are the best choice. Most versions are quite affordable. A double-ended steel scribe that has a straight end and one bent to 90° is handy for marking in tight areas (these are often called picks as well). These will wear down faster on hard metals than High-Speed Steel (HSS) or carbide-tipped scribes. Carbide scribes often have a replaceable tip and include a magnet, which makes identifying ferrous metals easy. A prick punch is similar to a center punch, but with a sharper point; these may be used like a scribe for lines or gently tapped to mark a center point. If a deep impression is needed, a center punch can follow. Sometimes a simple heavy-duty awl is a useful substitute for a prick punch; the thinner body offers extra reach.

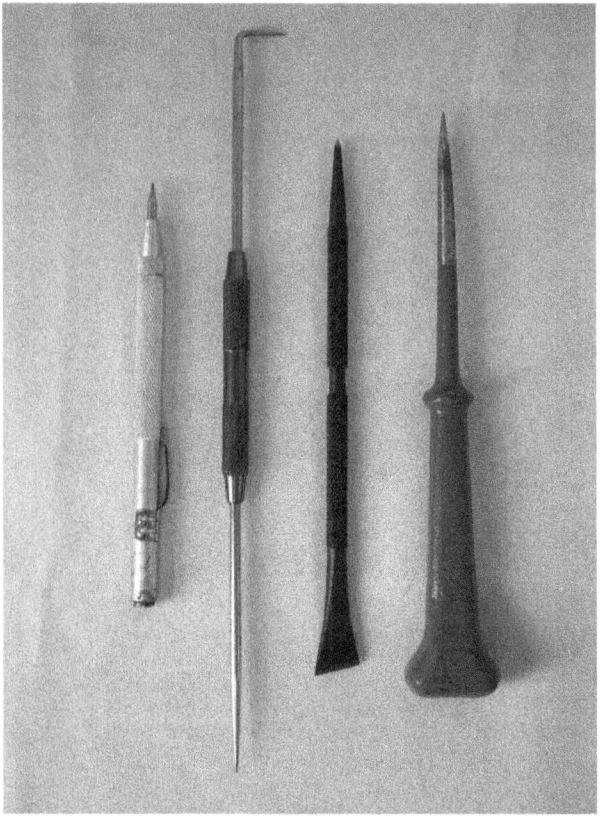

Figure 1.11 Hand scribes from left to right—a carbide scribe with magnet, a double-ended HSS scribe, HSS scribe with scraper/blade, and a scratch awl.

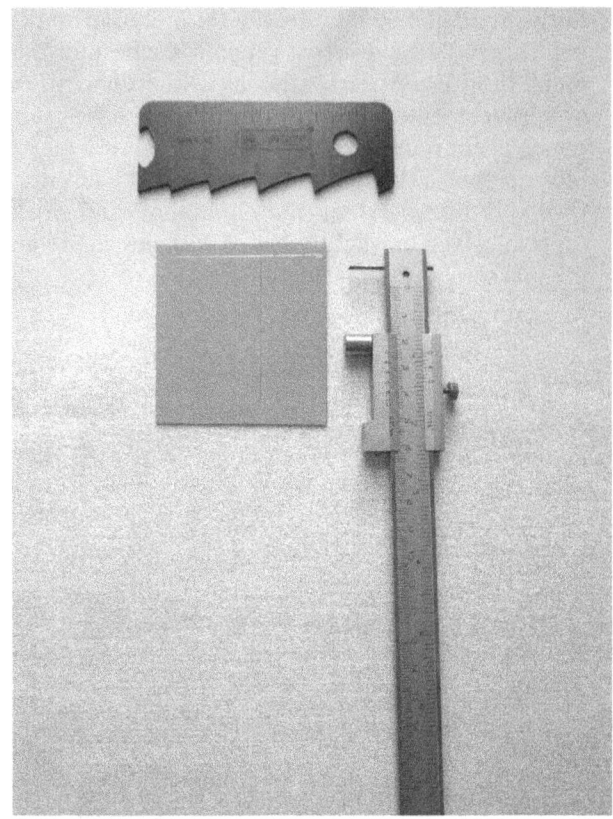

Figure 1.12 At the top of the photo is a hardened steel offset scribe and to the right a marking caliper. The painted steel sample shows each tool's respective score line.

- Marking caliper—Also referred to as a scribing caliper, these are an adaptation of a vernier caliper used to mark an accurate measurement rather than finding one. They are excellent for marking a line along which a series of holes will be drilled, or for a welded member inset from an edge.
- Offset scribe—These simple little tools made from hardened steel make marking offsets at fixed distances from an edge quick and easy by simply butting an adjacent notch to the edge, then sliding it along to make the score mark. They do not offer the variability of a marking caliper but mark common distances.
- Transfer screw—These are a means of accurately marking a surface to install hardware with blind threads, such as a knob or pull. The transfer screws thread into the hardware which is then tapped with a soft-face mallet or pressed in place to mark the surface that will need to be drilled. Unthreaded versions called dowel centers or blind hole spot plugs can be used for pinned hardware.
- Transfer punch—These are longer versions of spotting plugs. These are usually sold in sets with 1/64" increments. They slide through a drilled hole onto the surface below to mark center for drilling or punching.

MEASURING AND LAYOUT TOOLS FOR METAL WORKING • 9

Figure 1.13a An example of transfer screws threaded into a hanging bracket and the marks made on the back of an aluminum project box as well as the transfer screw set.

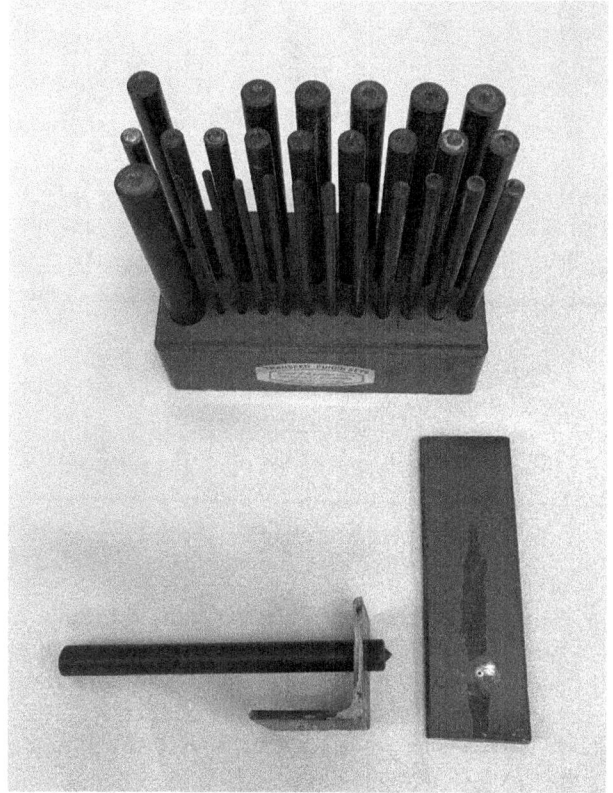

Figure 1.13b An example of a transfer punch used to mark steel strap for drilling to mount a tab and the full transfer punch set (1/8" to 1/2" by 64ths).

- Trammel set—As in wood working, trammels are used for laying out large circles. For metal working, the set can be used with steel pins for scoring; sets designed to hold soap stone are also available.
- Center finder—These are simple devices with a V-shaped metal head and a blade that traverses the vertex of the head. They are commonly used to mark center on solid rounds. This is especially useful when drilling on center such as for setting up in a lathe or drilling through for an axle.
- Machinist straight edge—These generally have no rule etched or printed; they are precision ground along their length and used to check the flatness of a surface. One with a beveled edge can be used for marking layout lines as well.
- Machinist square—These unruled squares are high precision and available in a few styles. Solid squares either have a flared base similar to those used for wood working or are machined flat. Those with a flare generally stay upright when the short leg is used as a base. Machined squares are similar to a carpenter's square, but thicker; these are also available with a beveled edge and are well suited for scribing. Double squares have a sliding leg, similar to a combination square but set at 90°. These may have a single rule or dual rule from center.
- Machinist combo square—These are sets that include a standard try/miter-square head, a protractor head, and a circle-center finder. The advantage to these is covering a multitude of tasks without buying separate tools; the downside is the need to reconfigure the tool as tasks change. While low-cost versions are suitable for occasional use, the precision of a brand name tool is a worthwhile investment.

10 • FABRICATION FOR THEATRE AND ENTERTAINMENT

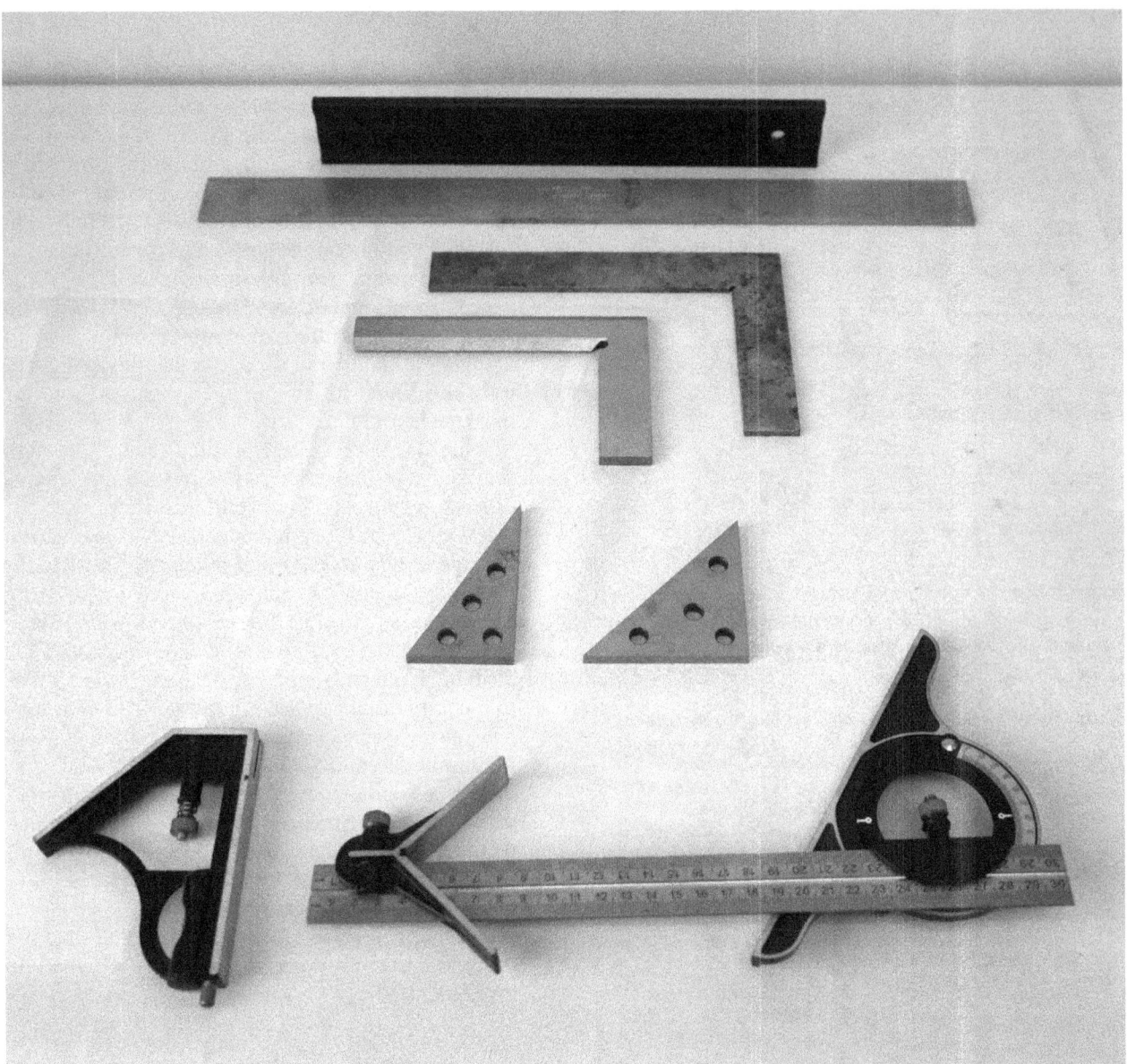

Figure 1.14 Machinist layout tools from top to bottom—aluminum and steel straight edges, machinist squares, angle blocks, and combo square set with the center finder on the left of the rule and the protractor on the right. The standard head has been removed for clarity.

- Swing blade protractor—These are usually made from stainless steel and consist of a rectangular plate with the arc-shaped scale of a protractor and a swing arm with an indicator held in place by a knurled nut. Essentially, they are a very small swing-head T-square and used in a similar way: the head is placed along the material edge and the arm is used to mark the set angle. Though these are not the most accurate means of finding or developing an angle, when used with care they work well for small items.

- Pipe center finder—This simple tool consists of a sliding center punch in a V-shaped guide that often includes a level. Those with a level can also be used to divide the circumference into equal segments. Place the base over a pipe, tube, or rod and gently strike the cap on the rod to mark center, or slide it along while pushing on the top cap to scribe a mark. These work best with a bit of marking fluid.

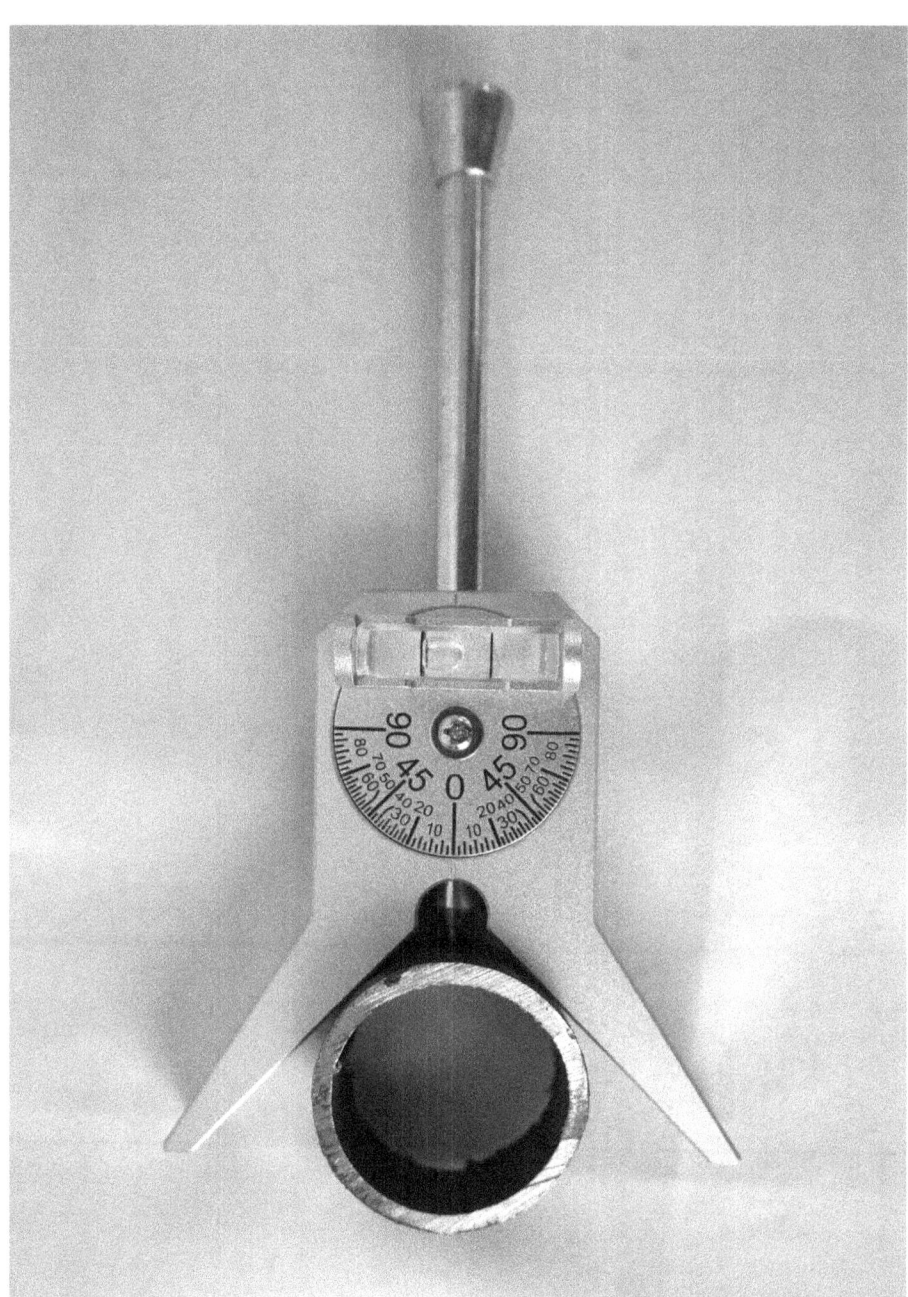

Figure 1.15 An example of a pipe center finder on a small section of pipe. This version can be used to evenly divide the circumference of the pipe by setting the appropriate degree offset on the compass wheel and move the base until the bubble reads level, then strike again. The pipe does need to be fixed in a vise for this to work well.

Chapter 2

Metal Alloys

Metal has become a standard fabrication material for large scale projects. Commercial scene shops use metal for a wide variety of projects from large armatures to small props and even costume pieces for animatronic characters. Metal is a fabulous medium because it can be shaped and hold that shape, permanently affixed via welding or brazing (unlike wood), and cast or milled into dimensional shapes that will be as durable as their base metal.

There are far too many metal alloys available to list all of them in this text. Only a certain portion of them are really suitable to entertainment fabrication. This text is intended to introduce those that are most applicable or may be encountered in venues. Some of the alloys listed may find rare application in the industry but are included because they have special properties that could be useful to fabricators who may be less familiar with them.

Material cost is an additional consideration for many shops. While steel can have a comparable cost to wood for some projects due to less material being needed overall, aluminum is usually much more expensive. The value benefit of aluminum comes from its light weight and ability to be exposed to the elements with little to no impact. It will be left to the creator or technical designer to determine if metal is the appropriate value proposition for a given project.

COMMERCIAL FORMS AND PROCESSES OF STEEL AND ALUMINUM

There are several processes by which various metal shapes are made. One is casting, where molten metal is poured into a mold for the desired object, then allowed to cool and solidify followed by the removal of the mold. While it is possible to do limited aluminum casting in a well-equipped shop, most shops will need to outsource to a commercial or art foundry if a batch of cast product is needed for a special application. Wrought shapes are made by forcing semi-solid to solid metal into shape via some form of applied pressure. These are the metal sections that will be used by most fabricators.

- Casting—This process requires a pattern with the proper shrinkage allowances (i.e. slightly oversized) unique to the metal to be cast so as to achieve an exact match to the desired finished product. Foundries typically use molds made from sand; the customer may do the finishing or outsource to a machine shop. Some examples that may be regularly encountered in entertainment are older counterweight bricks that were cast from gray iron (and were therefore brittle) and iron pipe fittings such as floor flanges and other threaded pipe fittings that are generally made from ductile iron which is strong and machinable. A version of casting that uses permanent dies and injects the metal into the mold is die casting. This process yields smooth, strong, and dense products. Die cast aluminum is used in many hardware and machine parts, some power tools use die cast housings, and many theatrical lighting instruments make extensive use of die cast aluminum.
- Forging—While historically forging referred only to shaping metal with a hammer on an anvil (and still does), at an industrial level, this is the process by which hot metal is pounded with or into a die to form the desired shape. This is often referred to as "drop forging" because die forming machines often use a drop-hammer to press the metal into the die. This pounding alters the arrangement of the metal's grain from a crystalline structure to more linear

form which increases its strength (since the grain structure follows the shape of the forged object) and is applicable to many types of metal. Since the cost of the dies is great, drop-forged shapes in entertainment will be limited to commercial items such as tools and mounting hardware. There are instances when hand forging steel is the right solution to one-off or small batch pieces of hardware or decoration. Some examples are discussed in Chapter 11.
- Rolling—Most of the steel that is used in the entertainment industry is rolled. Usually the more ductile alloys of steel (1010, 1018, or 1020) are available in cold-rolled sheet and bar, at least in the smaller sizes and shapes. This cold forming is beneficial to the steel's internal structure; much like forging, rolling realigns the molecular structure and increases tensile strength to a significant degree. Note that the lower carbon and manganese content of cold-rolled shapes allows easy welding. Hot rolling is used to manufacture steel shapes that are either too large for cold-rolling or formed from high-carbon manganese alloys which are not ductile enough for cold-rolling. Hot-rolled steel shapes are generally cheaper than cold-rolled and more easily shaped cold in the shop. Rolling is also commonly used to form aluminum sheets and bars. An ingot (up to 25" thick) is heated, then rolled to an intermediate thickness of approximately 1". The hot-rolled plates may then be cold-rolled to the desired sheet thickness or shape; cold-rolling imparts significant strength gains.
- Extruding—Many aluminum shapes that are useful in entertainment are extruded, a process practically unique to aluminum. In its simplest form, extrusion is the technique of pushing the aluminum through a shaping die. Heating the aluminum (well below its melting point) reduces its yield strength and helps it flow during the extrusion process. The friction generated by the process generates the rest of the heat needed for forming. Aluminum extrusions that require high strength must be made from a heat-treatable alloy since there is no way to cold work these shapes in order to gain strength. While extruding aluminum in-house is likely impossible, many shops have custom dies made and aluminum extruded for a particular shape. Extrusions may have elaborate cross-sections and much fabricating time may be saved by using a specialized extrusion instead of building up a shape from numerous parts or machining it down from solid stock.
- Drawing—This is a similar process to extruding, but the metal is pulled through the die instead of being pushed. This is often done to create a smooth surface after material is roll formed. Higher grades of wire, steel tubing, and rod are commonly drawn products. One drawn product that may be encountered in entertainment (when precision is needed) is round tubing that has been Drawn Over a Mandrel (known as DOM). In this case, both the interior surface and exterior surface are compressed simultaneously. This process has much the same effect on hollow shapes as cold-rolling has on rod and bar, creating a very strong and smooth-finished product inside and out.

The following alloys of steel and aluminum will solve most metal working requirements. If confronted with a problem that these alloys will not solve, consult the various steel and aluminum handbooks and check with the suppliers. Somewhere out there is an alloy that will be just the right solution to a project.

STEEL

Steel is a combination of carbon and iron that is malleable to some degree. This malleability—the ability to be bent or pressed into a desired shape without failure—makes steel an ideal material for scenic fabrication as well as artistic endeavors such as blacksmithing. Variations in the amount of carbon and additions of other alloying elements make it possible to manufacture innumerable variants. The entertainment industry is most likely to opt for a fairly narrow range of alloys that are easy to form, weld, and machine. One major drawback to steel is a lack of corrosion resistance. Because of the way steel is manufactured and preserved, it also often needs to be cleaned prior to fabrication, then preserved again (usually by painting) to prevent oxidation. While some steel alloys will begin to oxidize within hours of being cleaned, especially in humid regions, the most common types of mild steel used in entertainment will tolerate fairly long indoor storage before oxidation begins. In addition, mild oxidation does not change the structural properties or ability to weld these alloys to any significant extent. Steel is a cost-effective, approachable material and most shops and fabricators can learn to use it fairly easily.

Steel Alloy Selection Aids

The following "rules of thumb" are helpful in understanding steel alloys.
- Carbon—Higher carbon content equates to higher strength and hardness but becomes more brittle making it harder to work cold and sometimes more difficult to weld.
- Manganese—Higher manganese content also increases strength and hardness without making the

alloy brittle, but like carbon makes the alloy harder to work cold and can change how the material takes to welding.
- Nickel—Introducing nickel to an alloy adds toughness and corrosion resistance. In small quantities, it does not change the mechanical properties noticeably. As the percentage increases, such as in stainless steel, nickel helps maintain malleability when other brittle elements, such as chromium, are added.
- Chromium—This element adds surface hardness, toughness, and corrosion resistance. Likely the only chromium-containing alloys that will be encountered in the entertainment industry will be a few types of stainless steel.
- Copper—This is another element that can add strength without affecting welding or cold-working but is mostly added to mild steel in very small quantities to help resist corrosion.
- Lead—While many are familiar with the dangers of lead, in small quantities it can add machinability to some alloys without reducing strength. Any lead-containing alloy should be handled with extra care.

Mild Steel

Mild steel refers to a variety of alloys which are the most useful general purpose types for entertainment projects. These alloys are offered in the broadest array of shapes that are easy to cut, shape, and weld, while being sufficiently strong for almost every purpose outside of building a roller coaster. Alloy numbers for mild steel are assigned by the American Iron and Steel Institute (AISI) and generally indicate carbon content: 1010 for example having a lower carbon content than 1035. Mild steel is broadly referred to as carbon steel and therefore is thought of as plain steel. Mild steel is manufactured in two primary forms: structural steel has a reasonably uniform chemical composition, complete internal soundness, and no significant surface defects, while merchant bar is a variety manufactured for non-critical uses that may require bending, forming, punching, and/or welding. Merchant bar may have surface defects and minor internal flaws. As examples, structural steel (A-36) is primarily going to be found in permanent installations such as a rigging grid, where merchant bar (M1020) would be used for decorative applications such as railings, decorative grills, and other non-permanent items.
- MT 1010 and 1020—These are the most commonly used types of steel in the industry. Both are merchant grade steel, most often formed into tubing referred to as mechanical tubing or Hot Rolled Electrically Welded (HREW) due to the manufacturing process. Sections are available as round, square, and rectangular tube in a wide assortment of sizes from 1/2″ up to 6″ or 8″ for some shapes and tend to have fairly thin walls (varies by size). The main difference between 1010 and 1020 is the yield strength: 32 vs. 38 ksi. For most scenic use, this will not be relevant, but if the tubing is intended to be used in a structure that will support performers, the difference could be critical and should be accounted for in the engineering of the design. Mechanical tubing can be easily bent to quite small radii when proper equipment that supports the thin walls is used.
- A500—This is cold-formed structural tube with a much higher yield strength than mechanical tube. As well, these sections have a narrower range of sizes from about 1 1/4″ to 12″ or larger, though the largest sizes are unlikely to be encountered. The step up to structural tubing may be needed for long spans or very strong columns. While A500 can be bent, the radius of the bends should be subtle and done using a proper rolling machine.
- M1020—Merchant bar is often found in smaller, hot-rolled solids and thinner sections of angles and tees. Merchant bar is indistinguishable from hot-rolled A36, thus the buyer must specify when ordering if the supply yard can furnish both. If the steel is to be used for any engineered purpose, the tensile strength of merchant bars is a good bit lower than A36. Merchant bar is also good for cold forming when an appropriate radius is observed per thickness; otherwise cold working can lead to cracking.
- A36—This is the common designation for structural steel and tends to be supplied hot-rolled in larger sections of angles, I-beams, and channels. It can be used for scenery when larger sections are needed. It welds as well as any other mild steel. Again, the buyer may need to specify A36 when ordering small sections of some shapes.
- 1018—This is a general-purpose steel with a medium manganese content that can be casehardened (the ability to obtain a tough, hard outer surface while retaining a malleable core). Much of the cold-rolled or cold drawn steel available in the smaller sizes used for entertainment fabrication is 1018. Due to its manganese content, it machines well and is a great choice for parts that require good wear resistance and need to be welded such as revolve pivots or axles. Cold drawn 1018 has a significantly higher yield strength at 54 vs. 36K psi for hot-rolled merchant bar. 1018 is best shaped hot, as it can be brittle when bent cold.
- 1045—This is a high-strength carbon steel that is most often supplied as cold-drawn bars and rods. Applications in entertainment include custom parts for automated scenery or purchased as axles, gears, and fasteners.

- A53—This is the designation for steel pipe and applies to black pipe and galvanized pipe. Though pipe is similar to structural tube, there are key differences; the main difference is dimension. Pipe is sized based on historic specifications for wall thickness and internal diameter when pipes were made from lead, thus modern steel pipe does not match the named dimension due to the increased strength it provides. For example, the most commonly used pipe in theatre, 1 1/2" schedule 40 has a 1.9" outside diameter, and a 1.6" internal diameter. Pipe is available in three types: F, E, and S as well as two grades: A and B. Type F is the most common type found in the entertainment industry, especially in counterweight rigging systems.
- A15—This is the designation for deformed reinforcing bars (re-bar). Due to the surface texture and ease of shaping, re-bar is sometimes sought out as a decorative element for scenic units or environments. While these are quite strong in their original application (encased in concrete), they tend to be brittle when welded (unless special filler metals are used) and thus not good candidates for vertical structure or spans.

Alloy Steel

- 4130—This indicates weldable chromoly steel with a high yield strength: 50K psi rolled and up to 70K psi drawn. It is mostly available as round tube, but sheet, rod, and rectangular sections are available. It is often supplied with a traceable lot number making 4130 excellent for critical applications (this is why it is used for race car and light aircraft frames). One important note: it is best welded via TIG or OAF processes.
- 4140—This harder, more brittle alloy needs to be purchased annealed in order for it to be welded (4140 HT is hardened and tempered and should be avoided) and needs to be preheated before welding and slow cooled much like cast iron. It requires low hydrogen filler such as ER80S. Because it is highly wear resistant, it is an excellent option for drive shafts and other moving parts of automation equipment. It is available in sheets, bars, rods, or tubes. TIG welding is the best option, but it can be MIG-welded when shielding gas containing a higher percentage of Argon (85%–90%) is used.

Steel Finishes

- Plain oxide—This is the most common and inexpensive finish. This is steel that has developed a gray oxide surface during manufacture. It usually has some degree of loose scale and varying amounts of rust depending upon the source. For many metal working operations this oxide coating must be wire-brushed or ground off, particularly when brazing, since it interferes with the flow of the filler and may interact chemically with molten brass. The mill finish also needs to be removed prior to painting since the oxide is an unstable base that will lead to paint peeling, especially if exposed to the elements.
- Oiled and pickled—When a clean steel surface is desired, steel should be ordered oiled and pickled. The pickling process (a hot acid bath) removes the mill scale and the oil prevents oxidation. The end-user needs to clean the oil off prior to finishing. Oiled and pickled finishes are most often found on sheet steels and tubing.
- Finish coated—Some steel is available from the supplier painted or plated. Sheet steel is the most likely to be available with a variety of painted or powder-coated finishes as well as zinc or nickel plated. While little plated material is used in theatre due to its cost, the brilliant metallic effect can be worth the expense. It is a common means of distracting the eye with magic props for example. Paint can never approach the brilliance of plating.

ALUMINUM

Aluminum is the second most used metal in many industries world-wide and finds extensive use in the entertainment world. Although it is considerably more expensive on a per pound basis, it has about three times the volume of steel. This means that in many situations much lighter structures made of aluminum are actually stronger than those made of steel. For theatre and entertainment use, particularly touring shows with elaborate structures, light-weight combined with strength is extremely important. Another key factor that makes aluminum attractive is its corrosion resistance. Aluminum naturally forms a very durable oxidized surface quite quickly; this allows it to be used in a number of projects with no further protection. One downside regarding aluminum oxide: it melts at about 3600° compared to most aluminum alloys that melt at only 1200°–1300°. Due to this, aluminum requires complete removal of surface oxide before welding.

Alloys

Like steel, aluminum may be purchased in a variety of chemical compositions or alloys. Practically speaking, #6061 and #6063, which are wrought alloys, will be the most commonly encountered types in entertainment

shops. Cast alloys use a three digit numbering system addended by the alloying compound(s) indicator, e.g. 300.3. Though cast parts may occasionally be found in entertainment, the specific alloy will rarely be known or relevant.
- Heat-treatable alloys—While there are an array of heat-treatable alloys available, only two are particularly likely to be encountered in the entertainment industry. Each alloy will be designated with a heat treatment category; for the most readily available alloys, these will labeled T1–T10.
  - 6061 is a medium-strength aluminum alloy that has been extruded (the process of pushing metal through a die to give it a specific cross-section) into many structural shapes. It is very useful for platform and stage machinery applications. 6061, depending on its temper, has a tensile strength of between 35,000 and 45,000 psi. T6 is the most commonly used temper in entertainment and is readily available from suppliers; in fact it is common enough that it is sometimes referred to as multipurpose aluminum. 6061 is produced in almost every shape possible, from rods and bars, special shapes such as hex bar and half rounds to U-channels and tees.
  - 6063 has a tensile strength between 32,000 and 36,000 psi and is common in T-5 and T-6 tempers. Because many truck trailers are made from this alloy, it is readily available in most of the same shapes as 6061. Many companies choose 6063 for custom extrusions. It is more corrosion resistant than 6061 and may be a better choice for outdoor use. It otherwise behaves and welds much like 6061.
  - 2024 is a high-strength alloy that is sometimes used for gears, wheels, and hardware. While it is heat-treatable, it is not weldable and thus will not be used for many projects. It is machinable making it a good choice for bolted or riveted components that need to be strong, light, and corrosion resistant. 2024 may offer 40,000–47,000 psi yield strengths.
  - 7075 is another high-strength alloy that can be heat treated but is not weldable. It may be encountered in machined hardware such as truss clamps and brackets. Various tempers offer 50,000–70,000 psi yield strengths with a higher stiffness than 2024.
- 1100—This is most common of the 1000 series alloys and is near pure. The lack of alloying compounds lowers the tensile strength to about 13,000 psi. It is easy to work, bend, shape, fasten and is very ductile. It is used in many extrusions. Certain processes, such as die extrusion, can actually double the strength. Pure aluminum cannot be tempered but is easy to form and readily welded. This is not a disadvantage; it is excellent for decorative projects and lower cost than wrought alloys. It is available in sheet and plate form and offers the highest corrosion resistance. It can be machined but may clog cutting tools; it is also very hard to sand and grind due to clogging media. 2011 is a similar alloy that is better suited to machining when high strength is not required.
- 3003—This alloy is sometimes considered an economy grade and may also be listed as formable aluminum. It has slightly less corrosion resistance than 1100 or 6061 and is not tempered. It is an excellent choice for props and non-structural projects where cutting and shaping are the primary needs. An array of shapes from textured sheets, such as diamond tread, and weave to honeycomb panels that are great for signs and other exhibit work are available. 3004 and 3005 are similar alloys and may be available (likely special order) that add 10%–20% strength over 3003 and may be valuable for some special projects.
- 5052—This alloy is commonly used for marine and large vehicle applications due to its very high corrosion resistance while remaining weldable. It is available in a relatively narrow range of shapes, primarily tube, bar, and sheet. It offers yield strengths from 29,000 to 41,000 psi. It is a very good choice for outdoor installations, especially those that may be near salt water.

Aluminum Surfaces

While most aluminum has a standard mill finish, which may not be entirely free from stains and oil residue, sheet aluminum may have one face that is bright and unblemished and a mill finish on the reverse. Mill finish is the most common and will be adequate for most projects. Other surface finishes, such as swirls or raised texture, may be offered on sheets as well. Aluminum is also available in a variety of painted, plated, and anodized surfaces; of note are short sections available at hardware stores and home centers. These may be sealed with a clear coating that makes them a poor choice for welding due to the finish needing to be removed, which is labor intensive.

OTHER USEFUL METALS

Along with the most common metals (steel and aluminum), stainless steel, weathering steel, copper and its alloys (brass and bronze) can be very useful metals to explore. All are well suited to props and scenic adornments. Because these alloys are less common, the author has not included dedicated chapters for shapes and uses. These characteristics are included here.

Stainless Steel

Though stainless steel will likely not be a regularly used material in most shops, it may be the material of choice for certain applications. Many fabricators are leery of stainless because they have heard how difficult it is to work with. Those rumors are only true if the fabricator cannot determine the alloy and thus the properties it is most likely to exhibit. While it is true that most stainless steel sheet will distort more while welding than mild steel, that should not be intimidating to the experienced weldor that knows how to control heat and use proper fixtures and welding techniques to minimize its impact. Even shops that do not TIG weld can consider stainless for smaller projects where bolted or riveted seams can be used. There are a few stainless alloys that are readily available from both steel suppliers and industrial catalog suppliers that are quite practical for entertainment use.

Figure 2.1 An example stainless steel framing for scenery to be used at a water park.

- 304—This is often referred to as multipurpose stainless because it is found in an array of manufactured products from cookware to supply plumbing in chemical plants. It has a relatively low yield strength (25,000–30,000 psi) making it fairly easy to shape. It can be purchased in a wider variety of shapes than other alloys. Bars, strips, rolls, sheets (even textured), tubes (round and square), rods, angles, and tees are readily available. In addition, many shapes are offered with different finishes from mill finish to highly polished. It is not heat-treatable and is essentially non-magnetic. Being the most readily available, shops that are interested in the unique look that stainless provides would be well served by 304. For shops with more advanced machinery, 303 is a more easily machinable variant that may be chosen for custom hardware.

- 316—This alloy contains molybdenum and is most commonly encountered in fasteners designated for use where they will be exposed to salt water. It is the second most common grade of stainless used in industry. In addition, this highly corrosion resistant alloy is available as bars, foils, strips, sheets, tubes, rods, and angles making it quite versatile for use in outdoor structures, especially those near a coast. One note for 316 stainless is that it should not be preheated before welding. Welds also require back gas; for this reason bolted structures are the easiest to make from 316. Using 316 alloy fasteners will prevent any galvanic response.

- 321—This is the best alloy for welded products because it maintains its corrosion resistance around the weld area better than other alloys due to the addition of titanium. Welding can be done without back gas, but weld quality will be lower. Otherwise 321 is similar to 304.

- 416—This is the most easily machinable variety and has a yield strength up to 40,000 psi. It is available as bars, sheets, and rods. One advantage to 416 is that it is magnetic and heat-treatable. It is somewhat less than ideal for welded products unless the finish product can be heat treated.

In most cases stainless is going to be used for nonstructural applications where the member is either exposed to the environment or its visual impact is a component of the design. Most shapes can be used to make display frames, custom furniture, lighting fixtures, or decorative objects. Tube may be used in place of mild steel when a structure will be exposed to the elements; this would likely need to be outsourced by most shops. Thin gauge stainless sheet makes an excellent facing surface because it can be polished, textured (such as with a sanded swirl), or left in its milled state while providing a clean modern look. It can be installed over many substrates with liquid adhesives or adhesive films.

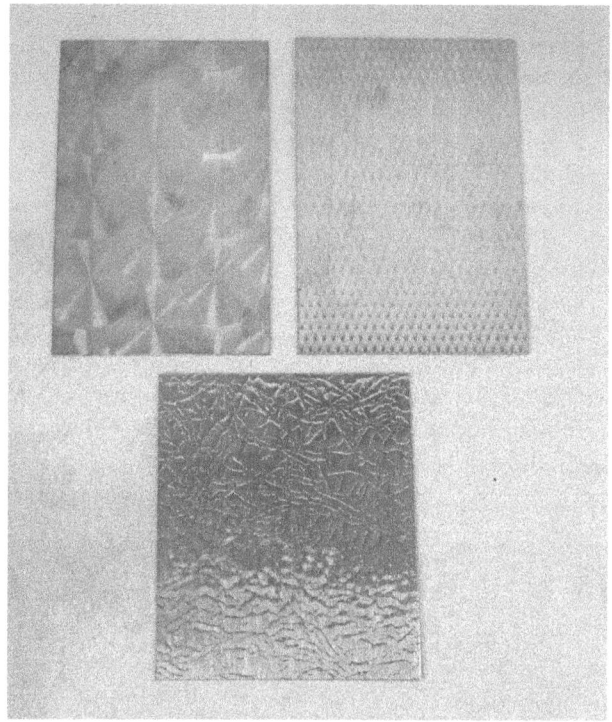

Figure 2.2 Examples of textured stainless steel sheet showing machine turned swirls, a stamped wave texture and a leather texture.

Weathering Steel

Some steel alloys are engineered to build a thick layer of rust, ideally sealing the surface from further oxidation, much like aluminum. The original alloy, COR-TEN, was developed by U.S. Steel but has in some usage come to refer to other weathering steel alloys. While these steels are "preserved" by this process, the oxidation is fairly delicate and can be removed by light abrasion, unlike aluminum oxide, and make these unlikely to be used where movement or high vibration are likely. These alloys are ideal for outdoor displays where the oxidation is a benefit. For example, many abandoned rail lines that have been converted to walking and biking paths use bridges made from weathering steel because they will not require painting while still being attractive. One challenge is presented by welding; any exposed welds are unlikely to weather at the same rate or in a similar manner to the steel; containing welds to unseen areas is best. Another consideration is that when fully exposed to the elements, these will continually erode and the run-off can stain surrounding materials. These are primarily available as plate, channel, and beams.

Figure 2.3 A sculptural fountain designed by Doug Hendrickson at the Metal Museum in Memphis, TN. The base has been made from weathering steel. The sculpture is an artistic expression of ALS, thus the extensive erosion is intentional and caused by the consistent exposure to air and moving water.

Though there are multiple ASTM designations for weathering steel, there are two that are most common.
- A242—This is the original weathering steel and is produced in type 1 and type 2. Type 2 is the more likely candidate for entertainment projects as it is intended for exterior finishes.
- A588—This is a newer alloy of weathering steel that offers higher tensile strength which offers no specific advantage to entertainment use unless it is the alloy available locally.

Cast Iron

Cast iron products are not going to be produced in house by an entertainment shop, nor is a shop likely to order custom castings. Regardless, cast iron can still be a very useful metal when one considers the array of architectural castings available. It is easy to order items like

park bench ends, machinery bases, and decorative castings for doors, tables, or even bird baths. Cast iron bases are also an easy way to attach decorative steel hand railings. There are many varieties of cast iron in industry, but there are three types that are most common.
- Gray—This is the most used type of cast iron and can be found in cookware, old toys, and decorative objects (e.g. a pot-belly stove). It can be machined fairly well, but it is brittle and a bit difficult to weld. Though heavy, it is exceptionally durable and a great option for permanent installations where the look of wrought iron (not the same product) is needed such as replicating the iron work of New Orleans.
- Malleable—This is a heat-treatable version that is often found in machinery components because of its resilience. Though much harder to break than gray iron, severe impact will cause it to fracture. It too can be somewhat difficult to weld, but when done with the right welding rod, the component can often be machined to near original.
- Ductile—This is the most durable type of cast iron and unlikely to be used for anything decorative. It is, on the other hand, regularly found in the housings for gear reduction boxes in automation and winch systems. While this iron is very difficult to break, if it happens attempting to repair it by welding will likely be unsuccessful. Gear boxes most often contain oil that will impede welding; even if very clean, the finished weld will make the area far weaker and should not be put back into critical service.

Figure 2.4 Gates, headers, and a balcony rail made with decorative cast iron panels for a production of *Much Ado About Nothing* at the University of Memphis.

Copper and Copper Alloys

Copper and its alloys can be particularly useful to properties and other decorative items because they are relatively easy to shape and they polish well. Brass and bronze are excellent for pipe and fittings because they are more corrosion resistant than steel and find many uses as bushings and bearings in motion applications.
- Pure alloys—Sheet, pipe, and tubing are mostly pure copper. Copper tube stands out because one

of its most common uses is for plumbing and it is readily available. Other solid shapes may have to be acquired from an industrial supplier, though copper sheet can often be found at commercial roofing fabricators and sheet metal shops. Examples of working with copper are shown in Chapter 11.
- ○ Copper plumbing tube is often referred to as pipe in order to distinguish it from medical tubing and refrigeration tubing, though ASTM does designate copper plumbing as tube. Copper plumbing has an OD that is always 1/8″ larger than nominal (named) size. For example, 1/2″ copper will have an OD of 5/8″. Refrigeration tubing (ACR) is specified by actual OD and is not compatible with plumbing fittings. Copper tubing may be sold annealed making it flexible (most often in coils) but may be purchased in straight runs or drawn, which like other metals, increases yield strength and rigidity. Annealed copper can be easily flared or belled to make connections whereas rigid pipe will require a slip fitting of some kind. Copper plumbing pipe can be used for compressed air or water in special effect systems; if used for such an application, the type of tube and its working pressure must be known as it varies significantly between types. There are three commonly available designations for copper plumbing.
    - ▪ Type M and type L are what is most often found in hardware stores and home centers, the difference being type L has a thicker wall and about 50% higher pressure rating than M. L is more available in annealed coils; these are much less likely to kink than annealed type M coils.
    - ▪ Type K is the only copper plumbing that can be used under ground and has a higher pressure rating than either L or M. Unless the tubing is being used to convey pressure, type M or L will be preferable for the lower cost.
- ○ Alloy 122 is weldable and commonly only sold as tubing for industrial systems such as non-potable water, air, or hydraulic oil. It is usually available as thin-wall straight sections or thick-wall annealed coils. Any application requiring hard transfer lines, such as oil return lines in automated scenery that uses hydraulics, would be well served by 122 copper.
- ○ Solid shapes such as sheets, bars, and other solid shapes are made from two common alloys: 110 and 145. Sheet may be sold by gauge, mils, or by ounces per square foot which can make deciding on the proper thickness a bit more difficult. It also may be available in six tempers from 060 annealed (dead soft) to H04 (hard). Sheets may also be sold with textures such as a hammered finish or with a patina. Copper does need to be clear coated to prevent natural darkening (oxidation) or from developing a green patina if exposed to moisture.
    - ▪ Alloy 110 is a multipurpose alloy that is good for cold forming. It can also be readily annealed for easy shaping; it will work harden as it's shaped. It offers good electrical conductivity but lousy machinability. It can be soldered or brazed, but not welded. It is available as sheets, rods, and bars with polished and unpolished finishes. Sheets of 110 are the most applicable to decorative work in entertainment. It can easily be cut and formed into decor like leaves, flowers, or a weather vane or used to make more practical elements such as lighting fixtures or hardware for props.
    - ▪ Alloy 145 is machinable and well suited to making decorative, but more durable hardware such as brackets, latches, or hinges. It is common for copper fasteners such as rivets and nuts/bolts. Like 110 it can be soldered or brazed; it cannot be welded. It is most likely to be used for OAF torch tips. It is available as rods and bars.
- • Copper alloys—Like other metals, the addition of other elements changes the properties of the resulting alloy. Brass and bronze are the two most common copper alloys applicable to entertainment fabrication.
  - ○ Brass is primarily an alloy of copper and zinc. Two common places to encounter brass are scenic models and small props (formable brass) or in plumbing parts (yellow brass). Many pneumatic motion systems or water effects use brass fittings because they are corrosion resistant. Like black iron fittings they are available in low pressure types that are rated at 125 or 250 psi (cast brass) and medium pressure types that are rated at 1000 psi (machined). High-pressure fittings are available as well. The main distinction of brass fittings is size: long lengths of brass pipe are not available; typically nipples will not exceed 12″ in length. As well, the diameter of brass fittings will typically not exceed 2″ ID. Unthreaded pipe and socket fittings used for brazed joints are also available; these are well suited to water effects as they will not develop leaks over time like threaded fittings can.
    - ▪ Yellow brass is mostly encountered as cast brass in decorative hardware and plumbing fixtures. It has a high zinc content of about 35% making it quite durable. It is somewhat difficult to machine with cutters, but sands and grinds well when using silicon carbide

stones or closed-coat grinding belts designed for non-ferrous metals. It is available as sheets and its bright coloring makes it attractive for props and other decorative objects. Yellow brass polishes to a very high sheen and is solderable. Because it tends to be more brittle than other alloys, it is not a good choice for cold forming.

- Alloy 260 formable brass is also known as cartridge brass due to its common use as shell casings for ammunition and is the alloy most often found in hobby brass used for modeling and other small projects. It contains about 30% zinc and is the best choice of brass alloy for cold forming. Small pieces are readily available from hobby supply stores and industrial supply catalogs. This alloy offers the most varieties of shape making it excellent for properties construction and even costume applications. Yield strength varies by shape and many shapes are unrated. It can be welded, soldered, or brazed.

Figure 2.5 Soldered hobby brass used to make scale scenery for a model of *Hamlet*. Scenic design and model by Dave Nofsinger.
Source: Photo courtesy of Dave Nofsinger.

- Alloy 360 free cutting brass is designed for machining and is used for brass hardware such as nuts, bolts, and lock parts. It has a very low yield strength (15K psi) and is essentially yellow brass with the addition of about 2.5% lead to increase machinability. It is an excellent choice for making custom-machined hardware that also needs a highly polished finish. It is available in rod, bar, and hex shapes from industrial catalog suppliers. It can be soldered or brazed but is not heat-treatable. Though the lead content is fairly low, precautions should be taken to avoid lead exposure if the brass is to be worked, especially by sanding.

- Alloys 330 and 353 are designated as formable and machinable. Both alloys are primarily available as sheet and rod. Both can be soldered or brazed; neither can be heat treated. Alloy 353 is a good choice for prop hardware such as decorative hinges, fake locks, and appliques that may need to be both machined and cold formed. Alloy 330 commonly has a higher yield strength.

- Alloy 385 is sometimes referred to as architectural brass because it has commonly used in formed hand rails and other press formed decorative objects such as furniture hardware. This alloy contains iron and lead in addition to the copper and zinc. It is available as rods, bars, angles, and channels making it quite versatile. It can be soldered and brazed but not heat treated. It is very soft (16,000 psi yield), machines very well and hot forms well when using a gas forge. It is not good for cold bending. Though the lead content is fairly low, precautions should be taken to avoid lead exposure if the brass is to be worked, especially by sanding or heating.

- Bronze—Historically this is a blend of copper and tin but other alloying metals such as aluminum are more common to contemporary bronze. Most bronze alloys are more ductile than aluminum making them a good choice when the ability to shape the material outweighs the need for welding while retaining a similar resistance to corrosion.
  - Silicon bronze is a very durable alloy that can be cast or hot formed such as by forging or hot bending. It also machines very well. It is corrosion resistant unless exposed to saltwater or coastal air and polishes well. While it may find little use in entertainment, its ability to be forged to shape much like steel, but at a much lower temperature, or easily machined when compared to brass, makes it suitable for decorative custom hardware. In addition, silicon bronze is an excellent candidate for cast metal parts. Though this capability will almost always need to be outsourced, there are many small foundries around the U.S. that will accept small batch projects.

Figure 2.6 Decorative bronze castings on the author's house; designed and cast by the author.

- Bearing bronze (800 and 900 series) are variants that are suitable for moving components and most can be machined for custom applications. For example, 840 and 841 are oil-filled, self-lubricating, powdered varieties that can be used as wear plates, bushings, and guides. Some varieties may be welded, but most are braze or solder only. Heat treat capability varies by type as well. These alloys are mostly available as sheets, tube, and rod. They contain various amounts of lead, thus any dust generated during use should be handled properly during maintenance or replacement. The only likely application is in mechanized or automated scenery. While ball or roller bearings may be preferred for high-speed applications, bronze sleeve bearings need far less space, are much lower cost and long lasting in low-speed applications.

- Aluminum bronze is also called marine bronze due to its resistance to corrosion in saltwater environments. It is unlikely to find significant use in entertainment but may be encountered in hardware.

Ordering Metal

When ordering metal products, the supplier needs specific data: shape, size (nominal or actual dimensions and/or gauge), alloy, and finish for each separate item. By ordering standard lengths (usually 20′ or more), buyers can often keep cost lower by avoiding cutting charges. Many hardware stores and home centers offer short sections of many types and shapes of metal, but at a significantly higher cost per unit. For a rarely used shape or type, this may be a good option.

Figure 2.7 A bronze sleeve bearing pressed into a steel disc for use in the author's roll bender.

Chapter 3

Steel Shapes and Applications

Steel is available in an array of shapes that all offer many variants. Solid shapes range from hexagon bar to tees, angles, and straps. Hollow sections range from round pipe to square and rectangular tube. Each shape offers various sizes and thicknesses to meet almost any need. This chapter is intended to introduce the reader to the shapes available while identifying those most appropriate for entertainment and possibly more importantly, outlining common applications for these. Long-time fabricators may already be familiar with many steel shapes, but for the shop or technician considering a move into steel, this chapter should provide enough information to help decide how applicable steel may be to a given project. Though many of the sizes of steel listed here are well beyond those that would be used to fabricate entertainment structures, for many companies that will be fabricating for installations in buildings currently under construction, having an understanding of the steel being used in the building will be helpful in knowing what can be installed and what will be required to do so. The reader may wish to consult a local or regional steel distributor for recommendations for availability and specific uses of any steel section.

HOLLOW SECTIONS

A wide range of shapes, sizes, and thicknesses of pipe and tubing are readily available. Steel tubing is one of the most common metal products used in theatre and opera but in many cases has been superseded by aluminum tube in other parts of the industry such as exhibits and themed entertainment. These sections are specified by external dimension(s) and wall thickness (by gauge). Structural tubing exists in the form of Hollow Structural Sections (HSS), these are only available in a somewhat limited range of sizes, some of which are far too large and heavy for application in the entertainment industry. More common in the industry is mechanical tubing. These can be used in walkable and moving structures, but engineering properties are not provided by the SCM. This data is readily available in *Structural Design for the Stage* for users who need it (data derived from Steel Tube Institute of North America *Handbook of Welded Carbon Steel Mechanical Tubing*).

Square and Rectangular

Much of the tubing used in our industry is Electric Resistance Welded (ERW), either Cold-Rolled (thinner walls under .065″) or Hot-Rolled (thicker walls .065″ and over). For any project where tight manufacturing tolerance and/or pristine surface finish are not required, ERW tubing is the cost-effective solution. A more refined choice, sink drawn (cold worked) square and rectangular tubing is also available. ERW has moderate yield strength of 32K psi or 38K psi depending on if it is MT1010 or MT1020, respectively. Structural tube has a yield strength of 46K psi.

- Square mechanical tubing—This product ranges in size from 3/8″ to as large as 6″ with as many as eight wall thicknesses per size, matching sheet metal gauge. 16 ga (.065″)–8 ga (.165″) are shared across most sizes up to 3″. Standard lengths are 20 or 24 ft.
  - ERW square tubing has many uses in entertainment fabrication. One of the most common uses is to frame flats with 1″–1 1/2″ tubing in place of 1×3 or 1×4 lumber. Smaller sizes are well suited to railing pickets and furniture. Larger sizes can replace lumber for platform framing and legs or frame very tall flats. Light gauge tubing, up to

about 14 ga, can be bent in a manual roll bender or draw bender; thicker sections will require powered machinery. Square sections are less likely to be used solo for horizontal spans; they are typically used as top and bottom chords on space frames or trusses when used for long spans. Cast-iron floor flanges are available to fit smaller sizes of square tubing, making anchoring railings much easier. The author chose to drill and tap the university inventory for set screws making them easy to reuse.

Figure 3.1 1″ square tube used for space frame platforms and decorative trusses for the set of *Working* at the University of Memphis.

- Rectangular mechanical tubing—These sections range in size from 5/8″×3/8″ to as large as 8″×4″ with as many as eight wall thicknesses per size; 16 ga (.065″) to 8 ga (.165″) are shared across most sizes up to 3″. Sizes under 2″×1″ and over 4″×2″ may be special order at many suppliers. Standard lengths are 20 or 24 ft.

  ○ These sections can be well suited to the top of railings, the sides of ladders, platform framing, and as stringers for stair units. Like square sections, these can easily be bent in a roll bender. Dies for tubing benders are much less common for rectangular sections.

STEEL SHAPES AND APPLICATIONS • **27**

Figure 3.2 The decking for *Metamorphoses* at the University of Memphis was framed with 3"×1" 16 ga ERW tubing allowing the platforms to overhang the pool. This created hidden entrances and exits for the cast. The upstage stairs were framed with larger 6"×2" 11 ga tubing, allowing them to appear to be floating.

- Square structural tubing—These are heavier wall, higher yield tubes available in sizes from 1 1/4" to 12" but can be ordered as large as 22" or more. Listed wall thicknesses are fractional for these sections (starting at 1/8") and refer to nominal size not the actual thickness (e.g. 1/8" nominal wall is .116" thick). Lengths are typically between 20 and 40 ft in 2 ft increments but may be available up to 60 ft in larger size sections.
  ○ Structural tubing is not commonly encountered in entertainment shops but can be a very good candidate for columns and may be found in some permanent installations such as theme park rides, or large outdoor facades.
- Rectangular structural tubing—Like structural square tubing, these heavier wall sections are normally available in sizes from 2"×1" to 12"×8" but can be ordered as large as 20"×12". These share the same wall thicknesses and available lengths as square sections.
  ○ These are unlikely to be required for most entertainment applications but may be used for permanently installed projects or for long spans where the depth of a truss is unsuitable.

Round Tube

While mechanical tubing (ERW) is the most widely used hollow round product, other options are available for precision tubing. If only the exterior tolerance is a factor, sink drawn tubing is a moderate cost option, but less readily available at steel warehouses. Drawn over mandrel (DOM) tubing is manufactured to stricter internal and external tolerances, has a better surface finish, and provides increased yield strength over ERW. The next step up in tolerance and surface finish is Cold Drawn Seamless round tubing. DOM and seamless tubing both have the advantage of a smooth interior finish; ERW and sink drawn retain the internal welding flash at the seam.

- Mechanical tubing (ERW)—This is the most common round steel product used for scenic applications. Round ERW ranges in size from 3/8" OD up to 12 1/2" OD, with 1/2" OD to 6" OD being most available. These sections may have up to 11 variants of wall thickness from .049" to .5", with wall thicknesses up to .375" being the most common. Standard lengths are 20 or 24 ft.
  - Round tubing may be used like pipe for lightweight structures such as railing (both the top and pickets if coped joints are used), furniture, or ladder rungs. Seamless tubing is available in telescoping sizes that can be used for simple effects. Most types of light gauge tubing can be bent relatively easily with simple equipment such as a conduit bender or roll bender (though it can be hard to keep round tube running straight). Tight radii will require a dedicated draw bender.

Figure 3.3 A jungle gym made from square and round HREW for a production of *Do Black Patent Leather Shoes Really Reflect Up* at the University of Memphis.

- Structural—These tubes are available to match pipe sizes starting at 1.315" OD matching 1" pipe and that match mechanical tubing starting at 2 1/2" diameter. Structural round sections are not for pressure applications; they are reserved for structural purposes. Listed wall thickness for these sections is in the same range of thickness as the other structural tube varieties.
  - Structural round tubing is excellent when the strength of pipe is needed in an even dimensional size; as an example 2" structural round tubing has a 2" OD vs. the closest pipe section 1 1/2" that has a 1.9" OD. The author has used 4" OD structural tube as the center column for an all steel spiral stair unit for example. Structural round tubes also have a higher yield strength than pipe.
- DOM tubing—These are smooth, strong versions of tube that range in size from 1/4" OD up to 12" OD. Listed wall thickness for these sections is in the same range of thickness as ERW varieties, often produced in random lengths up to 24 ft. Strengthwise, DOM falls between ERW and structural tubing but has a much finer surface.
  - The smooth interior allows some infrastructure, such as air or hydraulic lines, to be run damage free. The extra stiffness of DOM tubing makes it ideal for projects where small round tube is needed, but the flexibility or softness of ERW would not suffice. Depending on the steel alloy, DOM tubing is sometimes used for structural applications such as frames for small aircraft.
- Seamless—Mechanical tubing is available in two seamless varieties: hot drawn (HDS) or cold drawn (CDS). Like DOM, the cold drawing process increases yield strength. CDS tubing is available from 1/4" OD to 10" OD. While smaller sizes are available with wall thicknesses matching ERW, larger sizes may be available up to 1 1/2" wall thickness. Hot drawn varieties range in size from 3" OD to 26" OD and typically have thicker walls from .435" up to 4" for the largest diameters. These sections are often produced in random lengths up to 24 ft.
  - For the entertainment industry, thin wall, smaller diameter tube can be an excellent choice for unpainted units where bare steel is part of the aesthetic. Like DOM, the smooth interior allows hoses or other effect parts to be inside the structure.

Conduit

One of the most common types of steel tubing is electrical conduit. This is sold in three forms: rigid (or heavy wall), EMT (Electrical Metallic Tubing or thin wall) and flexible. All are galvanized which can be an advantage, but brazing or welding should be avoided.

- Rigid—This conduit is sold in nominal internal diameters from 1/2" to 6" with ODs that match

black and galvanized pipe. Though rigid conduit will thread into pipe fittings it cannot be substituted for pipe. It has a slightly thinner wall and is not rated for structural use nor to hold pressure.
  - For many scenic applications where the strength of pipe is not required, the lower cost may make rigid conduit a good option, such as for bottom pipe in a drop. Being somewhat easier to bend also makes it an attractive option for curved units such light-weight curtains. Rigid conduit could also be used for decorative railings when combined with slip fittings for pipe.
- EMT—Thin wall conduit is available in nominal internal diameters from 1/2" at .042" wall up to 4" at .083" wall. The thin wall makes fairly large sizes easy to bend with a manual bender. EMT can be joined with either compression or set screw fittings and a variety of fitting shapes such as elbows and offsets are available for all sizes. While EMT and its related hardware should not be used for weight-bearing applications, it is excellent for props and set dressing. Sections are available in 10- and 20-ft lengths.

Figure 3.4 EMT conduit used as a decorative element on the walls for the set of *The Physicists* at the University of Memphis.

- Flexible—Galvanized flexible steel conduit is available in sizes from 5/16" to 2". This conduit is most likely to only be used for decorative purposes, such as set dressing, but some creative thinking can find artistic uses as well such as a movable armature for a sculpture.

Figure 3.5 Flexible conduit being used to create texture on a giant nest for Sesame Street at Adirondack Studios. The conduit provides a flexible base for a resin build up. The flexible conduit was chosen for its relatively low cost and durability.

Pipe

The following section refers to full length sections. A discussion of fittings and short sections (pipe nipples) follows the main section. Steel pipe is available as black pipe and galvanized pipe. Both are manufactured to ASTM A53 standard and come in three types: F, E, and S as well as two grades: A and B. Both E and S types have a higher yield strength than Type F. Black pipe is corrosion resistant, but not to the extent that galvanized pipe is. The blackening process is a chemical treatment that forms a hard magnetite coating on the surface. While it is resistant to rusting in low to moderate exposure to humidity, it will rust when exposed to the elements. Pipe diameters are specified by nominal inside diameter and thickness schedule, thus neither the ID nor OD of the pipe will match the named size. Standard length for pipe sections is 21 ft; larger diameters may be available in 42 ft sections as well. Black pipe is available with either unfinished ends or threaded ends. Galvanized pipe is typically threaded on each end and delivered with a straight coupling. Lengths under 10 ft are mostly identified as pipe nipples and do not ship with the coupling.

- Pipe types—Though type will not always be relevant to entertainment use, having the information is useful when ordering because a steel warehouse may have different stock than a plumbing supply house.
    - Type F, grade A is manufactured with a furnace butt weld. This is the most common type found in the entertainment industry, especially as battens in counterweight rigging systems. It has a 30K psi yield strength and though not likely to be used in permanent welded structures, its strength and availability make this pipe suitable for most temporary entertainment use.
    - Type E is electric resistance welded like ERW tubing. Grade A has a 30K psi yield strength and is better for cold bending. The minimum recommended radius for bend up to 90° is 12× the nominal diameter. Grade B pipe has a 35K psi yield strength due to slightly higher carbon and manganese content. It too can be bent at 12× ID, but it will be more difficult to do. Type E pipe is often used for permanent welded structures such as catwalks in a venue.
    - Type S is a seamless pipe formed by piercing and drawing. While this pipe tends to have a much more consistent ID, it is high cost and mostly found as schedule 160 high pressure pipe (rated up to 3000 psi) used in industrial systems.
- Pipe schedules—Though the ASTM recognizes a full schedule of pipe wall thicknesses from schedule 5 to 160, the most commonly available pipe is sold in three wall thicknesses (or strengths): standard weight (schedule 40), extra strong (schedule 80), and double-extra strong (similar to but not matching schedule 120). These main three are also the only types that the *SCM* provides design values for; design values for schedule 10, 40, 80, and double extra strong are also available in *Structural Design for the Stage*. Wall thickness increases with diameter, as pipe is pressure rated. Since the external diameter is used as the spec size for tooling, the internal diameter may not be consistent like ERW as ASTM A530 allows the wall thickness to vary by 20% over or 12.5% under for pipes 1/8″–2 1/2″.
    - Schedule 10 pipe is available from 1/8″ ID to 2″ ID at many steel warehouses and can be ordered up to 4″ ID. Schedule 10 pipe is commonly used for sprinkler systems, but in coastal areas stainless steel may be the most available type because it is preferred for marine and low pressure transfer systems. It is likely that mechanical or structural round tubing will serve the needs of entertainment applications better due to many choices of external dimensions and variety of wall thicknesses. It is also unlikely the need for a piping system that cannot be served by more readily available schedule 40 pipe will arise. It is well suited to decorative use such as pipe framed furniture.
    - Schedule 40, standard weight pipe, is available from 1/8″ ID up to 16″ ID. This is the most commonly encountered pipe weight used in entertainment. It can be used for both plumbing systems (air, water, or oil) and structural projects such as pipe grids, platform legs, or hand rails. One unique application is to use pipe for rollers or axles; there are flanged bearings that fit the ID of schedule 40 pipe.
    - Schedule 80 extra strong pipe is available from 1/4″ ID up to 16″ ID. It may be encountered in counterweight rigging systems when battens need to span slightly farther between lift lines than the recommended 8′–10′ for schedule 40.
    - Double extra strong pipe is available from 2″ ID up to 8″ ID. It is sometimes incorrectly referred to as schedule 120. Due to the smallest available size having a nearly 2.4″ OD, this pipe will likely only be used for special applications.

Pipe will resist moderate stress from any direction better than any other shape of equivalent mass and may be used as structure or for decorative purposes. It is much harder to bend than ERW tube; pipe over 3/4″ ID will most likely require a hydraulic bender. Many examples that demonstrate the strength of pipe can be encountered in performance venues such as pipe grids, battens, and supports or rails for catwalks. Some nesting may be possible by mixing strengths. One example that has been common in theatre is using 2 1/2″

double strong (1.77″ ID) to sleeve over 1 1/4″ schedule 40 (1.66″ OD) to make a simple but effective center pivot for revolve. As well, threaded pipe can be used for special projects such as compressed air storage.

Figure 3.6a A number of elements in the adaptation of *Hamlet: Fall of the Sparrow* at the University of Memphis used 1 1/2″ schedule 40 pipe. Both the legs for the upper level and the forced perspective ceiling grid are built from pipe.

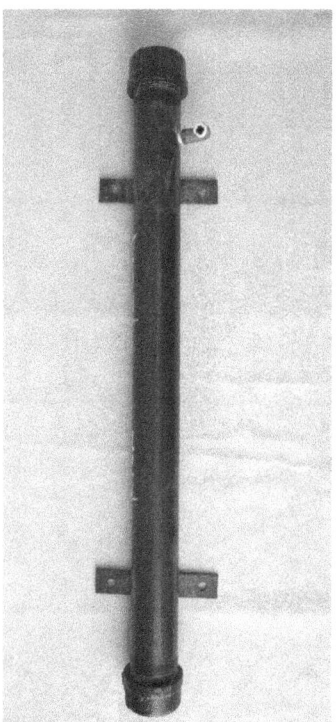

Figure 3.6b A compressed air storage tank made to mount under a 2×4 framed platform. It holds enough compressed air to operate multiple cycles of pneumatic brakes attached to a small wagon. The pipe was drilled and tapped for 1/8″ NPT fittings. Pressure did not exceed 80 psi.

Pipe Fittings

Any discussion of pipe would be incomplete without at least an overview of the many types of fittings available for joining pipe. The most common varieties are threaded fittings, which are available in iron and steel depending on application. Threaded fittings should not be used for structures, especially overhead. In limited cases, some structural slip fittings are suitable for overhead use when manufacturer design limitations are followed.

- Threaded pipe fittings—These fittings are available in a wide variety of shapes, the most common being: caps, couplings, unions, elbows, tees, and floor flanges. There are many others that allow the interconnectivity of different pipe sizes. Supplier catalogs, such as those from Grainger and McMaster-Carr, are excellent resources for discovering available fittings. For pressure applications, fittings must be matched to pipe schedule. Though threaded fittings should be avoided in most structural applications, they are still quite useful in many areas of the entertainment industry.

- Low-pressure iron (class 125 or 150 indicating max psi) fittings are widely available at hardware stores, home centers, and industrial suppliers in both black iron or galvanized finishes. These will be the most commonly used threaded fittings as they are most available and intended to be used with schedule 40 pipe.
- Medium pressure (class 300) fittings are predominantly black iron, but a narrower range of types are available galvanized. These are designed to be used with schedule 80 pipe and are well suited to special applications such as compressed air storage where there may be need for a higher pressure than 125 or 150 psi.
- High-pressure fittings jump to 3000 psi and may be steel or galvanized steel. The only likely use for these high pressure fittings in entertainment would be hard plumbed hydraulic supplies for mechanized or automated systems. Theatres that have hydraulic orchestra lifts may have hard plumbed lines that use these fittings as well.
- Gray iron fittings are not for use in pressurized systems. The most likely place to encounter gray iron used for pipe is threaded floor flanges. These too may be plain or galvanized finish.
- Brass and bronze fittings are discussed in the copper and copper alloys section of Chapter 2.

• Welded fittings—Unthreaded fittings are available to match various types of pipe but schedule 40 and 80 fittings will be the most likely candidates for entertainment use. These are butt-welded and often used in HVAC applications but can be used where a smooth finish at the joint is required (e.g. hand railings). High pressure welded fittings are socket welded and unlikely to be found in entertainment. Welded fittings are not galvanized and should only be installed by a certified welder if used for pressure or other critical applications.

• Decorative fittings—Decorator grade threaded fittings match pipe threads but are designed for lightweight objects such as furniture or shelving. These may be gray iron or an undisclosed ferrous alloy. These are sold in a wider variety of configurations than those for plumbing, including 3- and 4-way corners or 5- and 6-way intersects offering versatility that heavy duty pipe fittings do not.

Figure 3.7 A table designed by the author using schedule 10 pipe and decorative fittings.

- Slip fittings—These fittings use grub screws (set screws) to hold pipe in place and thus cannot be used for plumbing. They are readily available for most pipes up to 2″ ID from companies such as Kee Klamp (nodular iron fittings) or Hollaender (aluminum fittings for steel or aluminum pipe). The Hollaender website even has an entertainment applications section. These are primarily designed for building safety railings and racking in industrial settings, but often find a variety uses in entertainment fabrication. There are far too many variants to list, and the catalogs are readily available from the manufacturers. These can be used for overhung loads (such as a lighting side-arm on a vertical pipe) when proper design factors are applied (provided by the manufacturer) or to assemble a variety of structures. Some fittings have a fixed depth socket while others may slide along a pipe or drop over much like a Rota-lock. There are a number of swivel fittings and even flanges to build stairs. They truly are one of the most versatile means of building with pipe. There are also decorative (non-rated) slip fittings that fit ERW tubing, but these are mostly available as floor flanges.

Figure 3.8a Five variations of ductile iron slip fittings for 1 1/2″ pipe (top and middle) and slip-fit flanges for square tube (bottom).

Figure 3.8b Decorative "scaffolding" on the set of *Elektra* at the University of Memphis, constructed from a mix of iron slip fittings and scaffold clamps.

- Pipe clamps—Though not quite the same as pipe fittings, these are the pieces of structural hardware that can be used for joining pipe that are encountered across the entertainment industry. The following clamps are all designed for pipes that will intersect on different planes. These are mostly designed for smaller pipe from 1 1/4″ to 2″, making them well matched to much of the pipe used in entertainment.

- Scaffold clamps are often referred to as cheeseboroughs and are one of the strongest and most common pieces of hardware used with steel pipe. There are two styles: 90° fixed and swivel. Both have their place, but a note of caution with swivel types: there is play in the swivel joint that can make noise when used on structures that will be interacted with. These are not to be used for overhead lifting (dynamic loading), but most are suitable for static loads overhead when manufacturer guidelines are followed. If the manufacture of the hardware is unknown, and structural data cannot be acquired, the author would recommend they NOT be used for load bearing structures. A common example of how these clamps are often used would be to attach a pipe that spans the opening of a pipe grid in order to add an extra hanging position. These can also be used to assemble scaffold style scenery when rated.
- Rota-lock clamps are well suited to horizontal grids or for adding horizontal cross pipes to a vertical pipe (the tensioning bolt should always be at the top of a mounted cross pipe). The manufacturer does not recommend them for use with overhung loads and they are not suitable for supporting suspended loads such as a lighting tail-down. Their downside is the need for one of the pipes to slide through the U-connector while holding the locking wedge in place; it is most helpful if the sliding pipe is rather short.
- Cross clamps are formed steel plates that bolt together at the four corners. These are for horizontal use and best suited to permanent installs such as pipe grids.

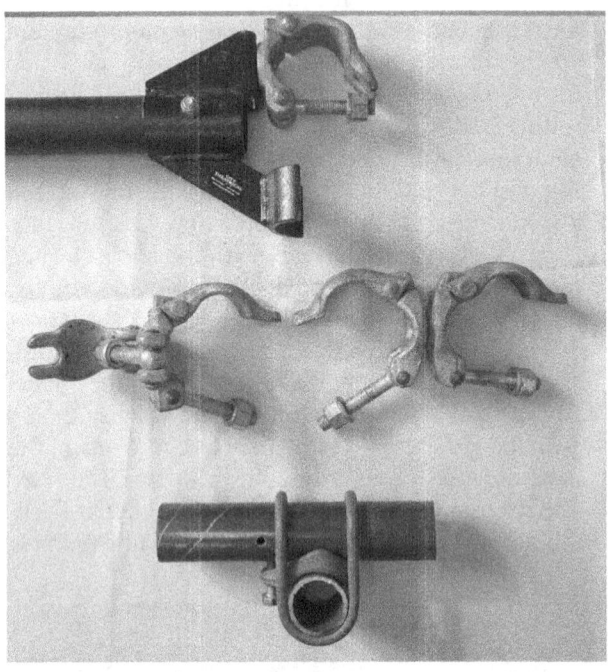

Figure 3.9a From top, a purchased lighting side arm with a half-clamp, a pair of standard scaffold clamps (fixed on the left, swivel on the right) and an assembled Rota-lock.

Figure 3.9b The set for *Godspell* at the University of Memphis, showing scaffold constructed primarily from schedule 40 pipe and scaffold clamps.

Ducting

There are two common types of metal ducting, snap seam, and spiral. Spiral duct is much more durable and is used for dust collection systems and fume extraction. While many shops will encounter it in those systems, its combination of light weight, relative strength due to its spiral design (the ribbed seams act like an I-beam flange) and availability of very large diameters makes it an interesting material for scenic use. Being galvanized makes it resistant to rust, and easy to paint. Spiral duct cuts well with a dry cutting circular saw or jig saw. Though these are quite sturdy, they are not strong enough to be load bearing.

Steel Studs

While steel studs may not be an enclosed hollow, they are a modified U-shaped and light gauge making them similar to rectangular tubing. Steel studs are sized to replace standard wooden framing members and are available as non-structural type suitable for non-load bearing wall framing and as load bearing studs with .033″–.097″ walls (20–12 ga). Bridging members are available to brace tall walls. Unlike framing with lumber, top and bottom plates are differently shaped members (track) that are an open U-shape. Assembly requires self-piercing screws. Some of the benefits of steel studs are a complete lack of warping and other flaws, meeting fire code for some indoor event complexes, and they are lighter than lumber. Sizes are slightly different that lumber with 3 5/8″ being the odd one, but 2 1/2″, 6″, and 8″ are easy to apply sizes; steel studs are available up to 12″. Non-structural studs can be cut with snips, but a dry cutting saw is required for thicker gauges and will always provide a tidier cut. There are also abrasive blades just for steel stud, but they will leave a small, sharp burr.

SOLID SECTIONS

Like hollow shapes, an array of shapes, sizes, and thicknesses of solid shapes are available. While these shapes may find less use in theatre and opera scenery, shops that fabricate exhibits, themed structures, and properties will find many uses for solid steel shapes. These sections are specified differently by shape, but generally a width and thickness for each shape will cover most of the needed information. Nearly all solid shapes that will be encountered are processed from A36 steel or merchant bar for which design data is readily available in both the *SCM* and *Structural Design for the Stage* for users that need it. Like tubing, some shapes will offer both hot and cold-rolled forms, with cold finished pieces having a higher yield strength.

- Bars—Steel bars are available in several types of steel, in a wide range of sizes. Bars may be further processed by cold-rolling or made into shapes such as squares, rounds, or hexagons. Merchant quality bar and cold-rolled 1018 (one of many variants listed as special bar quality) are the most common steel bar varieties. As in other shapes, cold-rolled bars are manufactured to higher tolerances and have an increased yield strength. Merchant bar is the cost-effective choice for many applications. It is easy to machine and shape and thus has many uses in fabrication. Standard length for these sections is 20 ft. For bars, the preferred practice is to specify width in 1/4″ increments, and thickness and diameter in 1/8″ increments. Shorter lengths are readily available at hardware stores and some supply houses. The variety of bar shapes makes them extremely useful. They should be used so that the primary stress is parallel to their longest axis or in tension when possible. Often bars are welded together to make special shapes.
  - Round bar, sometimes referred to as rod or pencil rod, is available in a variety of steel alloys and sizes. Sizes are available from 1/8″ to 5/8″ in 1/16″ increments; up to 1″ in 1/8″ increments and up to 2″ by 1/4″ increments. Standard length for these sections is 20 ft. Shorter lengths of small diameter rod are readily available at hardware stores and some supply houses. For structural purposes, design data must be derived from cross-sectional area and the allowable tensile stress for the given alloy.
    - For standard scenic or other construction, hot-rolled merchant bar may be used for tension members or as decorative metal work (it cold bends very well). For more demanding use, such as axles or guides in machinery, 1018 cold-rolled is an excellent choice. In most cases, heating will be required for bending cold finish rods, especially for tight radius bends. Short pieces of rod can be used as guide pins in place of dowels and are much stronger. Rod can also be threaded easily or turned down to size in a metal lathe.
  - Square and rectangular bar (often called strap when thin) are often lumped together as rectangular bar. These are available in very large sizes, but 1/4″–3/8″ are likely as thick as most shops will use. Thicknesses are available 1/8″–1/2″ in 1/16″ increments, up to 1 1/2″ in 1/8″ increments and up to 2 1/2″ in 1/4″ increments. Maximum available width will vary by thickness; for thicknesses up to 3/8″, width will be 12″ or less. Standard

length for these sections is 20 ft. Shorter lengths of small dimension sections are readily available at hardware stores and some supply houses. For structural purposes, design data must be derived from cross-sectional area and the allowable tensile stress for the given alloy.

- Square bar sizes start at 1/4″ and are often used in decorative grillwork since the shape allows for easy bending while still providing clean edges. They can also be used for hand rail pickets, locking pins that slide but do not rotate, and for furniture frames. Sizes between 1/4″ and 1/2″ are likely the most useable sizes as larger bars get quite heavy and square tube becomes the better option.
- Rectangular sections have many uses, but two of the most common are as door sills on flown walls and custom mounting tabs or brackets. In addition, strap can be used as edge banding on wood faces to add durability or to the ends of steel grating to prevent snagging (such as where a walk connects to stairs). Strap may be bent and/or welded to make corner irons, scenery bumpers, or curved decorative furniture components. When mounted on edge, rectangular bar can become a track for grooved wheels or as guides for moving scenery.
  o Special shapes such hexagons and ovals will find less use. Hex bar is sometimes used for custom coffin-lock keys. Hex bar is usually cold-rolled and much stiffer than round bar. The ends of hex bar can be turned in a lathe more readily than square bar for use as an axle or other pivot point that will not rotate in its mounts.
- Angles—While tube steel is one of the top contenders for framing, angles are sometimes the better solution. While angles are not very good for long spans when used solo, they can be combined with other components to create long spans, such as when used in bar-truss. Angles are available in two varieties, both of which are hot-rolled A36. Sizes are defined by the length of legs (may be unequal) and thickness.
  o Bar-sized angles are smaller angles that are hot-rolled low carbon steel. Sizes range from 1/2″ to 1″ leg in 1/8″ increments and up to 2″×2″ in 1/4″ increments. Under 1″ leg all share 1/8″ thickness, 1″–2″ angles offer 1/8″, 3/16″, and 1/4″ thicknesses. Unequal legs are available from 1″×5/8″×1/8″ to 2 1/2″×1 1/2″ with similar thickness groupings. Standard length for bars sizes is 20″.
    ▪ These sections are small enough to be of great use in scenic construction as well as in stage machinery and equipment. For other uses, such as platform framing or columns the designer must remember that angles are hard to bend but easy to twist. Angles are very strong when adequately braced such as when used in opposing pairs (tee shapes) or where the weak axis leg is braced (for example platform framing with intermediate toggles connecting the vertical legs). Angles can also be bent with a one leg in or out along a fairly large radius. See cold bending in Chapter 11 for examples. When placed with the hypotenuse down, equal leg angles work well as track for V-groove casters. Angles 1″ and under may be carefully bent in this orientation, but this must be done by hand-using jig blocks. Angles are also easy to lap over the edge of plywood to add significant durability. The 1/8″ minimum thickness also makes it much easier to weld without worry of burn through.
  o Structural angles are available in a larger array of sizes than bar-size angles. Similarly these may have legs of equal or unequal length. Equal leg length angles are available in sizes from 2″×2″×1/8″ up to 8″×8″×1 1/8″; uneven leg angles are available from 2 1/2″×1 1/2″×3/16″ to 9″×4″×5/8″. Smaller sizes up to about 2 1/2″ × 2 1/2″×3/16″ are well suited to theatre and opera scenery with large moving units being a common application. Larger sizes are more likely to be found as part of structure of an entertainment venue. Some sizes may be available galvanized. The standard length for these sections is 20' but can be ordered at 40'.
    ▪ Structural angles are less common to scenic fabrication but they have certain advantages. They are somewhat easier to use for bolted structures than tube steel because drilling is through a single face, avoiding alignment issues and angles do not crush like a hollow sections can. Angles also allow lapped joints when a perpendicular section is tucked under one leg. Larger angles can be rolled by machinery, but when not used for load bearing purposes, they may be kerfed to create tighter curves than rolled angle. Some examples of kerf cut aluminum angle are shown in Figure 11.27a and b.
- I-beams—These are most commonly found in the structure of a building, but small beams can be useful, even if heavy. Two features of I-beams make them well suited to structural use: the vertical web in the center resists vertical loads, while the top and bottom flanges resist lateral forces. This configuration uses much less steel than an equivalent strength hollow section. There are two main types of I-beam: wide flange and standard. Wide flange

beams increase resistance to bending and require less lateral bracing. I-beams are commonly used as horizontal members but may also be used as columns. These sections are designated by height and weight per foot (plf): e.g. a 3×5.7# S-shape would be 3″ tall and 5.7# pounds per linear foot.

- Junior I-beams are lighter, thinner sections that are similar in profile to S-types and are available from 3″×2.9# to 12″×11.8#; these do not have multiple weights per foot as do other types. The lighter weight and slightly narrower flange of these sections may have an advantage in entertainment fabrication because they retain adequate strength for typical loadings in the industry and their thinner profile makes them easier to drill through when needed. For comparison, a 4″×7.7# S-type beam has a 2.663″ wide flange and a .193″ thick web whereas a 4″×3.24# junior beam has a 2.25″ wide flange and a .092″ thick web.
  - These are excellent for long spans where legging is undesirable and a truss would be too tall. The advantages over wood beams (sawn or engineered) are the compactness of a metal I-beam, very high strength per height, and much less need for lateral bracing (possibly none if the beams are interconnected by say a floor).
- S-shapes (also known as American standard beams) have a slope of approximately 16 2/3% (2 over 12) on the inner flange surfaces. This profile is common to commercial construction and are often found throughout entertainment venues in rigging grids, catwalks, and other building structure. In many cases, these beams may be used as attachment points for scenic and lighting structures. Though the sloped flange can add difficulty to attachment, specialized hardware is available such as beam clamps and beveled washers that match the flange slope allowing bolt heads or nuts to rest flat. Trollies are readily available to use these profiles for moving heavy loads. The lighter size designations of 3″, 4″, 5″, and 6″ beams are the most likely candidates for scenic fabrication projects, but S sections are available up to 24″×121#.
- W-shapes have essentially parallel inner and outer flange surfaces. Though these sections are significantly wider than S designations, the nearly flat inner flange surface can be an advantage for bolted connections or when the beam will be filled for aesthetic purposes or for easy attachment of other materials. This is often done with dimensional lumber; W-shapes eliminate the need to bevel the filler boards to fit the flange. Oddly the lightest section designation is 6″×9#, both shorter 4″ and 5″ sections are heavier per linear foot. Outside of building construction, most fabricators will never encounter a W beam.
- M-shapes are members that are not classified in ASTM because they are limited production (or somewhat custom) items that may not be readily available in steel warehouses. These sections typically have cross-section features that do not meet the criteria for other listed shapes. Sizes range from 3″×2.9# up to 12.5″×12.4#. If available locally, some W shapes could be useful as they may be lighter, slimmer, and/or have flatter flange profiles. Design data for the use of some M-shapes as beams is provided in the *SCM*.
- HP-shapes are also known as bearing piles and are unlikely to be used for entertainment fabrication projects. They are similar to W-shapes except their webs and flanges are of equal thickness and the depth and flange width are nominally equal for a given designation. Due to their nearly square shape, they are often used as columns and as head block beams in entertainment venues. They are available from 8″×36# up to 18″×204#.

• Channels—Steel channels are essentially half of an I-beam, but with a full thickness web. Like I-beams, they are designated by height and weight per foot except for bar sizes. All channel sizes have flange slopes that match their I-beam equivalents. Since channels have half the flange material of an I-beam, they are best used where the main stress is pressing against the smooth face of the main web toward the flanges. If used in a vertical application they will require adequate bracing to prevent lateral buckling.

- Bar-size channels, like bar-size angles, are smaller and thinner sections than structural channels. These are made in 19 sizes from 3/4″ to 2 1/2″ widths and may be listed by dimensions or by height and plf.
  - These are small enough to be useful in steel-framed scenery such as platforms or automated/mechanized units and the machinery that moves them. In addition they can be used as very heavy duty planking on steel structures, but at higher cost than grating.
- Junior channels are characterized by having a very thin web in proportion to their size. These are available in 10″–12″ sizes that are used commercially these as stair stringers. In some cases, these could be viable for supporting long span scenery if properly braced.

- Standard channels are mid-sized sections available from 3"×3.41# to 15"×50#. Channels are often slightly lighter (by 1 or 2 lb/ft) than equivalent strength rectangular tubing but require more lateral bracing. This is usually not a weight penalty; for example a platform frame would require toggles to support flooring with either shape as a perimeter frame. 3" through 6" channels in the lowest plf sizes are more than adequate for the modest loads found in most entertainment applications.
    - Although these are not produced in sizes smaller than 3", there are possible uses such as long platform spans or slip stages. They also make excellent machinery bases, caster plates on very heavy wagons and stair treads (though junior channels are preferred). Another advantage to channel over rectangular tube is having only one surface to drill though when a bolted connection is needed.
- Ship and car channels are characterized by a very thick web which makes them the strongest types of channels. They are available in 3" to 10" sizes at one-inch intervals and in larger sizes at two-inch intervals. The only likely place to encounter these sections would be in grids for counterweight rigging systems.

- Tees—Because most tees are split from I-beams, they share many properties and are designated by WT-, MT-, and ST-types. Like those I-beams, tees are specified by depth and pounds per linear foot. Tees have a structural dis-advantage when compared to I-beams; the removal of the bottom web significantly decreases the amount of material available to resist tensile and lateral forces created when used as a beam. This can be overcome to some extent by inverting the T (web up) and connecting the web members.
    - Bar-size tees, like bar-size channel, are smaller and thinner. Sizes range from 1 1/2" to 2 1/2" with

Figure 3.10 6"×8.2plf American standard channel used for the frame of a CNC router table (per CNC manufacturer specs); note wedge washers used to level bolt heads.

the stem height being of equal length and thicknesses of either 3/16″ or 1/4″. These are quite suitable for lighter duty projects such as tracks or as center spans (toggles) inside an angle iron frame.
- Bar-sized tees are the most often encountered type in entertainment, traditionally as the guides for counterweight arbors. Design data for bar-size sections can be derived from cross-sectional area and the allowable stress of a given alloy.
  ○ ST-types range in size from 1.5″×3.75# to 12″×60.5#. The sections have tapered flanges that may be difficult to use in entertainment scenarios as they are difficult to fasten to and the tapered flange at the web may preclude their use as guides.
    - For entertainment fabrication the advantage of a structural tee is the availability of very short sections (as small as 1.5″) that are thicker and stronger than bar-sized tees. These can be used in place of similarly sized angles while providing higher resistance to twisting.
  ○ WT-types range in size from 2″×6.5# to 22″×167.5#, the majority of which are well beyond the scope of most entertainment industry use. These sections have the widest and thickest available flanges that are flat for most of their width.
  ○ MT-types range in size from 2″×3# to 6.5×6.2#. These sections may find specialized use in the industry as guides and tracks for example. These sections may have wide, thin flanges that are flat for most of their width.

Plate and Sheet

Plate and sheet are to metal what plywood is to lumber. They may be used as a high-strength, heat-resistant covering material or as a source for parts and pieces. Both are available with various finishes and textures. Most steel plate is rolled from A-36 steel and is defined as sections over 1/4″ thick when wider than 8″. Below that threshold it is considered steel bar. Thinner sections become strips and sheets. For structural plates, the preferred practice is to specify thickness in 1/16″ increments up to 3/8″ thick, 1/8″ increments for 3/8″ to 1″ thicknesses, and 1/4″ increments over 1″ thick.
- Thin plate—These can be fairly easily cut into custom shapes with a plasma cutter (or torch or jig saw). For entertainment shops, this is really anything over 16 ga and most likely to be 14–11 ga sheets. These thicknesses are well suited to many purposes. They can be welded to as bases for the armature components of organic sculptures or cut into arc-shaped strips that can be welded to a rolled bar for custom tees or angles. These are also thicknesses than can be used in a heavy duty manual brake for making structural shapes like steps or mounting brackets that need to be custom shaped. Thicker plate such as 1/4″–3/8″ may be cut to shape as well, but these thicknesses are also available as wide bar stock (10″–12″ wide) that are easier move and handle. Projects requiring modules that must be cut from full-sized sheets this thick are most like going to be jobbed out.
  ○ One type of plate that stands out and may wish to be purchased in full sheets is diamond tread. For example, 11 ga sheets are within the threshold of maneuverability for most shops, can easily be cut with a plasma cutter or saw, and are excellent for custom stairs or landings. An example can be seen in Figure 11.56a. Similarly, traction tread is punched and flanged 16 or 11 ga sheet that provides enhanced traction over diamond tread and will not hold water when used outdoors.

Figure 3.11 A diamond tread access stair and landing.

- Raised floor plates—These are a special subset of plate steel. These plates are specified by nominal thickness and weight per square foot. Plates are available from 18 to 12 ga and from 1/8" to 1" thicknesses. While they are for structural use, design data must be acquired from the manufacturer as it is not provided by the *SCM*.
- Sheet metal—For entertainment shops, sheet metal will usually be 16 ga and under even though by manufacturing standards sheet is 1/4" thick and under. Sheet steel offers more options than thicker sheets, including mill finish, galvanized, or textured.
  - Sheet metal has many uses from small props such as lanterns to decorative items like leaves and even light-duty hardware such as a French cleat for a large painting. Sheet steel can also be shaped into domes, cones, and similar shapes with the right tools (see Chapter 11 for details). Shops that build automation equipment for scenery will often use thin sheet to guard moving parts.
  - Textured sheets can be used as decorative surfaces. While diamond pattern plate can be used for walkable surfaces, light gauge, diamond tread sheet could be used as decoration such as for a bar, or over a plywood surface to imitate diamond plate. Other raised textures available include basket weave, diamond quilt (like back splash in an old diner), swirls, and even leather texture. Like other thin sheets, these can be formed on a brake, but they cannot be hammer formed without damage to the texture.
  - Corrugated sheets are readily available since they are usually used for siding or roofing. They are low cost and light weight, lending themselves

Figure 3.12 Corrugated sheet used to cover the wall on the set for *Bat Boy* at the University of Memphis.

to a variety of decorative purposes in entertainment. These sheets are always galvanized, so care should be used if any welding is required. Resistance welding produces the least amount of fumes and works well on very thin sheets. These sheets can be tricky to cut with any tool other than a metal-cutting circular saw or powered bypass shears, though small cuts can be made with snips or a jig saw when needed. Other roofing and siding shapes are available, but most have a painted finish and can only be screwed in place.

- Punched sheets are for decorative projects and are often used for radiator covers. They are excellent for privacy screens and other decorative panels in displays and exhibits. They can easily be backed with colored plastic or sandwich fabric between two sheets for interesting translucent panels.

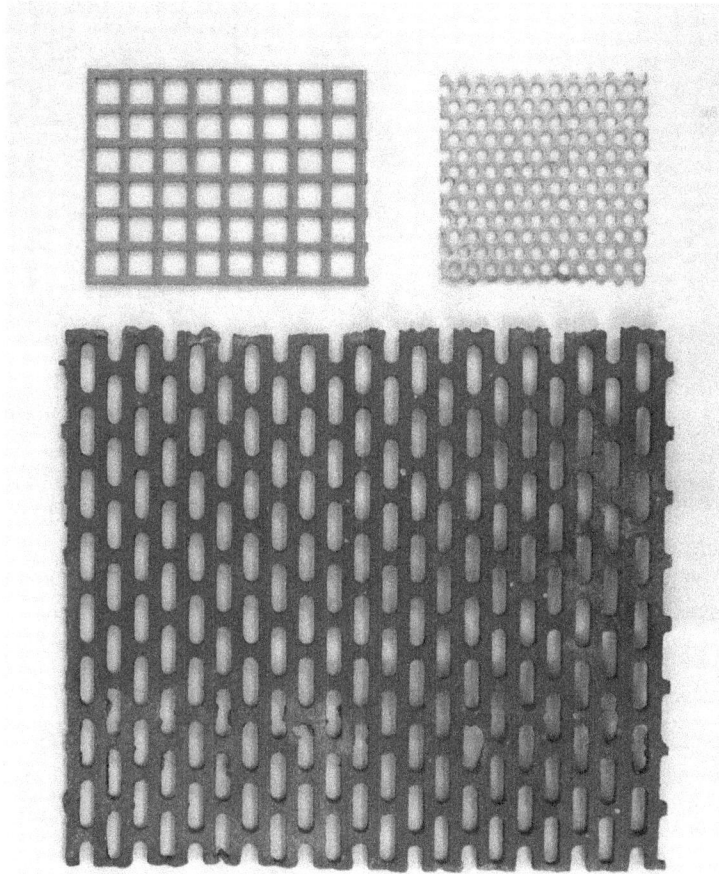

Figure 3.13 Samples of punched steel clockwise from top—square-punched 16 ga, round-punched 16 ga, and slot-punched 11 ga steel.

Special Sheets and Similar Products

Beyond flat sheets, steel is available further processed into textured and perforated sheets. Related are wire-mesh products that may be sold in panels or rolls.

- Expanded steel—These sheets are punched and stretched to make diamond-shaped openings in offset rows. Depending on form it can be used for work surfaces, protective covers, or walkable surfaces. Sheets are specified by thickness and opening size or open area percentage as well as raised or flattened. Raised style is better for traction but has sharp edges that require care when handling. Sheets can also be Long Way Mesh (LWM) which are the most common or Short Way Mesh (SWM) which are less common and will likely be special order.
- Raised sheets can be tricky to specify as the listed thickness usually refers to the thickness at the knuckle, not the thickness of the strands. The strand thickness and opening size are the key dimensions, especially if the sheet will be used as a walkable surface. Lighter gauge sheets are not span rated so any such use must have significant support determined by a qualified person.

42 • FABRICATION FOR THEATRE AND ENTERTAINMENT

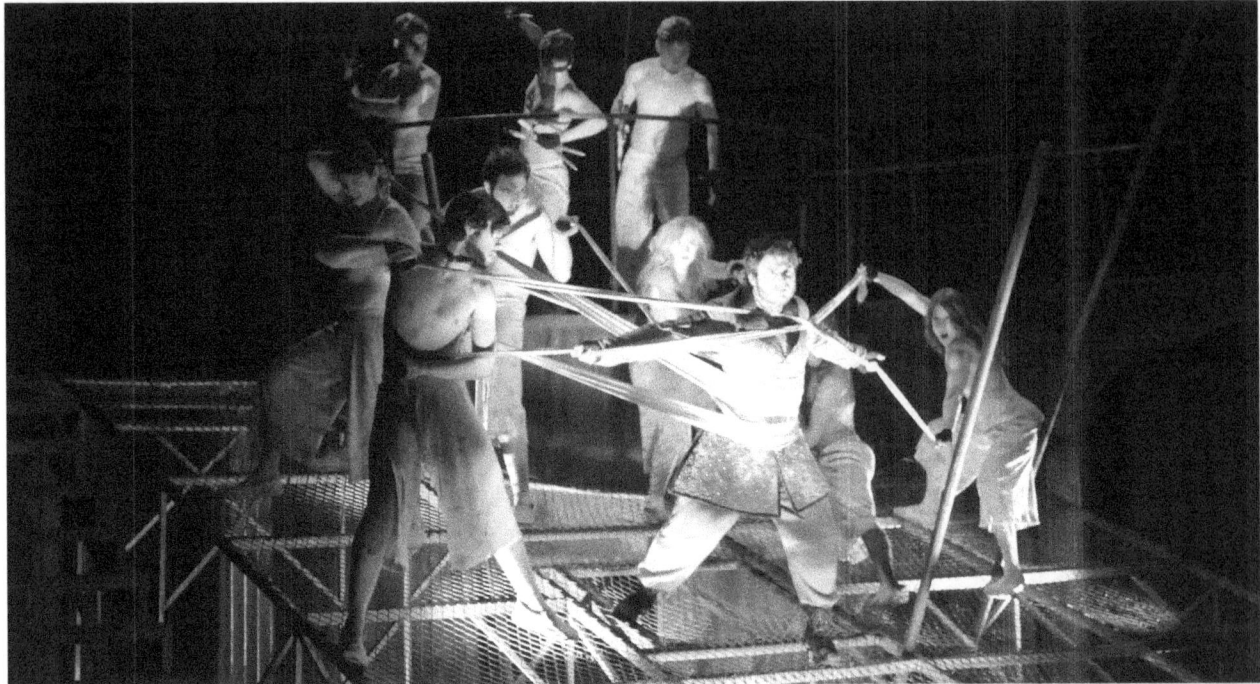

Figure 3.14 Raised expanded steel used for a raked acting platform. The steel was coated with elastomeric to cover sharp edges without reducing traction.

○ Flattened sheets are raised sheets that have been rolled flat to an even thickness, thus the knuckle and strand thickness are the same. These have essentially the same opening size as the original sheet. These sheets are great for work tables, security cages, and decorative panels.

○ Grating is very heavy gauge-expanded steel that is meant to be used on walkable surfaces. These sheets are span rated for both concentrated and evenly distributed loads. Their advantage is being lighter and lower cost than bar grating, but they retain sharp edges from processing that bar grating does not have.

Figure 3.15 A stage floor section made from expanded grating for a production of *Measure for Measure* at the University of Memphis.

- Bar grating—For longer walkable spans such as catwalks, industrial mezzanines, and scenic units that require up-lighting, bar grating is the best solution. Two styles are common: riveted and welded. Both are fabricated from vertically oriented rectangular bar. Riveted grating consists of zig-zag bars between straight bars. These may have a flat surface or be serrated for extra traction. Welded bar grating consists of parallel bars connected by perpendicular rod or bar set flush to the surface. Bar grating relies on bar size for span, thus grating made from 1 1/2″ × 1/4″ bar will have a higher load rating than one made from 1″ × 3/16″ bar. Steel bar grating is very heavy and high cost; in many scenic applications it has been replaced by aluminum grating to save weight. Welded bar grating is also available galvanized or powder coated. Stainless bar grating is also available.
    - Welded grating may have either a plain or serrated top and consist of bearing bars made from vertically oriented rectangular bar that is connected by round or twisted square bar cross ties pressed into notches and then welded.
    - Press-lock grating uses dovetail slots in the bearing bars to connect cross ties made from smaller bar sections. The advantage to this style grating is the much narrower space between bearing bars (3/16″–1/4″) that make it ADA compliant when bearing bars are perpendicular to direction of travel (though they run parallel to length of the panel). Press-lock is also popular for steel pathways where carts with casters or material handling equipment need to traverse.
- Wire mesh—Steel mesh is available in an extensive number of types and sizes/weights from very thin mesh that can be molded by hand, to welded bar mesh used to reinforce concrete. Mesh products may be available in plain steel or galvanized and as rolls or sheets depending on gauge. The variety of types can make specifying mesh for load bearing use somewhat difficult; consulting a vendor is very helpful.
    - Square opening wire mesh offers the widest variety of types. Square mesh is sold in sheets and rolls (often referred to as hardware cloth) and may be woven or welded. Woven mesh further offers plain weave like a basket or crimped wire weaves in which the wires have a zig-zag pattern between intersects. Mesh with openings under 1″ are specified by squares per inch; larger are defined by opening size and wire gauge. Fencing and reinforcement mesh for concrete is also available as rolls and sheets and are made with heavier gauge wire, up to about 8ga. Reinforcement mesh has 6″ openings while fencing is usually 3″–4″. One advantage to rolls of reinforcement mesh is the availability of very wide sizes; 7′ wide is not uncommon.
    - Rectangular mesh is welded and available in rolls or sheets typically with 1″×2″ or 2″×4″ openings. Rolls use light gauge wire (typically 16 or 18 ga) and are available in 36″ or 48″ widths of varying length. Sheets are fabricated with heavy gauge wire (14 ga or larger); fencing panels for example are made with 6 ga wire and may be as large as 50″×16′.
    - Decorative patterns are available primarily as woven sheets with double square, round, and rhomboid, in addition to square and rectangular openings. These are excellent for exhibits, display panels, or privacy screens. They can also be backed or used to sandwich other materials such as fabric or translucent plastic.
    - Poultry mesh is essentially standardized with 1″ hexagonal openings and may use between 23 and 20 ga wire. This is sold in rolls of varying width and length at home centers, farm stores, and industrial suppliers. It is excellent for supporting cloth covered sculptural shapes or for holding artificial greenery.

Figure 3.16 Welded bar grating used for lighting catwalks.

Proprietary Shapes

Several companies make special steel shapes that make up a variety of structural systems. Several are quite useful for entertainment use.

- Strut channel—Often referred to as Unistrut, a very recognizable brand name, there are other

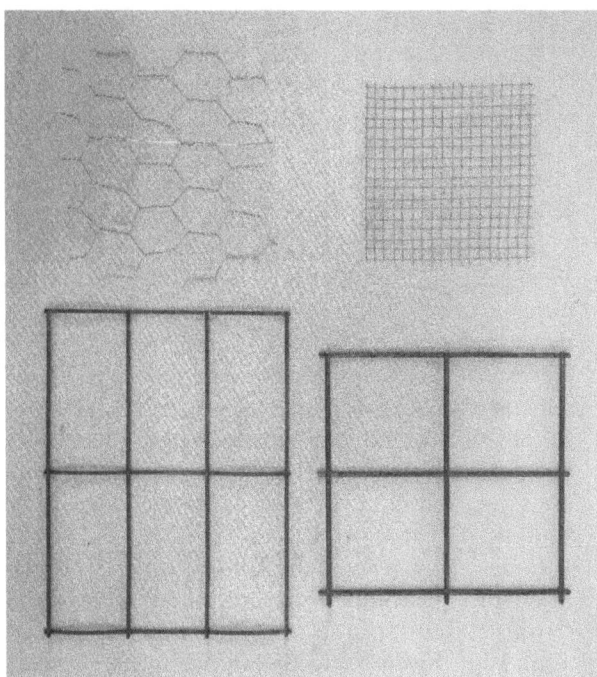

Figure 3.17a Samples of steel wire cloth clockwise from top—poultry cloth, 4×4 galvanized hardware cloth, 3"×3" 11 ga carbon steel mesh, and 2"×4" 14 ga galvanized mesh.

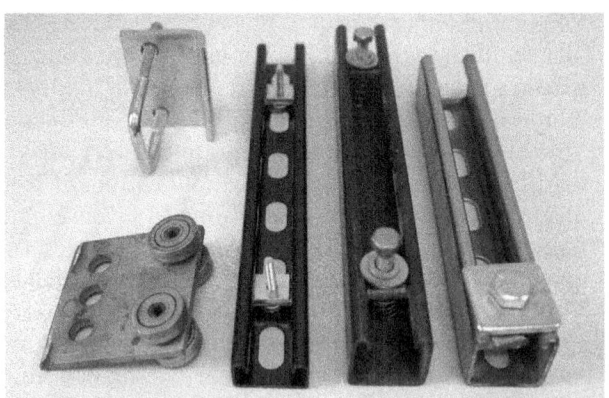

Figure 3.18 On the left are a trolley and a beam clamp for 1 5/8" strut. Examples of strut from left—low profile slotted strut with mounting studs, a standard 1 5/8" square strut with quick fit 3/8"-16 nuts and slotted square strut with 1/2"-13 nut, bolt, and square washer.

Figure 3.17b The pit rail at the University of Memphis. The lower portion uses 3"×3" 11 ga steel mesh to protect the orchestra from loose objects.

manufactures that produce similar products. It is probably the most used proprietary steel shape in theatre.
- ○ Struts are available in a few widths, with 1 5/8" being the most common, and may be available with three wall thicknesses and two depths (of single strut). Other widths include 13/16", 1 1/4", and 1 1/2".
- ○ An array of connectors and other hardware designed for strut channel makes it a versatile, modular material. Nuts and threaded studs are available with many inch and metric threads, along with square washers and shaped plates that are sized to match the strut making attachment quick and easy.
- ○ Struts may be painted or plated, solid or punched. Punched struts offer round holes, short or long round end slots and rectangular slots along the back for easy mounting. Beyond single struts, manufacturers offer an array of welded configurations such as back-to-back, horizontally stacked, S-shape and others depending on strut series.
- ○ Many scenic and stage equipment items may be made with this material. Some small converted spaces and black boxes use them as lighting positions, overhead rigging points, and tracks for scenery when no fly space is available (though the rollers are quite loud). Manufacturers offer hardware to assemble stairways, racks, and platforms. Strut frames are like having a giant erector set. The advantage of the material is that it only takes simple cutting and bolting to use. The dis-advantage is that it requires many relatively expensive fittings and the final result might look a little too industrial for some design situations. There are also capping strips to fill spaces between mounts to clean up the look a bit.
- Steel track—Almost all of the steel track used in entertainment is for overhead applications. For that reason, only track that has a listed load rating from the manufacturer should be used. There are two U.S. manufacturers of track commonly used in entertainment venues: Automated Devices Company and H&H Specialties. Both companies offer at least two sizes of steel track each of which have different variants based on per linear foot loading requirements. The most common track size is 2 1/2" × 2 3/4" capable of up to 50# per foot loading depending on manufacturer.
  - ○ Theatre tracks generally use centered hanging brackets and offer splice brackets to extend their length. Other bolt-on hardware allows them to operate curtains or light-weight scenery via off-stage ropes or motors. Carriers have synthetic wheels so they operate quietly. There are steel door carriers available from other suppliers that will fit curtain tracks, but care should be used to not overload the track. Steel curtain track is for straight-line use.
  - ○ Door track should be used for heavy units. Door track is available in more size and load carrying abilities; track is available rated for a 5000 lb unit on two carriers. These tracks may be center mounted or wall mounted (single and double track) or hang on centerline. Some door track is so close in size to smaller curtain track that parts may interchange so the user must confirm which type of track is in use. Some light duty door track may offer radius units.

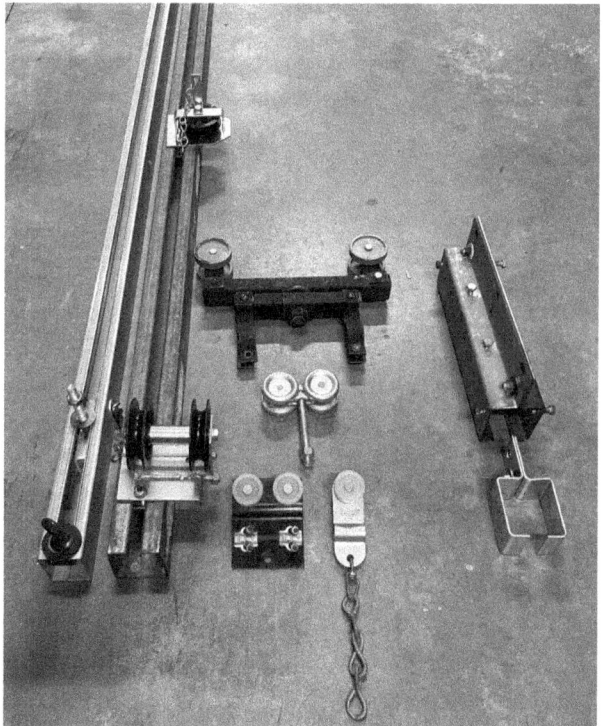

Figure 3.19 An example of door track on the left with a door carrier and track stop. To the right is a sample of theatrical curtain track shown with a "double-down" and "turn-around" pulley set installed. To the right of the track are various carriers for curtains and scenery including an all steel door truck that can be shared between the two styles of track. Farthest to the right are examples of curtain track hardware: a hanger bracket and a splice bracket with adjustment screws.

- Telescopic tube—Telespar is brand name manufactured by the Unistrut Company, but a few other manufacturers make similar products. These may be perforated or unperforated. Perforated tubes are available in sizes from 1 1/2"×1 1/2" up to 2 1/2"×2 1/2" with 3/8" holes on all four sides punched every 1" on center for easy bolting or pinning. Plain tubes are available round or square (square in telescoping sizes from 3/4" to 2 1/2"; round in 3/4" and 1" OD). Both types of square tube are available in a plain or galvanized finish. Additional hardware such as tees, face mounted angles, inside angles, base plates, and joining straps add to the material's versatility. This can be a great material for theatrical scenery, especially for smaller companies that may need to disassemble and store much of their stock. Variable height platform legging or fabric-covered masking units that can be adapted to different sizes when used for touring are examples.
- Slotted angle—These are manufactured from punched and formed sheet steel and are available in various sizes: 1 1/2" equal length leg is common at home centers. 2 1/4"×1 1/2" up to 3 3/16"×1 5/8" unequal leg sizes are usually available from industrial suppliers. These have a variety of holes and/or slots punched into them so pieces may be easily bolted together and are galvanized or powder coated for corrosion resistance. Special shears are sold to cleanly cut the angle. Slotted angle may be an option for companies without welding capability that need the benefits of steel; it is also highly reusable. Slotted angle is well suited to building storage racks and shelves and can be used for both upright and horizontal components. Corner plates for reinforcing 90° joints and punched flats for use as diagonal bracing are also available. Flats may also be a good material for custom brackets.

Chain

No discussion of steel for use in entertainment would be complete without including chain. A wide variety of chain types are available. Many readers will be familiar with chain used in entertainment rigging but may be unaware of the variety of types that can find other homes in the industry. There are essentially two types of chain: lifting and non-lifting. The key distinction is essentially dynamic use; many types of utility chain are rated for hanging, but not movement. Only chain for non-lifting applications will be discussed in this section. Chain of unknown origin should be assumed to be ungraded and thus never used for critical applications.
- Welded link—This is a very common style and some types offer tangle resistant (shorter, more oval links) or lay-flat links (with a 90° twist). They are also available plated and un-plated.
  - Graded chain is used for load binding and/or towing depending on grade. Three grades, 30, 40/43, and 70 (transport chain) are available and are the strongest type of non-lifting chain. For example, a 1/4" grade 30 chain is rated for 1300 lb whereas the same diameter utility chain is rated for 800 lb. These are available in many home centers, farm stores and catalog suppliers. Because graded chain may appear the same as utility chain but has a significantly higher cost, it should be stored separately in labeled containers or tagged/marked.
  - Utility chain is lighter duty chain that is hard to differentiate (or maybe impossible) from graded chain once out of the manufacturer's packaging. Utility chain in addition to metallic coatings can be powder coated which is excellent for barriers or decoration. Cut-resistant chains are hardened and may have links with round or square sections.

Figure 3.20 Slotted angle used to make storage shelving for greenery.

Some welded-link style utility chain may be provided with a working load rating. If the manufacturers design factor is unknown, it should be assumed to be 1:1 and the appropriate design factor then added for the application.

- Jack chain — These light duty figure-8 shaped chains are most commonly encountered on traveler curtains but can serve other purposes such as for retaining a hinged lid on a trunk or to hang small light fixtures for example. It is sized by wire gauge, thus trade size 8 uses 8 ga wire. These have much lower weight ratings than other wire chains; for example trade size 6 may have only an 88 lb load rating. Double jack chains overlap the loop ends making them less likely to tangle.
- Lamp chain — This light duty chain is used for hanging lamps and chandeliers. Unlike other chain, it is available in unique shapes such as oval, long oval, or gothic and may be made from round wire or twisted square wire. Other alloys such as brass and aluminum offer links with decorative stampings. Like other wire chain it is sized and weight rated based on the wire gauge and base metal. These are available in many plated finishes and colors. In addition to lighting use, these may also find a variety of uses in properties and craft shops.
- Wire chain — For hanging light to medium weight objects wire chain is often sufficient. Two styles are common: lock-link chains have loops that are bound end to end so they do not slide or twist; coiled wire chains have a loop at each end with the wire ends twisted in the center. While these are not as common as welded link chains, they are fairly low cost and can be rated up to a 580 lb load.
- Flat link chains — Sash chain and plumbers chain are quite similar other than shape. Both are made from stamped and punch sheet that is folded over to create the link. Sash chain has a tear drop shape, while plumbers chain has an oval shape. Both are available in plated steel as well as brass, aluminum and stainless. They are excellent for props, such as for a drop front desk, but also for small mechanical effects because they roll well over pulley sheaves.

RESOURCES

- *Handbook of Welded Carbon Steel Mechanical Tubing* — This volume is published by The Steel Tube Institute. The handbook provides manufacturing specs, design values, and recommend practice for fabrication for hollow steel sections (HSS) and mechanical tubing.
  - www.steeltubeinstitute.org

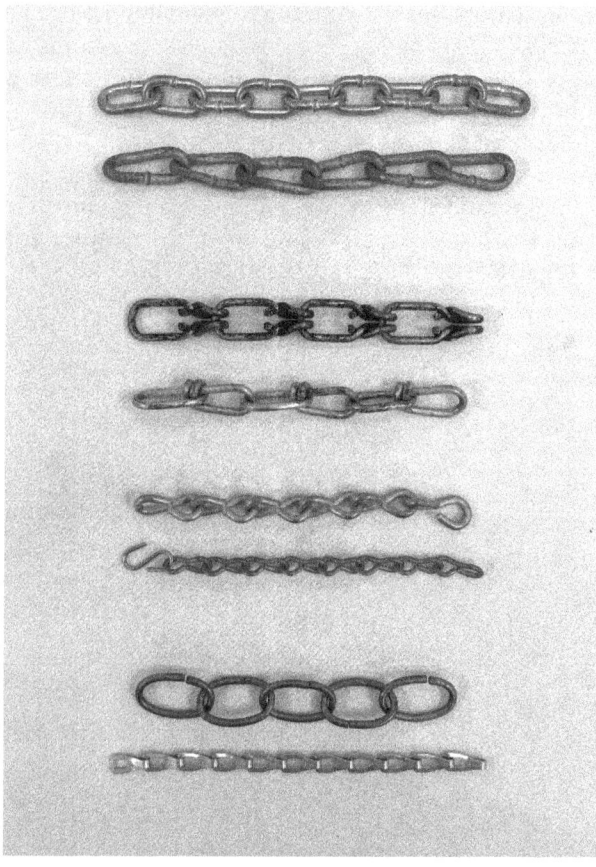

Figure 3.21 Examples of hanging chains from top—3/16″ utility chain and lay-flat chain, two types of wire chain (lock-link and coiled), two sizes of jack chain, followed by lamp chain and sash chain.

- McNichols — This vendor offers a wide variety of punched steel sheets, hardware cloth, and other woven products, as well as expanded steel and tread way grating.
  - www.mcnichols.com
- McMaster-Carr — This is an industrial supplier that offers thousands of products related to metal fabrication, including strut channel and accessories, raw materials in small quantities as well as tools and fasteners. The company offers a print catalog, app, and web site.
  - www.mcmaster.com
- Grainger — This is a large industrial supplier that offers thousands of products related to metal fabrication, including fasteners, chain, door track, and raw materials in small quantities. For those who work at a large company, state facility, or college/university it is likely that the organization has an account with Grainger. The company offers a print catalog, app, and web site.
  - www.grainger.com

- Unistrut—This is an international manufacturer of strut channel and accessories that is a sub-brand of Atkore. They catalog offers all the information a user could need to determine which strut variant and hardware is best for a given project.
  - www.unistrut.com
- Automated Devices Company—This manufacturer makes tracks, carriers, and related hardware for theatrical curtains in a variety of types and sizes. I addition they offer motorized and automated systems.
  - www.adctracks.com
- H&H Specialties—This company is a division of Texas Scenic that manufactures steel and aluminum tracks for theatrical curtains as well as the related carriers and hardware in a variety of types and sizes.
  - www.texasscenic.com

Chapter 4

Aluminum Shapes and Applications

Aluminum has been widely adopted across various areas of the entertainment industry. For many, the aluminum trusses used in touring will be the most notable usage, but aluminum's properties make it an excellent material for use far beyond truss. The two major benefits of aluminum that make it so attractive are its light weight per volume and its very durable oxidation that reduces or eliminates the need to paint it. It does have a few drawbacks such as higher cost than steel by weight, its somewhat lower impact durability and being generally trickier for new weldors than steel. It may not be the first material that a shop adopts, but experienced weldors can learn to tame aluminum without too much trouble.

Aluminum is about 1/3 of the weight of steel by volume but also has about 1/3 of the stiffness of steel, thus structures that need to resist bending will require members with more mass. This does not mean a one to one increase; structures designed properly for aluminum's characteristics can still be 40%–50% lighter than a steel structure of similar capacity. Likely the most important design consideration when using aluminum for structures is the significant reduction in yield strength of the weld-affected area. While welded aluminum structures can be re-tempered, doing so requires a tempering oven large enough to house the entire unit; for most shops, finding and enlisting a company to do this would be difficult and unlikely to be cost-effective. This type of work is generally reserved for aircraft and high-end race cars. As well, aluminum can be somewhat riskier to bend. When bending is required, the easiest solution is to use a non-tempered alloy that will not crack as it stretches. Tubing generally requires a much larger minimum radius than steel, thus roll bending is often more effective than draw bending, but draw bending can be done on certain shapes.

Most shapes will be similar to steel, but there may be variables such as thickness, or more commonly the corner or edge profile. While steel is bent or rolled to shape, many aluminum shapes are extruded. This allows for different edge finishes, thus many shapes may be available with both rounded and square edges.

One important note for purchasing aluminum: for small projects it is often handy to purchase small sections in short lengths from a home center. The buyer will pay a premium for this convenience and these may be clear coated. Any clear coating will need to be removed over a significant area if any welding is to be done. It will likely be impossible to match the original finish after; buying uncoated aluminum should always be a priority when welding.

HOLLOW SECTIONS

Aluminum offers fewer options for hollow shapes than steel, but the key shapes of round, square, and rectangular tubing are available in enough sizes to be quite valuable to fabrication. In many shops, aluminum square tubing is the primary metal member instead of steel. These sections are specified by external dimension(s) and wall thickness (in inches or mm). For designing structures, the design values can be found in the *Aluminum Design Manual* or in *Structural Design for the Stage*, though those familiar with using wood or steel data may be surprised by the added complexity of welded aluminum structures.

- Tubing—Aluminum tubing is extruded from various alloys, including 3003-H14 (cold worked), 6061-T6, and 6063-T5 with 6061-T6 being the most common. Tubing is predominately extruded but drawn sections of round tube are available. These are stiffer and have more consistent dimensions. Square and rectangular tubing is available with either a square corner or a rounded corner, though both options may not be available in every size. Typically smaller sizes intended for decorative use will have square corners and may be listed as architectural, while large sizes intended for structural applications will mostly have rounded corners. Tubing is generally produced in 20' lengths.

- Square tube sizes range from 3/4" up to 8" with two wall thicknesses under 1" and up to four wall thicknesses for sizes 3" and up.
  - These will have many of the same applications as steel tube, but render lighter units that will not rust. Like steel, aluminum square tube is common for large framed structures that need to be suspended (where the lighter weight is a big advantage) or where they will be exposed to weather. Because of the extrusion process, some sizes of rectangular tube will nest, such as 3/4" being able to nest into 1" that has an 1/8" wall.

Figure 4.1 A hybrid cart at ATOMIC (www.atomicdesign.tv) with modular aluminum sides made from 2" square corner aluminum tube.

- Rectangular tubing ranges in size from 1/2"×1" up to 5"×8". Generally any rectangular tube under 2" width will have an 1/8" wall, while sizes over 2" wide, especially larger depths, can have up to a 3/8" wall.
  - These sections are great for light-weight spans or where add strength is needed in one axis compared to square. Because of the extrusion process, some sizes of rectangular tube will nest; for example 1"×1 1/2"×1/8" will fit tightly into 1 1/2"×2"×1/4"; these sections do exhibit very different strength properties so this usage would be limited.

Figure 4.2 A custom walk-board fabricated from 1"×3"×1/8" rectangular tube at Accurate Staging in Nashville, TN. These fit the support walls fabricated by the company and are primarily used to support lighting and audio equipment, thus being fit on the lower rung.

- Round tube offers diameters as small as 1/4" OD but these are generally softer alloys that are untempered for easy bending. Tempered tubing sold in straight runs will start at 1/2" diameter and run up to 12" diameter. Almost all sizes offer at least three wall thicknesses .049" up to 1/2". Tubes may be available in 6061-T6, 6063-T5 as well as 3003, 2024 high strength and some 5xxx series when higher corrosion resistance is required.
  - Truss is the most common use for round tube as mentioned, but it is an excellent material for railings, platform legs, and custom structures such as unique add-ons to truss. As well, there are many sizes of aluminum tube that will nest (because thicker walls are more common in aluminum than steel) while remaining usably light weight. Like steel tubing and pipe, round aluminum tube can be an excellent choice for short columns.

Figure 4.3a Custom follow spot chairs manufactured from aluminum tube.

Figure 4.3b Aluminum tube for scaffold style framing called "walls" at Accurate Staging in Nashville. These are used to support the company's modular staging as shown. These units are stocked in various standard heights to make assembly easy.

- ○ Other shapes include ovals, double wall tube (coaxial shape with four connecting ribs), and hex tube. Ovals make especially nice welded hand railing while double wall tube and hex tube offer unique properties for exhibits and displays.
- Pipe — Aluminum pipe is sold in the same diameters as steel, but more schedule types are commonly available from Schedule 5–160 in either 6061-T6 or 6063-T5 alloys. Like other round sections, pipe will resist moderate stress from any direction. More care must be used when bending aluminum pipe; round tube is usually a better option when curved pieces are needed as properly sized compensating dies are available for many tubing benders. Aluminum pipe is common in unthreaded 20 ft lengths as schedule 40 and 80.
  - ○ In addition to threaded fittings, slip fittings are readily available for most pipes up to 2″ ID from companies such as Hollaender (aluminum fittings for steel or aluminum pipe). The Hollaender website even has an entertainment applications section. These are primarily designed for building safety railings in industrial settings but often find a variety of uses in entertainment fabrication. There are far too many variants to list, and the catalogs are readily available from the manufacturers. These can be used for overhung loads when proper design factors are applied (provided by the manufacturer), for pipes that span between welded structures or as a side arm on a vertical pipe that is properly secured at both ends.
  - ○ Pipe clamps are similar to the scaffold clamps used with steel but offer more varieties, such as bolt-on half clamps. They are mostly designed for typical truss-sized pipe and tubing from 1 1/4″ OD to 2 1/2″ OD, making them well matched to entertainment use. These are most often found on equipment that will be attached to truss. In addition they can be used to build tube and pipe structures much like cheeseboroughs are used with steel.

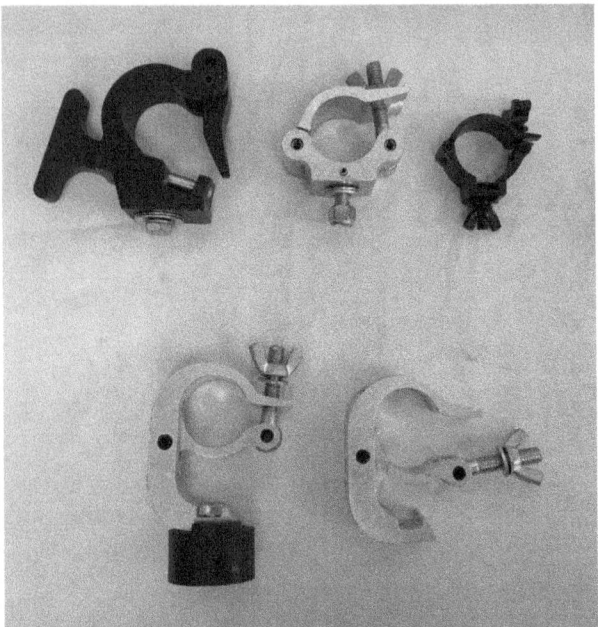

Figure 4.4 The top row of clamps from left—a self-holding style clamp (tongue drops in place), a heavy-gauge clamp for 2″ pipe and a light-duty clamp for 1 1/2″ pipe. On the bottom are examples of another style of self-holding clamp designed for a 12 mm bolt; one has a fitting for threading 1 1/2″ pipe for a tail down.

Pipe Fittings

Like steel pipe, threaded fittings are available for aluminum pipe. Similarly, these should not be used for overhead structures. In limited cases, some structural slip fittings are suitable for overhead use when manufacturer design limitations are followed. These fittings are available in essentially the same variety of shapes as those for steel. Supplier catalogs, such as those from McMaster-Carr, are excellent resources for discovering available fittings. For pressure applications, fittings must be matched to the pipe.

- Threaded fittings—Low pressure aluminum fittings have a 150 psi maximum and may be available from industrial plumbing supply vendors and industrial catalog suppliers. These pipes are excellent for air or water transfer for effects where the plumbing may be exposed to the elements and/or the lighter weight may be an advantage.
- Welded fittings—Threadless fittings are available to match schedule 10 and 40 and are excellent candidates for entertainment use. Schedule 10 thin wall offers both butt weld and socket weld fittings, whereas standard wall fittings are butt-welded. These can be used where a smooth finish at the joint is required, in hand railings for example. Welded fittings should only be installed by a certified welder if used for pressure applications.
- Slip fittings—These fittings use grub screws (set screws) to hold pipe in place and thus cannot be used for plumbing. They are readily available for most pipes up to 2″ ID from Hollaender (aluminum fittings for steel or aluminum pipe). The Hollaender website even has an entertainment applications section. These are primarily designed for building safety railings and racking in industrial settings but often find a variety of uses in entertainment fabrication. There are far too many variants to list, and the catalogs are readily available from the manufacturers. These can be used for overhung loads (such as a lighting side arm on a vertical pipe) when proper design factors are applied (provided by the manufacturer) or to assemble a variety of structures. Some fittings have a fixed depth socket while others may slide along a pipe or drop over much like a Rota-lock. They truly are one of the most versatile means of building with pipe. Hollaender offers anodized aluminum pipe to work with their fittings.

SOLID SECTIONS

Like steel, many shapes are available in aluminum; some will find extensive use across the entertainment industry, while others (especially smaller sections) will find more limited use, mostly for properties and decorative items. Also like steel, some shapes will be manufactured via two methods: extrusion which is the most common and by cold forming which imparts slightly higher stiffness. Solid shapes tend to be available in a wider array of alloys, especially shorter pieces (6′ or less) available from industrial catalog suppliers. While not all shapes will be available in multiple alloys, most will be available in 2024, 6061, 6063, and 7075. Fewer shapes are available in 5xxx series alloys.

- Bars—Aluminum bars include rectangles, squares, rounds, and specialty shapes that may be extruded or cold formed. These are generally available in 12′–16′ lengths. The smaller sizes can be used in scenery or properties as they are; larger sections are often the raw material for machined parts, especially 7075 bars. Many shapes are also available in high tolerance versions that have much smoother surfaces and are exceptionally consistent in size. These are often drawn and offer higher stiffness. Bars may also be available in metric sizes, especially from catalog suppliers.
  ○ Rectangle and square bar sizes range from 1/4″ to 4″ for squares and from 1/8″×1/2″ to 3″×6″ for rectangles. Strips can be ordered coiled in a

variety of widths and thicknesses when very long runs are required.

- Thinner flats, often referred to as strap, can be roll bent to match radius cut sheets to make custom tee or angle or as edge banding on curved plate, such as for a reveal on a sign. Thicker squares and bars can be used for furniture and projects that require arcs (solid shapes bend well). Though this is best done using softer alloys, these can be readily cold formed to tighter radii than hollow sections for curved elements.

○ Round bars (or rods) are generally those sections with a diameter of 3/16″ or larger; smaller diameters are considered wire.

- Rod is rarely used for any significant structure but is an excellent choice for curved shapes because it is easy to bend in many types of bender, though care should be used to avoid cracking. Even helixes are an option with practice.

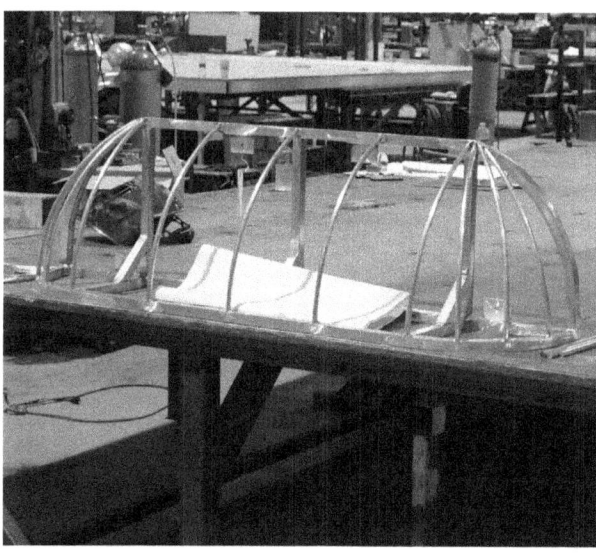

Figure 4.5 An aluminum awning in progress at Adirondack Studios made from 1″ square corner tube and solid round rod.

○ Unique shapes of bar are available such as half-round, hex, and zees. These can be used as trim work or as sculptural elements.
- Angles—These are extruded in two types: American Standard, designated by L, which match steel angles and square edge, designated by LS, that do not have the rounded edges but retain a small fillet on the interior of the vertex. While 6061 and 6063 will be the most readily available, catalog suppliers stock L angles in 2024 and 7075 alloys. LS equal leg angles range in size from 3/4″×3/4″×1/8″ up to 4″×4″×1/4″, while L angles range from 1 1/2″×1 1/2″×1/8″ to 8″×8″×1″. Unequal leg L angles range in size from 1 3/4″×1 1/4″×1/8″ up to 8″×6″×3/4″, while LS angles range in size from 1″×3/4″×1/8″ to 5″×4″×1/8″. The 16 ft lengths are standard for LS angles, 24 ft lengths for L angles.

○ Thinner angles are frequently applied to the edges of road boxes, speaker cabinets, and counters to provide protection or aesthetic trim. In some cases, larger and thicker angles may be a better option than square tube for bolted assemblies. These may also be riveted to sheets to make a reveal when aluminum welding capability is unavailable. This works quite well when a mitered and bent corner is used and the perimeter is seamed along a straight edge. See Chapter 11 for an example. Angles also make very good dual axis guides, for example slide-out units under a deck.

- Trim—Aluminum is extruded in a variety of trim shapes such as angles, U-shapes, and tees. What distinguishes these from other similar shapes is the overall size and thickness. Most trim pieces are 1/16″ thick or less and rarely exceed 2″ in any dimension.

○ While these are unlikely to be welded, they can be applied with adhesive, tape, or mechanical fasteners. Metal trim pieces are used much like their wood counterparts to create decorative contrast, especially on props. These light pieces can also be used as the structure for props or decor that does not need to support significant weight.

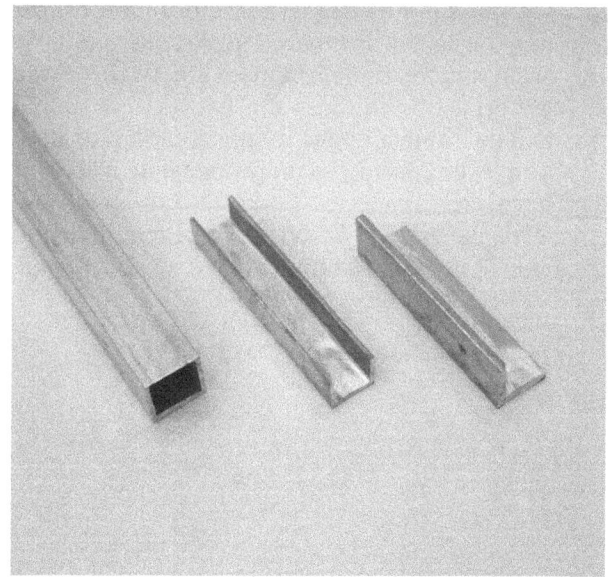

Figure 4.6 Examples of aluminum trim from left—1/2″ square tube, 3/8″×1/2″ channel, and 1/2″ angle.

- I-beams—Aluminum is extruded in a variety of I-beam shapes, usually from 6061 or 6063 alloy with a T6 temper. Some sections may be more useful to entertainment fabrication than their steel counterparts due to lighter weight or unique shape. Like steel I-beams, these are used in situations where the primary stress is parallel to the web. The flanges add significant lateral strength thus requiring less bracing than channel. Standard length is 25 ft.
  - Aluminum Association (AA) Standard beams offer more sizes and are shaped closer to wide flange steel beams but with very flat webs making bolted connections easier. Sizes are slightly lighter than the American Standard counterparts and more available than those that match Junior or S-shapes.
    - The availability of small sizes and the flat flange make these the best choice when aluminum is needed for moderate to long spans, but the depth of a truss is unworkable.
  - American Standard (AS) beams offer the same shapes as Junior steel beams but are lighter per linear foot. Sizes offer 2–3 weights (plf) per beam size much like steel.
    - These are excellent where a steel beam is too heavy or the strength of steel is not required. Many if the same hardware pieces will fit these beams, such as a beam clips or clamps, though users should be aware that mixing metals for permanent installation can cause a galvanic response leading to corrosion at the point of contact.
  - Wide flange beams are square or nearly square with tapered flanges. While the square profile may be useful in some applications, similarly sized square tubing is more likely to be the material of choice as the flat face of tubing makes it much easier to attach materials and/or may be considered more appealing when left uncovered.
  - Wide flange Army/Navy (AN) beams are available in the same widths as standard wide flange beams but have flat flanges. The key difference is that only the largest sizes (4″ and 5″) are square; smaller beams are taller than they are wide.
    - These would be an excellent choice when lateral bracing needs to be kept to a minimum on a long span. Flat flanges make attachment much easier than standard wide flange beams or rectangular tube since they can be easily bolted. They are likely to be special order only from most suppliers.
- Channels—These sections are available in four types extruded from 6061 or 6063. Standard length for channels is 25 ft. Channels are an example of how aluminum differs from steel. Using a channel that is 40% deeper than the required steel section could provide the same strength while weighing about 50% less than the steel member.
  - Aluminum Association channels have square edges and flat flanges. These are available in sizes from 2″D×1″W to 14″D×6″W. Shorter lengths of these channels up to about 4″D are available from catalog suppliers.
  - American Standard channels match steel shapes with rounded edges and sloped flanges. These range in size from 2″D×1.22 plf (1.4″ wide) to 15″D×17.3 plf (3.76″ wide). These are available in fairly large sizes (up to 12″D) from catalog suppliers and many sizes are available from commercial metal suppliers.
  - Car and ship channels have a much wider flange than American Standards with a similar slope and thicker webs. These range in size from 3″D×2.23 plf (2″ wide) to 10″D×10.1 plf (3.625″ wide). These sections are much less likely to be used in entertainment fabrication due to their significant weight per section.
  - Canadian channels are similar to Aluminum Association channels but with slightly wider flanges. These range in size from 2″×7.06 plf (1.46″ wide) to 12″×10.3 plf (3″ wide). Availability of these sections will depend on supplier and region.

BUILD 11

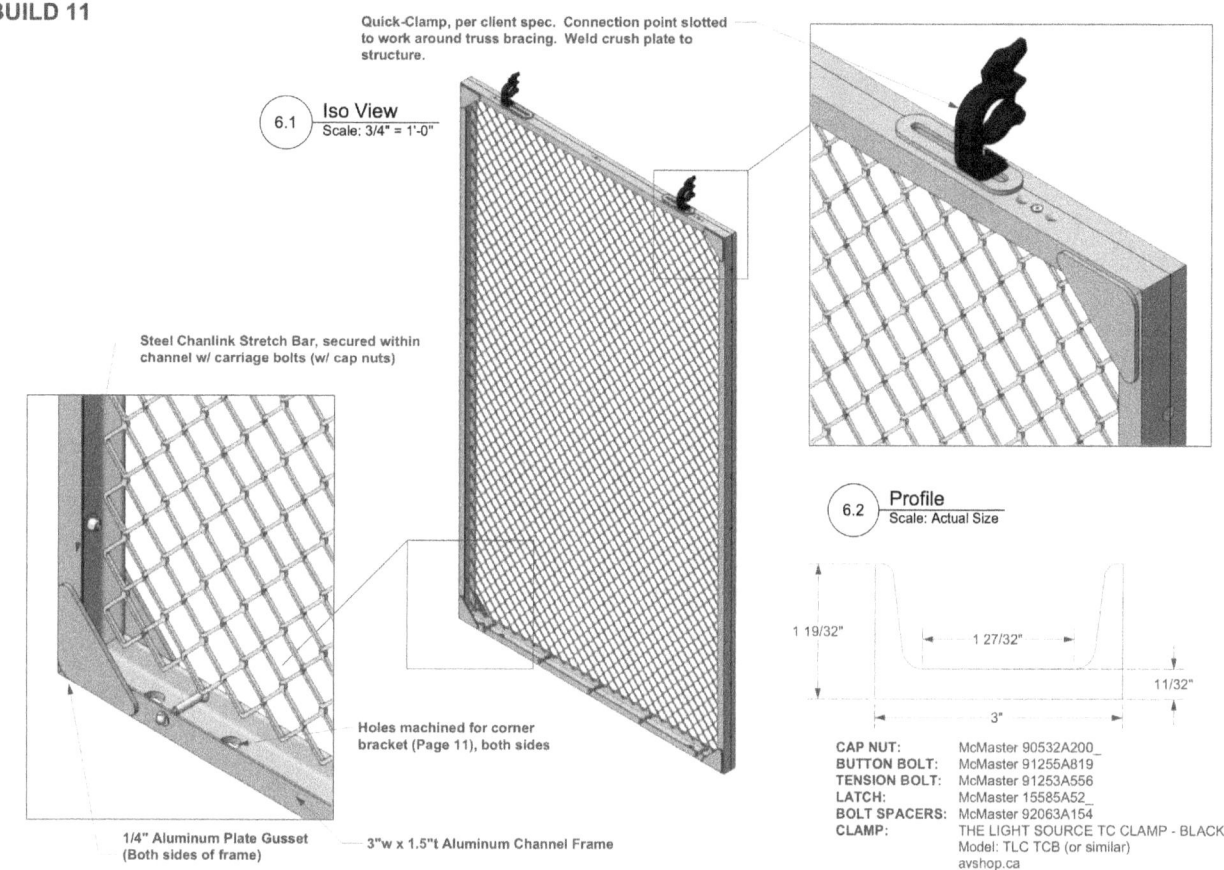

Figure 4.7 A sample panel for a wrestling cage for a televised event designed by Jake Lacher at Accurate Staging, Nashville. The wall panels use 3"×2.07 plf American Standard channel.
Source: Photo courtesy of Jake Lacher.

- Tees—Aluminum tees are available in two common types: Aluminum Association (AA) Standard and Army/Navy (AN). Like other sections, AA tees have square edges. AA sizes range from 3/4"W×3/4"D×.31 plf to 2.5"W×2.5"D×1.77 plf and a few very large sizes up to 6.5"W×10"D×10.5 plf. AN tees start at 1.25"W×1.5"D×.384 plf to 3"W×6"D×3.24 plf and also offer some very large sizes up to 6"W×8"D×11.2 plf. Availability of any size will vary by supplier, with many being special order.
  ○ Tees are regularly found as the guides for counterweight arbors in modern rigging systems because they can be custom-ordered in lengths that nearly eliminate seams. They can also be used for stiffening large panels (much like a wooden hog-trough) or for supporting the seams of facing materials such as lauan on a large flats framed with square or rectangular tube when easy attachment points are needed on the rear face. Tees allow hardware to be easily attached by drilling through the web for example. These combine well with angle perimeter framing as internal toggles that are less likely to twist than angle. Army navy tees offer a number of sizes with extra deep flanges that may support higher loads with proper lateral bracing.
- Zees—Aluminum manufacturers offer zee-shaped sections. Unlike Z-shaped steel roof purlins, aluminum zees are much like a channel with one flange flipped. These are available from 1 3/4"W× 1 3/4"D×1.09 plf to 5"W×3 1/4"D×6.19 plf. Unique to these sections is the width measurement referring to a single flange, making the overall width nearly double the listed size.
  ○ The flat nature of these flanges can make these very useful for attachment points (such as a hanging ledge) or for supporting removable panels when integrated as a surrounding frame.

PLATE AND SHEET

Aluminum plate and sheet divide at 1/4" thickness with anything thinner being sheet. Both are manufactured in a wide selection of alloys and tempers. For most shops, precut flat sheets will be the standard though coiled sheets are available in very long lengths (these are common to companies than manufacture semi trailers for example) that could be useful for skinning very tall flats. Sheet thickness is typically specified in thousandths of an inch, while plate is most often specified in 1/8″ increments. Cut sheets and plates may be available up to 144″ long and may be available up to 72″ wide.

- Plate—In aluminum, plate is readily available in thicknesses from 1/4″ to 1″ in widths from 24″ to 72″ and lengths from 72″ to 144″. Plate usually offers a very wide variety of alloys at suppliers because of the multitude of applications. Plate is common in 1100, 3003 as well as various 5xxx alloys. Some applications, such as tread plate, are likely to be 6061.
- Sheet—Aluminum sheet is available in a much wider array of alloys than hollow sections. 6061

Figure 4.8a Large "bird houses" in progress for Bavarian Blast Waterpark in Frankenmuth, MI at Adirondack Studios. These are made from 6061 aluminum sheet.

Figure 4.8b Triangular aluminum sections design to bolt together to form hexagon panels that were then attached to overhead truss for a rock and roll tour.
Source: Photo courtesy of Erica Causi.

is common and available with various options, including hard anodized (a gray finish like cooking pots) that is very stiff. When forming is required, 3003 sheets are much less likely to have surface cracks when bent in a brake if proper dies are used. 2024 and 7075 are excellent choices when wear resistance is required, such as for making custom guides (these alloys cannot be welded). Some sheets are sold with a sealed paper cover that prevents oxidation. These save a step as there is no need to clean them, simply peel the protective cover just before welding. Another option for most alloys is a polished (with either a brushed or shiny) surface or unpolished (mill finish) which most fabricators will use for a surface match to other shapes used in a project. Like bar, tight tolerance sheets are available for special projects; these may be required for automated units for example.

- Textured sheets can be used as decorative surfaces and are often adhered to non-metallic surfaces for reduce cost and weight over a solid metal surface. While diamond pattern plate can be used for walkable surfaces, diamond tread sheet would be used as decoration such as for a bar, or over a plywood surface to imitate diamond plate. Textured sheets are common with basket weave, diamond, and tread style surfaces. Like other thin sheet these can be formed on a brake, but they cannot be hammer formed without damage to the texture.
- Punched sheets tend to be sold in smaller sizes than solid sheet or plate (approximately 3'×5') and are primarily used for decorative projects. They are excellent for privacy screens and other decorative panels in displays and exhibits. They can easily be backed with or sandwich fabric or plastics for interesting translucent panels. Punched shapes may be squares, ovals, union jack or diamonds.

58 • FABRICATION FOR THEATRE AND ENTERTAINMENT

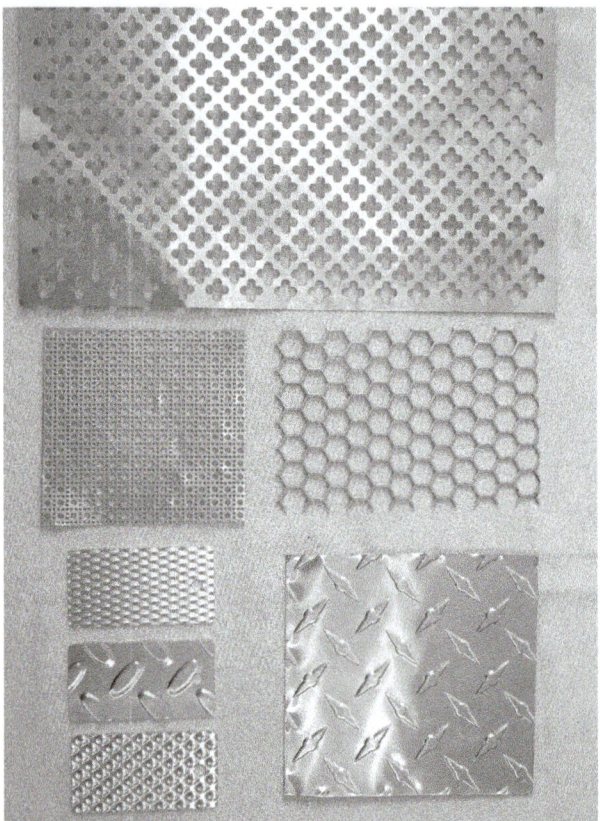

Figure 4.9 Samples of three patterns of punched aluminum sheets at top, and four patterns of textured sheets at the bottom.

- Laminate—Some manufacturers of high pressure laminate (HPL) also make aluminum laminate. Theses thin sheets are usually anodized on one face and have a mill finish on the other to aid bonding to a substrate. Some offer a subtle surface texture

Figure 4.10 Aluminum laminate swatches showing hard-anodized gray and copper colors.

such as ribbing. Though intended to be used on a flat surface, flat finish sheets with no backer can be bent to follow a shallow radius. For tighter radii, the material could be passed through a slip roll (while protecting the face) to be installed on a curved face. These are usually available as 4′×8′ and 4′×10′ sheets.

- Foils—While food service foil may be the first product that comes to mind, industrial foils in both standard 1100 and corrosion resistant 5052 are available up to .002″ but are also available in thickness similar to heavy duty food service foil which ranges from .0009″ to .0013″. Industrial foils are also available with a self-adhesive backing, making them very easy to install. Those in the lighting world will be familiar with black-painted foils used for masking and light leaks. While commonly acquired from theatrical suppliers, industrial catalog suppliers, such as McMaster-Carr also sell it. Industrial foil should not be used for food!
  ○ When bonded with fabric, foils can make an easily paintable material that holds its form. All thicknesses, especially self-adhesive types, of foil are excellent for skinning non-metallic materials that need to appear metallic. Those who build effects for magic acts often use contrasting polished foil and flat black painted foil to make an effect, such as a disappearance table, appear thinner than it actually is when placed in front of a black background. When applying foil, the user should be aware that the texture of the underlying material will translate through.

SPECIAL PRODUCTS

- Grating—Aluminum grating requires applying its unique design properties to make efficient use of material. These characteristics allow for a few more styles of grating to be available. Its corrosion resistance is also a significant advantage when exposed to the elements; painted steel grating is subject to wear and thus much repainting.
  ○ Bar grating is offered with either a smooth or serrated top surface. Like steel, the depth of the bar provides span rating, thus aluminum grating will always be deeper than the equivalent steel for the same load rating, typically by about 40%. Standard panel length is 3′×12′.
    ▪ Press-lock aluminum grating is manufactured much like its steel counterpart with smaller perpendicular bars pressed into dovetail slots in the bearing bars. The primary difference is load and span rating. Aluminum panels require shorter maximum span distances and

approximately 50% lower loading per square foot of the same thickness compared to steel.
- Swage-lock grating is unique to aluminum because it is able to be compressed in order to lock components together instead of welding or press-fitting. The bearing bars may be standard bar, but extruded I-bar and T-bar shaped bearing bars increase load capability without increasing thickness. T-bar types may have raised edges to improve traction.

Figure 4.11 Swage-lock aluminum bar grating at Accurate Staging, Nashville. The grating will be used in the companies modular platforming, allowing for uplighting and other effects.

- Plank grating is mostly unique to aluminum because it can be extruded, edge formed, and then punched. These C-shaped planks are punched with a pattern of circles or diamonds that are then flared to improve traction and increase the stiffness of the plank.
  - These are usually used for scaffold planks but can be ordered in custom lengths that could make them easy to integrate into scenery as a span requiring a very thin section profile.

- Expanded sheet—Aluminum sheet is offered in many of the same smaller sizes of expanded sheets as steel; flattened sheets are somewhat more available than raised and produced in 1100 and 3003 alloy (not for walkable surfaces). Designer shapes, such as a seashell shape openings, are available as well. Grating thicknesses (with span ratings) are made from 5052 alloy.
- Wire cloth—Aluminum wire cloth is much like its steel counterpart, but mostly available with square openings under 1″ with plain or crimped wire but some designer styles are sold as well. A similar product is plaster mesh; this is very thin expanded sheet with very small diamond openings sold in rolls

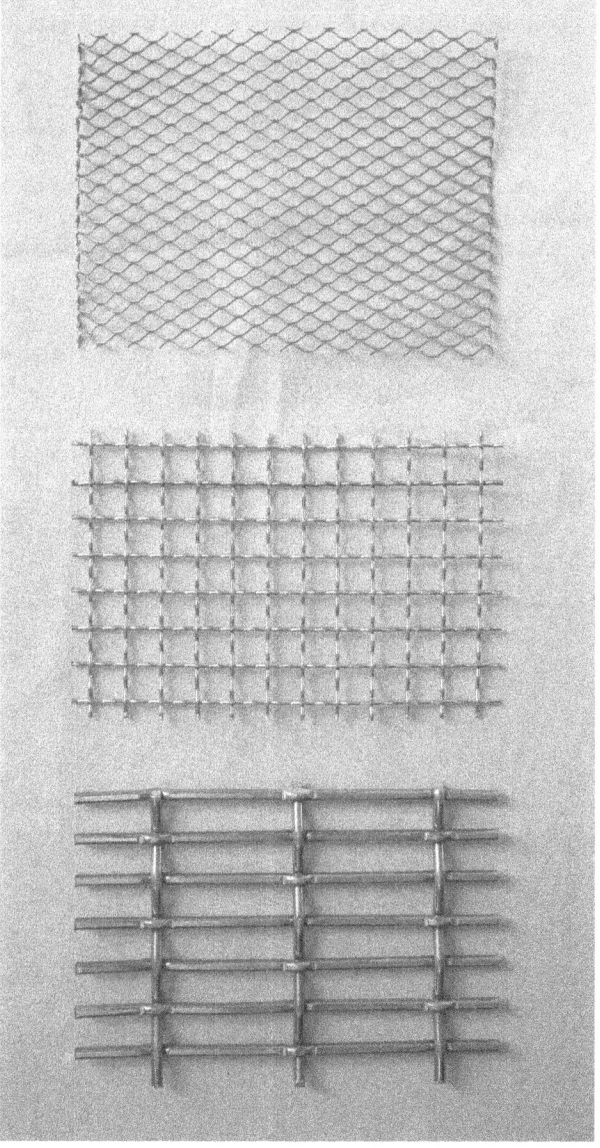

Figure 4.12 Examples of aluminum mesh from top—lath mesh, 2×2 crimped mesh and 11 ga welded-wire decorative mesh.

or sheets. It is commonly used in place of lath to hold plaster or stucco and can be used for similar applications in scenery to apply a surface coating. It can also be formed to contours relatively easily and could be a decorative surface in itself.

- Extrusions—While many standard shapes are manufactured via an extrusion process, the term is more often associated with complex shapes. Some are available from suppliers as stock shapes, but ordering custom extrusions is also relatively common.
  - T-slot framing is one of the most common stock extrusions and used for bolt together structures. These are square, rectangular (may have multiple slots in the wide face), or quarter round and have T-slots on some or all faces (faces without slots are designed to be trim). The slot can hold either the head of a fastener, the tab on a bracket or a hex nut when used with proper length bolts. As well, they are often drilled and tapped to hold compatible hardware in place or make stops for sliding hardware. Many inch and metric sizes are available. Small versions are commonly used for the framing for 3D printers, while larger extrusions are used for modular display framing or equipment housings. There is an array of compatible hardware available to connect these much like steel strut channel.
  - Modular deck framing is another common use for extrusions in entertainment. These maybe designed for a variety of platform thickness as well as single- or double-sided decking. Larger units tend to have a single deck face to be used on legging similar to scaffolding while thinner platforms may be decked on both faces and drop into a perimeter angle or zee frame allowing for easy changes for floor color or texture.

Figure 4.14 Modular platforming using a custom extrusion at Accurate Staging, Nashville. The inherent groove is designed to hold the head of a hex bolt for quick, strong installation of handrail. It also allows mounting of custom facings or other decorative items.

  - Perforated tube framing is similar to Telspar but not available in nesting sizes. In addition to perforated square tube that can be bolted or pinned to, the extrusion process allows these to be available with a single flange or U-shape flange on one face that allow for easy mounting of display or divider panels.
- Track—Aluminum is often the material of choice for track because it can be extruded in shapes that are ideal for bending, while retaining needed

Figure 4.13 Examples of 1 1/2" square T-slot framing and 1 1/2"×3" double T-slot framing. A close look shows the center of the square framing tapped for mounting.

strength. Many types of aluminum track are shaped like I-beams with the addition of medial flanges. This design makes them resistant to bending in two axes and the flat flanges provide smooth surfaces for both carrier wheels and mounting clamps. As well, some companies offer C-shaped track that matches HD steel curtain track; these provide a lighter-weight solution that is compatible with the same carrier hardware as their steel counterparts. Other shapes such as low-profile track that can be integrated into ceiling panels and double channels that are a single unit are available as well.

Figure 4.15 Three examples of aluminum track and a pair of carriers. The taller U-shaped track is much stiffer than the shorter version requiring fewer pick up points, though it does not have a higher load rating per linear foot. The I-shaped track is one of the most common patterns used for curved curtain tracks. This is the smaller of the two most common sizes.

- Aluminum honeycomb—These panels feature hexagonal openings that, when skinned, act like a multi-axis I-beam. They are sold as un-skinned cores to add light-weight support inside hollow structures and as faced panels. These are most often aluminum skins that may then be painted or have other materials, such as wood, plastic, or print media applied. Some companies offer hybrid panels that use advanced materials, such as carbon fiber or aramid as the facing. Aluminum honeycombs are an excellent upgrade from plastic and wood panels for signage as they won't warp or sag from heat, nor will they degrade when exposed to the elements (though the surface treatment may hold up differently). While stock panels are flat and can be used for vertical or horizontal applications (and may have a span rating for loads), many companies offer curved panels by special order that make excellent

exhibit material or can be used as column segments. An excellent example of hybrid use would be to create a large counter or reception desk by using cultured stone bonded to a honeycomb core. This can give the impression of a very large stone slab that is about 70% lighter than solid stone.

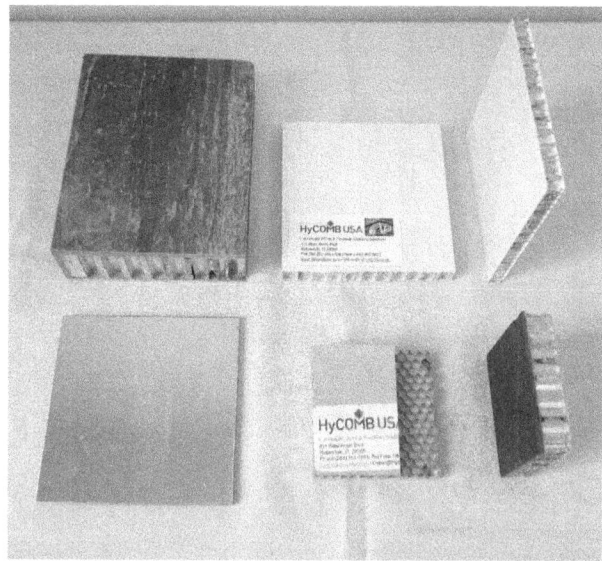

Figure 4.16 Samples of aluminum honeycomb with various materials as the bonded surface. Clockwise from upper left—1 1/2" core with cultured stone surface, two examples of Aramid textile (resin cured) as the bonded surface, two examples of cores bonded to porcelain (one with cutaway revealing the core) and a 1/4" panel with mill finish aluminum face.

RESOURCES

- *Aluminum Design Manual*—This is published by the AA and offers design values for most structural aluminum shapes. This is some of the data from which the aluminum design values used in *Structural Design for the Stage* are derived.
  - www.aluminum.org
- McNichols—This vendor offers a wide variety of punched aluminum sheets, and woven products, as well as aluminum bar grating and punched tread way planks.
  - www.mcnichols.com
- WilsonArt—This company is a manufacturer of HPL and aluminum laminate. They also offer excellent technical data for their products.
  - www.wilsonart.com
- Formica—This company is a manufacturer of HPL and aluminum laminate. Formica products are available for order at many home centers.
  - www.formica.com

Chapter 5

Hand Tools and Manual Machines

This section is intended to be a quick reference of hand tools that are specific to metal fabrication. While the vast majority of work done in the various shops in the entertainment world will be done with machinery and power tools, there are many hand tools that can be used to refine fit and finish. Unlike wood working, there are many manually powered machines available for metal working; since these use no electricity, they are included here. These are especially important to display work that will be seen up close. More common hand tools that would be shared across areas are not included here as there are many resources that cover them. Though there is not an included section for Personal Protection Equipment (PPE) in this chapter, one should remember that at the very least, safety glasses and/or a face shield should be worn anytime a striking motion is used to operate a hand tool. In addition, the reader should refer to Chapter 13 for specifics of PPE use.

HAND TOOLS

Fewer hand tools are dedicated to metal working than wood working, but most are quite specialized and serve a purpose that cannot be done without them.

Cutting Tools

- Hack saw—While a portable bandsaw is the "go to" for many metal cutting jobs, a shop should never be without a hack saw or two. They are available in different styles, but the two main ones to have are a mini saw that allows the blade to stick out of the front a bit and a full frame saw that holds the blade in tension either inline or at a 45° angle for access to tight spots. Typically hack saw blades are installed to cut only on the push stroke but the mini saw is often better used on the pull stroke. Blades are specified by length and teeth per inch (TPI). Higher tooth counts are generally used for thin metal and lower counts for thick. Lower TPI blades always work better with aluminum; fewer teeth allow chips to clear more easily.

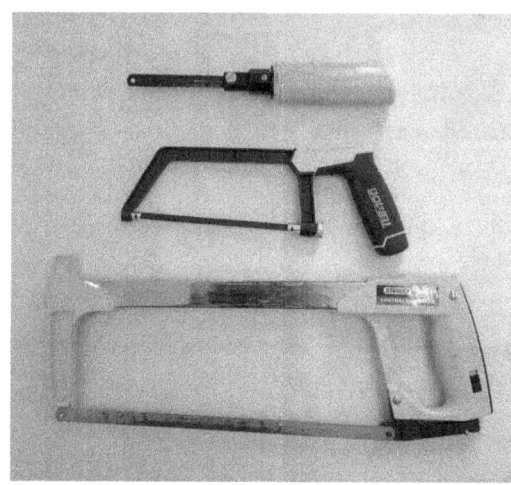

Figure 5.1 From top to bottom—a close quarters hack saw, a 6" mini hack saw frame and a full-sized 12" frame. This full-size frame also stores spare blades in the upper span.

- Aviation snips—These are similar to sheet metal shears but are easier to use because of their compound design. The jaws use a bypass style cut and are designed for left-hand curves or right-hand curves. Some versions may have extra short or extra-long blades that are best for straight cuts. Handles may be inline, offset, or vertical. These are best used for thin sheets up to about 18ga steel or 16ga aluminum. One note for the user: the serrated blades do leave a slightly rough edge that may need to be dressed.

64 • FABRICATION FOR THEATRE AND ENTERTAINMENT

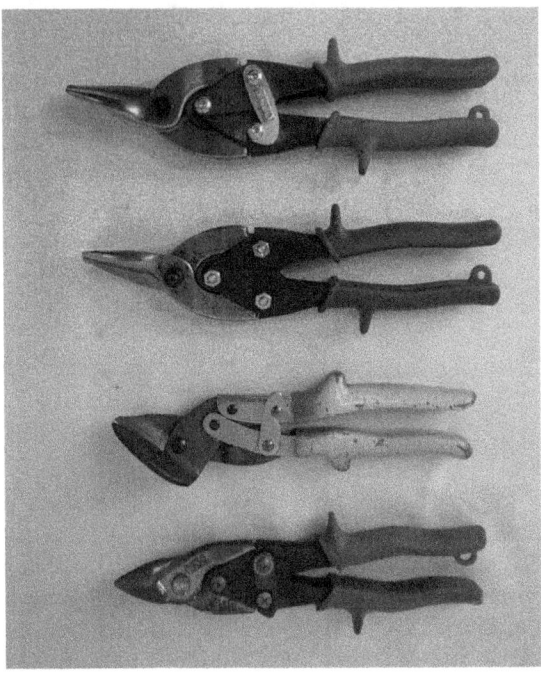

Figure 5.2 Top to bottom—right cutting, left cutting, offset snips or "throatless" and finally "Bird's beak" snips.

- Nibblers—These pliers like cutters are available in two styles. Punching nibblers have a square jaw that is often used to make the rectangular holes required for low voltage switches. Bypass nibblers are hand-held shears used to cut out shapes, much like aviation snips, without deforming the off-cuts.

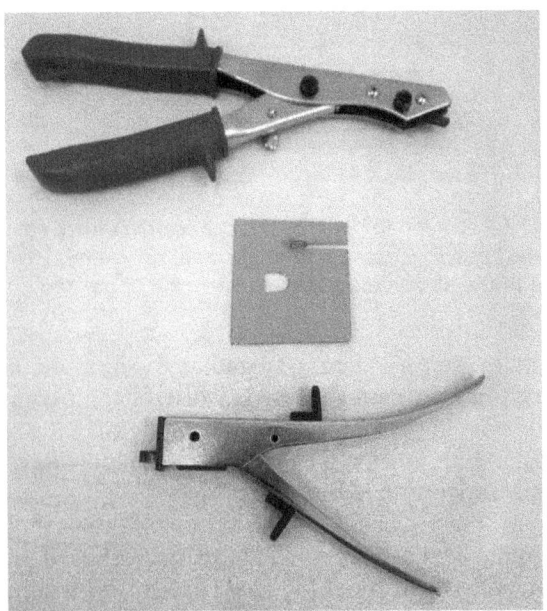

Figure 5.3 Double cut nibblers (top) and punching nibblers (bottom) as well as respective sample cuts.

- Pipe and tubing cutters—These cutters have two guide wheels to hold the tool perpendicular to the tube and a cutting wheel that is tightened during the rotation of the tool. Screw feed tools must make a 360° rotation and often have a built-in ream because all of these cutters compress the tubing and make an internal burr that should be removed when used for plumbing. Ratcheting style cutters have a pivoting internal head and are useful in tight quarters. Single size, tight-quarters cutters are self-adjusting and can only be rotated one way. There are also chain type tubing cutters, often referred to as muffler cutters, that are similar to a locking chain clamp, but with cutting wheels on every other link. The advantage to these is that they cut fairly large tube and do not require a full 360° rotation.

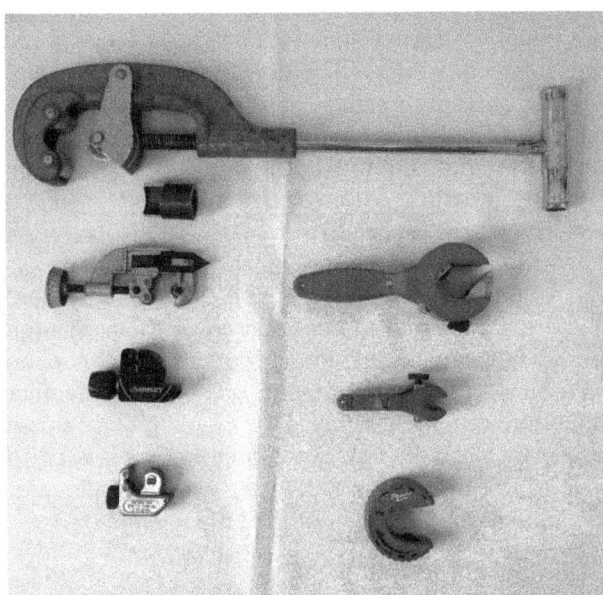

Figure 5.4 A pipe cutter (top) with a cut-away section of pipe showing the internal burr made while cutting, a screw feed cutter with ream and two small screw feed cutters (left column), and large and small ratcheting cutters followed by a close quarters cutter for 1" tube (right column).

Shaping

- Through punches—These hole-making tools are for sheet metal and make a far cleaner hole than drills or hole saws. They also tend to leave a duller edge that needs little deburring.
  - Swing-arm punches, often called Whitney punches, may be hand-held or bench mounted. Much like a rivet nut tool, there are interchangeable punch mandrels and nose pieces to punch various diameter holes. Bench-mounted units

will punch larger holes and/or punch through thicker sheet. These are for punching fairly small holes.
  ○ Knock-out punches (a.k.a. chassis punches) require a pilot hole be drilled to allow the threaded mandrel to pass through. A hollow die is mounted on the mandrel before passing through the pilot hole; a cutting die is then threaded onto the mandrel. The mandrel has a hex or square head allowing the use of a wrench or socket to pull the cutting die through the metal. The most common punches are used for 3/4" to about 2" diameter holes, but square and rectangular punches sized to fit common low voltage switch bodies are also available.

- Dimple dies—These cone-shaped dies are used after a hole is punched in sheet metal to flare one face. When small dies are used, the raised flares can be used to improve traction on sheet metal steps; when larger dies are used, dimpling significantly stiffens the sheet, often eliminating the need for welded stiffeners. Small dies or those used on soft metal may be used in an arbor press; heavier use will require a hydraulic press.
- Hammers—There are many more hammers for metal working than wood working. They may be made from a variety of materials, but the two most common to metal working will be steel and brass. Steel hammers are for driving pins, bending, or forming hot metal. Brass hammers are used to

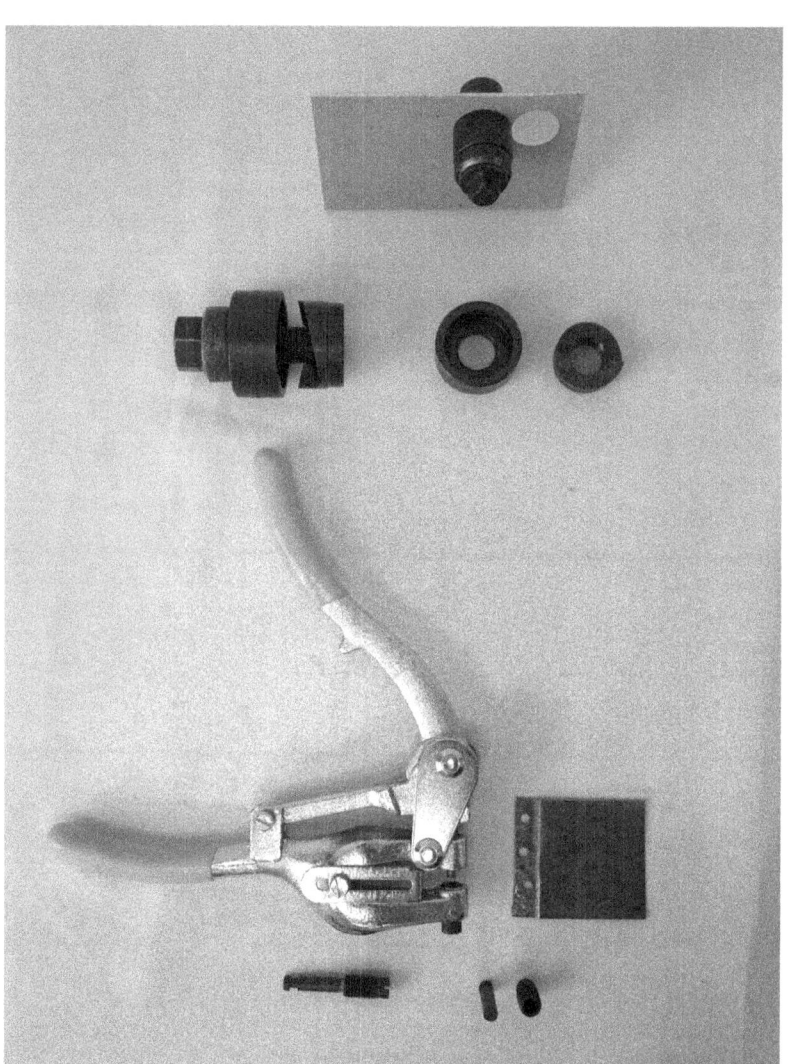

Figure 5.5 A set of knock-out punches (top) showing the smallest punch ready to cut, a large set assembled on a drawbar as well as a punch and die with a hand-held swing-arm punch (bottom) shown with a pair of punch/die sets and a punched sample.

Figure 5.6 A dimple die in a hydraulic press with a sample flared hole as well as a larger example showing the two components.

- Cross peen and straight peen hammers have a linear peening end designed for many uses: this can create an indentation to guide a bend, be used to stretch hot metal or create grooves when used with a backing die. Their linear nature (especially cross peens) makes small versions great for peening welds. There are various types of cross peen hammers with the German pattern being the most common.
- Dead-blow hammers are generally a plastic head loosely filled with steel shot whose inertia prevents the head from bouncing. Many are all plastic, but for working with metal dual-head hammers with a soft plastic face and a harder brass face are quite useful for assembly. The soft face can persuade parts into place without move metal objects into place (such as bolts or dowel pins) without damage. As well, in places where sparks could be dangerous, brass or other non-sparking hammers may be required. Steel hammers should only strike tools designed to do so; hammer faces should not be struck against each other as they may split or chip. Hammers for metal working are also offered with many more weights than claw hammers for wood. For example, cross peen hammers may be as small as a few ounces, to as large as three pounds with many sizes in between. This allows the hammer to exert the effort, not the user, when handled properly.
- Ball peen hammers are one of the most common to encounter in the metal shop, but surprisingly many new to fabrication are unaware of the purpose of the ball end of the hammer, which is to "peen" over, that is intentionally mushroom, things like rivets. To do so, the ball end should be struck against the pin end until it begins to flare, and then the ball is moved off center to press the flare down to the surface.

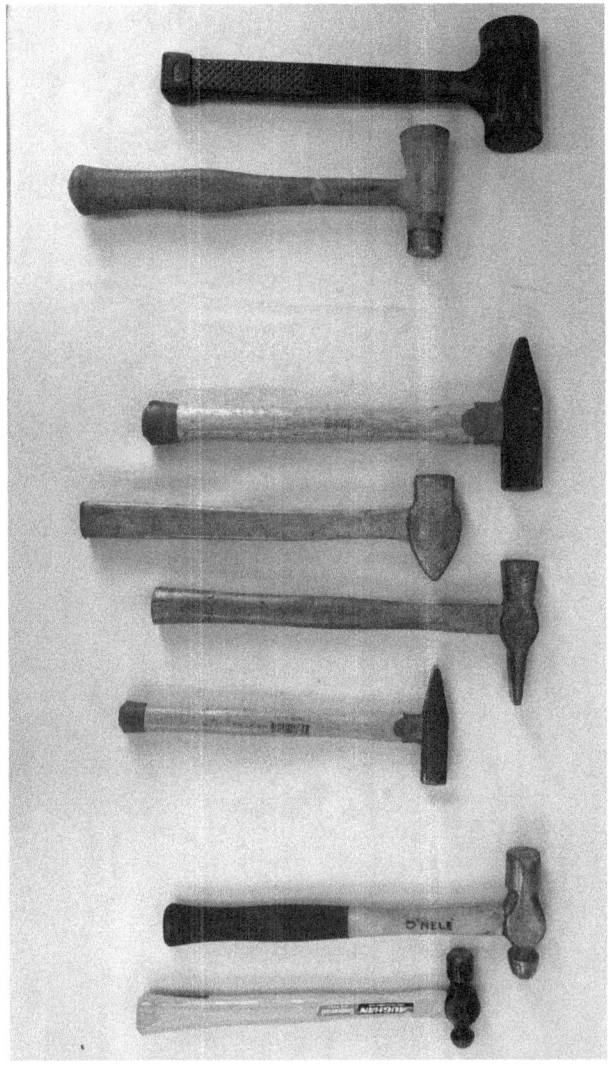

Figure 5.7 Metal working hammers from top to bottom—a pair of dead-blow hammers (one with a non-sparking brass face), four sizes and patterns of cross peen hammer and two sizes of ball peen hammer.

marring, and brass face can be used to drive chisels or remove steel dowel pins and similar objects. As well, dead-blow ball peen hammers can be easier to control than traditional steel hammers.
- Shaping hammers are those designed for specific purposes such as texturing or repairing sheet metal.
  - Texturing hammers are mostly used for jewelry making but can be excellent for prop and craft projects. These have imprinted heads with patterns that may mimic bark, pebbles, cross-hatches, and more. They work very well to texture soft metals such as aluminum and annealed copper. Texturing hammers can also be made from cheap hammers by grinding grooves, welding beads on the head, and/or carving waves with a burr.
  - Sheet metal is often worked with special hammers such as a rounding or planishing hammer, for use with a dolly or raising stake, and nylon teardrop hammers that are used with a shot filled leather bag. All can make compound curves.
  - Auto-body hammers are sold in sets and are used to repair damaged sheet metal. Each hammer has a specific use; many are used while the metal is being backed by a specially shaped dolly that keeps the metal from moving too far.

Figure 5.8b Texturing hammers made by the author. Each is made from a cheap, worn hammer. Example of each hammer's texture can be seen below on a sheet metal sample.

- Punches—These have a variety of functions in metal working from marking, to driving to alignment. Punches may be made from tool steel, brass, or in some cases aluminum.
  - Center and prick punches are similar and are both marking punches. A typical center punch has a steep bevel and is meant to make a small divot used to start a twist drill without drifting. A prick punch can be used as an awl to mark a line, or tapped to mark a point, though usually it is not intended to make a deep impression like a center punch. While many styles are struck with a hammer, spring-loaded versions can be quick and easy to use.
  - Drift punches are long tapered punches with a blunt end that are used to align holes. These are best used to align units that have multiple holes so that one can be used for the drift, and the other for the bolt.
  - Pin punches are diameter specific and designed to remove dowel pins and, in some cases, fasteners that have rusted in place. These are available in steel, brass, and aluminum. Softer punches are less likely to damage the pin or the bore, though may bend or break if struck too hard.
  - Rolled pin punches have reduced noses intended to fit into the center of rolled spring steel pins. The punches are almost always steel.

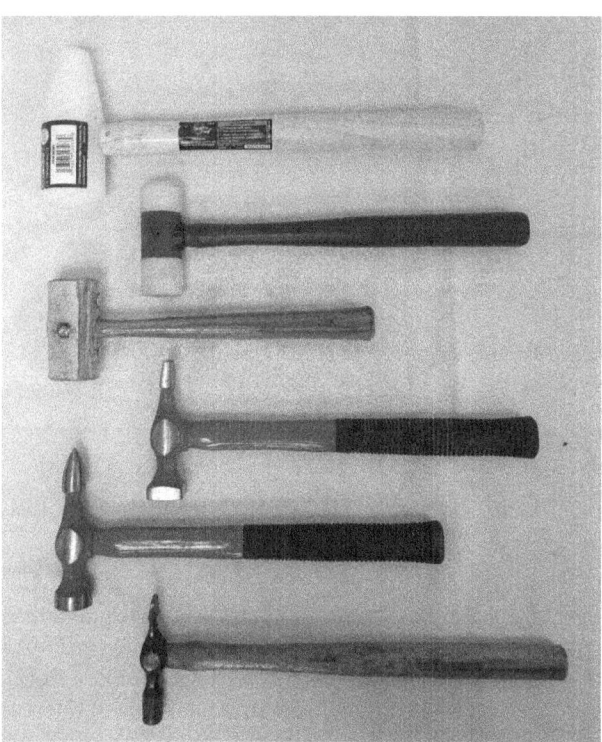

Figure 5.8a Examples of shaping hammers from top—a teardrop nylon hammer, a flat and domed nylon hammer, a raw hide mallet, an auto-body cross peen, an auto-body picking hammer, and a jewelers hammer.

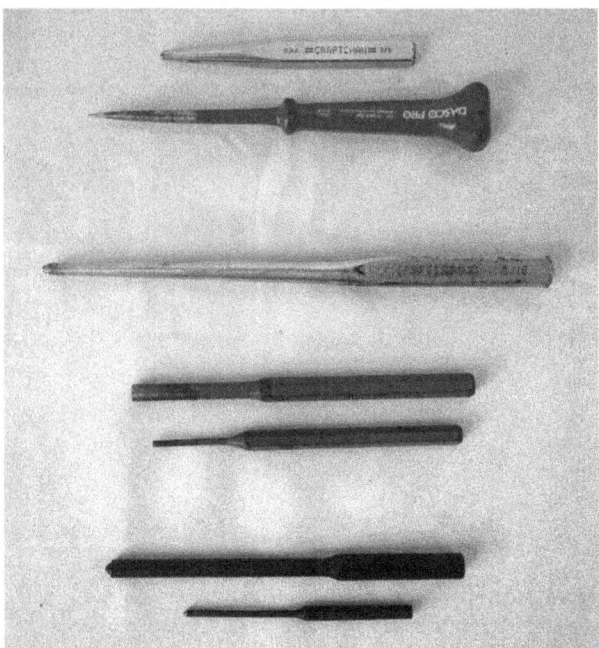

Figure 5.9 Punches from top to bottom—a center punch, the awl that the author uses as a prick punch, a drift punch, a pair of pin punches, and a pair of roll pin punches. Note the inset ball end on the roll pin punched that center the punch on hollow pins.

- Letter/number stamps—These sets of stamps are for permanent marking and labeling. They are hardened steel and are able to stamp into mild steel and soft metals when struck with a hammer.
- Chisels—These are primarily for cutting or etching (sometimes called chasing) metal.
  - Cold chisels are common in shops but often unused or misused. These are used for cutting small sections when struck with a hammer. The metal to be cut should be on a sacrificial plate (the plate will be scarred). An important note: these are sold with different cutting angles based on use. Steel and hard metals are cut with a more blunt tip (55°–70°), while soft metals are best cut with a sharper angle (30°–45°). Examples of how a cold chisel may be helpful include cutting wire rope when bypass cable cutters are unavailable or to cut perpendicular to the threads at the end of a bolt to prevent the nut from coming off (e.g. from vibration).
  - Cape chisels are used to cut shallow grooves into metal. They are an excellent way to make a scoring line to be used in a sheet brake on short sections. These can also be used to make permanent registration marks for component assembly.
  - Diamond point chisels are for cleaning weld bead spatter or oxidation from inside corners.
  - Round nose and cross cut chisels are similar to cape chisels but cut a wider, rounded groove. These are best used in soft metals for short distances and can make a nice relief groove for hand bending.

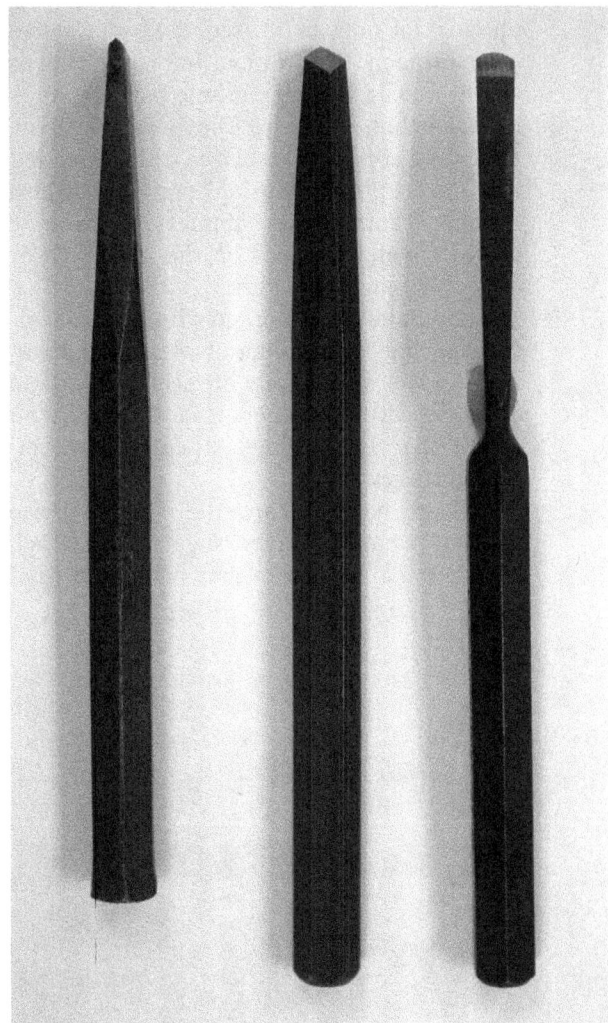

Figure 5.10 Metal cutting chisels from left to right—a cold chisel, a diamond point chisel, and a round nose chisel.

- Forming dies—Various tools are available for hand shaping sheet metal cold. Much like a blacksmith would hammer against an anvil; these dies are used in conjunction with a hammer to shape sheet metal.
  - Dollies are hand-held or vise-mounted steel shapes used behind sheet metal while hammering from the front. These are primarily used in auto body and sculpture, but they are fairly low cost and worth the investment if a curvy sheet metal project arises.

HAND TOOLS AND MANUAL MACHINES • 69

- Shot bags are leather bags filled with fine steel shot (or sometimes sand) used as backing when shaping sheet metal with hammers. It is intended to conform to the hammer strikes making rough doming easier. Shapes formed on a shot bag are usually refined in an English wheel or with dollies.
- Dapping punch and block sets consist of a steel block with a series of concave insets and matching dies that are used to push the metal into the recesses (via hammer). These are mostly used by jewelers but can be excellent in the prop shop for making small details on regal furniture or fantasy props. For example, one could make a series of round raised areas (like rivet heads) along a strip of copper as decorative banding. Blacksmiths use a very large iron block, called a swage block, for the same purpose on bigger pieces of metal.

Figure 5.12 Shaping stakes made by the author for various projects. From left—a sinking and doming stake (convex and concave ends), a pair of curved Tees, a 3/4" Tee, a pair of veining chisels and a veining stake.

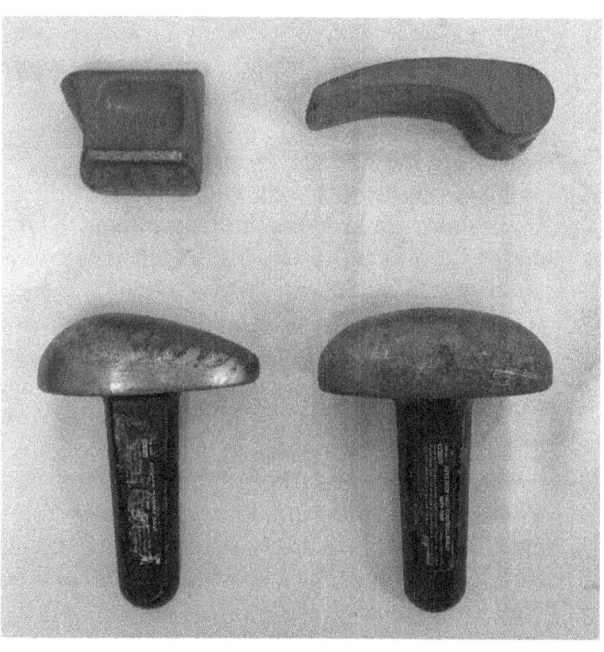

Figure 5.11 The top pair of dollies is hand-held and used with shaping hammers for final smoothing. The bottom pair of dollies mount in a vise and are used for initial hammer forming.

- Benders—There are many tools designed for bending metal and most are relatively low cost and easy to acquire.
  - Brake line benders are not only small tools designed to bend hollow tube but can also be used for thick wire or soft metal rod (not steel) of equivalent size. They are easy to use, though they don't work well for radii larger than their integrated die.

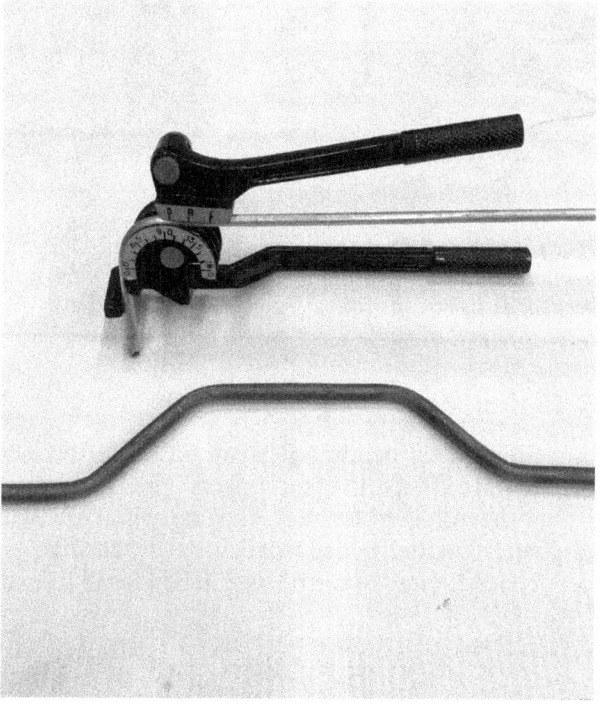

Figure 5.13 A brake line bender and examples of bends in 3/8" copper tube and 1/4" aluminum rod.

- Stakes—These are forming dies for cold forming soft metals that are often shop made for a specific purpose. Larger shaping dies, similar to small anvils, that can be held in a vice are also available for purchase. Stakes can be used for grooving/veining, creating beads or rounding over edges and raising or sinking an area to make contrasting texture. An example of a veining stake can be seen in use in Figure 11.67a–d.

- Conduit benders are essentially a much larger version of a brake line bender. They have a hook end to grab the tubing, a long lever handle, and a foot pad to add stability. These usually have indicators on the casting used to align the bender for different types of bend such as a back-to-back (long U shape), offsets, and saddles. They also have degree marks. Examples can be seen in Figure 11.28.
- Wire bending jigs are smaller metal blocks that attach to a work bench for bending wire into sharp angles, curves, and loops. They are often used by jewelry makers but are an excellent tool to keep in any shop.

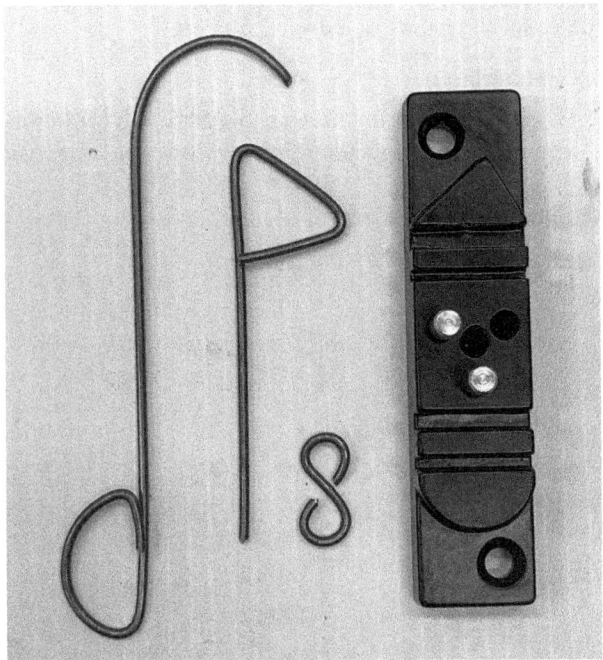

Figure 5.14 Example shapes made with the small wire bending jig at the right. The D-ring and triangle shapes were made using the matching bends on the jig. The longer radius was made with the pins by spacing out short bends.

- Shop-made bending jigs can be made for any required shape, but one with two pins is excellent to keep handy for making rings. Similarly, bar stock can be welded to a base to make sharper bends. Examples can be seen in Figures 11.22 and 11.47.
- Scroll benders are bench-mounted (or vise-mounted) tools for making a variety of shapes in rod, bar, and strap. They can be used to make eye loops with a little practice. An example can be seen in Figure 11.25.
• Blacksmithing tools—While it is unlikely that an entertainment shop would have a full smithy set up somewhere, a few key tools used by blacksmiths can be very handy for any metal worker.
  - Tongs are used in blacksmithing rather than pliers because they have longer handles for more leverage and they keep ones hand away from a very hot fire. As well, they are made with different jaw shapes to hold different shapes of steel. Even when welding this can be an advantage, for example needing to hold square bar in place for a tack weld, one could use tongs designed for square bar. In cases where metal is heated with a rosebud to be bent or otherwise shaped, the long handles of tongs are far safer than pliers and allow easy movement to a shaping surface versus locking the metal in a vise, for example. Most vises and pliers are also not meant to be heated and cooled repeatedly.
  - Anvils are the primary forming tool in a smithy and can be just as handy in any metal shop. A single-horn anvil is the most common. High-quality tool steel anvils are expensive; a cast anvil would suffice for many shops. The face (large flat portion) can be used for straightening or hot shaping, the horn can be used to shape bends, and the step can be used for cutting (such as with a cold chisel) to avoid damaging the anvil face. The two holes in an anvil have special purposes as well. The Hardie hole (large and square) is designed to hold tools such as a hot cut chisel, rivet buck for solid rivets or a bending fork (for shaping tight curves). The Pritchel hole (small and round) is traditionally used for punching but can be used to make quick bends in rod stock too. Anvils are best mounted on either a solid wood block, or a metal stand with wood cushion.
  - Swage blocks are essentially very large dapping blocks used by blacksmiths to shape steel. While they are unusual in an entertainment shop, they can occasionally be found for reasonable prices at estate sales. There are quite useful for hot forming steel and cold forming soft metals.

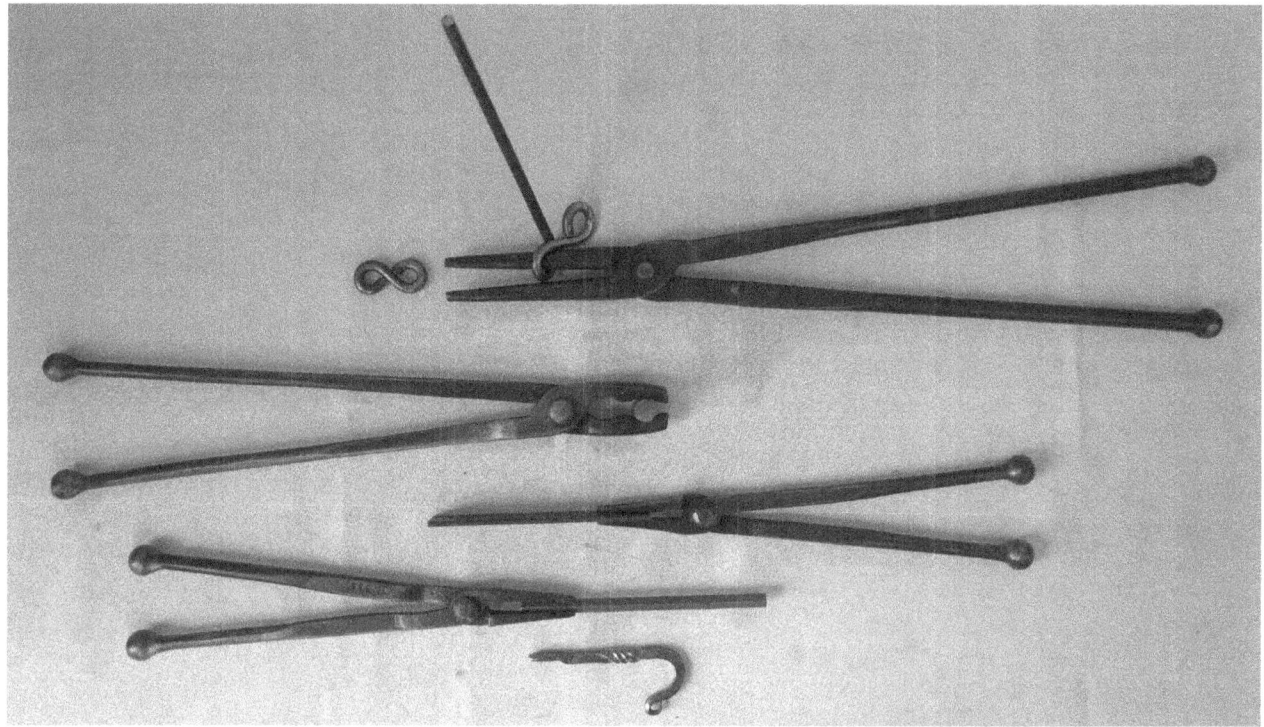

Figure 5.15 Examples of common blacksmith's tongs and the shapes they make or hold. From top—ring tongs and example S-rings, wolf-jaw tongs will hold round stock parallel or perpendicular, flat jaw tongs for strap and V-groove tongs for square bar with an example of a forged hook that was held with the above tongs for both forming and twisting.

Work Holding

- Pliers—There are a variety of pliers and similar tools that are useful when working with metal, especially sheet metal.
  - Seaming pliers can be used both as a miniature brake and to finish and crimp folded sheets. They are available in a few varieties with different-width jaws and may have inline or offset handles.
  - Flanging plier or "jogglers" are for making lapped seams in thin sheet metal by crimping a slight jog into the end of the sheet. They usually include a punch to prep for rosette welds.
  - Wire forming pliers have round, stepped jaws that often have six different diameters. They are excellent for forming small wire into loops.
  - Glass pliers have rubber coated tips and a set screw that can set clamping pressure. These are excellent for bending small metals without damaging the surface.

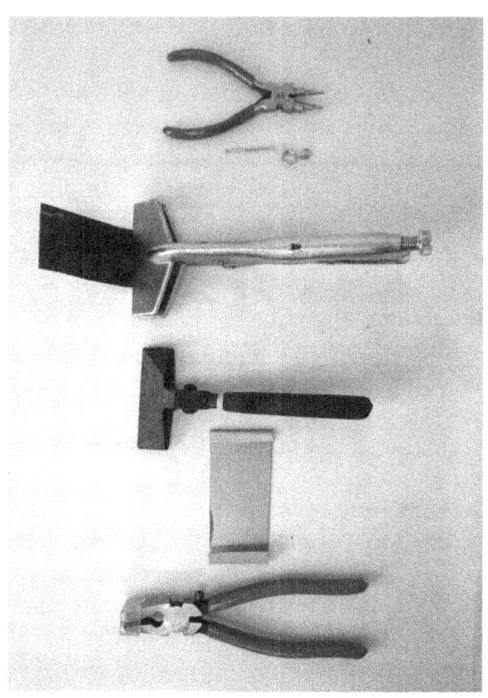

Figure 5.16 Pliers for shaping metal from top to bottom—wire bending pliers, locking and regular seaming pliers, and glass pliers. Between the seaming and glass pliers is a sample of 18ga sheet worked by each.

- Clamps—Clamps for metal working need to be all metal to resist heat and be safe from welding spatter. They should not be heated beyond a point where they cannot be handled without gloves to avoid damage.
  - C-clamps (also known as G-clamps) are probably the most ubiquitous clamp in shops. They are strong and affordable but can be awkward to install. They are also available with an extended throat depth; though not as strong as a regular C-clamp, they are especially useful. Because metals tend to have no give, one can over torque a C-clamp bending its casting. Care should be taken when stick welding or using flux-cored wire because spatter from these can clog the threads of a C-clamp.
  - Quick locking clamps have been around for a long time and the most common are pliers style. There are a few unique versions specific to welding.
    - C-clamp styles are sometimes referred to as welding clamps because they are nearly synonymous with fixtures for welding. These are available with and without pivoting pads on the tips. They are available in a range of capacities and reach. Strong Hand Tools offers table mounting brackets for these making them able to mimic a vise.
    - Offset jaw pliers are designed for butt welding. They have U-shaped jaws that allow them to clamp to two pieces while providing access for tack welding.
    - Chain clamps are designed specifically for working with pipe and tube. These will not mar the surface due to a lack of teeth. As well, they will not collapse thin-walled tube like a pipe wrench can.
    - Pipe jaw pliers are like a locking pipe wrench, but with beak-shaped jaws. These are well suited to handling pipe and tube when hot.
  - F-style clamps are one of the most common welding clamps. They can be used much like a C-clamp but have variable reach making them more versatile. The threads are vulnerable to spatter.
  - Strong Hand Tools is a rare example of citing a brand name tool because they hold patents on a number of clamps specific to welding including two and three axis quick clamps for square tube, locking pipe pliers, expanding pliers, and pipe fit-up clamps for butt welding.
  - Butt-welding clamps are small clamps designed to hold thin sheet in place for butt welding. They make a very small gap between the sheets forming a root weld. These can be seen in use in Figure 11.5a.

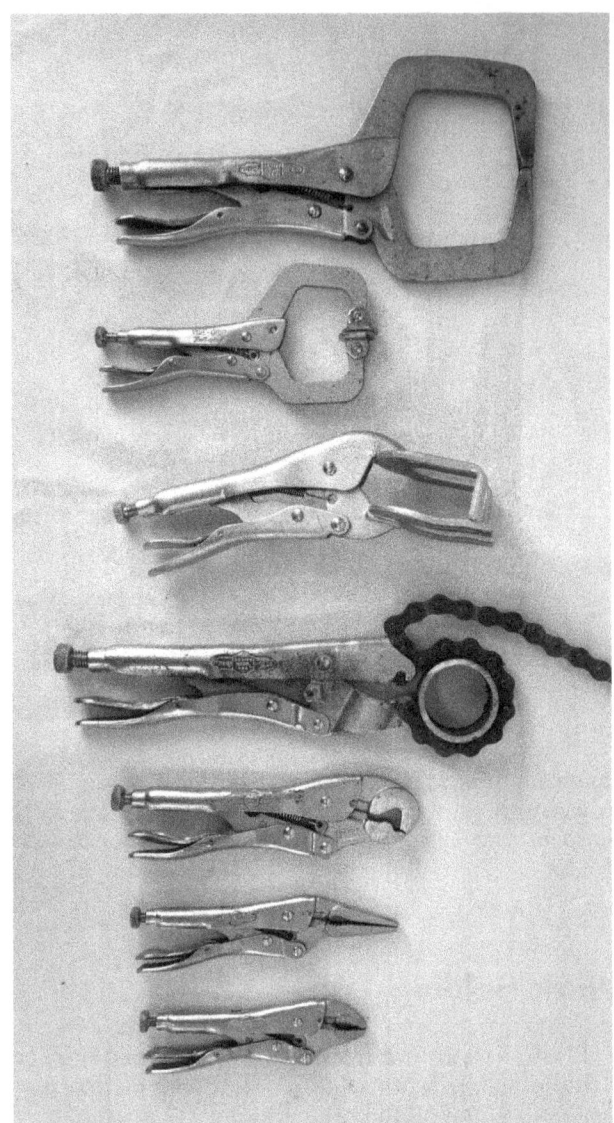

Figure 5.17 Locking pliers from top to bottom—11" C-Clamp with fixed ends, 6" C-clamp with self-aligning pads, offset pliers, a chain clamp, hex nut pliers, needle nose pliers and standard jaw pliers.

  - Cantilever clamps are unique in that they operate somewhat like scissors. Their advantage is strength; unlike C-clamps, the frame will not twist.
  - Toggle clamps are available in many varieties, but only a few versions are useful as hold downs. The lever action of these clamps makes them fast and easy to use once mounted. They may be mounted on a work table, or as part of a movable jig. The most useful varieties for welding are the 90° hold down (horizontal mount) and the sliding rod type that may be mounted horizontally or vertically. Both have internally threaded mandrels that make mounting a custom foot quite

HAND TOOLS AND MANUAL MACHINES • **73**

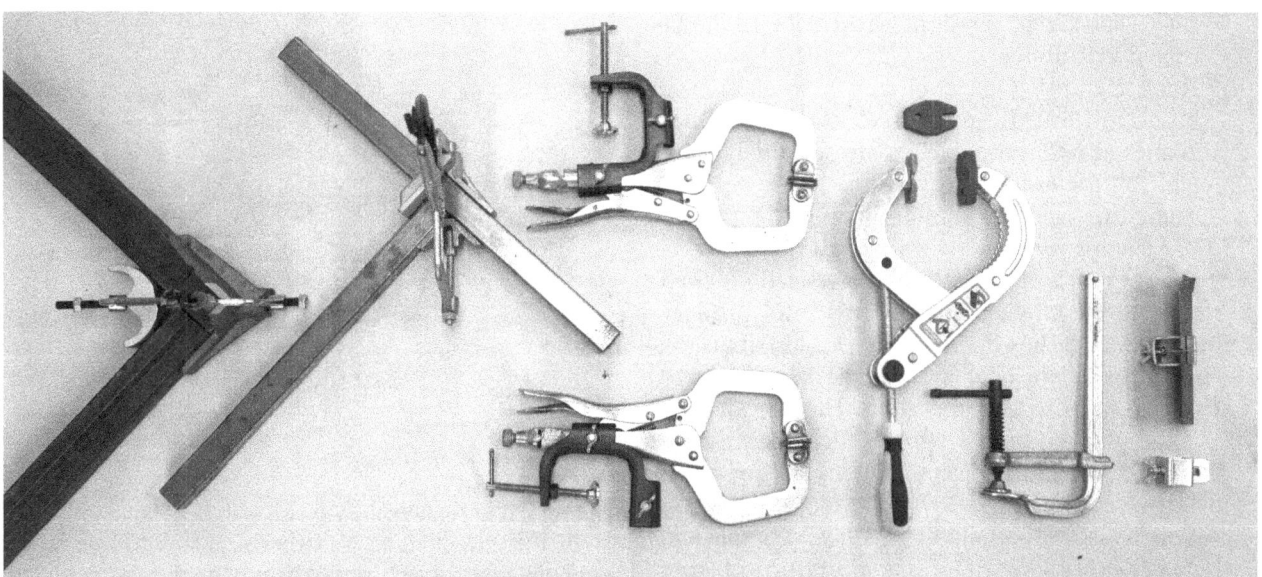

Figure 5.18 From left to right—large and small 90° quick clamps, table mounting brackets for locking C-clamps, a cantilever style clamp, and F-style clamp and butt-welding clamps for sheet metal.

Figure 5.19 Hold down style toggle clamps used on a drilling jig to quickly hold material. The clamp on the lower right is another version called a toggle plier. The threaded stud to adjust grip is under the table.

easy. They are an excellent way to set up a jig for repeat assemblies.
- Rack clamps—One company, Carver & Co., based in the U.K. makes rack clamps and bar clamps (1 or 2 moveable ends, respectively) specifically for hold large sections when welding. These are used in a similar manner to pipe and bar clamps for wood working, but these have a deeper reach and use regularly spaced notched to hold the moving end(s) in place for primary adjustment. They do have one U.S. distributor.

- Vises—These are one of the most common and strongest ways to hold materials. They should not take the place of proper fixtures for large projects but may be used to hold smaller items for tack welding, shaping, or cutting.
  - Bench vises are available in a few varieties and nearly every shop has one or more. A mechanics or utility vise is the most common to encounter; some have integral pipe jaws below the flat jaws. A mechanics vise is the larger frame, more durable of the two. Most shops will opt for a vise with a pivoting base for versatility. Utility vises can have quick-release jaws that make setup much faster. Other versions include rotating head

Figure 5.20b A multipurpose vise with both flat and pipe jaws. The advantage to this style vise is the ability to hole pipe and other objects vertically or at an accessible angle.

multipurpose vises and small versions that can clamp to a work table.
  - Pipe vises are available in two varieties, yoke style with jaws and versions that use a chain attached to a threaded drawbar for tightening. Both are equally useful when threading pipe.

Figure 5.20a 4" mechanics vise and a 5" quick release utility vise.

Figure 5.21a An example of a chain vise with a 4" pipe in place.

Figure 5.21b An example of a yoke-style pipe vise holding a 1 1/4" pipe for tightening a threaded cap.

- Tilting and rotating vises are used when a cut needs to be made off axis on a mill. These can also be used for drilling on an angle after a baseline has been cut for the drill point to bite into. Tilting vises raise the vice body; a rotating vise keeps the body on a horizontal axis and rotates the head to either side.

Figure 5.22 A 4" tilting machinist vise.

These can also hold pipe when using it to hot form rings.
- Machinist vices are precision tools mostly used on vertical mills. They are an excellent choice for use on a drill press as well, but they are much more expensive than standard drill press vises. A unique feature of these vises is having jaws that are ground smooth to prevent scoring material.
  - A standard machinist vise is similar to a drill press vise, being low profile and designed to be clamped to the machine table. The primary differences are strength and precision. A machinist vice is designed to have exceptionally parallel jaws with very little tolerance for lateral or vertical movement. See Chapter 12 for examples of a machinist vise in use.
  - A fractal vise is unlikely to be found outside of a machine shop, but it is an exceptionally interesting design intended to hold irregular shapes for machining. The jaws are a series of nested C-shapes that slide long one another to conform to the object. These are also exceptionally expensive.
- Post-style vises are found in blacksmith shops and are designed with a leg to transfer load (and impacts) to the floor instead of the work table or the internals of the vise. They can often be found used for reasonable prices and are an excellent upgrade if a shop forms metal, especially steel, in to odd shapes on a regular basis.
- Accessories for vises improve or expand their performance.
  - Soft jaws are often made from aluminum or plastic and may additionally have rubber padding. Many shops make covers for vise jaws from copper sheet or very thin steel sheet to prevent marring.
  - Vise brakes have two components: one half has a blade or fingers and the other half a V-shaped face. These are excellent for a shop that makes small objects or that rarely needs a brake.

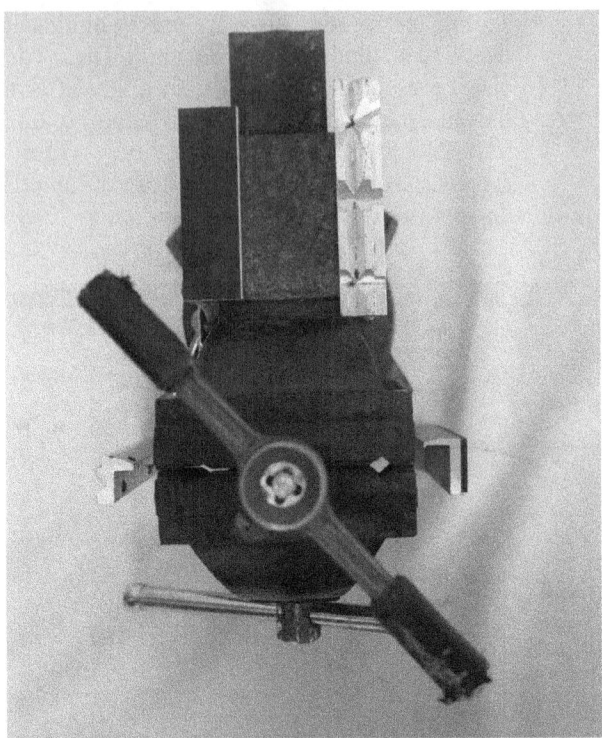

Figure 5.23 In the vise are plastic soft jaws with multiple grooves (good for holding without damage) and on the back of the vise a soft-face aluminum insert and an aluminum insert with multiple grooves.

Figure 5.24 Magnetic welding helpers: top—a spring-loaded welding "finger", middle magnetic tab holder on top of the pipe being held in place by magnetic V-pads (Sample beside) and bottom—a magnetic ground for a welder.

- Magnetic tools—Magnets are excellent when working with steel because they are fast and fairly accurate. A variety of magnetic tools are available to weldors. One important note: overheating these tools can lead to the loss of there magnetic properties; this is especially true of the steel tools with embedded rare-earth magnets.
  - Magnetic grounding devices make grounding to projects in wooden jigs very easy. Most are a disc magnet with a copper center pin that can replace a spring clamp, or be clamped to. Another style has the contact mounted on a spring-loaded arm allowing it to hold small items in place while providing a local ground.
  - Tab holders are small tools designed to hold a tab perpendicular to a surface making tack welding easy.
  - Tubing holders have flexible magnetic pads mounted on a magnetic base, making them helpful when butt-welding tube, or setting up a coped joint to weld.
  - A spring finger has a magnetic base and a bent metal rod that is hinged and mounted on magnetic base. Like a traditional welding finger, it is designed to hold small pieces in place for tack welding.
  - Magnetic angles are available as 45°/90°, 30°/60°/90°, and multi-angle types. Another handy magnet style is the flexible angle. Some companies offering "switchable" versions that make releasing the magnet easier.

Figure 5.25 Magnetic angles: top left—an adjustable magnet with insert pin for holding at 45°, top right—a multi-angle magnet, middle—a mid-sized magnet holding tube in place with a mini magnet aligning a section of 1/4" square rod, and bottom—a large 90° magnetic angle.

  - Magnetic torch rests are another tool MIG and TIG weldors should consider. While these do not hold materials in place, they keep the welding torch safe and within easy reach. Some have a positionable arm, offer small bins to hold other

HAND TOOLS AND MANUAL MACHINES • 77

tools such as MIG pliers, and/or have cable control for easier torch handling.
- Wooden jigs—Using a custom jig is one of the most common ways to hold complex shapes when welding. These can be a flat sheet of plywood with wood blocks that hold components in place, or three dimensional "bucks" that components clamp to. Like other jigs, they are used for repetition work where duplicates need to match. One trick the author prefers is to cut a hole though the plywood at all welded junctions (usually with a hole saw) to reduce charring and smoke generated for overheating the plywood. Best practice is also to only use these jigs for tack welding; final welds made off the jig will further reduce damage to the wood. Figure 11.51a and b shows this methodology being used on a large scale by blocking components to the floor.

Fastening

Metal will often be welded, but a number of other fastening methods are quite viable depending on need. The pros and cons of various fasteners are discussed in Chapter 9.
- Rivet gun—Though this is not a tool to assemble large items, it is invaluable when a blind rivet is the best fastener for a given project. Because different-sized rivets use different diameter stems, the nose piece of the rivet gun must be matched to the diameter of the mandrel. Small pliers style rivet guns are the most common but larger versions that resemble a bolt cutter can set larger rivets overall and set all rivets with less effort. A pantograph-style push riveter can also be used for long reach.
- Rivet nut gun—Rivet nuts are a type of threaded insert that collapse like a large rivet and compress the inner and outer surface of the material. They are ideal for adding threads in thin materials that cannot be tapped. Each size of rivet nut uses a unique nose and mandrel.

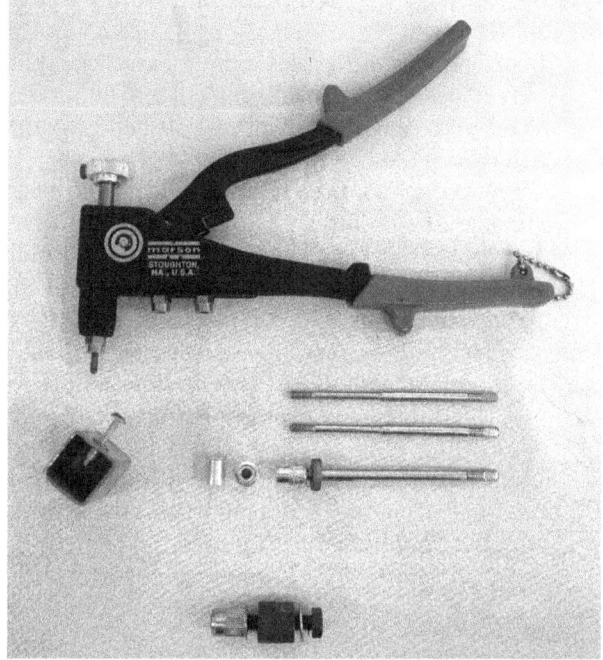

Figure 5.27 Top to bottom—a rivet nut setting tool followed by a set nut in 1" square tube and the interchangeable mandrels for setting various thread sizes; at bottom a wrench-operated rivet nut setting tool. This style is common for large rivet nuts such as the 5/16-18 nut shown.

- Rivet buck—This is a simple tool used for setting solid rivets (hot rivets). Most mount in a vise or to an anvil, but some are held against a rivet head, while the tail end is peened over. Most fabricators will never encounter hot rivets, which is a bit of a bummer in the author's opinion. They are not only decorative, they hold materials in place tightly, will not vibrate loose like a bolt and nut may, while still being a "pinned" connection that allows a tiny bit of movement making joints more resilient. There are limited application for rivets in scenic construction.
- Steel stud tools—Crimpers are the main tool that will be used to quickly join a steel stud to a base channel or to install blocking between studs. Their advantage is that they leave nothing protruding

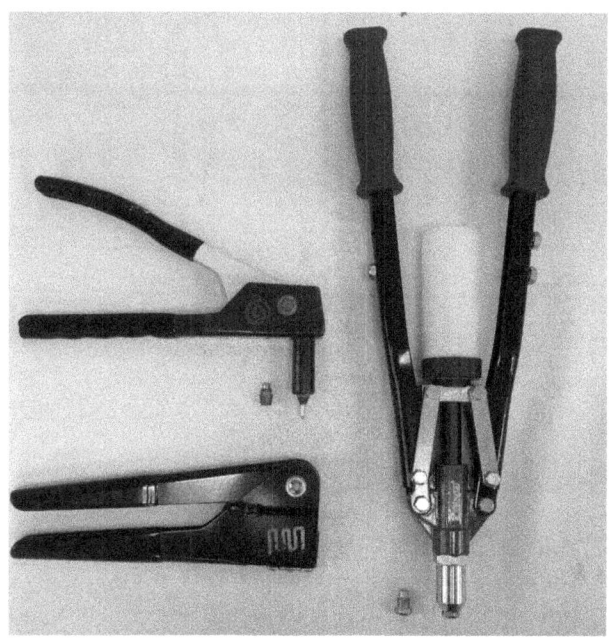

Figure 5.26 On the left are pliers-type rivet tools, one with a long-reach nose for up to 3/16" rivets. On the right is a lever-style install tool for larger rivets up to 5/16".

from the surface unlike a self-drilling screw that must be accounted for when facing. While steel studs are primarily used in commercial construction they can be an excellent option for exhibits that need to be fire retardant or permanent immersive installations that require light duty partitions. There are also punches for steel studs to allow for the pass through of wiring or plumbing.

- Damaged fastener removers—There are a few tools designed specifically for this task. Most are quite affordable and easy to use. If the fastener broke during removal, the application of penetrating oil or heat is likely required before attempting to use a remover.
  - Broken bolt removers are similar to a socket but have helical "teeth" inside that cut into either the shank of a bolt, or a stripped bolt head to grip and twist it out.
  - Screw extractors, often referred to as "easy outs," are similar to a thread tap with a square drive and a tapered spiral with helical "teeth" that cut in to the fastener needing to be removed. Though these are called screw extractors, they are designed to remove machine screws and bolts, not wood screws. These require a hole to be drilled into the fastener first and most only work with right-hand threaded bolts. There are square versions that are driven into the drilled hole with a hammer and then twisted; these work with left- and right-hand threads.

- Pipe wrenches—While many technicians have used a standard pipe wrench and know it will only grab when rotated properly, they may not know that it should always make three points of contact to prevent crushing the pipe. Internal pipe wrenches are often unknown tools in fabrications shops, but for any company that uses threaded pipe fittings, these low-cost tools should be in the tool room. They are simple and the only way to install and remove a close nipple without damage.

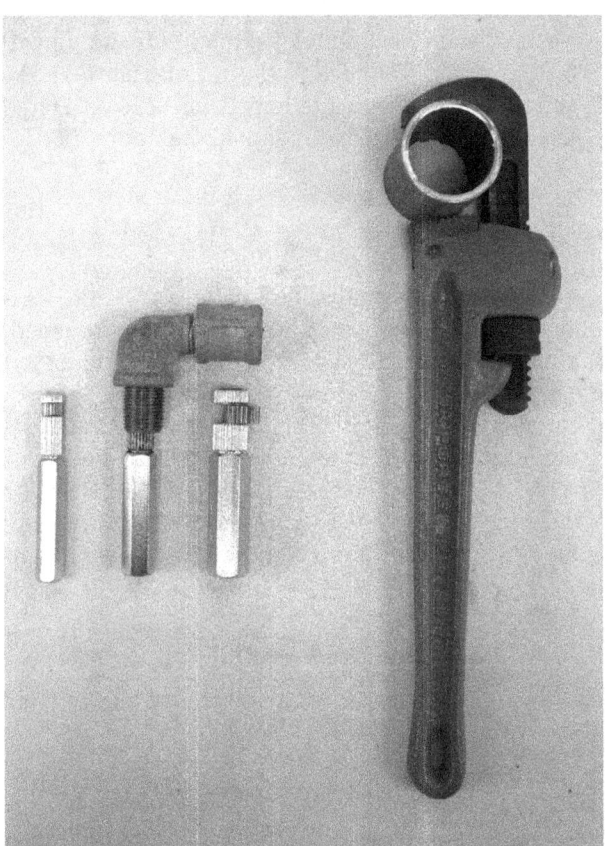

Figure 5.29 On the left are examples of internal pipe wrenches and on the right a standard pipe wrench showing a three-point bite.

Threading

- Thread gauges—These are used to find thread pitch. There are different styles: sets with folding leaves and cards with pitch gauges along the perimeter and pass-through holes in the faces to determine diameter. Another useful tool is a test string of studs with both male and female threads that can quickly be used to check the fit of a nut or bolt.

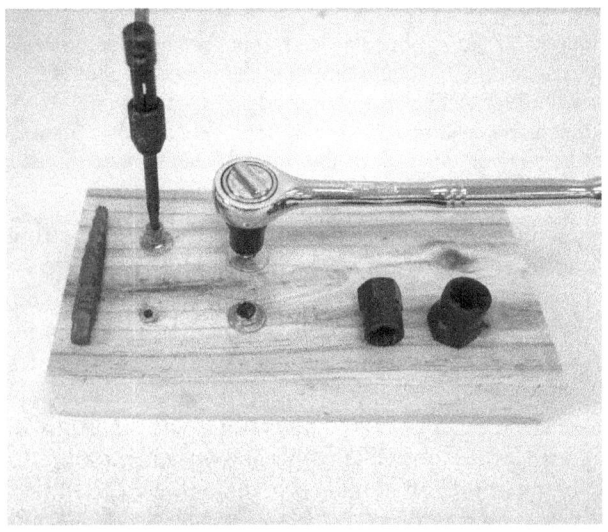

Figure 5.28 On the left are examples of broken lag bolts that have been drilled to prepare for the helical screw extractor shown in use. On the right are lags with stripped heads, with the top one being extracted by a broken bolt remover and two further examples of the removers.

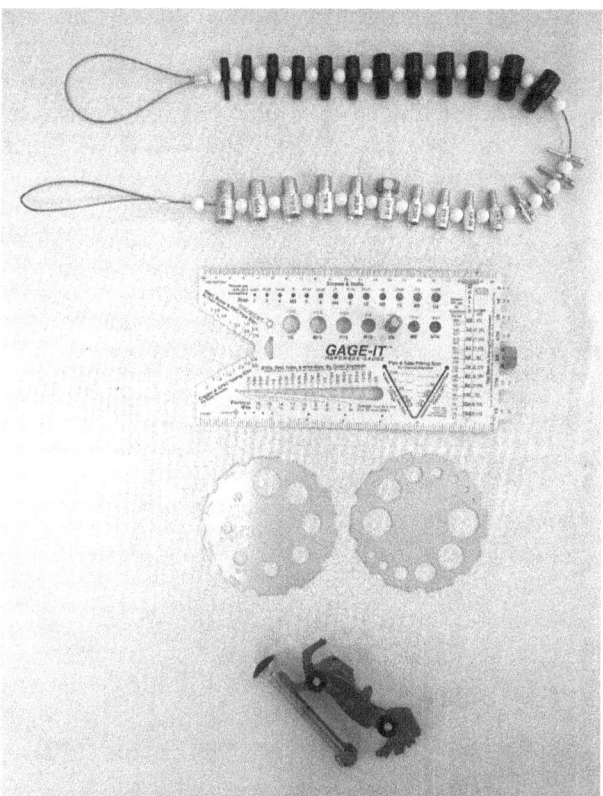

Figure 5.30 Thread checking tools from top to bottom—a set of thread checkers on a cable, light weight plastic gauge (front and rear) with references in metric and imperial, a set of pass-through gauges with thread pitch gauges, and leaf gauges (metric and imperial).

- Manual tap and die—The most common way to cut threads in most shops is using a manual tap and die set. Taps are for cutting internal threads, while dies are for cutting external threads. The majority of sets for cutting bolt threads have taper taps designed for pass-through threading. While sets are available that exceed 1/2″ diameter, for most shops cutting such large threads manually is impractical. One trick when tapping a hollow object, like tube, is to cover the tap with grease (the thicker the grease the better) to catch swarf and prevent it from dropping inside. Another note is to spin the tap or die backwards after 1/4–1/2 rotation to break the swarf free and remove it from the cutting area.
    - Bolt taps are available in three main types and may have straight flutes (most common) or helical flutes which clear chips better. Figure 11.20 demonstrates tapping a blind hole.
        - Taper taps have long tapered noses that cut very shallow threads to start and increase cutting depth as the tap moves into the cut. They are used for through tapping, or to start threads in a blind hole.
        - Plug taps have a short taper at the nose and are intended to follow a taper tap in a blind hole cutting all but the last 3–5 threads.
        - Bottoming taps follow plug taps and cut threads to within 1–2 turns of the bottom of a blind hole.
    - Other taps are available that shops may find useful.
        - Pipe taps up to about 1/2″ pipe use same or similar handles as bolt taps; above that most fit into a ratcheting system that is paired with ratcheting dies. NPT taps do not cut a taper–the taper is only on the male fitting.
        - Lamp tube taps are available for the two standard sizes of lamp tube, 1/8″-27 NPS and 1/4″-18 NPS. They are excellent for repairing lamp bases or making custom bases.
    - Holders for taps are available in multiple styles.
        - Sliding T-handle holders are common for smaller taps and may be fixed or ratcheting. Some have a recess to connect to a square drive ratchet.
        - Self-aligning tap holders add an outer sleeve, usually with a notch, making it useable on both flat and round faces. These help ensure the tap remains perpendicular to the surface.
        - Dual handle tap holders provide more leverage but may hold small taps slightly off center. Die holders may also have a conversion die to hold taps.
        - Sets of socket adapters convert standard square drive ratchets into tap holders.
        - Hand tappers are similar to an arbor press in that they have a C-shaped frame with a quill, though the handle drives the tap rotation, not the feed. Tools should include a set of adapters that thread into the quill and are sized to match common taps.
    - Twist drills sized specifically to match each size of tap ensure that threads are cut to the proper depth without over-stressing the tap. Many tap and die sets include drills, but sets of tap drills are available separately.

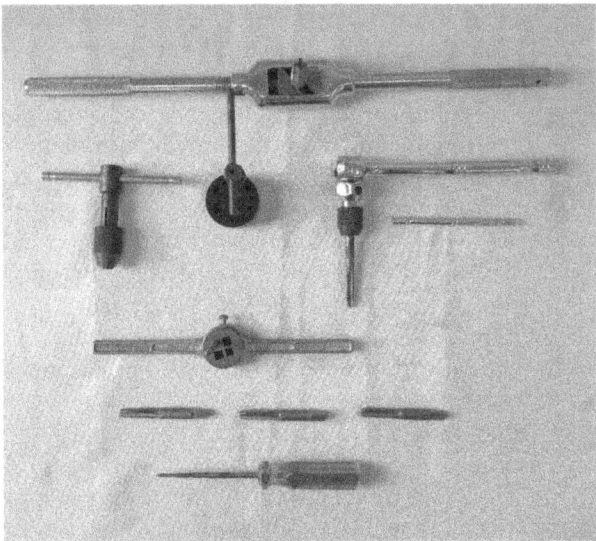

Figure 5.31 Tapping tools from top to bottom—a large tap holder and tap for 1/2" NPT pipe, various styles of tap handles and a tapping guide block (center), a hex-die holder and tap adapter, a set of taps (L to R—taper, plug, bottoming) and a threading screw driver for thin sheet (used often by electricians).

including the U.S. The two systems are not interchangeable.
- Lamp dies are available in two standard sizes for making custom tubing or to repair existing tubes. 1/8"-27 NPS and 1/4"-18 NPS dies require different holders.

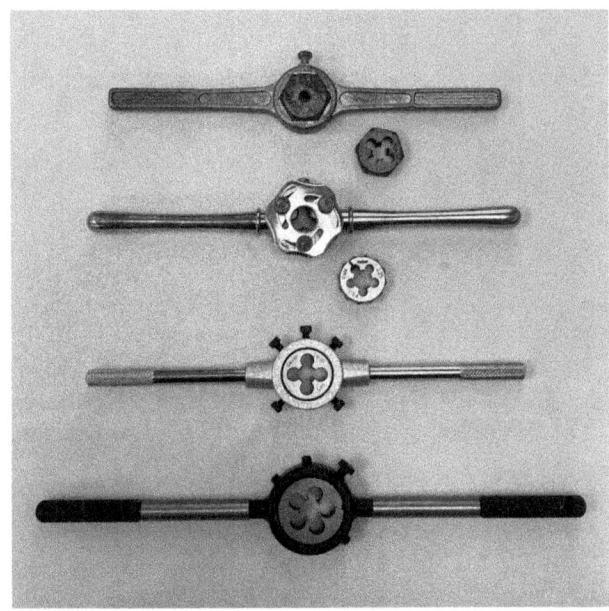

Figure 5.32 Threading dies top to bottom—a standard 1" hex die holder with a self-aligning die and an example of a standard hex die; a 12 point die holder with an irising guide for alignment with an example adjustable die; a 1 1/8" round die holder with a 1/8"-27tpi die for lamp tube; and a 1 1/2" round die holder with die.

- ○ Dies are mostly available in either round or hex shapes, though 12-point dies may be found. There are a variety of die holder sizes for round dies; most hex dies and holders are 1" across.
  - Standard dies can be tricky to start. Dies need to be very level to properly cut concentric threads. It can also be difficult to identify the proper side to start the die from unless clearly labeled. Self-guiding dies are extra thick to slide onto the rod or stud holding the die level to start the threads properly. Adjustable dies have a split and a set-screw that allow them to be adjusted to slightly over- or under-cut the thread diameter.
  - Split dies are designed for repairing or extending threads. The dies hinge open to be installed along the threaded area. To close properly, the threaded area must be undamaged. These may also require a slotted die wrench.
  - Pipe dies that are most likely to be encountered in entertainment fabrication are National Pipe Thread (NPT) that create steeply tapered threads and commonly used in the U.S., and British Standard Pipe Thread (BSP) that may be straight (BSPP) or tapered (BSPT) which are used in many countries,

- Thread repair—Damaged threads are high on the list of annoyances for many fabricators, especially in shops where bolts are reused. There are a few solutions to repairing threads that work well.
  - ○ Thread restorers are available as sets that contain taps and dies; the primary difference is that these are not designed to cut new threads and can be damaged by attempting such. These tools have much larger flutes, which are especially helpful on rusted or dirt-covered fasteners, and do not taper like cutting tools. Dies can be somewhat difficult to start if the first few threads are damaged. These fit the same tap and die holders as cutting tools.
  - ○ Thread files are typically double-ended, square bars with eight thread patterns each and are used much like any other file, but the thread grooves need to match the thread count and be aligned to

the angle of those on the bolt or other fastener. These only work on external threads. These are often the best way to repair the threads at the tip of a bolt so the repair die can be used to complete the job.
- Universal thread repair tools use a pair of blades that either clamp on (external threads) or expand into (internal threads) and are then twisted past the damaged area cutting away any mushrooming. These are also available for pipe up to 2 1/2" internal and 6" external. These can be difficult to use on the starting threads and may take multiple passes on hardened alloys.

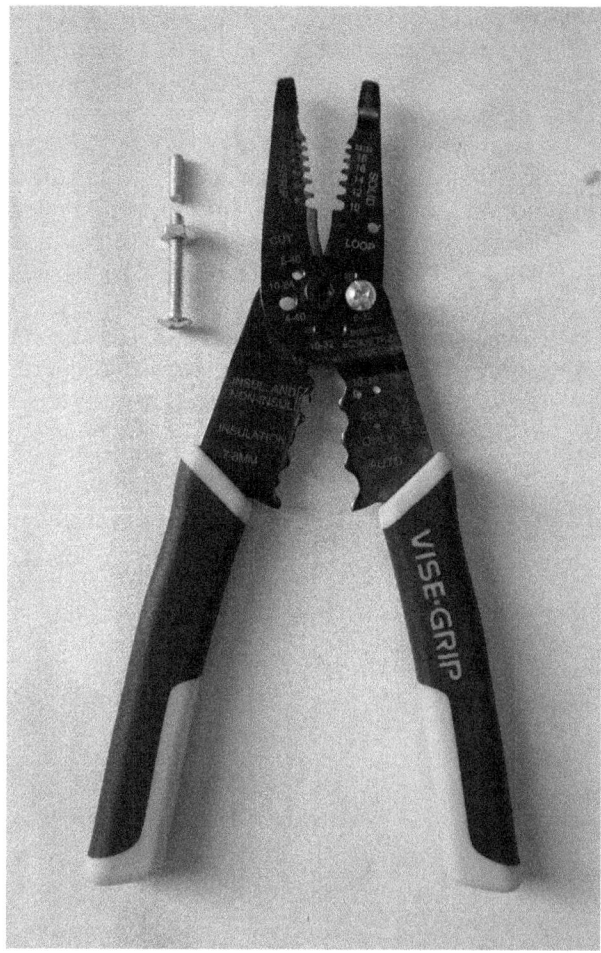

Figure 5.34 An electrical crimper/stripper with a machine screw in place and a cut screw with nut demonstrating the usable threads.

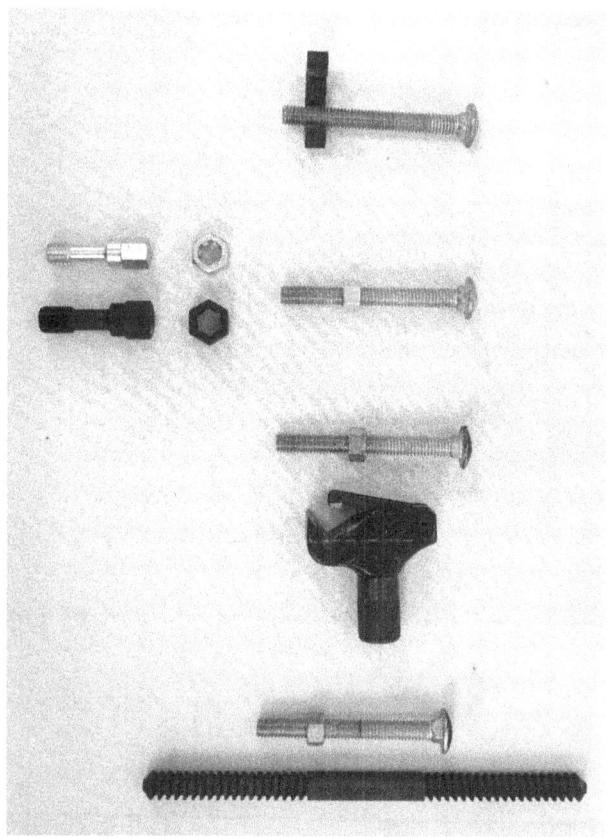

Figure 5.33 Thread repair tools top to bottom—a split hex die, thread restorers, a universal thread repair tool, and a thread file (without its protective handle). All bolts shown have some threads that have been repaired with each tool except the split die.

- Electrical pliers—Many crimper/stripper pliers can be used to cut small machine screws and to repair the threads after. Many users seem to miss this feature.

Finishing

- Files—Metal files are available in "full size" files (lengths and widths vary), mid-sized files, and needle files, making it easy to find a fit for any project. Files can be tricky to use with aluminum or other soft metals, as they tend to clog. The application of dry lubricant (usually sold in stick form) or chalk helps keep the file from clogging. An important note: file only cut on the push stroke; applying pressure on the return stroke will round over the cutting edge rendering the file mostly useless.
  - Shapes include flat, half round (usually tapered), square, triangle, round, and some other specialized shapes. Most files have a tapered tang that will fit a variety of file handles.

- American cut files have three general types: smoothing, second cut, and bastard, listed fine to coarse. Second and bastard cut files may be single or double cut. Double cut files can be easier to work with as they are less likely to drift, but single cut files can be used with a draw motion (holding the file at each end and pulled toward the user). Cut determines both cutting speed and final finish, much like the coarseness of sand paper. American cut files are a great choice for steel and other hard metals. Swiss cut files are double cut and numbered 00-6, coarse to smooth. These are often used on softer metals like copper and bronze, or for fine finishing work.
- File cards are wire brushes with very short, stiff bristles used to clean debris from the file teeth without dulling the file.
- File handles are available made from wood with metal inserts that thread onto the tang of a file and plastic handles with shaped inserts to match various file tangs and slip on.
• Sanding blocks—Sanding blocks for metal working are mostly used to smooth surfaces that have been repaired with filler or for sanding primer before final painting. They are not really designed to remove metal the way a file or grinder can. They are unique in that many are quite long and thus useful for ensuring a very flat surface. As well, flexible blocks make finishing curved shapes much easier. These are often used wet to reduce dust.

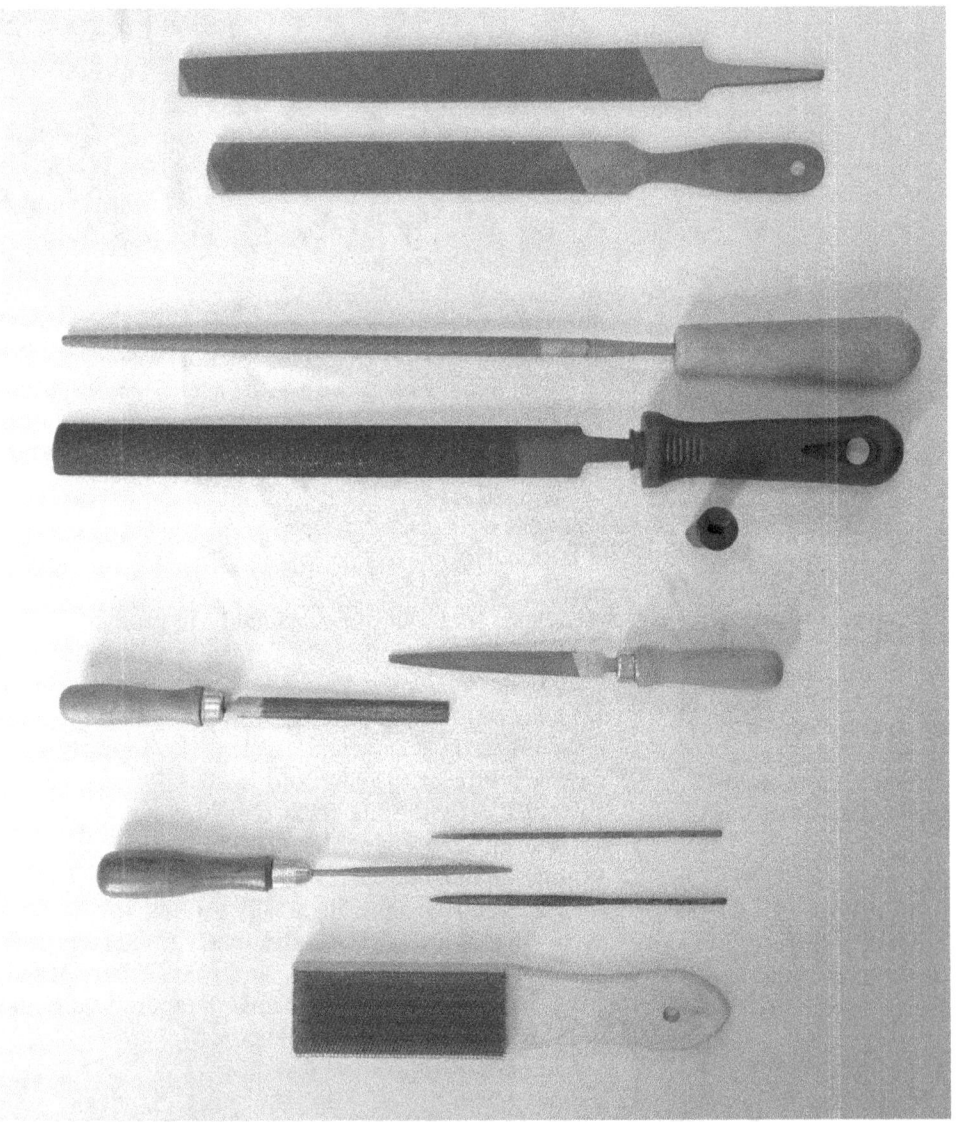

Figure 5.35 From top to bottom—a plain tang single cut bastard file, a double cut bastard file with integral handle, a double cut 2nd cut file with thread on wood handle, a double cut 2nd half round file with a push on plastic handle, a pair of mid-sized smoothing files, a trio of needle files (one with a clamp-on handle), and a file card.

Welding

- MIG pliers—These are a multi-tool for MIG welding. The large jaws are used to remove the shielding nozzle (rarely needed unless threaded), and the small jaws for contact tip replacement. The square needle-nose tips are used to clean the shielding nozzle when build up occurs. They also have a cutter to nip off the ball end of the wire to avoid cold starts.
- Welding spoon—These are thick copper shapes that attach to a handle used to back up open root welds or for plugging holes in thin sheet.
- Plug welding pliers—These are a version of locking pliers that have one forked jaw and one copper plate jaw similar to a welding spoon. Some companies offer a shielding nozzle with guide pins that match the notch in the pliers to easily align a MIG welder for plug welding thin panels.
- Chipping hammer—These are simple hammers with either a point and chisel or chisel and wire brush for removing slag from flux-cored and stick welds. These can also be used to peen a weld while it is cooling.
- Wire brush—These are a must in a metal shop. Carbon steel bristles are for general use such as removing rust, slag remnants, or smoke from stick or flux-cored welding. Shops that weld aluminum should have stainless steel bristle brushes for each welder to remove oxidation just before welding; these brushes should not be used for other tasks. The author labels with marker on multiple sides as an attempt to prevent mixed use.
- Bottle wrench—These are flat steel multi-tools for working with compressed gas. The main use will be using them to connect a regulator to a bottle, but they have slots sized to connect oxy/acetylene hoses to the torch or regulator and a punched square hole near one end for old-style acetylene valves that are used on some HVAC and jewelers sets.
- Tip cleaners—These sets are also called tip drills and are used to maintain torch tips. Most OAF sets come with drills, but they are easily damaged; having a spare set is ideal. These have an array of very small wire files that fit the orifice sizes of torch tips to remove carbon. They may also be used to clean MIG contact tips.

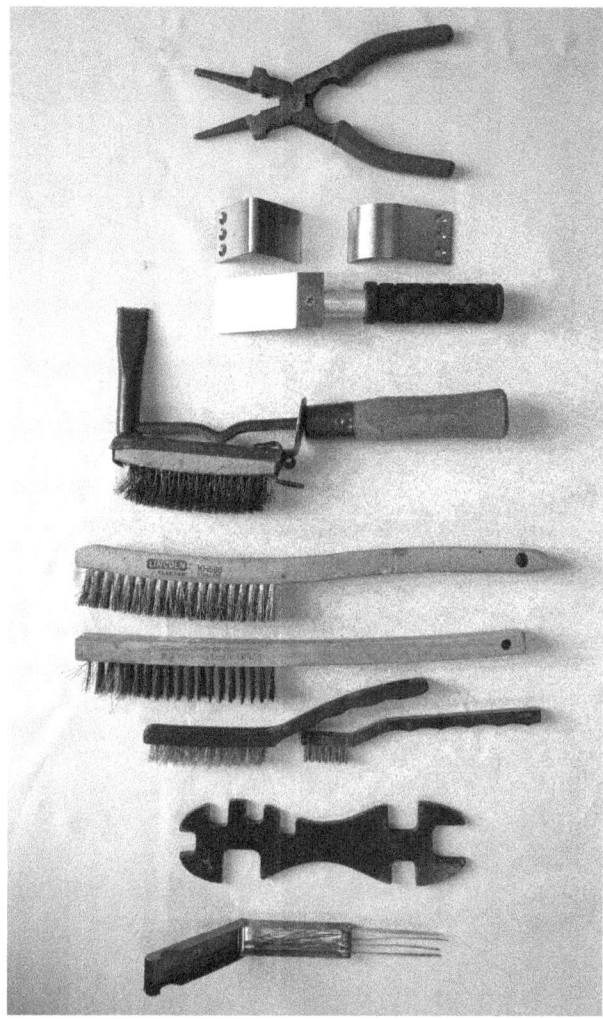

Figure 5.36 From top to bottom—MIG pliers, a welding spoon set, a chipping hammer with wire brush, a stainless wire brush for cleaning aluminum, a carbon steel wire brush, small brass and stainless brushes, a bottle wrench, and a set of tip drills.

- Welding guides—Though technically not a hand tool, some manufacturers offer quick reference guides and phone apps for setting up welding machine parameters for various materials. Miller offers very easy-to-use sliding calculators for various processes.

84 • FABRICATION FOR THEATRE AND ENTERTAINMENT

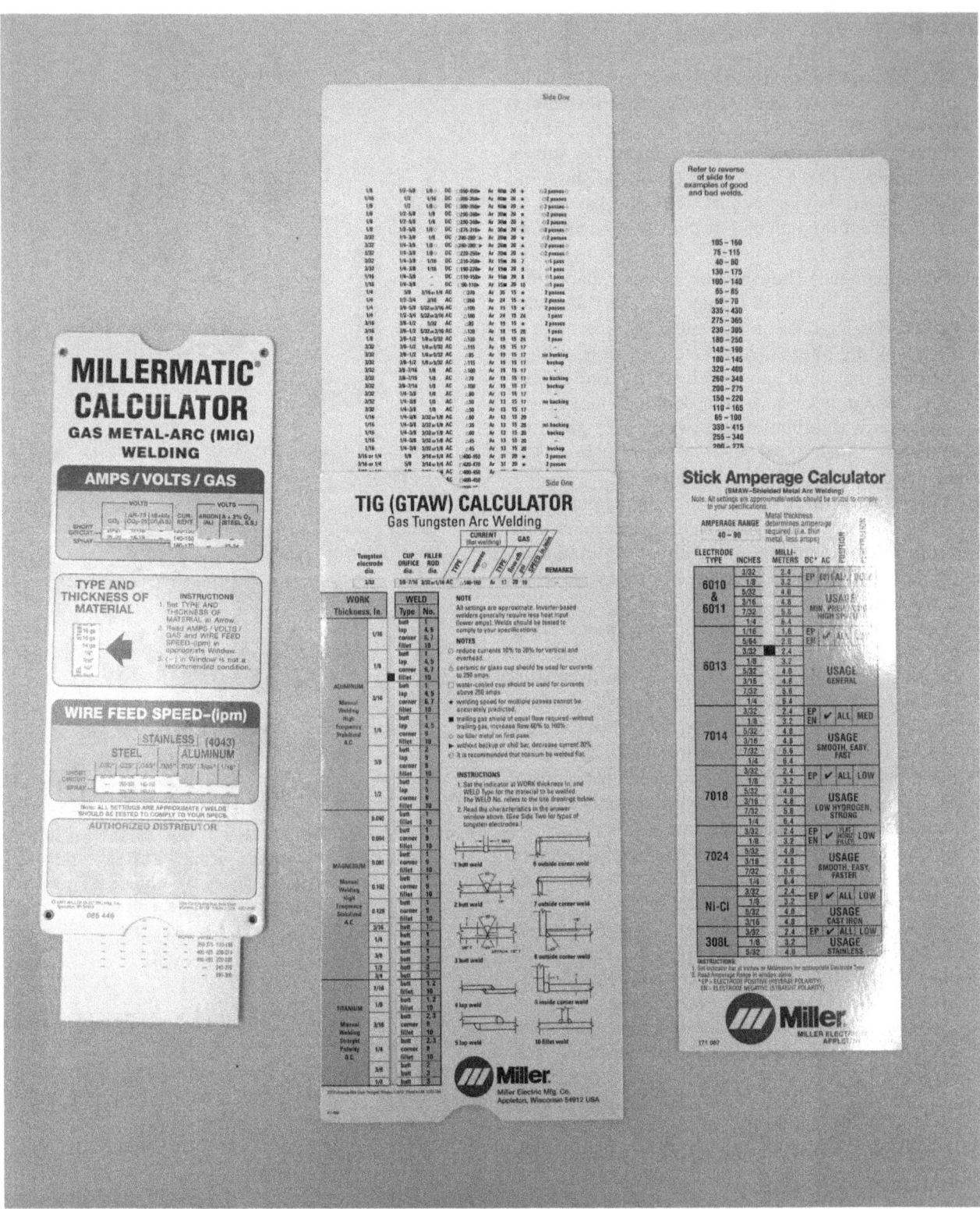

Figure 5.37 From left to right—a MIG welding chart for steel, stainless, and aluminum showing the settings for 16ga mild steel. The reverse offers settings for flux cored welding. A TIG welding chart showing settings for aluminum; settings for steel and stainless are on the reverse side. A stick welding calculator showing settings for 6013 filler rod.

MANUAL MACHINES

Unlike wood working, there are a number of manually operated machines for cutting, bending, and shaping metal. Many of these have powered counterparts, but often the cost puts them out of reach for smaller shops. Unless a shop does large production runs or uses large sections of metal on a regular basis, manual machines are likely well matched to typical projects and more cost effective.

Cutting

- Shears—A variety of manual shears make quick work of cutting various metal shapes.
  - Bench shears are available with 6"–12" throats and often include a rod shear. These generally cut much thicker sheet or strap than other shears but are mostly for 14ga and thinner steel.

Figure 5.38 The author's 12" bench shear and hold down table. This bench shear also has a rod cutter (the hole toward the rear of the blade face).

- Throatless shears are so named for their ability to continually pass a sheet through by offsetting the waste piece much like aviation snips. The most popular style is bypass shear, often referred to as Beverly shears for the company that invented them and still makes them. Lighter duty style shears use two rotating cutting wheels which fit against one another much like the blades of scissors to both pull the metal through and cut it.

Figure 5.39a A bypass style throatless shear mounted on a portable base.

Figure 5.39b The author's rotary shear mounted on a stand with other forming tools.

- Stomp shears are for cutting large sheets and named after the large pedal that is used to operate the shear. The function of these consists of two stages: the hold plate slides down to press the sheet tight to the table (this is usually done with light foot pressure) and then the blade will be engaged requiring the operator to "stomp" on the pedal to complete the cut. Most shears have a maximum capacity of 16ga.

Figure 5.40 A stomp shear in the metal shop at Meow Wolf.

- Slotted angle shears are unusual tools designed for one purpose: to cut slotted angle to easily make bolt together structures. These tools are quite expensive, and they make a far superior cut in slotted angle that requires no deburring.

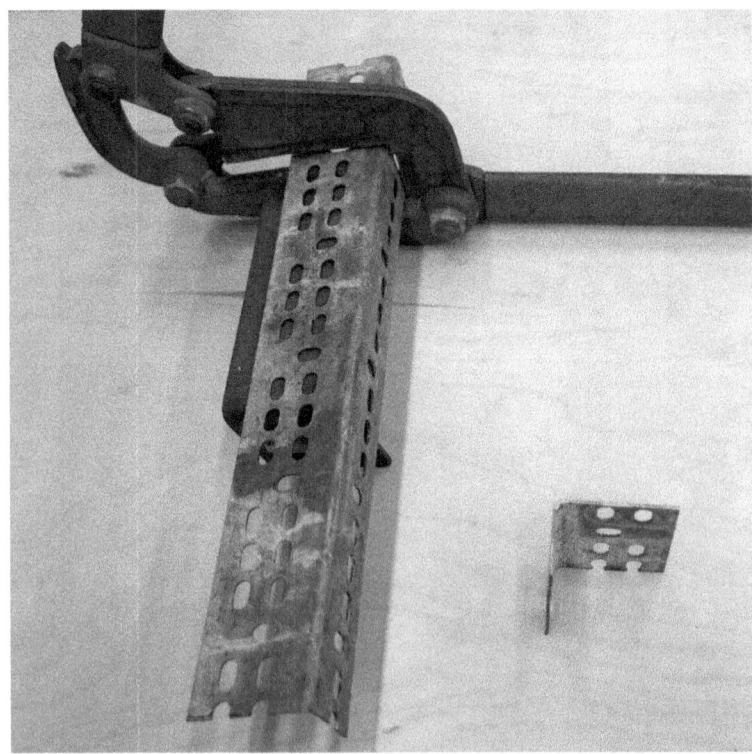

Figure 5.41 A slotted angle shear and an example of freshly sheared steel.

- Corner notcher—These cut a V-shape notch into material, usually angle, allowing it to be quickly bent to 90° and welded without the need to make two miter cuts and weld separate pieces. They do produce a radius on the outside corner, which may not be ideal for some projects, but round corners can save a lot of scrapes and bruises!

Figure 5.42 An example of corner notcher in the shop at Meow Wolf.

- Iron worker—This is a multipurpose tool designed to shear rod, bar, strap, and angle as well as punch any flat stock. While their capacity is much lower than their larger, hydraulically powered cousins, they are far more affordable and quite suitable to small shops.
- Tubing notcher—A punch-type tubing notcher is designed to shear an arc-shaped cope in the end of tube and pipe to prepare them for welding. These are the middle ground between an end-mill notcher and a hole saw notcher. They are heavy duty, but much slower than an end-mill notcher, and are more durable than hole saw notchers.

Shaping

- Hossfeld—This is a somewhat "universal" bending tool for metal. It can bend round pipe and tube, square tube, and solid stock such as angle and rod. For a smaller shop that does not have space for stand-alone tools for each function, a Hossfeld bender may be ideal. There is even an option to add hydraulic power for bending thick bar or large pipe. Many interchangeable dies are available. These machines will make long- and short-radius bends, eye bends, 90° bends, and scrolls. Similar benders for thin-wall tube that use compensating dies (to prevent crushing) are available as well and operate in the same manner using a long lever. Examples in Chapter 11 show the machine in use.
- Pipe bender—These are simple machines for bending pipe that incorporate a hydraulic jack and curved dies that are similar to a conduit bender, but more durable. The die is placed on the head of the jack and the pipe slid into the support frame. The jack is then extended until the required bend is complete.

Figure 5.43 A hydraulic pipe bender set with an end roller and bending die set out. The rest of the parts have been left in the case because they are quite heavy.

- Manual tubing roller—These are commercially available, but not difficult to build for a moderately experienced fabricator. Most use two spaced bottom rollers to support the tube with a top roller centered between them that provides the pressure for bending and has an attached crank handle to drive the material through. One design uses a hydraulic jack under the out-feed roller to control the bend radius. Examples of the author's roll bender in use are shown in Chapter 11.
- Slip roll—This is a sheet metal tool used to bend long, smooth curves. Most also have grooves for rolling heavy wire or thin rod. Some have rollers that can be disconnected at one end allowing the machine to roll closed cylinders. A slip roll can also be used for texturing soft metals; very coarse sandpaper, metal mesh, or other hard items can be layered with thin aluminum or copper and sandwiched between paperboard. The soft backing of paperboard helps embed the texture and prevent damage to the rolls.

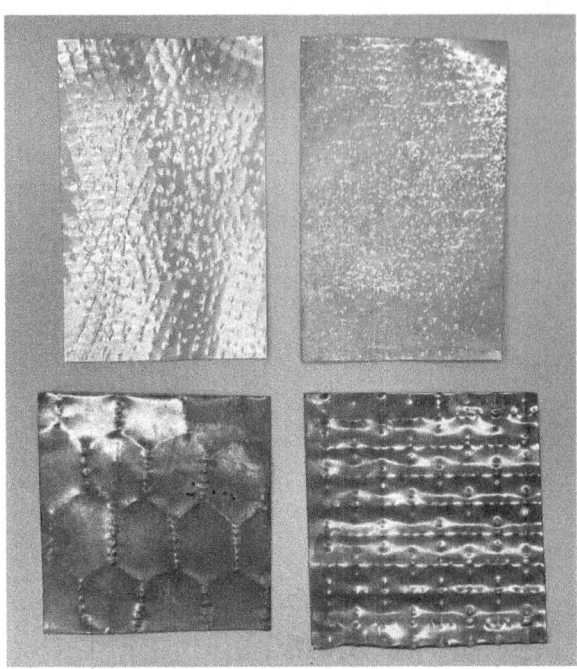

Figure 5.44b Examples of thin aluminum flashing (top) textured with diamond mesh and very coarse sandpaper, as well as 16 ounce copper (bottom) embossed with poultry cloth and hardware cloth using a slip roll.

- Brake—These are mostly used for sheet metal, but press brakes can be added to a hydraulic press to bend much thicker metal. There are two types: a straight brake that bends angles in sheets across the full width of the brake or a box (or pan) brake with removable "fingers" of various widths. These are the more desirable type as they can bend multiple sides on the same sheet without interference. Sheet metal brakes may be either bench or floor mounted. Bench-mounted units are lighter duty and may bend up to 16ga steel or slightly thicker aluminum, while floor brakes may bend up to 12ga steel. Press brakes are capable of much thicker but narrower metal. Examples of both a box brake and a press brake in use are shown in Chapter 11.

Figure 5.44a A 36" manual slip roll for 18ga sheet at full width. This machine will also roll 16ga at half width and includes grooves for rolling round bar.

HAND TOOLS AND MANUAL MACHINES • 89

Figure 5.45a A bench-mounted straight brake. This 18" brake is the most basic version available using C-clamps to hold the brake bar in place. These work quite well for occasional use on thin sheet.

Figure 5.45b A bench-mounted box brake at the University of Memphis. This brake will bend a 24" piece of 18ga steel or slightly thicker aluminum or narrow pieces of steel.

Figure 5.45c A 48" box brake at Meow Wolf. This brake is rated for up to 12ga mild steel.

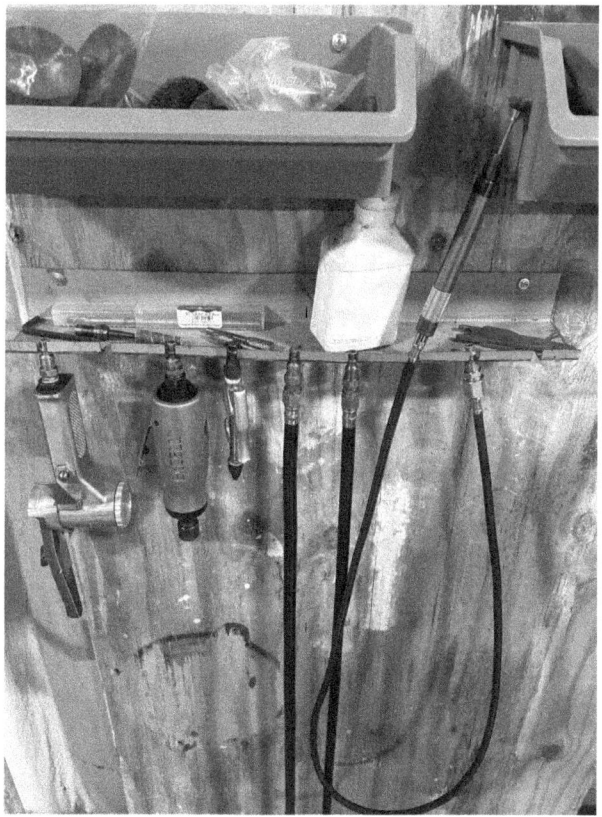

Figure 5.45d A rack for storing pneumatic tools. The sheet was first drilled, then bent in a brake, and finally the front flange cut to make rounded slots.

- Shrinker and stretcher—These are unique to working with sheet metal and are designed to help the fabricator make long radius bends in thin strap or angles and to slightly dome a sheet metal circle. The teeth in the jaws do leave a marred surface that can later be hammered, ground, or filed for a smooth finish. They are excellent for making metal trim from sheet metal. Examples of what these machines can do are shown in Figure 11.43.
- Bead roller—This is another sheet metal specific tool that is less common in entertainment shops but is almost a necessity for large sheet metal projects. The interchangeable dies can be used to create offsets for lapped seams, fold, or radius edges and add raised beads to the face of a sheet increasing its stiffness. A powered version can be seen in Figure 7.13.
- English wheel—This is possibly the most traditional tool associated with sheet metal work. It is designed for smoothing and stretching dished panels after initial forming. The top wheel is always flat, while the anvil wheels below have varying radius tops (the wheels are a consistent diameter on centerline) to match the work piece.

Figure 5.46b The completed copper altar in *Iphigenia and Other Daughters* at the University of Memphis.

Figure 5.46a The author and Michael "Jonz" Jones shaping a copper panel with an English wheel for use as an altar.

Presses

- Arbor press—This manual press can be fitted with dies for pressing pins in or out, assembling press-fit units, or shaping. These are specified by tons of pressure the frame can generate and withstand. The bottom die of the press has multiple slots to support material as needed. A manual C-frame press is a similar to an arbor press but generally has a fabricated frame with a much deeper throat than an arbor press and with a lower capacity. C-frame is a more common configuration for electric-hydraulic presses. An example of a 1-ton press can be seen in Figure 11.41.
- Hydraulic press—These are quite common in shops and have a multitude of uses. They can be used to press-fit assemblies, straighten bent items, and install/remove bearing and seals as well as punching and shearing with accessories. Small, bench-mounted models usually have an A-shaped frame, while floor standing models have an H-shaped frame. Most presses are shipped with cast iron press plates. While these may hold up well for many uses, they can fracture and it is quite scary when they do. A press that will see on-going heavy use should be upgraded to cut steel press plates.

Figure 5.47 The author's hydraulic press converted with an air-operated hydraulic jack (that retains manual function). The press has been welded to a riser for more comfortable use.

Chapter 6

Power Tools

In this text, power tool refers to portable tools used for fabrication; machinery refers to stationary tools. This chapter is intended to introduce both the most common power tools for metal working as well as a few that may be unfamiliar, but useful to the entertainment industry. There are not as many variants of metal working tools as there are for wood working. Many of the cutting tools operate in a similar manner to their wood working counterparts; shaping tools on the other hand use the pliability of metal to their advantage. Duplication of certain tools can also increase shop efficiency. Having multiple angle grinders, for example, is quite common. In addition to duplication, many power tools offer variants such as size, capacity, or additional features. These variants should be included in estimating return on investment. For example, a variable speed bench grinder is more expensive than a fixed speed unit but is more versatile. Another example would be choosing a dry cutting saw over an abrasive saw; the dry cutting saw is more expensive, but labor is saved by less clean up (deburring) time after each cut. Tool choice should add to the quality of the finished product as well as adding speed and efficiency to the production process. The list below is not exhaustive but thorough.

A quick reminder about Personal Protection Equipment (PPE): any tool that creates flying debris, particulate that could be inhaled, or loud noise poses a risk. Proper PPE is the best way to reduce risk. Eye, ear, and respiratory protection may not all be necessary with every tool, but they should be readily available as most fabrication requires the use of multiple tools. At minimum, safety glasses (and/or a face shield) should be worn in the metal fabrication area at all times and hearing protection should be at the ready. Some specific hazards are noted in this section, but readers should familiarize themselves with the recommendations in Chapter 13 for specifics of PPE use before embarking on fabrication projects.

CUTTING, SHEARING, AND PUNCHING

The primary means for cutting metal, much like wood, is to use various saws. Many metal cutting saws are similar to their wood cutting relatives, but most operate slower. In addition metal can be drilled, punched, and sheared, making some of the machines for metal working quite different from those used for wood.

- Dry cut saw—These portable saws are often mounted to a bench making them easier to use with long sticks of material. With either a 12″ or 14″ diameter carbide toothed blade, they will cut the majority of the sizes and shapes used by industry. These saws are best suited to thinner steel but cut aluminum well also. The main advantage is providing a nearly burr-free cut while making very few sparks. Another advantage is the ability to cut to their full depth for the life of the blade. The downside to these saws is that they are very loud. Tooth count varies a bit by the thickness of the metal being cut. Thicker steel will increase wear. These saws plunge cut like a miter saw but do take a bit more of a delicate hand when cutting. Pressure should be such that few to no sparks are being produced while the blade is advancing. Hollow sections can be a bit odd; the saw will take longer to cut through the portions that are horizontal than it will to cut through the walls.

Figure 6.1 A dry cutting portable metal cut-off saw at the University of Memphis (the guard has been held back only to show blade detail). Like most portable saws, the material must be clamped at an angle to cut a miter.

Figure 6.2 The author's abrasive saw mounted to a portable frame. This saw is most often used with roller stands for long material.

- Abrasive saw—These portable saws may also be bench mounted. Nearly all use a 14" blade and are nearly synonymous with cutting steel. For very thick steel, these are often a better choice than dry cut saws; thick sections impart significant wear and dry cut blades are quite expensive compared to abrasive blades. These do produce a spark, will not cut aluminum, and the depth of cut gets shallower as the blade wears away. While not as loud as a dry cutting saw, these are still very loud. The biggest downside is the very sharp burr left at the cut that needs to be removed before further processing. Cutting also requires a bit of getting used to; very thick sections will require a slight plunge, release just a bit, and repeat in order to not stall some saws.

- Metal cutting circular saw—These are available both corded and cordless. Like the dry cutting bench saw, these cut sheet metal and tube steel nearly burr free. For long cuts in sheet, they are far superior to abrasive blades.

Figure 6.3 A metal cutting circular saw in the process of cutting 18 ga sheet steel.

- Miter Saw—Slow-speed miter saws are much like their wood cutting cousins but operate at about 1/2 the RPMs of a wood cutting saw. There are few options available, and most have a fairly small capacity. These are still suitable for most light fabrication with aluminum. One key component is running a Triple Chipboard (TC) blade with a 0° to −6° hook angle.

Figure 6.4 A low speed (1600RPM) miter saw used for light duty aluminum cutting at ATOMIC (www.atomicdesign.tv). The advantage to the saw is being able to swing the saw to cut a miter instead of swinging the material into the room as many saws require.

- Portable bandsaw—These are often referred to as a Porta-Band as both a play on words and acknowledging that they were developed by Porter-Cable Corporation. A few varieties of this saw are available as both battery and corded versions. Most are variable speed making them easy to match to the material being cut. Though they cut slowly, they make no sparks and far less noise than other saws. Corded units tend to be deep cut style (4″–5″ capacity) while battery-powered units tend to be compact and subcompact (1 1/2″–3 1/2″ capacity). These can be challenging to make a straight cut with and pinching or twisting the blade can dislodge it from the tool. This can kink the blade, requiring it to be replaced. They are still and excellent tool because they are portable, make straight cuts with practice, and can be adapted to be small vertical saws used for contour cutting.

Figure 6.5a A deep cut, variable speed portable metal cutting bandsaw. This saw will cut just over a 4″ diameter.

Figure 6.5b A portable bandsaw converted with a table for contour cutting.

- Cut-off tool—These are typically pneumatic, though electric units are available, and use a 2″ or 3″ cutting wheel. Most are similar to a die grinder with an added shield and some die grinders are convertible. Right angle, long-reach tools typically use a 3″ blade. The advantage to standard tools with shaft being inline is compactness being able to cut in places an angle grinder will not reach.

Figure 6.7a An air nibbler being used to cut out oak leaves from 18 ga sheet steel.

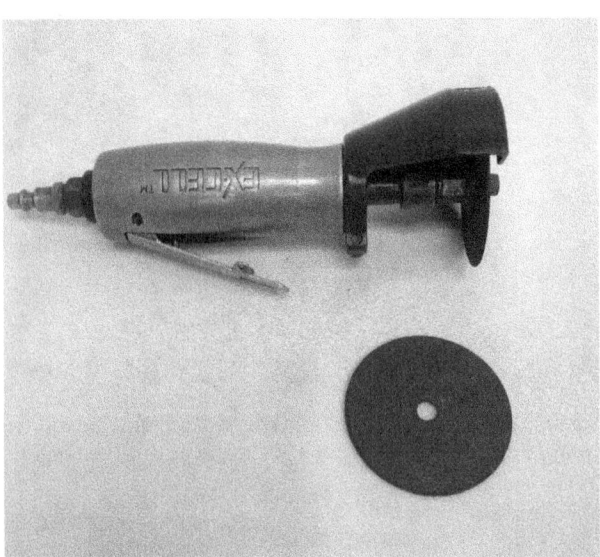

Figure 6.6 A standard pneumatic cut-off tool with front-mounted 3″ diameter blade.

- Nibbler—These tools are excellent for interior cuts in sheet metal because, like a jig saw, a drilled hole can allow the nose to pass through to start cutting but they produce a much cleaner cut with little to no distortion. These will also cut a very tight radius. The drawback to them is the off-cuts are small and very sharp. Pneumatic units are common, but battery and corded versions are available as well. Most have a capacity up to 16 ga. Drill-powered units are available but are less than ideal.

Figure 6.7b The oak leaves from Figure 6.7a on a finished sculpture. Though not a theatre piece it shows a good example of the detail a nibbler will cut.

- Double cut shear—These are also known as a slitting shears because they remove a small slice of the sheet (about 1/8″) which is a rather large kerf, so users should plan for this. Pneumatic, corded, and battery units are all available. These will cut a long radius, but are best for straight cuts with little to no distortion. Pneumatic shears are available as either pistol grip or inline styles. Capacity rarely exceeds 16 ga.

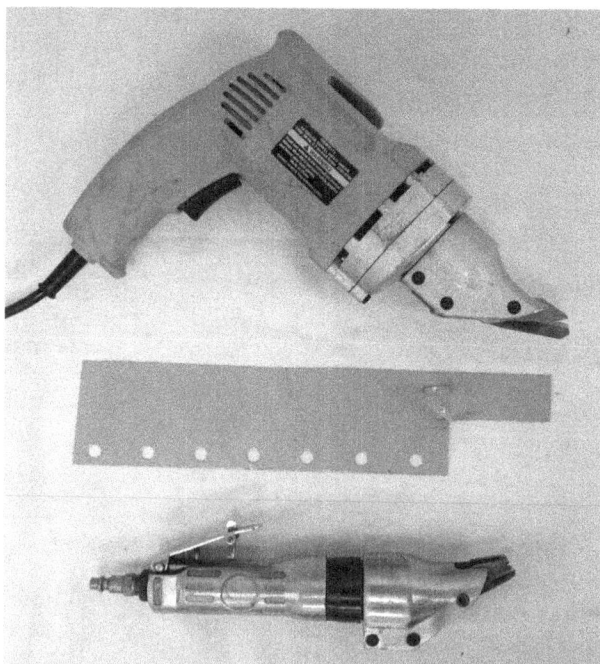

Figure 6.8 A set of electric pistol grip shears and inline pneumatic shears. The sample sheet shows the signature curlicue kerf these tools make when cutting.

- Throatless single cut shear—These operate much like a bench mounted shear, so the off-cut is pushed below the surface as the tool cuts. The advantage to these is the ability to cut a fairly tight radius, and some will cut much heavier sheet, up to 10 ga.

Figure 6.9 A portable throatless shear. This model will cut up to 16 ga steel.

- Air saw—These saws are primarily used in autobody work. They are similar to a jig saw, but with an inline blade. They cut quickly, with little distortion, no sparks and very little residual burr. They are designed for thin sheet and can cut easily through a vertical surface but the sheet needs to be well braced. The blades are unique to this style of saw.

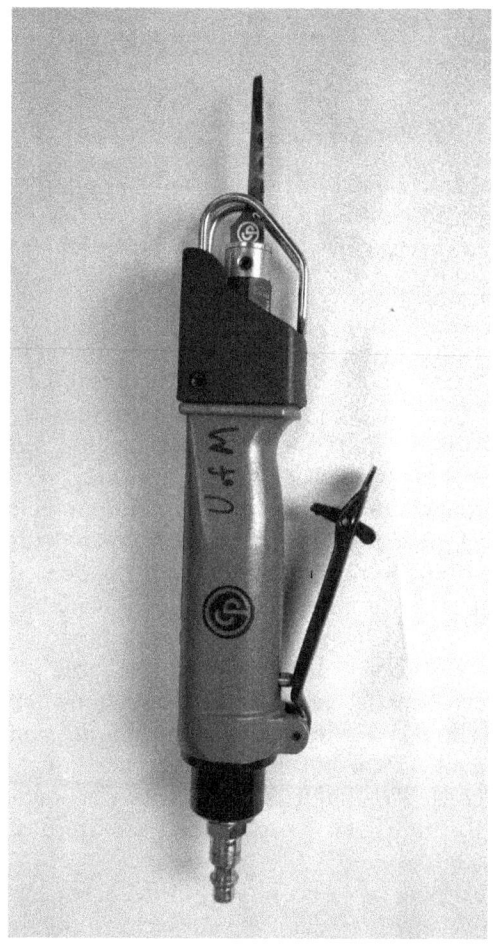

Figure 6.10 An air saw with a typical metal cutting scroll blade.

- Tubing notcher—This is technically an attachment for a drill, but mentioned here because it is unique to metal fabrication. These use a hole saw to cope the end of tubing to fit tight to another round tube for welding. Light duty versions are quite low cost; heavy duty jigs are two to three times the cost but will be long lasting. While they can be used on a drill press, it is quite easy to use excessive pressure, shearing the teeth off the hole saw. A manual drill allows the user to feel the cutting action extending the life of the hole saw. Very low RPM and cutting oil are essential.

Figure 6.11 On the left is a light duty tubing notcher set to cut an angled intersect and on the right a heavy duty notcher that has been mounted to a clamping plate for portability.

Figure 6.12 A magnetic base drill shown with annular cutter and sample steel plate.

- Drills—Most readers will be familiar with standard drills but there are variants of these tools that are less common but quite useful. Beyond electric and battery-powered drills, pneumatic drills can be very useful at work stations as they are lighter than their electrically driven counterparts and never overheat. Most tend to run at higher speeds, but geared units that are appropriate for metal are available. Right angle (or tight quarters) drills are commonly paired with stubby drill bits and are available for any power source. Users should be aware that when using any hand-held drill with metal, there is an increased risk of the bit binding on break-though; this can cause wrist injuries. Drills with a secondary handle allowing for two-handed use are best for metal working.
- Magnetic drill press—These have a switchable magnetic base that allows them to be attached directly to steel for drilling. They are excellent for center drilling large sheets, drilling in steel pieces or units that won't fit on a drill press. Like a drill press, they make a very straight cut. Because of this, some users will fabricate a steel jig plate to attach the drill to non-magnetic metals in order to achieve clean, perpendicular holes. Many units offer an optional traditional chuck for use with twist drills, but the more common choice is to mount an annular cutter directly to the quill. They are available cordless, but the high amp draw of the motor makes corded units preferable. Most will mount up to a 1 1/2" annular cutter and/or 3/4" twist drill.

SHAPING

- Flanger—These pneumatic tools usually include a punch. They are used to make offsets along the edge of a sheet for creating lapped seams. The punch is typically 7/32" or 8 mm; sized for plug welding thin sheet up to 16 ga. Such a joint can be seen in Figures 11.6a and 11.6b.
- Air hammer—These tools are essentially powered chisels. Pointed and flat chisels are typically used to remove welding slag or dross from plasma cutting. Cutting chisels can be used to shear sheet metal, slit tubing, or cut the heads from tubular rivets to remove them. Rivet setting chisels are used to form heads on solid rivets after heating (these are better suited to rivet specific hammers though). Round

chisels are for hammering out rusty fasteners such as steel dowel pins. While not a precision tool, they are handy for some tasks and are low cost.

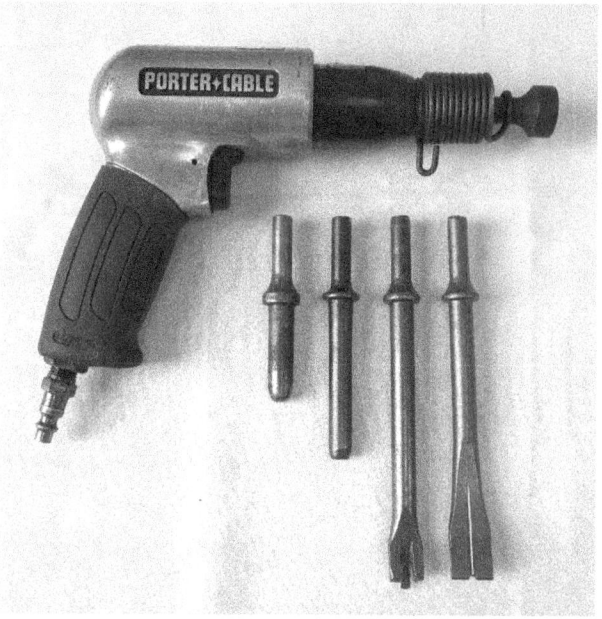

Figure 6.13 An air hammer with a smoothing bit installed and chisels below. Chisels from left to right—sinking bit for shaping sheet metal, a rivet setter for solid rivets, sheet metal shear, and rivet cutter.

- Planisher—Planishing is the act of quickly "slapping" the surface of sheet metal while it is being backed with a shaping dolly. This is often done to remove imperfections from hammer work. Unlike using a hammer, planishing tools strike more surface area and are designed for smoothing. While most planishers are mounted on a C-shaped frame, much like an English wheel, hand-held tools are available and are excellent for small areas.
- Pneumatic riveter—While there are pneumatic riveters similar to air hammers for setting solid rivets, most shops will opt for an air operated hydraulic blind riveter. The advantages to these are reduced hand fatigue, speed, and increased capacity over a manual riveter. They are compatible with the same blind rivets as hand-held models.
- Needle scaler—These are designed to remove heavy rust, scale, paint, or welding slag. While most projects will not require one, they are fairly low cost and excellent for outdoor steel installations, especially those that may need repair. They operate similar to an air hammer, but with a bundle of steel "needles" in place of a single chisel and use a much shorter stroke. They may be inline or pistol grip style.

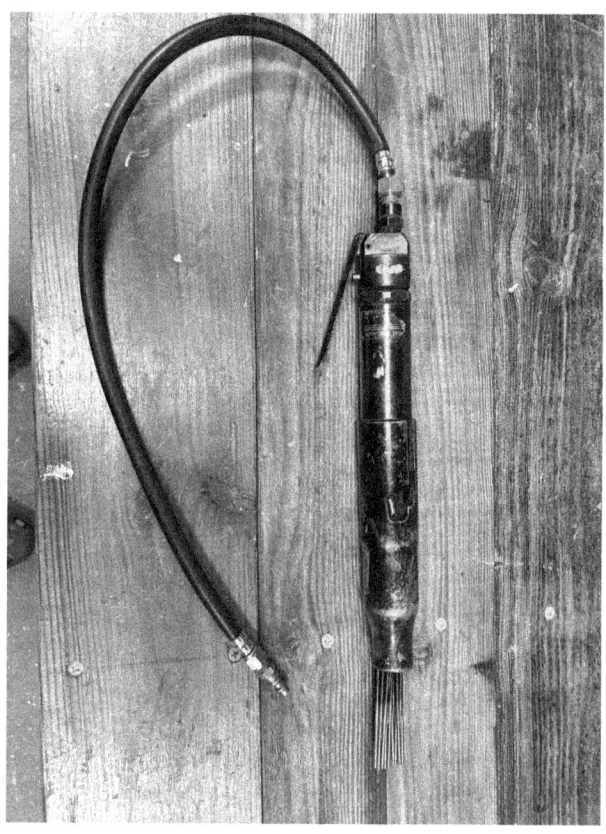

Figure 6.14 An inline needle scaler that has seen hard use in a restoration shop.

FINISHING TOOLS

- Bench grinder—These are one of the most common finishing tools in the metal area. They are offered with a standard speed of 3450 RPM motor, though slow-speed (1800 RPM) and variable speed grinders are also available. The most common sizes are 6″ and 8″. A few companies offer hybrid grinders that combine a stone wheel with a belt or a miniature machine with a 3″ wheel and flex shaft. These smaller grinders are very useful in props and craft shops. Grinding wheels may need to be dressed occasionally as they wear to reveal new abrasive. This is usually done with a stone or diamond dresser. With heavy (or improper) use, a wheel may need to be trued. This is typically done with a more aggressive dresser that uses cutting wheels.

Figure 6.15a A combination bench grinder that has both a traditional 6" stone wheel on the left and a 2" × 24" belt grinder on the right.

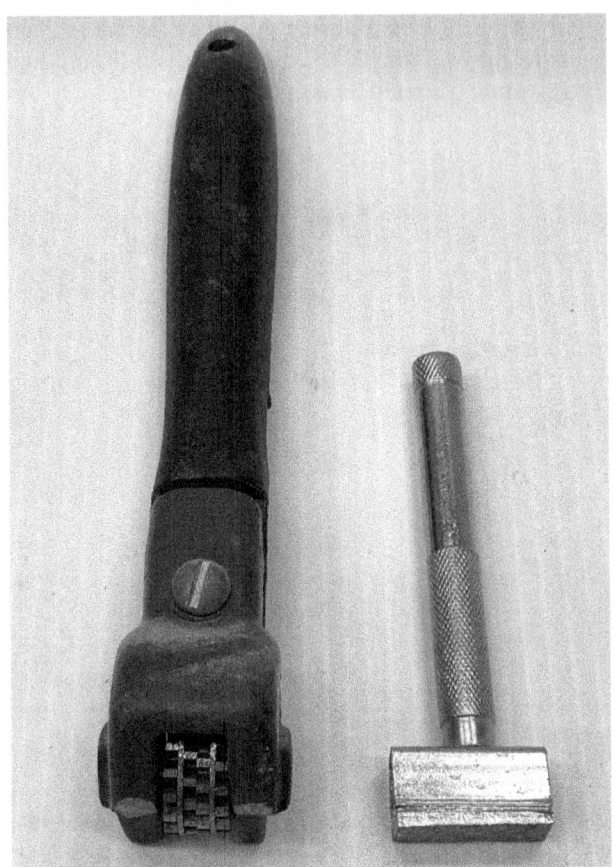

Figure 6.15c A wheel-type dresser on the left and a diamond dresser on the right.

Figure 6.15b An 8" variable speed bench grinder with a coarse grey silicon carbide wheel and fine grade white aluminum oxide wheel mounted.

Figure 6.15d Dressing a grinding wheel with a diamond dresser. The clear guard has been lifted for photo purposes.

- Angle grinder—These are likely one of the most used tools in fabrication. The interchangeable wheels allow them to grind, cut, deburr, and polish. Corded electric grinders are available from 4″ to 9″ diameters with fixed or variable speeds and are the standard in most shops. Battery and pneumatic grinders are typically 4 1/2″–5″. Amperage is a fairly good indicator of duty cycle for corded tools; pneumatic versions must be matched to a high CFM compressor. Battery grinders are best suited to touch ups or on-site repairs. Electric grinders offer two common trigger styles: paddle switch and thumb switch. Some units can be locked on for extended use.

- Pipe finisher—These can be dedicated machines or an attachment for an angle grinder. They consist of a grinding belt mounted on a spring tensioned metal frame that allows the belt to partially wrap around a pipe to remove burrs and black oxide coating to prepare for welding.

Figure 6.17 A pipe polisher accessory for an angle grinder. The author has mounted the angle grinder to a work table and added a foot pedal control.

Figure 6.16 A paddle switch grinder and a thumb switch grinder. The guard on the thumb switch grinder has been rotated for easier cutting.

- Air file—This term is used for two different tools depending on the source. It accurately names an air-powered file that does use hardened steel files. These are most commonly used by sculptors. The more common tool is a belt file, which is really miniature belt sander. Belt files are a favorite of metal artists and electric and pneumatic versions are available. The two common sizes use 3/8″ × 13″ or 1/2″ × 18″ belts. These are great for fine finishing work or for deburring the inside of tube steel.

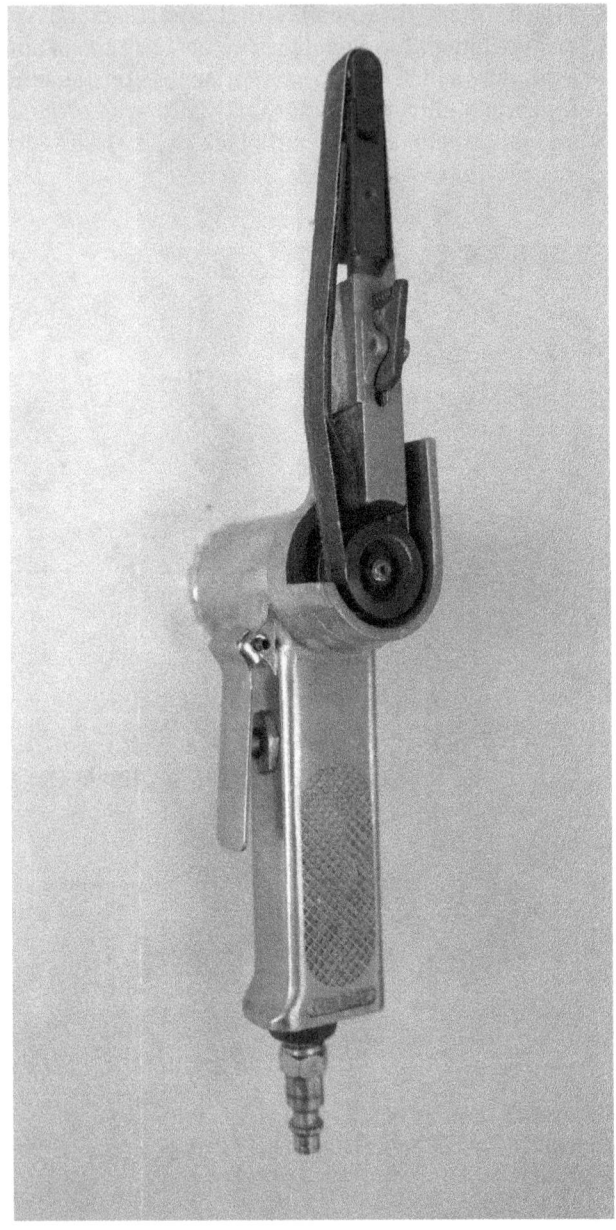

Figure 6.18 A compact air file with a 3/8″ wide belt. This version is variable speed.

used with 1/8″ and 1/4″ shank tools such as carbide burrs, mounted stones, and polishing points. Electric units, usually referred to as in inline grinders, are quieter but are much larger than air-driven ones. Both will achieve very high speeds from 10K to 25K RPMs. Right angle versions are best used as an orbital sander/polisher or for stripping paint. Backing pads are available from 1″ to 3″ in diameter and use screw-on pads that quickly interchange.

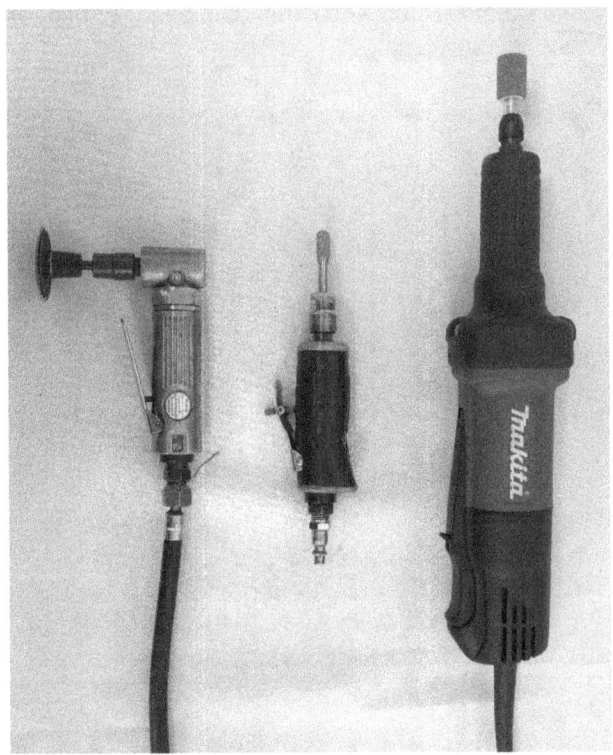

Figure 6.19 From left to right—a pneumatic right angle die grinder with a 2″ fiber disc, an inline pneumatic die grinder with carbide burr and an electric inline grinder with a mounted stone point.

- Rotary tool—These are synonymous with the brand name Dremel, but other manufacturers make similar tools. They are one of the most common detailing tools for small props. They can be used for sanding, carving, cutting, polishing, and drilling. Versions include corded and cordless, both may be variable speed up to 10K RPMs.
- Die grinder—Named due to their use in tool and die making, these are similar to rotary tools but are designed for larger, heavier use. Pneumatic versions are noisy, but fairly low cost and can be
- Pencil grinder—This little tool is essentially a pneumatic rotary tool. Most are variable speed with the twist of the dial and run at very high top speeds from 50K to 70K RPMs. They are an excellent detailing tool because they lack the bulk of an electric rotary tool and are much less expensive than a flex-shaft tool if the shop is already equipped with a heavy duty compressor. Most use a 1/8″ collet and can be used with carbide burrs, diamond burs, or mounted stones.

- Flex-shaft tool—These are the heavy duty version of a rotary tool, but with no direct drive option. They are the go to for detailers that need to use a rotary tool for extended periods. These are designed to hang from an arm and have a 24″–36″ flexible shaft that offers interchangeable hand-pieces (e.g. drill chuck vs. collet). Many of these units will run at speeds up to 18K RPMs and offer more power than hand-held types. They can be used with the same accessories as hand-held types. One manufacturer offers ultra-precision versions that are exceptionally well balanced and vibration free. While all name brand versions are more costly than rotary tools, they reduce hand fatigue and offer foot controls. These are commonly used for deburring or adding fine detail.

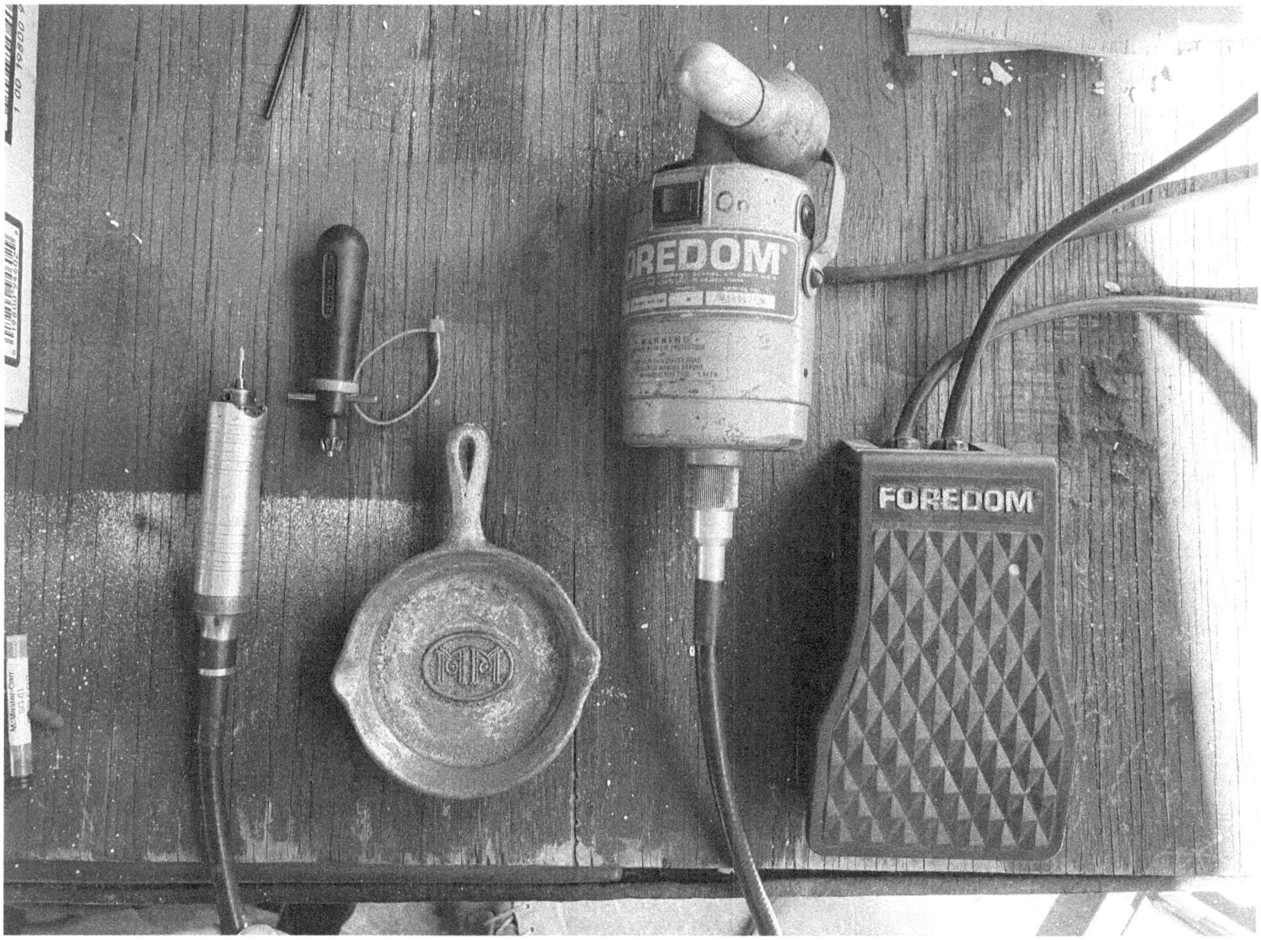

Figure 6.20 A pencil grinder with a carbide burr being used to clean the flash from the edges of a bronze casting.

Figure 6.21 A flex-shaft tool with a drill chuck hand-piece. Though staged for the photo, this machine is being used to deburr a novelty cast-iron pan using a carbide burr.

- Surfacing drum—These are excellent for stripping finishes, preparing for paint or polishing. The drums are 3″–4″ wide by 3″ diameter. Non-woven abrasive drums can be used for burnishing and polishing and bristle wheels will strip shallow contours.
- Drill sharpener—Though not a tool for finishing projects, a twist drill sharpener is a valuable tool because it saves both replacement costs and downtime. Machines designed for 118° and 135° bits are the best option for metal fabrications shops. Affordable machines will sharpen up to 3/4″ diameter bits quickly and easily. Other advantages to higher-end machines is the ability to grind split points and to adjust the relief angle, making a bit more or less aggressive as needed.

Figure 6.22 A drill bit sharpener that will sharpen 118° and 135° twist drills, back-grind split points and can adjust relief angle. The image shows how the included chuck fits into a setup slot that has sprung fingers to hold the flutes at the proper index as well as an additional chuck that will hold up to a 3/4″ bit.

Chapter 7

Machinery

In this text, machinery refers to stationary tools; power tool refers to a portable tool used for fabrication. The quality and scale of the machinery a shop purchases may vary with the business model it operates under as well as how important each is to the production process. Smaller "contractor" grade machines may be suitable in a community theatre scene shop, but industrial-quality machines are a must in a commercial fabrication shop. As a shop is starting out, trade-offs may be necessary; used machinery or lower horsepower machines with fewer features may later be upgraded, as these types of tools tend to hold market value.

A quick reminder about Personal Protection Equipment (PPE): any tool that creates flying debris, particulate that could be inhaled, or loud noise poses a risk. Proper PPE is the best way to reduce risk. Eye, ear, and respiratory protection may not all be necessary with every tool, but they should be readily available, as most fabrication requires the use of multiple tools. At minimum, safety glasses (and/or a face shield) should be worn in the metal fabrication area at all times, and hearing protection should be at the ready. Machines present specific risks. Guards and tool rests exist to help keep the operator safe, but proper training and use should be the primary safety mechanism. Sometimes overlooked risks include loose clothing or long hair and jewelry that could become entangled in moving parts. Wearing gloves when operating machinery can actually increase risk, depending on the machine. Some specific hazards are noted in this section, but readers should familiarize themselves with the specifics in Chapter 13 before embarking on fabrication projects.

Beyond PPE, operating machinery requires concentration, and operators should be trained on each machine and/or read the operator's manual prior to any use. This text is not intended to act as a substitute for proper training nor machine manuals. Only the operator should be in the control zone of the machine; all other personnel should be aware of material pathways and keep them clear. Operators should not be wearing in-ear music devices; you can hear a person with a raised voice through hearing protection, but in-ear devices can defeat that ability. Crew members should be trained to never distract any operator. Another item that improves safety and accuracy is task lighting. This is especially true on machines that have components above the work area, such as a drill press or bandsaw. Adding task lighting directly to the machine can greatly improve the operator's view. Magnetic and hard-mount versions are available from many tool suppliers.

A note about guards: machine guards are in place to be a reminder, not to ensure proper use. Guards certainly improve operator safety, but all machinery still relies on the attentiveness of the operator to ensure safe use.

CUTTING, SHEARING, AND PUNCHING

The primary means for cutting metal, much like wood, is to use various saws. Many metal-cutting saws are similar to their wood-cutting relatives, but most operate slower. In addition, metal can be drilled, punched, and sheared, making some of the machines for metal working quite different from those used for wood.

A note about cutting fluids. Many saws, drill presses, and machine tools use cutting fluid for both lubrication and cooling during operation. Machine owners should consult factory manuals for cutting fluid type options that will be compatible for the intended projects. Most fluid manufacturers recommend using purified or distilled water for best results and longest fluid life.

If the cooling system on the machine does not include a skimmer, one should be added. There are essentially three types of coolant, and all have a life span; they should be replenished following manufacturer recommendations.

- Soluble oil—These are oils that can be diluted (or emulsified) with water. They are one of the most common replacements for sulfured oils traditionally used (and still used for heavy cutting during machining). They perform very well but may be prone to microbial growth that leads to significant odor. A bit of liquid disinfectant or fungicide can delay or prevent this growth.
- Synthetic fluid—While these cutting fluids are unlikely to harbor microbes, they provide much less lubricity than soluble oils. They work well in bandsaws and in wet grinding operations but may not be optimal for steel cutting in a cold saw, for example.
- Semi-synthetic fluid—These are a hybrid of synthetic lubricant and soluble oil. They offer resistance to microbes and higher lubricity, making them an all-around choice for many operations.

Machines

- Cold cutting saw—These are one of the key machines in any large fabrication shop. They use toothed blades that are continuously cooled and lubricated with cutting fluid. These saws make a very clean cut, run fairly quietly, and make no sparks. They will also cut almost any cross-section within the cutting depth. Many saws have blades specified in metric units and use a four-bolt mount as opposed to a single-bolt arbor. RPMs will vary depending on material type.

Figure 7.1a and b Cold saws at ATOMIC (www.atomicdesign.tv) with long in-feed and out-feed tables with conveyor rollers make movement of heavy materials easy. The first saw is a high-speed saw for aluminum that does not cut miters; the second is a slow-speed saw (2 cutting speeds) for steel; this saw has a swing head to cut miters.

Key factors
- High-speed saws (1750–3200 RPM) are for cutting non-ferrous metals, while low-speed saws (under 250 RPM) are for cutting ferrous metals.
- The most common machines have 10″–14″ blades with cutting capacities from 2 3/4″ to 4″.
- Machines may be manual, semi-automatic, or fully automatic. Most shops will opt for a manual

machine due to cost, but for high production, a semi-automatic machine (pedal operated) that clamps and cuts in one step may be worth the increased production speed.

Safety considerations
- Like any saw, the operator must keep fingers clear and wear eye and ear protection.
- All materials must be tightly clamped; toothed blades can catch material, pulling it into the saw if not held tightly. This will often lead to breaking teeth or a blade plate.

Maintenance
- Blades must be selected to match the material. (See Chapter 10 for blade usage details.)
- Cutting/Cooling lubricant should be changed at regular intervals.

- Stationary abrasive—These are the industrial version of a portable abrasive saw, typically having a larger work surface and powered by an induction motor. Like the portable saw, they are primarily used to cut ferrous metals. They operate slightly quieter than their portable equivalents.

Key factors
- Machines typically use 12" or 14" diameter blades with a cutting capacity of approximately 3" or 4" and use 3 or 5 HP motors.
- Like a portable saw, the material must be pivoted to cut miters. Unlike portable saws, most cabinet saws use a fully rotating vise.

Safety considerations
- Like any saw, the operator must keep fingers clear and wear eye and ear protection.
- These saws generate significant heat and sparks; hot work protocols should be applied where applicable.
- Abrasive saws leave a very sharp burr at the cutting edge that should be removed before further processing.

Maintenance
- Abrasive blades lose diameter as they wear, thus reducing their cutting capacity. They may require replacing early when cutting large sections.
- Saw guards tend to have a build-up of dross over time. This should be removed from the guard before it interferes with the rotation of the blade.

- Horizontal bandsaw—These are another common saw in many large shops. The advantage to them is their versatility: like a cold saw, they will cut nearly any section shape that will fit, and they will cut

Figure 7.2 A stationary abrasive saw. Note the heavy guarding, foot-operated clamp, and induction motor.

Figure 7.3a A horizontal bandsaw at Meow Wolf; this saw has a fluid lubricant available and is variable speed.

Figure 7.3b A second horizontal bandsaw at Meow Wolf; this saw is a dry-cutting, two-speed machine.

almost any alloy. They are quiet and generate no sparks. They may use fluid cooling or solid stick lubricant or, for some alloys, run dry. Though very large capacity saws are available, the most versatile are those that have a swing table for cutting miters. A 6″–8″ cutting capacity is a reasonable size for most shops.

Key factors
- Blade guides are adjustable and should be set only slightly larger than the material to be cut (much like a vertical saw) to produce the straightest cuts.
- Some are variable speed to better accommodate alloys of different densities. Other machines may have three fixed speeds.
- Manual machines have a cutting feed controlled by an adjustable hydraulic circuit. Semi-automatic machines have a control panel to set blade speed and cutting feed rate but retain manual clamping.
- Industrial-grade machines have an automatic shut-off when the cut is complete.
- Larger saws may offer up to a 60° cut. Some smaller saws may be set up as a vertical saw using a bolt-on work surface.

Safety considerations
- Like any saw, the operator must keep fingers clear and wear eye protection. Most saws are quiet enough that the operator may not need ear protection.
- While stack cutting is an option on these machines, care should be taken to ensure all pieces are sufficiently clamped. This method should be avoided with round stock that can roll during cutting, which can jam and/or break the blade.

Maintenance
- Blade life increases with the use of coolant and/or lubricant. The additional cost of fluid cooling on the machine may be offset by the increased longevity of the blade in many cases.
- Blade type needs to be matched to the material. Chapter 10 provides information.

- Vertical bandsaw—There are a few options for vertical metal-cutting bandsaws.
  - Fixed frame saws may be two- or three-wheel, single-speed or variable-speed, and are almost identical to wood-cutting bandsaws. In some cases, variable-speed saws can be shared between these operations. Another option is to adapt a wood-cutting bandsaw for metal use by adding a speed reducer of some type, but the saw must be very heavy-duty for this option to be viable. Vertical saws are often considered contour saws because the user is able to manually feed the material in any orientation. Like a wood-cutting

bandsaw, the capable radius will be based on blade width.
- Gravity saws operate in a similar manner to horizontal saws in that gravity feeds the blade through the work piece. They also have automatic shutoff at the end of cutting. Many are four-speed saws, making them compatible with wood, ferrous metal, non-ferrous metal, and plastic; thus, the cutting capacity overall may be much larger than its capacity per material. Older saws may only cross cut at 90°. These are generally not well suited to stack cutting unless integrated into a large work station.
- Tilting frame saws are the most versatile of all metal-cutting saws. They are generally the only saw that offers the option of cutting compound angles. Many machines offer T-slot tables in addition to a traditional vise, allowing materials to be positioned in a myriad of ways. Though very expensive machines, they are semi-automatic with high production rates, making them well suited to large facilities.

Figure 7.4b A wood-cutting bandsaw converted to metal cutting by adding a gear reducer to the drive assembly (lower right in housing). This saw operates at approximately 325 (FPM), ideal for mild steel. The author has cut 1/2" steel on this machine; though not fast, it cuts cleanly.

Figure 7.4a A 14" metal cutting contour saw at Meow Wolf. This saw offers two speeds via belt change on the drive pulleys. This saw also has a blade welder; it is somewhat more cost-effective to make blades in house.

Figure 7.4c A gravity feed vertical bandsaw. This style saw uses a lever to manually move the saw up to load and allows the user precise control over engagement into the material. Though this saw only cuts at 90°, the currently available model from the same manufacturer has a moveable clamp that does pivot for cutting miters.

Figure 7.4d A tilt frame vertical bandsaw at Adirondack Studios. This style saw allows for very precise compound cuts and has a powered feed.

Key factors
- Metal-cutting contour saws are often lower horsepower than wood working saws because the speed reduction increases torque, yielding effective cutting.
- Ideal cutting speeds and tooth counts vary by material. The two most common materials for the industry are aluminum, which cuts very well at about 1200 FPM, and mild steel, which ideally cuts at 330 FPM. Using the same saw for both materials will require a variable-speed or two-speed machine and different blades.

Safety considerations
- For contour saws, like a wood-cutting bandsaw, the material is fed manually, so fingers must be kept clear of the cutting path. Eye protection is a must and hearing protection is recommended, especially while cutting steel.
- Steel in particular cuts slowly on a contour saw, which may tempt the operator to push harder than necessary. This can damage the machine or lead to injury.
- Gravity feed saws can slam into material (or fingers during set up) if the control lever is bumped too hard. Hands should be kept clear of the cutting path even when the saw is powered off, and the saw should be lowered to the material gently to engage the blade.

Maintenance
- Because blades operate dry, they may wear faster than lubricated blades on horizontal saws. Wax-based lubricant helps preserve blade life.
- Guide bearings should be checked for wear.
- Moving parts should be cleaned of any swarf regularly, especially below the work table.

- Shears—These machines use even and continuous pressure across a blade to cut metal. They generally leave no burr, make no sparks or heat, and cut with no kerf.
  - Sheet shears use hydraulic pistons to move the cutting blade and often require the operator to use a two-step operation process to ensure their hands are clear of the cutting area. This also requires the sheet to be fully supported as opposed to the operator holding it in place, as often happens with a manual shear.
  - Bar and rod shears are a bit more rare due to iron worker machines integrating this function. If bar, rod, and small strap steel are used on a regular basis, a dedicated shear requires much less space on the shop floor than an iron worker. Older machines used a flywheel to generate the energy required for cutting.

Figure 7.5a A large sheet metal shear on the shop floor at Adirondack Studios. This shop makes extensive use of aluminum sheets; thus, the 96" cutting capacity.

Figure 7.5b A flywheel-type bar and rod shear.

Safety considerations
- Like any machine that cuts, eye protection should still be worn even though there should be no flying debris.
- An odd possibility is material lift if not properly secured; otherwise, the material could flip up toward the user. The machine should employ an automatic hold down.
- Material must be in contact with hold-down bracing. Most shears have some means to keep material in place while cutting. If not in contact when the process is started, the material will slam into the hold-down and can pinch fingers.

Maintenance
- Sharp blades are key to the safe operation of shears. As well, only appropriate materials should be cut to avoid blade damage.

- Iron worker — These are multipurpose hydraulically operated machines that are primarily for punching and shearing, though some may offer bending dies as well. These will cut angle, tee, rod/bar, and strap steel faster than many saws with no heat or sparks. Shearing does slightly distort the material at the cut.

Figure 7.6 A 40 t iron worker on the shop floor at Adirondack Studios. The left end of the machine (as photographed) is for punches; on the right above, various dies can be inserted for shearing shapes such as bar and angle; on the lower right is a plate shear that is wide enough to cut miters when needed.

Key factors
- Capacity is rated in tons of pressure at the punch. Manufacturer specs will be required to determine the capacity of each function for a particular machine.
- Punches swing on a slight arc, which may be noticeable on thick metal. This is generally easy to correct with a ream.
- Some machines will notch the angle for bending and notch pipe for coped fitment.
- Third-party suppliers offer custom tooling for many brands of iron worker.

Safety considerations
- Because these are multipurpose machines, proper setup for each function is very important.
- Like other machines operated by hydraulics, these generate a huge amount of force so material needs to be properly aligned and/or secured.

Maintenance
- Punches wear faster than shearing blades but can often be resharpened, reducing their overall cost.
- Shear blades are long-lasting but can be prone to chipping if used on brittle material. Many machines use four-sided shear blades that can be rotated when dull to increase life.

- Drill press — These are primarily for boring. They are faster and more accurate than a hand-held drill. On manual machines, the mechanical advantage provided by the hand lever reduces operator stress; machines that have a self-feeding quill eliminate fatigue altogether (except for moving material). Drill presses create very straight holes because the quill keeps the bit vertical at all times while moving. As well, it is easy to create and attach a jig for consistency in repeated tasks. They are an especially good choice when a large twist drill or a step drill is required. One trick to accurate drilling is to mark the center with a punch, align the drill bit (or pilot bit), and apply a little pressure with the quill, then manually rotate the drill in the direction of cut a

Figure 7.7a A floor model drill press with multiple pitch pulleys netting 12 speeds ranging from 150 to 4200 RPM. This model has a T-slot bed shown with hold downs used to anchor a drill press vise.

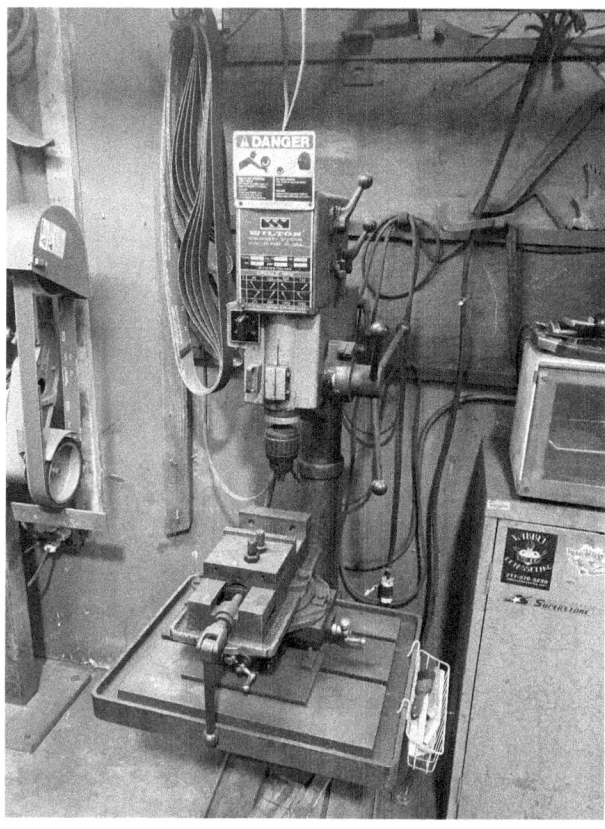

Figure 7.7b A geared head drill pressed with a machinist vise mounted to an X-Y table. This machine offers eight speeds from 85 to 1460 RPM and has manually fed quill.

revolution or two to start the cut. This will expand the center slightly, keeping the drill bit in place. Start the motor with the bit just touching the material (very light pressure) so that it cannot jump from the indentation.

Key Factors
- Horsepower for the most common machines in entertainment industry shops ranges from about 3/4 to 2 HP. Horsepower can be a bit of a double-edged sword: higher horsepower increases drilling capacity but also increases risk if materials are not properly secured. Metal shops often prefer machines driven by a 1750 RPM motor vs. wood working machines that typically use a 3450 RPM motor. Floor-standing models and bench-top machines can both be quite useful.
- Many have a table that can tilt, but this is rarely valuable in metal working. Tasks that require the material to be on a slant are usually better served by a mill. Some materials may be prepared on a mill, then through-drilled on a slant by a drill press.
- As a general rule, the larger the drill bit, the slower the operating speed. Material ultimately effects the proper speed for any bit. As a good rule of thumb, maximum drill speed should be 500 RPM in steel for a 1/2″ bit, and bit speed should be adjusted proportionally by bit diameter; thus, a 1/4″ bit has a maximum speed of 1000 RPM. These speeds can be doubled for aluminum.
- Chucks have a holding range; larger capacity chucks typically also have a larger minimum capacity (e.g. 1/4″–3/4″). Most machines for metal fabrication have a 1/2″–3/4″ capacity. Some machines allow easy changing of the chuck, but the majority do not.
- Table height adjustment may be a simple sliding clamp on the column or a rack and pinion mechanism. Both can rotate about the column. Typically the rack and pinion is preferred, especially on floor-standing machines where the table is much heavier.
- Power down feed is most common on geared-head machines, but some belt-driven machines also offer mechanized down feed. This feature can be quite useful for large projects that require repeated drilling.

Safety Considerations
- Operators should not wear gloves or, at the very least, keep them far away from the rotating chuck. There is a long list of glove-related injuries with drill presses listed by the Occupational Safety and Health Administration (OSHA).
- Materials should be firmly anchored when drilling, lest they become spinning projectiles. Loose materials can also slip as the bit breaks through, bending or shattering it. T-slot tables are preferred on machines for metal, as they allow the use of a machinist's hold-down kit.
- Always ensure the key has been cleared from the chuck lest it become a projectile.

Accessories
- Vises can be a good alternative to hold-down kits. A standard vise has long slots on each side that make it easy to bolt to the table and operates like a small bench vise. A cross-slide vise likewise bolts to the table but allows material to be accurately positioned after securing because of its X-Y movement. The X-Y movement is excellent for positioning but generally not robust enough for machining operations.
- T-slot clamping kits are used on machines with a T-slot table because they are the best option for material holding. T-nuts, studs, step blocks, and clamping bars combine to make an exceptionally versatile means of work holding. Sets do not

include bolts but use standard threads; thus, bolts can be added for holding fixtures and guides. These parts are shown in Figure 12.11 and can be seen in use in various examples in the milling section of Chapter 12.

Maintenance
- The quill and chuck need to be kept clean and lubricated (there is often an oil port on top of the quill or on the side of the quill housing). A bit of oil on the ring and jaws of the chuck prevents rust and ensures smooth operation.
- The table should be checked to ensure it is perpendicular to the quill because metal is far less forgiving of irregularities than wood. It also improves drilling efficiency.
- Drill press belts seem to wear faster than any other belt-driven machinery in the shop and should be checked each time the machine is operated and replaced when significant fraying or cracking is observed. Geared head machines need regular oil changes for the gear box and the oil level should be checked on a regular basis.

- Mill — These machines are for precision shaping of metal. They can drill, thread, and cut by various means with interchangeable cutters. Mills use collets for tool holding vs. a chuck, though chucks that match the collet mounting style are available. More details regarding using these machines are covered in Chapter 12.

Figure 7.8b The author's belt-driven mill/drill. This is a 2 HP machine with an 8"×22" table. Like a bench-top mill, the Z-axis is adjusted via moving the motor and quill.

Figure 7.8a A variable-speed bench-top drill/mill. This mill has two speed ranges, making it compatible with both hard materials such as steel and very soft materials like plastic. The Z-axis is adjusted by moving the motor and quill as a unit. It is shown with a hold-down kit.

Figure 7.8c A Bridgeport-style mill with an X and Y axis DRO at ATOMIC (www.atomicdesign.tv).

Key factors
- There are three common types of vertical mill: bench-top, mill/drill, and Bridgeport (or turret), which is both a brand name and a much-copied design. The major difference beyond size is versatility; the Bridgeport-style mill, especially "universal" mills that have a drive chuck for horizontal work, is much more versatile than other styles.
- Bed size and travel will determine the area of material that can be worked. In many cases, this does not limit the overall size of material that can be worked, but resetting material can make accuracy difficult to maintain.
- There are two common types of collets: R8 are the most common in the U.S., and ER type are the most common throughout Europe.

Safety considerations
- Operators should not wear work gloves or, at the very least, keep them far away from rotating parts. Nitrile gloves are a good option that will prevent metal slivers and maintain dexterity, keeping the operator's fingers safer.
- Material should be firmly anchored to prevent damage to the cutter. Milling operations are usually slow speed; thus, the tooling is more likely to be damaged than the work piece becoming a projectile. Hold-down kits are the most common means of attaching material, but vises and rotary tables may be used as well.
- Always ensure the wrench has been cleared from the drawbar lest it become a projectile.

Maintenance
- Table ways and quills should be kept clean and oiled to prevent wear, which can decrease machine accuracy.
- Lead screws also need to be kept clean and oiled to prevent wear. Worn lead screws add lash to milling operations, which is the amount of rotation the hand-wheel must be turned before the lead screw engages movement. Very worn lead screws may allow play in the table movement caused by the rotation of the cutter.

• Lathe—Metal lathes are much less common in entertainment fabrication shops but can be very useful in any shop that fabricates automated or mechanized scenery, props, or special effects; they are excellent for working with high-density plastics as well. These machines are less versatile than a mill but serve a purpose that no other machine can match. These can be used to make or adapt bushings and plain bearings, turn down shaft ends for custom fit, and center bore anything that will fit in the chuck. Sizes vary from compact benchtop models to large free standing models. More details regarding using these machines are covered in Chapter 12.

Figure 7.9a A bench lathe with a 7" swing and 19" bed. This machine uses a three-speed belt drive with change gears for both the turning speed and the feed rate of the lead screw for the carriage.

Figure 7.9b A gear-driven lathe with a 17" swing (with forward bed section removed) and 40" bed. This machine has a speed range from 60 to 2000 RPM and a 5 HP motor.

Key factors
- Swing and bed length are the terms used to define lathe capacity. Swing is the maximum diameter of a mounted work piece. Some machines increase swing via a removable section of bed or by having a sliding bed.
- Machines have three drive types: combination belt and gear drives that use interchangeable gears to set lead screw speed for thread cutting and/or cutter feed, geared drives that use only gears for all drive functions, and electronic variable speed drives that usually have two speed ranges. Combination drives will be the lowest cost option and suitable for a majority of projects but require more time invested when a speed change is required.

Safety considerations
- Loose clothing and/or gloves, as well as any other dangling item, present a significant risk of entanglement with a lathe.
- Sharp tooling prevents chipping or breaking of material.
- Cutting fluid may not be used for all operations, but when it is used, especially at high speed, the off-cast will be toward the operator; thus, a face shield and other protection may be required in addition to normal PPE on machines with no inherent shielding.
- Brittle metals like brass can shatter; a leather apron should be considered for many operations.
- Never clean a lathe while it is under power. Brushes, rags, and/or clothing could be caught, causing major injury.

Maintenance
- Sharp tools not only produce better finished work, but they are also safer.
- Lubricating bearings is critical because they operate under compressive load on a lathe.
- Ways and lead screws should be kept clean and oiled.
- The tail stock absolutely must lock firmly to the bed; thus, the bed should be clean and damage-free. As well, the tail stock locking mechanism should be checked regularly.

- Pipe notchers — There are two types of stationary machines for notching pipe and tube with a "fish-mouth" to prepare them for welding. The cutter should be matched to the OD of the material to be welded to, allowing smaller materials to be welded to larger ones when needed.
  - End mill notchers use large, spiral milling heads with carbide cutters to notch pipe and tube. The design is similar to the spiral heads used in jointers but designed for steel while running at a much lower RPM.

- Belt notchers have replaceable nose-wheels with differing diameters to match pipe or tube. These machines are primarily used to notch lighter gauge tubing, as pipe will increase belt wear significantly.

Figure 7.10 An end mill notcher, less the cutter, at Meow Wolf. Note the heavy-duty pipe vise that rotates for angled cutting of copes. The hand-wheel moves the cutter to set cutting depth, while the hand lever (lower left) moves the work piece into the cutter.

Safety considerations
- The guard should always be kept in place on end mill machines because they do create swarf. As well, this prevents loose clothing from being able to be caught in the moving cutter.
- Belt notchers add the generation of heat and sparks as well as dust that is an inhalation hazard.

Maintenance
- Most end mill notchers use a helical cutter head with replaceable carbide cutters. This allows them to be rotated as they dull and replaced when they are damaged or completely worn.
- Lubricating guides is important for smooth cutting.

BENDING AND SHAPING

There are a number of machines that take advantage of the plastic nature of metal and its ability to hold a form after shaping. This is one of the key elements where working with metal and working with wood differ. Though many of these machines will not be found in smaller shops, outsourcing is always an option for companies that need custom shapes but cannot justify owning specialized equipment. As well, some machines have manually operated equivalents that may be more economical.

- Roll bender—These machines are designed to make long radius bends in tubing. They use two powered drive wheels spaced about 6″–8″ apart to move the material through, while a third wheel centered between the drive wheels applies pressure to make the bend. These machines may have horizontal or vertical orientation. Each has pros and cons. The drive wheels need to match the profile of the material. The pressure die can be flat for square and rectangular tubes but needs to match the radius of round material to avoid flattening. These machines take some practice, as even those with a radius indicator are only somewhat accurate. When bending thin-wall tubing, care must be taken to make multiple passes to avoid collapsing the walls. Some machines may have dies for bending angle iron and channel.

Figure 7.11 A powered roll bender set up with dies for 2″ square tubing at Adirondack Studios.

- Power slip roll — Like a manual machine, these are designed to roll sheet metal into a curved panel. They are quite versatile, as the entire width need not be used, making it possible to roll smooth curves into fairly thick, narrow stock or make an open-ended cone. They should not be operated while wearing gloves; a caught glove can lead to a major injury. Material should be deburred prior to bending to avoid scarring the rollers.

Figure 7.12 A powered slip roll being used to make curved aluminum ribs at Adirondack Studios.

- Bead roller — Like the manually powered version, this machine can be used to create offsets for lapped seams, fold or radius edges, and add raised beads to the face of a sheet, increasing its stiffness. Powered machines like this one are often used with shearing dies to cut long or variable radius curves.

Figure 7.13 A motorized bead roller with a set of offset dies mounted and edge-forming and beading dies on its storage pegs at Meow Wolf.

- Hydraulic press—These are quite common in large shops and have a multitude of uses. They can be used to press-fit assemblies, straighten bent items, make custom bends, and install/remove bearings and seals, as well as for punching and shearing with accessories.

Figure 7.14a A 20 ton H-frame hydraulic press; the power unit is below and to the right. In the photo are also a press brake and bending dies.

Figure 7.14b A C-frame hydraulic press with a custom bending die installed. This press houses the pump atop the piston.

- Planishing hammer—This machine operates much like a person would use a hammer and dolly to finish smoothing curved sheet metal panels. The lower die (or dolly) should nearly match the shape to be smoothed, while the upper hammer head remains flat. Some machines are designed for interchangeable upper dies; these remain flat but vary in diameter. Caution should be used when operating a powered planishing hammer, as they can quite quickly stretch the metal too thin, creating distortion.
- Die bender—These machines are also referred to as a draw bender since they pull the material through/around the shaping dies. Much like a Hossfeld bender, these machines have interchangeable dies used to bend both pipe and tubing. They generally are not used for solid shapes. Most machines are fairly compact because the hydraulic ram does not need the lever length of a manual machine. Dies are typically specified by center-line radius. Machines may have vertical or horizontal orientations, much like roll benders. Set up and usage information can be found in Chapter 11.
  - Tubing requires the use of compensating dies that keep the walls from collapsing and make much tighter bends than pipe and may be designed to bend a full 180°.
  - Pipe may or may not employ a follower die depending on radius, and bends are usually much less than 90°. Threaded or welded elbows are a better solution when very tight radii are required.

Figure 7.15 A high-capacity horizontal die bender with a 1", 180° tubing die installed.

- Powered brake—Large, hydraulic-powered brakes are much faster than manual brakes and will bend much thicker sheets. Many have various angled bottom dies that take the guesswork out of bending to a specific angle. A brake can also be added to a powered hydraulic press.

Figure 7.16a An 88 ton hydraulic box brake at Adirondack Studios. This machine is capable of bending up to 10 ga steel.

Figure 7.16b The author's 20" press brake with standard and "goose-neck" dies mounted. The standard dies are for single bends; the goose-neck dies allow for a double bend. This brake is capable of bending a 2" wide piece of 1/2" bar stock but is more often used for thinner stock. The grooved wooden insert allows for bending short flanges on thin sheets that would not be supported by the V-shaped base.

GRINDING AND FINISHING

- Grinders—Stationary grinders are the larger and more durable versions of bench grinders and belt sanders. A variety of machine styles are available to suit a wide range of grinding tasks, making it easy to match a machine to a given shop's needs. All versions have tool rests that should be used for most grinding tasks. These should never exceed 1/8" between the rest and the media for safety.
  - Pedestal grinders are available between 3/4 and 3 HP. These mount between 8" and 12" diameter wheels.
    - Most grinders are 3450 or 3600 RPM, but 1800 RPM and variable-speed machines are available. Lower speed machines are more useful for sharpening and deburring and can be fitted with harder grinding stones. High-speed machines are best for heavy stock removal when hard stones are mounted and general deburring and some sharpening with softer stones.
    - Media available for pedestal grinders includes various grits of stone wheels, non-woven abrasives for deburring and buffing, flap wheels, and wire wheels (see Chapter 10).

Figure 7.17 An 8" pedestal grinder. This is an industrial-quality grinder, and it shows when compared to the 8" bench grinder shown in Figure 6.15b.

- Belt grinders are large stationary machines, usually mounted on a stand for accessibility. They are available in two basic configurations, but there are variants within each type and machines that are reconfigurable. The primary advantage of belt grinders over pedestal grinders is that belts are readily available that are compatible with aluminum, whereas the majority of rigid media for pedestal grinders are not. Belt grinders also have a platen that makes grinding a surface flat much easier than with a round wheel. Variable speed machines allow the operator to match the machine to the task; for example, running slower on softer metals helps reduce heat and clogging of the belt.
  - Vertical belt grinders are generally used for general grinding and shaping. The operator can work on the platen for flat edges and off the platen for convex shapes. Some machines have contouring wheels of various diameters for concave grinding; these are most often found in knife making, not general production.
  - Horizontal belt grinders are most useful for long edges. These are especially useful for deburring after plasma cutting or truing a slightly irregular edge.

Figure 7.18b A single-speed belt grinder is primarily used for heavy stock removal such as beveling for a weld. Note the moveable tool rest that allows the user greater accuracy when needed.

- Disc grinders (or sanders) are regularly used for metal working, especially for aluminum. Large diameter (20"–24") vertical machines are the most common for metal working; a variable speed unit with an adjustable table offers the most compatibility. Disc grinders are excellent for touch-up or adjustment on miters or quickly deburring or trimming curved pieces.

Figure 7.18a A vertical, variable-speed belt grinder with a long, flexible belt that is primarily used for finishing tasks. The exposed bottom wheel allows for some concave shaping.

Figure 7.19 A 20″ single-speed disc grinder used for aluminum fabrication.

- Polishers—Many shops have a variety of stationary polishing machines. Since polishing is accomplished in stages, machines may combine belt and wheel surfaces in one machine. Removal of oxidation and deburring are often accomplished with the same machines using coarse media such as a wire wheel.

Figure 7.20a A pedestal polisher fitted with a wire wheel for cleaning, and deburring and a high-density non-woven abrasive wheel for polishing.

Figure 7.20b A pedestal machine fitted with a long, flexible grinding belt and an interleaved flap wheel that combines cloth abrasive with non-woven abrasive.

- Abrasive blasting—These machines are an excellent option for preparing metal for welding or paint. They may also be used to work-harden soft metals after shaping. See Chapter 8 for details.
  - Cabinets are the best option for abrasive blasting of small- to medium-sized parts. Most operate using dry abrasive. Some machines mix water and abrasive, which helps keep parts cool (ideal for thin sheet metal), and they work slightly faster while generating essentially zero dust. Abrasive cabinets require a high CFM (10–20)

air supply. These may be side or front loading. Dry machines operate best when a dust collector is added. This keeps the fine dust that does not cut well and can cause clogging from being recirculated. Cabinets may have pedal- or trigger-operated blasting guns.

○ Portable blasters can be siphon tank style or small hand-held units. Both require some means of dust control, and the user (plus anyone in the area) must be wearing a dust mask and possibly extra PPE such as a jump suit and heavy-duty gloves. They also use much more media since it cannot be recycled. These still require fairly high CFM but can be run by a large portable compressor.

○ Pressure vessel blasters are primarily for soda blasting. The advantage to soda blasting is the friability of the media: it creates nearly no heat and will not etch the metal surface like harder media can. Soda also takes much longer to remove rust and finishes.

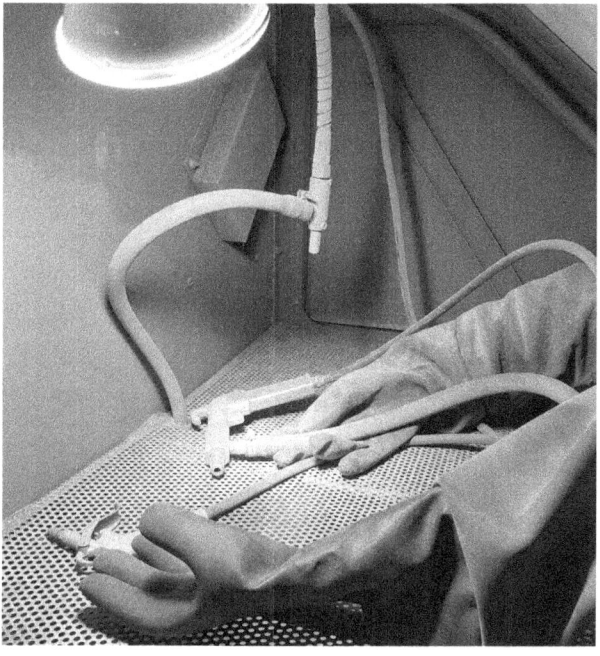

Figure 7.21b The interior of a typical blast cabinet showing the heavy duty gloves, hand-held blasting nozzle, and, on this machine, the center-mounted blasting nozzle and dusting nozzle for cleaning.

Figure 7.21a A typical end-loading abrasive blast cabinet. This unit is pedal operated and has a light and dust collector. It also has an optional center-mounted nozzle that allows the operator to hold a part with both hands.

Figure 7.21c A pressure tank-style soda blaster.

Auxiliary Machines

- Dust collection—Dust collectors designed for metal working machinery use metal bins to catch hot sparks. Heavy-duty filtering (usually cloth-based) is located after the induction fan. These are not to be used for welding fumes; they are designed for use with grinders and saws.
- Fume extraction—These machines are designed to remove fumes from welding. They may be wall-mounted, ceiling-mounted, or mobile. Portable units may have flexible hoses with a magnetically mounted intake or an articulated arm up to 12′–13′ long. Wall and ceiling mounts generally have shorter arms. Dual arms are available on some wall- and ceiling-mount units. There are welding tables with inherent down draft fume extraction, but these are often too small for entertainment projects.

Figure 7.22 A mobile fume extracting filter unit for welding at Meow Wolf.

Chapter 8

Welding and Related Processes

No one is likely to be able to learn to weld from a book, but knowing what is involved with each process can help the reader determine if it is an undertaking worth exploring or learning for their particular goals. In addition, it helps technical managers and designers understand the shop processes that may be used to achieve the final product. Learning the basics is fairly simple; mastering each welding process takes significant time and experience. Many welding seminars are available; they have been held at the United States Institute for Theatre Technology (USITT) annual conference, for example, and some artist cooperatives offer them as well. These are sufficient to get a feel for a process but not to become proficient; that takes practice and possibly further education, such as a class or two at a local community college or trade school. Knowing the kind of gear involved and how much practice will be needed helps the reader decide which capability they should add to their shop or technique they should learn. One important tip for new weldors: if you get frustrated, take a break. Welding requires being somewhat "Zen" to achieve good welds; working while frustrated will not improve the work.

For the sake of clarity, in this text, "welder" will only refer to a machine; "weldor" will be used to refer to the skilled person doing the welding. The term weldor sees rare to no contemporary use, but helps to clarify the text in this scenario. It is also important to note that many of the sample welds shown herein were made by the author, who is not a certified weldor, but has had his welds reviewed many times by other weldors from various industries. Readers should both physically test their own welds before applying them to any projects and consider having a qualified person review their work before embarking on any welding project beyond those for decorative use that would pose no harm to an observer should a weld fail. The author knows his limits and only fabricates using processes at which he has significant experience and only applies them based on his skill and comfort level.

Steel and aluminum are the most used metals in entertainment fabrication. Not only is the process of welding each quite different, even while using the same equipment, how the weld affects the metal is also different. A properly made weld on steel may increase the bond strength if done properly (i.e. weld filler tends to have a higher psi rating than the steel). Welding aluminum reduces the strength around the weld by more than half because the heat affects the temper of the material. As well, aluminum is much more susceptible to impurities in the weld. While all projects that will be used for critical applications should be welded by a qualified weldor, aluminum structures may be worth the extra investment to have sample welds tested if unique joints will be used. That should not dissuade experienced weldors from making the move to aluminum; aluminum is quite versatile and can be used for many projects that do not present life-safety concerns and can thus be done by a weldor without a certification.

GENERAL WELDING SAFETY

There are some general guidelines and items to be aware of when setting up a welding area. Protection particular to the weldor is covered in Chapter 13. Beyond protecting the weldor while operating, the welding station needs to be properly set up and the rest of the shop protected.
- Electrical safety—While electricity will always take the path of least resistance, there is a low risk of shock from a properly installed welder, though it is possible. Bare skin should not touch a metal

welding table while welding, especially the area between the ground clamp and the weld. As well, the machine should have a properly grounded electrical supply matched to the amperage requirement of the machine. High-frequency (HF) machines may require a separate ground.
- Heat safety—All welding processes create heat that could lead to burns if one is careless. The most common occurrence is grasping welded pieces that have not completely cooled. Metal in the welding area should be considered hot unless proven otherwise by holding a hand safely above, then possibly a quick touch if one is fairly sure there is no radiating heat. Working in shops without air conditioning can increase these factors. The Personal Protective Equipment (PPE) for welding is well insulated; on a hot day, this can lead to heat exhaustion. The same can be true if working outdoors. The weldor should stay well hydrated and take necessary breaks.
- Fire safety—National Fire Protection Association (NFPA) guidelines have been integrated into OSHA 1910.252 standard, requiring combustibles to be removed from within a 35-ft radius of any hot work. When a 35-ft radius cannot be fully cleared, all combustibles should be protected by welding screens, blankets or pads. Some situations and jurisdictions may require a fire watch, i.e. a qualified person on stand-by (often with a fire extinguisher) to watch for signs of fire. Fire watch is generally required to continue 1/2–1 hour beyond the cessation of hot work. Weldors should research standards and/or regulations within their jurisdiction, including those from local (e.g. municipal) oversight bodies.
- Ultraviolet (UV) safety—While the weldor is protected from UV radiation by PPE, there is still risk of eye damage from UV to the crew who would otherwise be at a safe distance. To protect passersby and crew who may be in the vicinity but not welding, properly shaded or opaque welding screens should be used to block the view of the welding area. This may not be possible for all users of the welding area, and thus, many shops require weldors to announce "welding!" to prevent accidental exposures.

Figure 8.1 A welding work station at ATOMIC (www.atomicdesign.tv). Note the welding screens that can be positioned as needed to protect other crew members. Extra screens are available as needed.

MATERIAL PREP

Before welding, most metals should have some prep work done, primarily the removal of preservatives, contaminants and oxidation. The processes will vary only slightly by material.
- Steel—There are a variety of reasons a that steel may require preparation for welding. Some steel is shipped pickled and oiled, which will contribute to welding fumes; other steel has enough scale that it can keep a weld from bonding or become embedded in the weld, creating a weakness that may not be visible.
  - Degreasing is the best means for preparing oiled steel for welding. While solvents will remove the oil quickly, it is not the safest means for doing so. Water-based degreasers are much safer, but slower. All degreasers should be used with protective gloves, and splash-resistant goggles may be required depending on how the product is applied; many should be used with an FFR respirator. Strong solvents, especially those with a low flash point and high Volitile Organic Compound (VOC) content, may require additional PPE. Users should fully read the manufacturer's Safety Data Sheet (SDS) before using any solvent.
    - Natural, light-duty degreasers are ideal if time allows. Many of these use water-soluble alcohols as surfactants and may cause mild skin irritation. At least one brand uses alcohol and sodium citrate as the primary surfactants, dramatically decreasing the risk of inhalation or skin contact hazards. These may take two to three passes to truly clean the steel enough to be paintable; thus, the time allowance is important. These carry the least risk and do not create hazardous or flammable waste.
    - Heavy-duty water-based degreasers, which use citrus, soy or pine oil, are a good middle ground. These clean quickly in one to two passes, but are much more hazardous than many might assume. Citrus- and soy-based solvents can have very high VOC content, be an inhalation hazard and cause chemical burns from skin contact. Always wear gloves (usually neoprene or nitrile) and any other PPE recommended by the manufacturer. These have the advantage of not creating hazardous or flammable waste when dry.
    - Solvents and acids such as naphtha, denatured alcohol, mineral spirits and phosphoric acid can be used to remove oil from steel, in some cases in one pass of a rag. Most commercially available metal prep chemicals contain phosphoric acid because it also removes light oxidation. The drawback is that most of these have some serious health risks and the solvents are flammable. Users should use these sparingly, read the SDS information before commencing use and ensure that others in the vicinity are properly protected as well. Most of these types of solvents have very high VOC content and create an inhalation risk across a large area unless used in a contained, properly ventilated space such as a booth.
  - Descaling is the removal of mill scale, which is a mix of iron oxides that form on hot-rolled steel such as A36 or 4130 as it interacts with the atmosphere during processing. While it acts as a temporary protective surface for shipping, the scale needs to be removed before welding and painting. This requires physically abrading the surface via sanding, abrasive blasting or with a wire wheel or cup brush. Thicker sections may be safe to descale with a belt sander or flap wheel, but thin-walled tubing is best descaled by hand with emery cloth; otherwise, there is a risk of weakening the wall in the weld area. A needle scaler may work well on very thick material.

Figure 8.2 Examples of three varieties of phosphoric-acid-based chemicals to treat rust, with a band of the original rust between each. From top—Metal prep scale remover (spray), naval gel (brush-on) and rust converter (brush or spray) have additives that bind remaining oxides to the base metal.

- Rust reduces conductivity, which can make welding difficult. While there are electrodes for stick welding that work well on rusted steel, most shops prefer MIG welding, which is less amenable to rust. Luckily, it is fairly easy to remove or treat.
  - Chemicals can either dissolve rust, such as naval jelly or phosphoric acid, or convert the oxidation into a permanently adhered primer for painting. Converted primer can prevent welding, and acid-based chemicals must be thoroughly rinsed away before any welding can take place. These also require chemical handling PPE, much like solvents. Users should always consult the appropriate SDS.
  - Physical removal of rust is the most common. Non-woven stripping wheels, wire wheels and cup brushes as well as abrasive blasting all work very well to remove rust and require no further processing before welding. The dust generated by abrasion is an inhalation hazard and PPE must be worn accordingly.

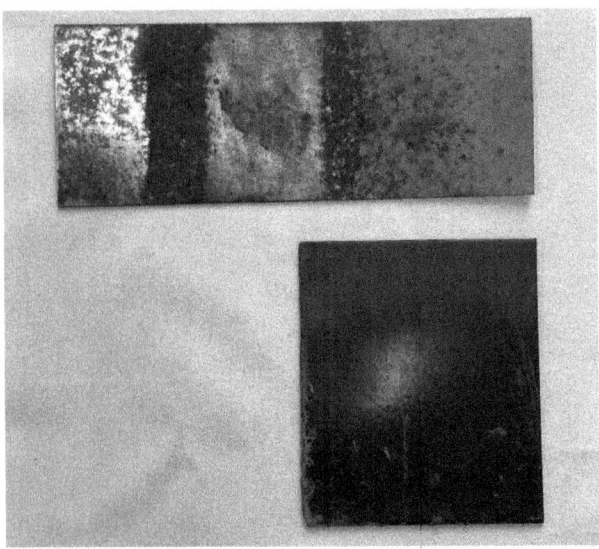

Figure 8.3 The top sample of steel shows the results of using various abrasives to remove rust. From left—A surface prep wheel (non-woven) leaves rust in pitted areas, followed by a wire wheel which removes rust very well and slightly polishes the surface, and lastly abrasive blasting with aluminum oxide that removes rust very well and leaves a slight surface texture to which paint adheres very well. Below is an example of abrasive blasting applied to commercial duty paint on steel (top edge). There is very little impact, suggesting grinding or a chemical stripper would be the better method to remove most paint.

- Aluminum—Removal of oxidation should be done as close to welding time as possible because the oxidation process is essentially immediate. Primary removal of oxidation should be done within an hour or two of welding. Even after the primary removal of oxidation, a quick scrub with a stainless steel bristle wire brush should happen immediately prior to welding. Alternatively, a quick cleaning with acetone may be an option.
  - Chemical oxidation removers are best used when a large area requires treatment, such as surfaces that will be painted or adhered to a substrate with non-solvent-based adhesives. Phosphoric acid baths are the most common (between a 4:1 and 10:1 dilution), and while a mild acid, they still must be handled and stored with great care. Like other chemicals, full removal must be attained before welding.
  - Physical removal of oxidation on aluminum is best done with plastic media like an uncoated, non-woven abrasive pad or a nylon bristle brush or wheel (fit to a grinder). Sanding, even with coated abrasive, is less than ideal for aluminum; the friable nature of most abrasive grits leaves remnants embedded in the surface that can lead to impurities in the weld.
- Abrasive blasting—While many refer to the process as "sand blasting," commonly available sand should never be used for abrasive blasting. Nearly all sand has a very high silica content; the dangers of inhaling silica dust are well documented. Use only abrasives intended for blasting. While abrasive blasting may be used on many materials, only its use on metal is covered here.
  - Machines for abrasive blasting can be either self-contained (cabinets) or non-recovery, such as a pressure vessel (these look like a 20-lb propane cylinder) or gravity-fed systems. Most shops need to do very little blasting and will opt for a medium-sized dry cabinet. Dustless cabinet systems that use a mix of water and abrasive are available, but add significant cost. The advantage of a wet system goes beyond the lack of dust; wet media is heavier and therefore has a bit more impact than dry media. As well, wet machines allow the user to vary the ratio of water to media, making them ideal for use on delicate surfaces and tend to leave a more polished finish. Portable gravity and pressure vessel blasters are far too messy for most entertainment applications.
    - Cabinets will have a hand-held blasting gun; some are trigger-operated, and some are foot pedal-operated. High-volume machines tend to use foot pedal controls. Some companies offer an additional mounted nozzle for foot-pedal-controlled machines so the operator can use two hands on objects. An example is shown in Figures 7.21a and 7.21b.
    - Nozzles for guns are most often ceramic and available in varying densities; high-density nozzles will cost more but last longer. Many companies offer an upgraded carbide nozzle that will far outlast ceramic nozzles, but these are very expensive.

- Safety concerns are fairly minimal when a cabinet is used. Quality cabinets will be available with a filtering vacuum system to remove dust from within the cabinet and have well-sealed doors to protect the operator. The vacuum system should be left running after blasting is complete, and while objects are being removed from the cabinet, to prevent exposure. As well, the cabinet gloves should be made specifically for abrasive blasting. A reminder when dealing with old paint—it may contain lead and should be tested before any work is done. Lead paint should only be removed by a qualified person or company that can contain the lead.
  - Primary usage for most shops will be cleaning away rust, contaminants, or scale and stripping paint from items that need repair work. Harder media can also be used to work-harden some metals like copper (shapes can have a polished front and blasted back). Similar to sanding media, finer mesh abrasives will remove material slower than coarse media, though there is no need to step through coarseness like there is when sanding. Blasting can start and finish with one mesh size.
  - Abrasive media should be chosen by the required properties: hardness, density and friability affect aggressiveness and longevity, while the shape of the media will affect surface finish. Most mineral-based media will require a little bit of surface cleaning after blasting to remove any remaining dust. Some manufacturers may offer mixed blasting media, such as glass bead/aluminum oxide.
    - Coal slag is one of the original alternatives to sand. It is low cost and effective, but may present a similar level of risk as silica. Coal slag contains many of the same impurities as coal, which could include arsenic, beryllium and lead. OSHA is pressing to remove coal slag from the market. When abrasive blasting is required, there are safer options.
    - Aluminum oxide has very hard grains with sharp edges that tend to be retained, is less friable than many other minerals, usually has a higher cost than slag, but it is much safer and can be cycled through a machine many times. It is one of the best options for cabinet use because it is readily available, moderately priced overall and a wide range of mesh sizes are available. Aluminum oxide is often used for etching as well, especially on soft materials.
    - Garnet is the abrasive of choice for water jet cutting, which makes its durability clear. It is slightly less sharp than aluminum oxide, thus a bit easier on surfaces. Being similar in cost to aluminum oxide, it is another very common choice for removing paint and rust from hard surfaces. It may be used for many cycles in a blast cabinet, and a wide range of mesh sizes are available.
    - Silicon carbide media nears diamond in hardness and is often used for etching using masking or templates. It is a very aggressive media and should be reserved for the removal of heavy paint coatings, deep rust, or removal of mill scale, and only on durable surfaces. It is about double the cost of aluminum oxide. And primarily available in only fine mesh sizes.
    - Alternative mineral-based media include iron silicate (copper slag), synthetic olivine and magnesium orthosilicate (brand name Green Diamond). These are similar in cost and performance to aluminum oxide, and some are reclaimed from other industrial processes, making them somewhat eco-friendly. Availability may vary by region and local suppliers. All are commonly used in industrial-scale blasters such as those used to prepare bridge beams for painting.
    - Steel shot is likely a rare choice and is similar to bead blasting, though the media is far more aggressive. If the primary goal is to remove mill scale, it is the perfect media, producing no dust that needs to be removed after. It may also be chosen to work-harden softer metals, though it will leave a distinctly textured surface. Steel grit is similar in use to silicon carbide as it is very aggressive, durable and leaves an aggressively etched finish suitable for thick coatings. Both are only slightly more expensive than aluminum oxide but are only available in a narrow range of mesh sizes.
    - Ground glass is moderately hard and dense with sharp edges and is quite effective at removing coatings while having little impact on the material surface. Ground glass is primarily used in cabinets or blast rooms where the media is collected and recycled. It is one of the lowest cost options but is only available in a narrow range of fairly large mesh sizes.
    - Walnut shell and corn cob meal are low-density and have a blocky shape, making them excellent for the removal of light coatings and contaminants from delicate surfaces. The low rate of friability makes them low-dust options as well. Corn cob meal is an excellent choice for work hardening copper, as it will somewhat polish the surfaces as it is working. These are often used in both gravity-fed and pressure vessels and are great for one-time use. They present no environmental hazard if used outdoors. Walnut shell is a tree nut and can be a risk to anyone allergic to tree nuts. Corn cob media is likely the lowest cost media available; walnut

shell is comparable in cost to glass beads. Both have a narrow range of mesh sizes available.
- Bead blasting uses manufactured media as opposed to crushed mineral. The benefit of using beads is the lower impact on the material surface; round beads tend not to etch like sharp media will. Most beads have fairly low friability. They tend to be incompatible with greasy or oily surfaces.
  - Ceramic beads are moderately aggressive and durable. If you have ever felt the unglazed foot of a porcelain plate, you can get a sense of the surface texture of these beads. They are an expensive option at nearly ten times the cost of aluminum oxide, but they do offer a fairly wide range of available mesh sizes.
  - Glass beads are best used to remove light oxidation or collected dirt. Glass bead is preferred for working with soft metals, as it leaves a very smooth matte finish that takes paint very well. They are also one of the lowest-cost media available with a wide range of mesh sizes available.
  - Plastic bead is the less environmentally friendly version of walnut shell. Though these may not always be round, the soft nature of the plastic makes them well-suited to delicate surfaces. Unlike walnut shells, they are easily reusable in a blast cabinet. They are similar in cost to aluminum oxide, with a moderate range of mesh sizes available.
- Alternatives to abrasive blasting are available and very effective for some applications. Their advantages may include lower environmental impact and/or increased user safety.
  - Dry ice is very friable, and its blocky shape makes it moderately aggressive. Dry ice works very well for removing build-up of dirt, oil and other contaminants but is not as useful on paint. The biggest advantage is clean up: only the removed contaminant remains. Dry ice blasting requires a specialized machine and is very expensive compared to soda. Dry ice quickly becomes CO_2 gas when introduced to the atmosphere, and therefore, proper ventilation is crucial. Dry ice also does not texture the surface in any way, possibly making it more difficult for paint or other coatings to adhere.
  - Soda is often chosen because particles have knife-like edges for good cutting while being soft and friable, creating virtually no surface impact on hard materials like metal. Soda blasting requires a pressure vessel machine. While it does create significant dust that should not be inhaled, along with the user needing sealed eye protection, the dust is otherwise not harmful. It is similar in cost per pound to aluminum oxide, but the inability to reuse the soda increases the overall cost significantly. Few mesh sizes are available.
  - Sponge blasting is a form of "dustless" blasting that uses a unique material. Soft, flexible beads that are impregnated with abrasives (often aluminum oxide) are shot through a large hose using high volumes of compressed air. As the "sponges" impact the surface, the flexibility presents abrasive from multiple directions in a large area (compared to mesh-sized particles), improving removal speed, with little impact on the surface. The environmentally friendly part is that these machines use a vacuum to collect the media and contaminants on the rebound and process the sponges for reuse. Though not a process that is shop-friendly, it may be an option to clean up an existing structure before it is renovated into a new entertainment venue.

COMMONALITIES OF WELDING PROCESSES

- Edge preparation—For most of the sections used for entertainment fabrication, the material is fairly thin; thus, the only edge prep needed will be to remove burrs. For instance, where very thick pieces are required (1/4″ and up), some amount of material may need to be removed, either as a bevel or groove, to achieve proper weld penetration.
- Weld properties—All welds share similar properties: a molten pool of metal created on each piece to be joined, and usually the addition of a filler metal that is used to combine and finish the weld pool. In addition, the way the weld bead is made is very similar between processes.
  - When arc welding, most texts describe the sound as similar to sizzling bacon. While that may be somewhat accurate, the sound is more complex than that. The sound will change with amperage and feed rate, regardless of the process, and each arc process sounds slightly different. The trick is to learn to connect the sound with the visual and recognize the components that make a good, strong weld. One can make a pretty good sizzle and still make a terrible weld.
  - Seeing the weld pool can be really tricky because of the shade glass. New welders using a variable

shade helmet may be tempted to reduce the shade setting to be able to see the weld pool better. DO NOT try this!! For most arc welding, the minimum shade really is 10 and often 11. Darker shades may be required depending on the amperage and welding process. An excellent chart that lists minimum protective shade for each process is available from OSHA at www.osha.gov/sites/defaultfiles/publications/OSHAfactsheet-eyeprotection-during-welding.PDF. If visibility is an issue, position is the likely culprit. The weldor's head needs to be fairly close and off to the side so that the weld pool is clearly in view. A beanie or cape helps protect the weldor's head from sparks when needed.
- Ensure the seam is visible while making the weld and that the weld pool connects to both pieces.
- Controlling heat is the key to a proper weld. Lack of heat can make a weld bead that looks ok but is actually sitting on top, too much heat can weaken the metal and even "boil" some away. Heat control methods will vary by process and involve some combination of machine setup and weldor control. When learning to weld, overheating a few practice welds helps the weldor find the proper melting threshold. For some processes, preheating the material to be welded is required. Temperature indicating sticks are an excellent way to determine proper preheating. These will melt at a given temperature. While the metal is being heated, the stick can be touched to it. Heat should be removed as soon as the stick melts.
- Making the weld will take significant practice to perfect. The tips below are further explained with examples in Chapter 11 techniques.
  - New weldors should practice using forehand (pushing away from the start) and backhand (pulling away from the start) welds on all the material types and shapes they intend to use. This should be done anytime a new material is introduced. It will help the weldor build a mental "database" of which technique works best for a given situation.
  - New weldors should also learn when it is ok to weave (swing slightly side-to-side) vs. using a stringer bead (pausing briefly to let the weld build) by trying each technique on a variety of materials. Observing how each affects the final weld will be valuable.
  - Watching how a weld cools indicates a lot about the weld too. It should cool evenly from the starting point to the finish with no spots or gaps visible. Dark areas that form quickly (especially in welding slag) indicate a void.
- Visual properties of the finished weld are generally similar.
  - The weld thickness should be about the same as the thickness of the material. A larger weld does not impart extra strength; overly large welding beads increase the heat-affected area and can weaken the surrounding material.
  - The end of the weld is often overlooked. A slight pause at the end of the weld allows it to build up to the full bead height, which can help prevent cracking. Where a member meets the face of another and will only be welded on one or two edges, wrapping the corners improves weld strength.
  - Proper filler metal should always be used. Scrap metal may be rusty or of unknown metallurgy, both of which risk an improper weld. Most importantly, DO NOT use a wire clothes hanger for filler metal. It is an unknown alloy

Figure 8.4 A 500° temperature indicating stick used to ensure proper preheat of cast iron before welding. The iron was heated with a welding tip on an OAF torch.

that could contain dangerous heavy metals, and they are painted, which creates hazardous fumes. If a gap needs to be filled due to poor fitment in non-critical applications while arc welding, adding a bit of matching TIG/OAF filler metal can be a solution.
- Joint types—The majority of the finished units produced for the industry will use some version of a butt joint, because a large percentage of what is being built uses hollow sections. A T-joint, miter joint, and even a coped joint for tubing are all versions of a butt joint, though the weld itself, may be a fillet or flat. When butting thick, solid pieces, an open root (slight gap) weld may be required, even with a beveled edge. Lap and corner joints are also a possibility and most often will be welded with a fillet.
- Position—This term refers to the position of the weld and materials, not the weldor and does not necessarily relate to a specific joint type. For example, butt welding square tubing usually requires both flat and vertical welds. A flat weld is one that is made on a horizontal plane. A vertical weld is just that; it is done on a vertical surface with a vertical travel. A horizontal weld is one done on a vertical surface, with a horizontal travel. An overhead (or out-of-position) weld is one that connects in some way to an overhead plane. As an example, this may be required when welding a coped round tubing on a unit that cannot be repositioned.

Figure 8.5 A welding "coupon" made to test all welding positions. This example has a horizontal weld joining two pieces of angle, a flat weld adding a strap tab to the bottom, horizontal and vertical fillets, and for good measure an "overhead" weld for the floating strap.

- Ergonomics—Hand placement and body position are not directly connected to weld quality, rather to the user's ability to create good welds. The focus should be on comfort so that work can be sustained over time without problems such as repetitive motion injury or backache. Many weldors prefer to be seated as much as possible, especially when TIG welding. This will not always be possible; planning the sequence of welds may allow for the least amount of awkward positioning. As well, strong tack welds may allow the unit to be maneuvered as opposed to the weldor's body.
- Welding circuits—Welders output current in three ways: two Direct Current settings and Alternating Current. All refer to positive and negative poles. Older welding books will refer to straight and reverse polarity DC; this comes from stick welding, where positive ground was predominant early on.
  - DCEN (Electrode Negative or "straight" polarity) is very good for stick welding thicker steel because the positive ground saturates the workpiece and is essentially "hotter" than the electrode. It is often used for FCAW wire feed welders as well.
  - DCEP (Electrode Positive or "reverse" polarity) is better for thin materials because heat is concentrated at the electrode, reducing the heat-affected zone, but creating a deeper weld due to high filler deposition. It is also preferred for overhead joints because the weld pool will set faster, reducing sag. This is the circuit for solid wire MIG welding because it provides better surface cleaning and pulls the metal ions to the field material.
  - AC current is used for TIG welding aluminum and some stick welding. When stick welding, AC provides the middle ground of penetration due to being split EN and EP and can reduce arc blow (wandering arc due to magnetism). TIG power supplies are designed to modify the AC sine wave to better suit the arc properties required for welding aluminum.
- Compressed gas cylinders—Since the welding processes most common to the industry require compressed gases, it is helpful to know how to properly handle them.
  - Cylinders should be stored, transported, and used while upright and secured. Cylinders should always have the transport cap protecting the valve in place until secured on the welder and the regulator connected. The user should be aware that fuel cylinders use a different diameter cap than other cylinders.

- Regulators are necessary and somewhat delicate parts of welding systems. The regulator needs to be matched to the gas type and the welding process (low output for oxygen on an OAF setup, for example). Some compressed gases are stored at over 2000 psi in the cylinder. The regulator is the only means of safely delivering the proper end pressure to the welding system. If a regulator shows any sign of not working properly, it should be replaced or repaired by a qualified vendor.
  - Fuel cylinders use left-hand threads, while other gases use right-hand threads. Acetylene cylinders are available with four types of threaded connections, though generally only two are used for industrial applications. When replacing, the user needs to order a cylinder with threads that match the regulator. See the OAF welding section below.
  - Cylinders require regular inspection. This is why most bottles (especially large bottles) are on lease; the inspection cost and liability are covered by the supplier. Small cylinders may be available for purchase, as many suppliers will simply trade them out when empty. Each bottle will have an array of data stamped or cast on the top. The most important thing to locate is the most recent inspection date (month and year) and the star that indicates a ten-year pressure test. Cylinders are available in various sizes. High-pressure gases, such as oxygen and shielding gases, are sized by cubic foot capacity and range from 40 to 400 CuF. Acetylene cylinders are a bit different due to the nature of their construction. While they may be sized by cubic foot, it is common for suppliers to use number/letter codes such as AC3 or AC4. For most shops, mid-sized cylinders from about 80 to 125 CuF (AC3 and AC4) will be the most common.
  - While cylinders are incredibly durable, they still need to be treated with respect. Never weld on or otherwise heat a cylinder. Do not hammer on or drop a cylinder. Cylinders should be rolled in the upright position or put on a hand truck when they need to be moved, never dragged.
  - When in use, the cylinder should be mounted to the welder or cart such that it cannot tip or fall, with the valve and regulator protected if possible.
- Filler metals—A variety of alloys and form factors are available for most materials.
  - Most wire-type filler (MIG and TIG) metal for steel will be die drawn and thus copper-coated. The highest quality fillers are vacuum melted, metallurgically pure, and are roll formed. For most applications in the entertainment industry (since we aren't building aircraft) store-shelf filler metals will be fine. Buyers should opt for any well-known name brand such as Hobart, Lincoln, Harris, and Washington Alloy. Copper coating of steel filler is less than ideal for super-critical applications, but fine for entertainment structures with one exception: 4130 chromoly. This is not a material that is encountered regularly, but it is worth mentioning that the copper coating on filler metal can be "absorbed" by the grain structure of 4130 and cause cracks. It's the one place where metallurgically pure filler is required. Some filler metals have a shelf life that should be adhered to, especially for critical applications such as in a unit that will be suspended overhead.
  - Dissimilar steel types can be welded with specialized alloys. Often this combination will be mild steel to stainless steel, in which case a stainless steel filler will be used. In rare cases this could be less common alloys such as high carbon steel, 4130 or stainless steel to any combination of these or mild steel. Lawson Products offers Cronatron 333 as both MIG welding wire (solid) that is used with 98% argon/2% oxygen shielding gas and flux-coated sticks for SMAW.
- Techniques—There are a number of techniques that help the weldor create good finished products regardless of the welding process chosen.
  - Grounding is key to a good arc weld. While steel can easily be welded on a clean steel table connected to the machine ground, when welding aluminum, the ground cable should always be connected directly to a clean spot on the material, not the table. Otherwise, the oxidation on the aluminum reduces conductivity and tends to arc to the table. Other metals will depend on their conductivity, but most can be welded on a clean, grounded table, with Stainless steel being the other exception.
  - Distortion cannot be completely eliminated in many cases, but it can be controlled to the level of almost no impact.
    - Clamping or using fixtures is the first step in controlling distortion. There are many commercially available clamps for welding, but when it comes to unique shapes, shop-made fixtures are the winner. This may be by using a punched steel table with wedges and dogs; some shops use a very thick steel table and tack-weld either fixture blocks to the table or the perimeter pieces of the unit to the table and grind them off once finished. Often a plywood top table works well because fixture blocks can be screwed to the table. The only

drawback is not being able to use the table as a grounding surface. The risk of fire is low when plywood tops are used with MIG or TIG welding. The greater amount of slag and sparks produced by stick welding makes it much less compatible.

- Magnets are a great solution to hold parts in place for tack welding, and there are a variety available for different tasks. These should not remain in place through the weld (they can be damaged by heat) and should not be expected to prevent distortion; they allow tack welding to hold members in position before final welding.
- Tacking welds and weld sequencing are the primary means of preventing distortion. When tacking, a criss-cross pattern helps equalize stress. Pieces should be checked for position after each tack; a few hammer taps may be used to move pieces into position. Welding sequence serves the same purpose, for example welding both sides of a perpendicular tab (after tack welding) will equalize stress. On hollow sections, welding opposite faces often works better than a continuous weld.
- Stitch welding is a technique used for sheet metal and long seams. Tacks are made first at the ends end and along the middle, then evenly distributed welds are made to control heat along the seam and often peened (tapped with a hammer) while cooling to help relieve stress.
- Using distortion to move a member into the finished position can be done with practice on parts that are made regularly. This method can reduce stress on the material, but takes either significant trial and error or an engineered solution.

○ Coupons and scrap material are the best means for learning to weld. Start with scrap pieces of the most common materials the shop plans to use (often thin-walled steel tubing). Once the weldor is comfortable making good, strong welds, destructive testing should be applied (use a big hammer!). A set of welding "coupons" is an excellent way to test both the welding skill of a new weldor and their ability to use proper techniques to keep everything true and square. These are small squares or rectangles that are intended to be welded into a cube or brick, while remaining square and true. Some coupon kits have themes like dice, and advanced kits may be in the shape of an animal head. Some sets cut as hollow frames allow for practicing tight quarters interior welds.

Figure 8.6 Example 16-ga steel welding coupons. On the left the die pieces have been removed from the sheet and tacked together; one side has been welded with an OAF torch. On the right are two complete coupon sheets; the top sheet can be folded, while the bottom sheet requires the weldor to support individual components while welding.

○ Making the weld may be done by creating a stringer bead, where the welding torch is moved in a straight line with a rhythm that creates the half-moon stacks (pause, move, pause, move...) or using a weave where the torch and filler material are swept slightly side to side while traveling, usually to distribute heat on thin material. Each technique has a place based on joint type, material thickness, and welding process.

○ Position refers to how the electrode/heat source relates to the material. Each process will vary somewhat, but typically for flat work, the source can lean slightly to one side (10°–30°) while for fillets, the source should bisect the total angle. Some processes may need the front-to-back tilt to be 0°, while others may allow up to 45°. For example, a MIG gun or OAF torch already has angularity, so the handle can be held level and the nozzle tilted slightly to one side. These can be a visual aid to the new stick weldor as well, to learn how to position the electrode.

WELDING AND RELATED PROCESSES • 135

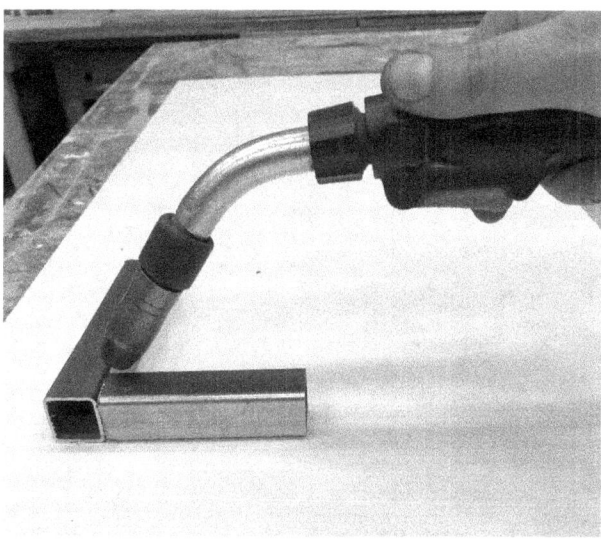

Figure 8.7a MIG torch held for flat and horizontal work. Note the slight tilt to the side for easier viewing while welding.

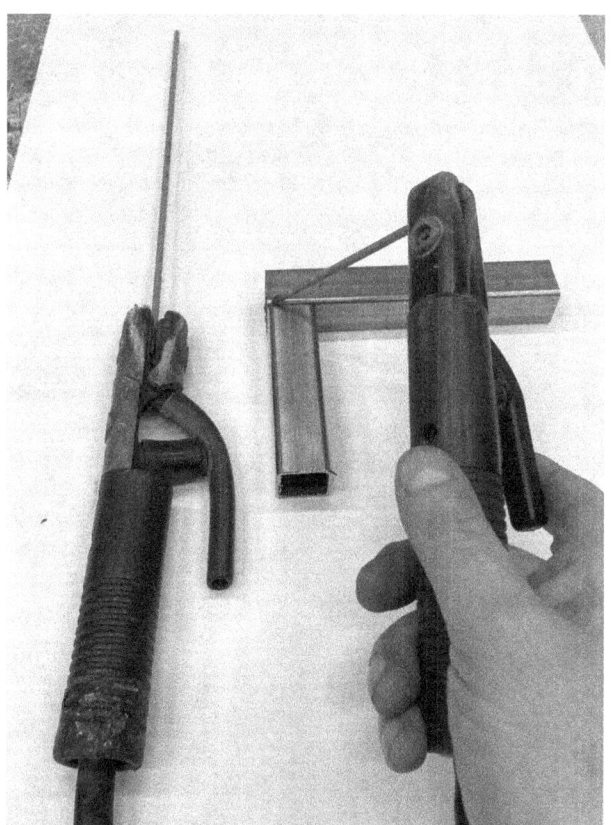

Figure 8.7b A stick electrode in position for a flat or horizontal weld. In this instance the holder is tilted at about a 45° angle to mimic the nozzle of a MIG machine. Alternatively, the electrode can be clamped in at a 45° angle, allowing the user to keep the holder flat or inserted parallel to the holder for overhead work, as shown on the left.

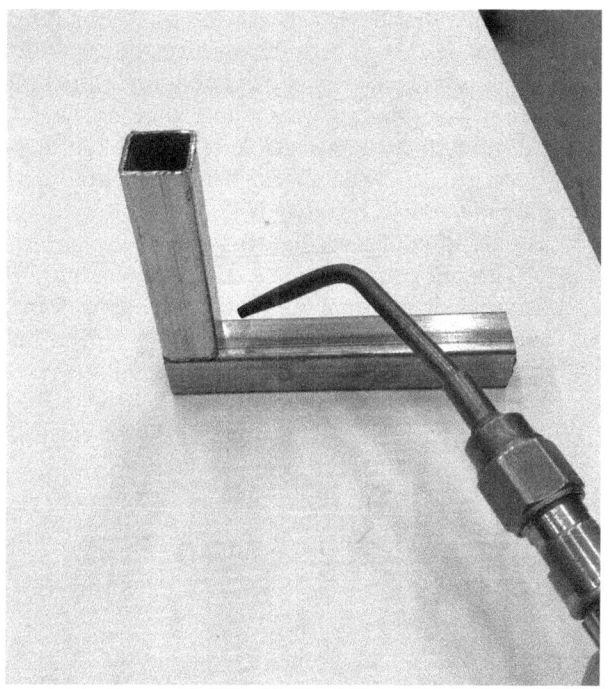

Figure 8.7c An OAF torch positioned for heating both components (which would require a tad bit of movement). Note the distance between the torch and material; the tip needs to be far enough away to prevent blow-back onto the tip and overheating the weld pool, which leads to popping.

○ Direction of travel can determine penetration and proper build of the weld bead. Vertical travel will most often be uphill to prevent the chilling weld from sagging into the weld pool; this is especially true for any process that produces slag. Weldors also refer to forehand and backhand travel. Forehand aims the heat source (or electrode) toward the direction of travel; with processes that include a hand-held filler rod, the rod travels ahead of the heat. Backhand travel aims the heat source away, and the filler rod follows.
○ Joining dissimilar thicknesses can be tricky, as somewhat higher current will be required to properly penetrate the thicker metal. Keep in mind the penetration into the thicker piece needs only to match that of the thinner. Extra depth of weld in the thicker piece yields no extra strength. In this instance, a slight weaving of the bead can help with a higher percentage of time held on the thicker material.
○ Venting may be required when a hollow section is to be fully welded at both ends. This vent need not be large and can often be welded closed once the member has cooled.
○ Repairing cracks is not a commonly encountered situation for most entertainment shops,

but units that have been on tour may be in need of repair. The author recommends only repairing minor cracks in steel and only when the unit is not load-bearing, nor going to be overhead. Aluminum with any visible crack is likely harboring other cracks that may not be visible, and the unit should be retired.
- Avoiding cracks can be tricky in some materials. Proper preheating when required, maintaining specific material temperature while welding, and proper cooling all play a role in preventing cracks at the weld. This can be difficult information to attain, though many books dedicated to welding have helpful information. Some of these are listed in Chapter 15.

WELDERS AND WELDING PROCESSES

There are some common factors that should be considered when choosing an arc welder of any type. All machines have a duty cycle. Machines are typically rated 60% duty cycle at the highest amperage setting, based on 10-minute cycle (6 min use/4 min rest). Choosing a welder with a higher maximum welding amperage than required for the most common material in the shop does two things: it ensures a high enough duty cycle and leaves room to grow into larger projects. When purchasing a welder, the electrical supply in the shop also needs to match the welder. Older, large machines can be 3-phase; most modern machines that will be found in a scene shop will be single-phase. Another valuable feature of new machines is offering variable input voltage (120–240 V), making these machines versatile for companies that may need to use them in more than one location. Major brands will offer better service and parts availability, as well as longevity. The buyer should be wary of discount brands; they tend to have lower longevity, poor weld performance and little availability of parts or service centers. They will often have a much lower duty cycle as well. Many low-cost wire feed machines may not be fitted for shielding gas.

METAL INERT GAS (MIG OR GMAW)

MIG welding, also know as Gas Metal Arc Welding (GMAW), is one of the most common welding processes in entertainment fabrication. For any shop starting into metal, MIG is the most likely first welder to be purchased. They are versatile, easy to learn, use and maintain. In addition, many machines can also use

Figure 8.8a A 200 amp Miller 211 MIG welder with spool gun (for aluminum). This machine is dual voltage: 120 or 240 V. This offers the flexibility to work in the metal shop or where there are no 240 V supplies.

Figure 8.8b A full frame MIG (CP200) 3-phase welder running CO_2. This machine could run the wire feed separately if needed for extended reach. Note the large hand-piece common to industrial MIG welders.

Figure 8.8c A wire feed separated from its power supply at the Metal Museum in Memphis, TN. This has been mounted on a crane arm, allowing access to most of the welding floor in this small shop.

flux-cored wire for gas-free welding; a process referred to as FCAW—Flux Cored Arc Welding. If the reader is not familiar with MIG welding, the machine uses a continuously fed spool of wire as both the electrode and the filler metal. While welding, a shielding gas surrounds the weld puddle, protecting it from impurities. The majority of portable machines use short arc transfer welding. This method is what makes MIG so versatile for all position welding. Spray transfer is reserved for very high amperage machines (above 200-A welding current) used mostly for industrial welding, such as bridge manufacturing.

- General considerations—Nearly all MIG machines will offer the same basic features and operate in the same manner. There are some details that can help choose the right machine and understand why MIG welding may be the best process for a given shop.
  - The advantages of the MIG process make it ideal for the most commonly encountered metals used in the entertainment industry: mild steel and aluminum. Most MIG welders can also be used with flux-cored wire for gas-free welding on steel, which is great for working outdoors. Other metals such as stainless steel, copper, silicon bronze, magnesium and titanium can be MIG welded too. MIG welding produces a more ductile weld than OAF or stick, which is great for scenery or display units that tour or get reconfigured regularly.
  - The few drawbacks to MIG welding are usually a worthwhile trade-off. MIG welding uses compressed gas to shield the weld pool. Gas cylinders require safe storage and handling. MIG torches generally have a fairly short reach up to about 15 ft. On some machines, the wire feed unit can be separate from the power and gas supply, adding to the reach of the machine overall; otherwise, a spool gun may be the best means to extend reach. These welders also have many moving parts, which may require a bit more maintenance. MIG welding can be somewhat harder to see the welding pool properly, especially when using flux-cored wire or a spool gun. Learning to position oneself to properly view the welding pool is a crucial skill for MIG welding. While filler metal for heavily rusted steel is available (ERS70-5), it is not compatible with short-arc transfer, which most MIG welders use.
  - Other considerations for MIG welding include matching the torch tip to the diameter of the filler wire as well as the drive wheels in the wire feed pinch roller. Many wheels are double grooved and can be flipped for different wire sizes. Filler wire should be kept clean, especially with open wire feeds. The welding torch usually has a plastic housing that is durable, but vulnerable where it meets the power source. Users need to avoid kinks in the torch liner. MIG welds are often not considered as visually attractive as those done with a TIG machine, especially when welding aluminum.
  - Machines offer various features that should be considered before purchase.
    - Many new machines offer automatic or semi-automatic setups. These machines range from automatic feed rate for steel based on filler diameter to full digital interfaces that set amperage and wire feed based on material choice. Manually controlled machines may have continuously variable amperage and speed controls or indexed current settings. Some machines offer a weld timer that can be set for spot, stitch or seam, allowing the weldor to easily weld very thin material.
    - Most shops will opt for a self-contained welder that has the wire feed integrated into the power supply cabinet. Mid-sized machines generally have transport wheels and mounting for the gas cylinder. Compact units require a cart and means to mount the cylinder when set up for

MIG. For many shops, the lower cost of the smaller machines offset the need to buy or build a cart. As well, many carts offer storage drawers. Separate power supply and wire feed welders are available, but are less maneuverable.
- Peak amperage and duty cycle are key factors when buying a machine. Most scenic applications will not require amperage above about 250 A. Most shops do not weld materials beyond a thickness that would require higher amperage, and higher peak amp machines may not offer low enough settings for thin material. The most popular mid-sized welders have a 250 A peak output.

• Technique—Below are tips and common procedures that will help the reader achieve proper welds.
  ○ Welder set up is the first step. Many new machines include a chart of current and wire speed settings per material thickness; others are automatic or semi-automatic. As an example, the feed rate would be reduced as the wire diameter increases, per the same thickness of base material. Cables should be checked, especially where the torch connects to the welder. Before the weld is started, the gas flow should be tested, the ground clamp in place, and the wire cut to proper stick-out (usually 3/16"–1/4"). Shielding gas cylinders should be closed at the end of the welding session.
  ○ Proper wire stick-out and feed rate not only affect the weld pool, allowing the necessary shielding, but also prevents wire burn back. Burn back can melt the wire into the contact tip, clogging it. As well, a small ball is usually formed on the end of the wire when a weld is complete. This should be clipped off before beginning a new weld to avoid making a cold-start (a spot where the material under the bead is not molten, but looks complete).
  ○ The direction and movement of the welding torch have a significant impact on the final weld.
    - Pushing the weld (forehand weld) with the torch tip pointed toward the direction of travel reduces weld penetration and is excellent for welding thin steel, approximately under 14 ga. Pushing is almost always used when MIG welding aluminum because this method also increases gas capture around the weld pool. Pulling the weld, with the tip pointed away from the direction of travel, increases the weld penetration and is thus helpful when welding thick material.
    - Speed of travel also affects penetration, the ability to melt filler and substrate, and the heated area. For this reason, the welding current and wire speed need to be matched to the task. For example, a lower current and wire speed may be needed when welding a hard-to-reach area to prevent burn-through, while a higher current and wire speed may work well on an easily accessible portion of the same material, reducing the heat-affected zone.
    - The weld motion controls not only where the weld meets the material, but also the heat-affected zone. Weaving (a zig-zag motion) is generally frowned upon by weldors who work with thick, structural steel, but may be required with thin materials to prevent burn-through. For example, weaving is common when making a T-joint with square steel tubing, where the radius of the edge creates a small gap to the end cut of the perpendicular tube. In this scenario, a 60/40 split that reduces weld time on the end cut prevents burn-through. With thicker metal, or joints like a lap or tee, a stringer bead is preferred to ensure good penetration of the weld.

Figure 8.9 An example of welding across the small gap created by the corner radius of the tube. The welding gun was tilted to about 45° toward the radius, and the pool allowed to flow into the gap.

- Vertical welds may be done from the bottom up or top down, depending on the material (not stick or FCAW). Thick material requires high deposition and should be built from the bottom up to prevent cold welds and inclusions. Thin materials can benefit from top-down welds, where the increased travel speed prevents burn-through.
  ○ When holding the MIG welding torch, using two hands is preferable for steadiness. Resting one hand on the table or material as a guide is often the best option. Also, many weldors prefer to pull their elbow in tight to their flank for extra stability when not welding on a table.
  ○ Tacking and stitch welding are easily achieved with MIG because there is no need to clean the

WELDING AND RELATED PROCESSES • **139**

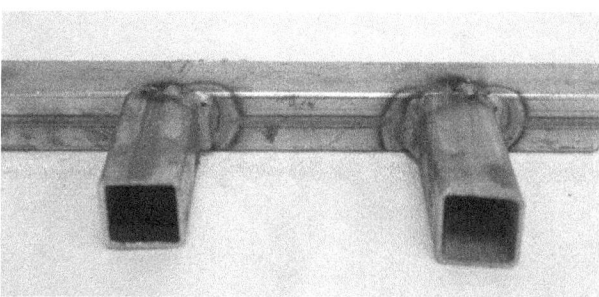

Figure 8.10 Vertical MIG welds on 16 ga square tube. The weld on the left was done bottom up and has a more rounded profile; the weld on the right was welded top down and has a bit of a concave shape.

Figure 8.11 A comfortable grip that allows for multidirectional travel while keeping the torch steady.

weld to restart. This allows the user to make a series of tack welds to hold all members in place before final welding, which leads to a much more square/true final product.
- Steel specifics — When MIG welding steel, gas flow can be relatively low, especially with Argon/CO_2 mix; approximately 15–20 cubic feet per hour (CFH). Most often a standard torch will be used, though a spool gun is a good option for extended reach.
  - Shielding gas options for steel are either 75% Argon/25% CO_2 or 100% CO_2. Pure CO_2 imparts slightly more spatter and a somewhat flatter weld bead. Welding speed will remain consistent throughout the entire weld.
  - The MIG nozzle needs to be kept clean both to ensure good contact with the wire and to allow the shielding gas to flow properly. Many weldors will keep a container of nozzle dip on hand to prevent the build-up of spatter on the MIG gun tip and shielding cup.
  - Filler metals for steel range from 60 to 120 ksi tensile strength, but 70 series fillers are the most common in entertainment shops because most of the steel used is mild steel.

- ER70S-2 is often chosen because it can weld in all positions and is compatible with light rust on mild steel.
- ER70S-3 is unlikely to be encountered in an entertainment shop, because the steel needs to be very clean, which shops often are not. It is a good choice for welding galvanized steel.
- ER70S-4 is excellent to weld with, but may need to be sourced from a commercial welding supplier. It is primarily used for structural steel like A36. It is a great choice for welding pipe and structural shapes.
- ER70S-6 is the most readily available alloy and can be found online, in big box stores and from welding suppliers. It is a great choice for entertainment shops because it has the best combination of characteristics: it is all-position, works well with thin sections and will weld through light rust. It requires slightly higher welding current and faster travel speeds than other alloys.

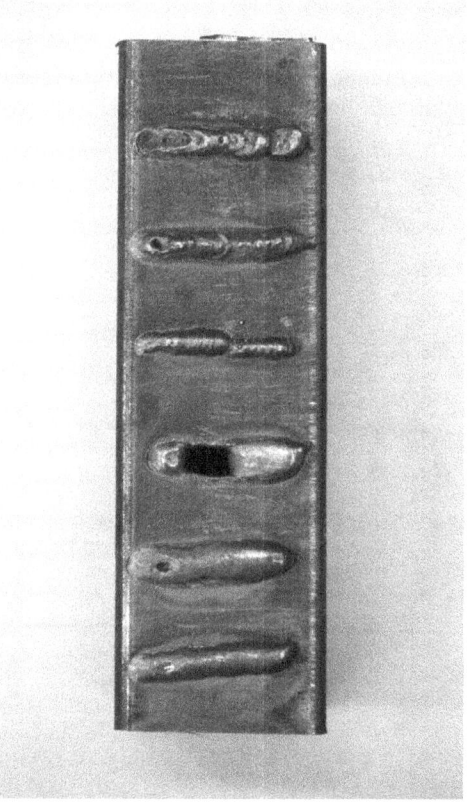

Figure 8.12 Examples of MIG weld errors from top — Welding with no gas, welding with far too much wire stick out (similar to no gas), amperage too low (small, peaked weld with little penetration), amperage too high (sunken even where not burned through), a weld with a crater at the end from pulling away too soon and finally, a proper weld.

- Aluminum specifics — MIG welding aluminum requires a higher gas flow, between 30 and 50 CFH, and almost always will be done with a spool gun, though shorter torch assemblies (under 10 ft) may be relined with a low-friction teflon liner to be compatible with aluminum wire, especially harder 5356. For high production shops where the small spools become cumbersome to continually stock and replace, a pull gun that synchronizes with the wire feeder may be worth the investment. These "push-pull" torches can have up to 35 ft of reach, but cost thousands of dollars. One trick peculiar to MIG welding aluminum is that the user must ramp the travel speed slightly after the initial bead is set due to the high heat conductivity of aluminum.

- The shielding gas used with aluminum is 100% argon.
- MIG welding aluminum produces a significant amount of nasty fumes and smoke; thus, a welding respirator is essential, even when a "smog-hog" is in use. This is why so many shops opt to TIG weld aluminum.
- Filler metals commonly used are mostly 4043 and 5356 because 1100 would be too soft to push, even from a spool gun. 4943 is less common; it is compatible with the same alloys as 4043, but provides a higher tensile strength. More details are available below in the Aluminum TIG welding specifics.
- Welding aluminum with MIG requires thorough cleaning and direct grounding. A bit of swirl or zig-zag motion may be needed to properly bond components, unlike steel.

Figure 8.13b Samples of aluminum MIG welds cut through and "hammer tested". The top sample of 1" square tube was welded with 5356 filler wire using the only settings provided on the welder for 4043 filler; while looking good, they clearly did not provide adequate penetration. The bottom sample of 1 1/2" was welded after a few practice welds and amperage adjustments; the welds survived five hammer blows while clamped in a vise.

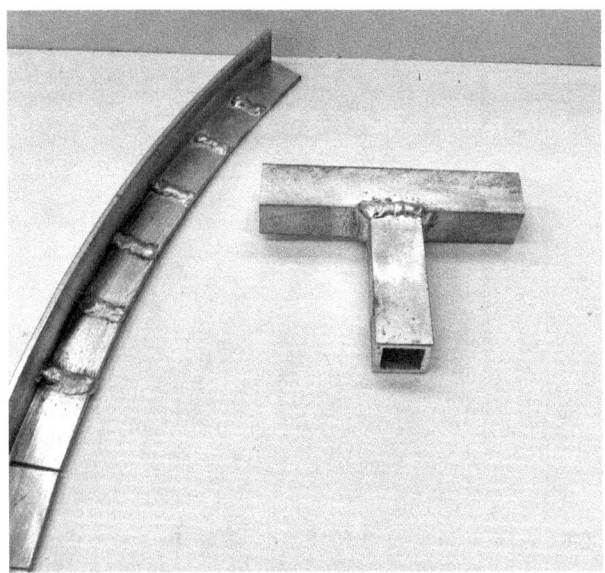

Figure 8.13a A sample of aluminum 1" square tube with a 1/8" wall MIG welded with 5356 filler. Alongside is a sample of aluminum angle with both MIG (nearest three welds) and TIG welds (rear three welds) showing some difference in the final appearance. Though not as aesthetically pleasing as TIG welds, MIG welds are very strong.

- Other metals—MIG welding is versatile and can be used with almost any weldable alloy, including titanium. For exhibit and properties fabrication, where more "exotic" metals may be used, MIG is an easily adapted process.
  - Stainless steel is not often used for fabricating scenic structures, but decorative elements, furniture and artistic signage that will be exposed to the elements could use stainless steel. As well, stainless steel fasteners may need to be welded in place. The most common alloy, 304L, can be welded with 308 wire, as can 308, 321 and 341 alloys. Stainless steel containing molybdenum, such as 316L (used for fasteners exposed to salt water) should be welded with 316LSi. Trimix

shielding gas (Helium 90%, Argon 7.5%, CO_2 2.5%) should be used when welding stainless.
- Bronze, copper, brass and cast iron can all be MIG brazed using silicon bronze wire (ERCuSi-A). It can also be used to braze copper alloys to steel. Copper and cast iron need to be preheated before welding, while bronze needs to be stitch-welded to avoid overheating, which will lead to cracks. ERCuSi wire is shielded with 100% argon.

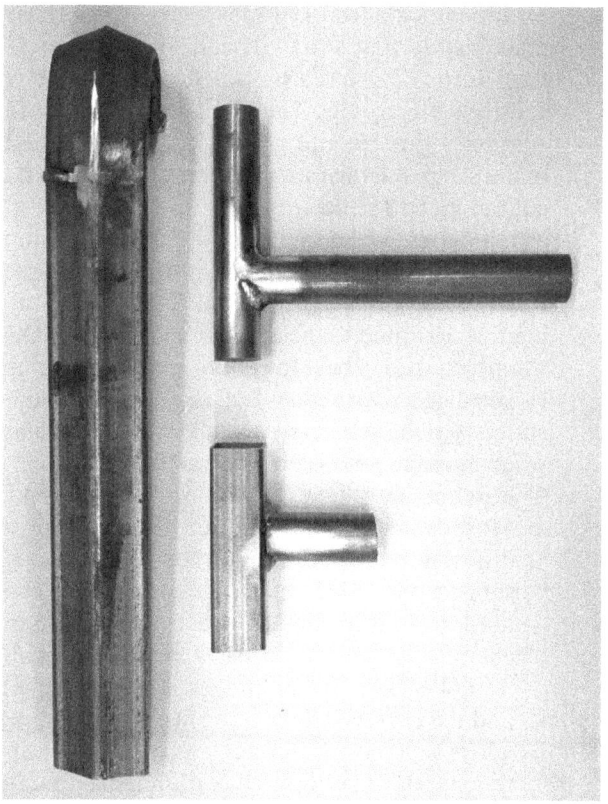

Figure 8.14 Examples of MIG brazing cast iron to steel, copper tube to steel tube and copper to copper.

- Flux-cored specifics (FCAW) — The differences between GMAW and FCAW are the wire and lack of shielding gas; flux-cored wire is a hollow metal tube filled with flux. Like stick electrodes, the flux composition varies but serves the same purpose: to protect the welding zone and finished weld. The process is applicable to ferrous metals, nickel-based alloys, and stainless steel. FCAW requires a faster wire feed rate than solid wire of the same diameter and works best when producing a stringer bead. Like stick welding, the process cannot be restarted on a cooled weld without removing slag and cleaning with a wire brush.
  - FCAW may use DCEN or DCEP (circuit polarity), depending on the alloy to be welded. The most commonly available wire used for mild steel, E71T-11, uses DCEN and requires no shielding. While DCEP is the default for MIG, most machines allow changing to DCEN via swapping power leads or bolted circuit plates in the welder (usually in the wire feed cabinet). Some welder manufacturers offer a closed tip guard for flux-cored welding that protects the gas orifices from being clogged by debris.
  - FCAW is better for welding moderately oxidized steel than solid wire. It is also better for windy conditions than stick welding, though still limited by torch length. New 120 V compact inverter-based machines are capable of welding fairly thick steel (up to 1/8″). When paired with the lack of a gas cylinder, it is easy to see why these are now being used in boom lifts on construction sites for things like steel door and window frames and other steel trim work. Some electrodes require or are compatible with shielding gas, but some will be negatively affected by shielding. The user should always check the manufacturer's specifications.
  - Alloy numbering ranges from 1000 series to 11000 series, but 6000 and 7000 are the most likely choices for entertainment use. Like stick electrodes, the series number refers to ksi tensile strength, the second number indicates position (either 0 for flat use or 1 for all positions) followed by T (tubular) and a two-digit alloy code. If you see GS in place of the last two digits, these

Figure 8.15 Examples of flux-cored welds. The example on the left shows the slag, spatter and soot created by FCAW welding, while the one on the right shows an FCAW weld after cleaning with a wire wheel. In the center is an open-root weld (partial) on 3/16″ steel; the slag was far less due to much higher heat input.

wires have been manufactured to brand-specific specs that are often undisclosed. This is common for off-brand filler metals; they are not recommended for critical applications.

TUNGSTEN INERT GAS (GTAW)

TIG welding, or Gas Tungsten Arc Welding (GTAW), is common in shops that work extensively with aluminum. Though MIG works quite well for aluminum, using a spool gun is unwieldy, and the welds may not be as pleasing to the eye. TIG offers greater control of welding heat and is therefore more useful for thin material (no stitch welding is needed if care is taken). For the uninitiated, the process uses a torch with a virtually non-consumable tungsten electrode to create the arc and a welding pool that is surrounded by shielding gas. The filler metal is manually added by the weldor; thus, it requires more practice than MIG to achieve a good weld, especially for non-ferrous metals.

- General considerations—TIG is an exceptionally versatile process that is somewhat more difficult to learn than other processes; those who have welded with an OAF torch have a leg up, as they are used to the two-handed process. TIG can also be an excellent way to braze.
  - The advantages of TIG welding are compatibility with essentially all weldable alloys and, in some cases, dissimilar metals. The precise heat control decreases both distortion and the heat-affected area. While TIG can provide high amperage for welding very thick metals, it is ideal for very thin metals, especially soft metals that require the most delicate touch. Most machines can double as a stick welder, and some multi-process machines can power a MIG wire feeder.
  - The disadvantages of TIG welding include the variety of consumables (including ceramic shielding cups that are delicate) that all need to be matched to the material. TIG welding requires bottled gas and coordination of current control via thumb or foot control while maintaining a consistent arc distance and manually adding the filler metal. It requires significant practice to make an attractive weld that also has proper penetration. If the tungsten makes contact with the weld pool, it will be compromised and must be reground.
  - Other considerations for TIG welding include torch type: water or air cooled. Torches rated above 200 A are water-cooled. Torch coolers should only be filled with distilled water (or distilled water and anti-freeze if used in unconditioned spaces). Repointing electrodes requires a very fine grit (400 or higher) dedicated grinding wheel (precision welding may require a diamond wheel) or a stand-alone tungsten grinder. Far more consumables are required for TIG welding than for other processes.
  - Machines can be DC only or AC/DC. DC TIG is used for ferrous metals and copper alloys; AC is used for aluminum, magnesium and other metals. Most new AC-capable machines will have an high frequency (HF), square-wave output. HF machine manuals often include a section on the importance of properly grounding these machines so that stray HF signals cannot backfeed into local circuits, which could damage sensitive electronics. The HF square-wave both stabilizes the arc and allows it to jump to the material to start without touching (which could contaminate the electrode).
  - Torch choice will depend on the most common needs of a shop. Some shops may opt for multiple torch types. Current can be adjusted via a thumb control mounted to the torch or a foot pedal. The thumb control is best for multi-position welding (vertical or overhead), but may not be well-suited to tight quarters. A pedal is difficult to use when standing and is best for table work.
    - Torches may have a fixed or flexible head. Most can be configured three ways by using a different back cap: full cap for 7" electrodes, short cap for 3 1/2" electrodes and stubby cap for 1 1/2" electrodes. (7" electrodes are often cut to fit.) Additional parts include the collet, collet body (standard and stubby lengths) and the cup (nozzle) of various lengths. Some alloys weld best with a gas lens, which replaces the standard collet body with a lensed body that helps make a stable area of shielding gas around the weld. These use a different collet and cup.
    - Air cooled torch sizes are #24 (80 amps), #9 (120 amps), #17 (150 amps), and #26 (200 amps) with #9 (because it is compact) and #17 (because of the amp range) being the most common; these also share common gas line fittings, collects and nozzles/lenses.
    - Water-cooled torch sizes are #20 (same size as a #9, but with a 250 amp capacity) and #18 (350 amps). Many TIG machines will require an add-on water cooler to be compatible. This is often preferred as internal coolers can be problematic, especially if they leak.
    - TIG torches use two types of machine connection: DINSE with external gas and water lines and Tweco (cam-lock style) with gas through the connector.

WELDING AND RELATED PROCESSES • 143

Figure 8.16a The TIG welder at the University of Memphis. It has a 200-A maximum output, foot pedal control and a WP17 (150 A) air-cooled torch.

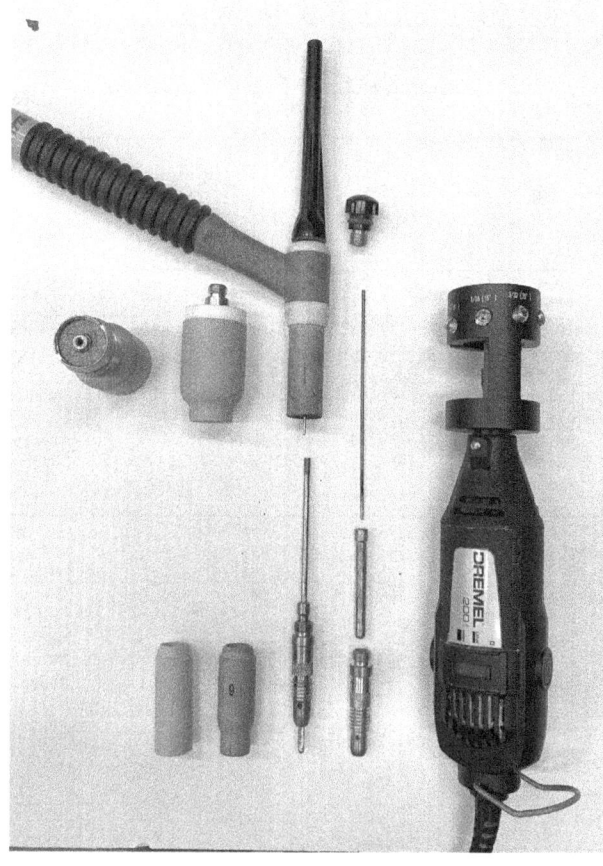

Figure 8.16b On the top left is an assembled TIG torch surrounded by parts including a close quarters back cap, examples of gas lenses and matching cups (left below torch) and collets, closers and cups (below). On the right is a tungsten grinding adapter mounted to a rotary tool.

- Techniques—For the metals most common to entertainment fabrication, argon is going to be the shielding gas of choice. Some alloys may benefit from helium or argon/helium mixes. Below is an outline of setup steps and welding techniques that will help get the reader started, but should not be substituted for proper training.
  o Setting up the torch for the material can involve many steps. Regardless of alloy, the electrode needs to be the proper diameter for the amp range. The collet and shielding cup need to be matched to the electrode diameter and the type of weld (e.g. a fillet may be done with a narrower cup than a horizontal weld). See Figures 8.17a and 8.17b.
    - The electrode stick out varies slightly by weld position: about 3× the electrode diameter for butt welds and up to 6× the diameter for fillets. The stickout may be extended slightly if a gas lens is used.
    - The point of the electrode needs to be properly ground for the current type and expected amperage. The point should be ground with the electrode parallel to the rotation of the grinding wheel. The general parameters of point grinding are: the point length should be 1.5×–2.5× the diameter, forming a 30°–60° angle. A blunt total angle (e.g. 60°) will keep the weld pool narrow and increase penetration; conversely, a sharp angle (as much as 30°) will widen the weld pool and reduce penetration. This may also be helpful on a fillet weld where the wider arc dispersion more readily engages both faces.
    - Electrodes should not be mixed between alloys once they have been used. Keep steel electrodes just for steel; ditto aluminum. Some weldors even keep collets and cups separate.

Electrode Type	Color Code	Compatible Metals	Process	Characteristics
Pure Tungsten	Green	Aluminum and Magnesium	AC	Best for low amp use. Excellent conductivity, good durability, lower longevity.
Ceriated 1.5%	Orange	Mild Steel. Titanium, Nickel, Stainless.	DC, Low amp AC	Easy arc strike, somewhat shorter life than 2%.
Ceriated 2%	Gray	Titanium, Copper, Magnesium, Aluminum, Nickel	AC/DC	Easy arc strike, best when low amperage is needed, very stable arc. Faster degradation at higher amperage range. Arc properties may be lost before electrode is worn away.
Thoriated .8%–1%*	Yellow	Mild Steel, Stainless	DC	Lower thorium content. Lower longevity.
Thoriated 2%*	Red	Mild Steel, Stainless, Copper	DC	Most common electrode. Good to very good longevity. Increased current capacity per size.
Lanthanated 1.5%	Gold	Stainless and Mild Steel; Titanium, Copper, Nickel.	AC/DC	Slightly less conductive (often used with lift start)
Lanthanated 2%	Dark Blue	Aluminum, Magnesium, Nickel, Copper, Stainless	AC/DC	Easy strike, good for HF use, good for low amperage use. Very good longevity. Best electrode for pulsed welding.
Mix Rare Earth (percentages vary by manufacturer)	Purple or other	"Universal", Very good performance with mild steel, Stainless, Nickel, Copper	AC/DC	Properties vary by manufacturer.
LaYZr (lanthium 1.5%, yttrium .08%, zirconium .08%)	Chartreuse	"Universal" Good to very good with Aluminum, Magnesium, Nickel and Stainless. Poor performance with mild steel.	AC/DC	Low to medium amp range. Very good for low amp starts.
Ziconiated .15% to .5%	Brown	Aluminum and Magnesium	AC	Special use for low contamination welds.
Ziconiated .8%	White	Aluminum and Magnesium	AC	Best for high amperage welding of thick materials and/or multiple passes. Balls very well for AC welding. Higher longevity that pure tungsten with similar weld properties.

* Indicates radio active element content.
Required shielding gas may vary by material type being welded and/or process (AC or DC) for a given tungsten.

Figure 8.17a The chart provides a general overview of electrode properties, compatibility with various metals and welding processes.

Electrode Diameter	Cup Size	Material Thickness	DC Amp Range	AC Amp Range (HF with Balance)	Recommended Point Size
.040" (1 mm)	6 to 8	.040" to .05" (1 mm to 1.27 mm)	15 to 80	10 to 60	0 to .020"
1/16" (1.6 mm)	7 to 10	.040" to 1/16" (1 mm to 1.6 mm)	70 to 150	30 to 120	0 to .030"
3/32" (2.4 mm)	8 to 12	.090" to 1/8" (2.3 mm to 3.2 mm)	150 to 250	60 to 180	.005" to .030"
1/8" (3.2 mm)	10 to 12	1/8" to 3/16" (3.2 mm to 3.8 mm)	250 to 400	100 to 250	.010" to .040"
5/32 (4 mm)	12	3/16" to 1/4" (3.8 mm to 6 mm)	400 to 500	160 to 320	.010" to .050"
3/16" (4.8 mm)	15	1/4" to 3/8"	500 to 750	190 to 390	.010 to .060"

Notes:
Amperage range will vary by electrode type and tip grind.
Pulsed use may increase maximum amperage capability.

Figure 8.17b The chart provides amp range, cup sizes and material thickness compatibility for various electrode diameters.

- Machine settings can vary significantly depending on the material. There are many variables in addition to amperage.
  - DC TIG is almost always DCEN. DCEP imparts significant extra heat at the electrode that can quickly consume the electrode. Typically, this mode is only used to form a ball on the end of the tungsten before AC welding. DC TIG is used to weld steel, cast iron and copper alloys. AC is used for aluminum, magnesium and stainless steel.
  - High frequency machines are huge plus for welding aluminum and allow for touchless start with all materials.

- Balance is used for AC welding and determines the amount of time the torch electrode is on the negative swing of the wave per cycle (relative wave lengths). This adjusts heat vs. cleaning cycle times.
- Shielding gas settings begin with setting a flow rate of 10–25 CFH (depending on welding current) and include adjusting pre- and post-roll, indicating the amount of time the gas will precede and follow the welding process. Pre-roll should be 1–2 seconds. While the torch is in post-roll, it should be held in position to continue shielding the weld and electrode until cool. Timing will vary based on welding amperage; many machines set this automatically. A rule of thumb formula for post-roll is 5 seconds minimum, adding an additional second for every 10 A increase above 50 A.
- Pulsing is a feature some machines offer for the TIG process that switches from a high amperage to a lower background amperage, effectively lowering the average. It is predominantly used for welding stainless steel but has other uses; it is not recommended for welding mild steel as it tends to create brittle welds. Slower pulse rates (less high amperage output) are great for low conductivity metals like stainless steel because the lower heating time reduces distortion. This can also be used for out-of-position, especially overhead, because it helps the puddle set faster. Some weldors use the feature at a very low rate (1–2 PPS) to time the addition of filler metal to make the nicely stacked weld many associate with TIG. High pulse rates reduce the effect of lowering the heat, but increase penetration and narrow the weld pool, reducing distortion, and on stainless it prevents the build-up of carbon. On some machines, the same controls are used for the dig percentage when stick welding.
  - Filler metal should be cleaned immediately prior to welding (even when stored in closed containers). This can be done with a quick wipe of denatured alcohol. For aluminum filler that has been stored for long periods, a quick rub with a non-woven pad and then a wipe with alcohol will ensure a better weld.
  - Ventilation requirements for TIG welding are different than other processes. Because the shielded area is much more sensitive to air movement, ventilation should be done by a light vacuum, such as a "smog hog" not from dilution ventilation, such as a fan. Because TIG welding produces far fewer fumes than other processes (especially if the base material is properly cleaned) there is less polluting product to be removed as well.
  - Starting the arc can be done by touching a copper "scratch block" by either dragging (like making a small check mark) or a tap (very lightly!) and is typical for older DC machines. High frequency allows a touch-free arc start, but the electrode may need to be slightly closer to the base metal than it would be during the welding process. This prevents any contamination of the electrode.
  - Forehand welding will be the most common technique for TIG welding. This technique ensures the pool abuts the chilled weld for continuity. Even when fusion welding, a forehand technique is used. The torch angle can be a bit complex; the majority of the time, the torch will be tilted at a 75° front to back. The side-to-side angle will vary based on weld position; 10°–25° off vertical for flat and lap welds, or near the bisector of an angle when creating a fillet.
  - TIG machines may be used to fusion weld (no added filler). This is usually done on a corner joint or by fusing flanges on the rear of a sheet metal joint. Most welds will use filler metal to ensure the best bond. When doing so, the weldor makes a molten pool then dips the filler, much like the OAF process.
  - A consistent arc length is crucial to TIG welding. The electrode cannot be moved away to create better visibility or less heat, as one can with an OAF torch. Likewise, too short an arc length can risk a dip into the weld pool or contact with the filler, which instantly pollutes the electrode.
  - The weld pool may need the weldor to make a small circular motion with the torch to get started, but straight travel thereafter. Generally, the filler rod is held at an acute angle (about 15°), which does two things: it opens the view of the weld pool and keeps the rod out of the radiant heat. Vertical welds often use a downward travel (opposite of OAF and stick). Backup bars may be required on thin material to reduce burn-through; these should not quite contact the back of the material to prevent both heat soak and/or bonding. Filler rods should be approximately the same diameter as the welded material thickness.
- Steel specifics—TIG welding steel is somewhat easier than other metals because it is less heat conductive than aluminum and less affected by heat than stainless steel.
  - Electrode preparation is straightforward. The electrode diameter should be about the same as the material thickness, with the tip ground to a

flat-ended point about 10%–20% of the diameter of the electrode. A blunt total angle (e.g. 60°) will keep the weld pool narrow and increase penetration; conversely, a sharp angle (as much as 30°) will widen the weld pool and reduce penetration. This may also be helpful on a fillet weld where the wider arc dispersion more readily engages both faces.
- DCEN will be the current mode of choice for steel. If the machine offers a pulse feature, it should be turned off for steel. If the machine does not offer HF touch-free starting, a copper "scratch block" will be required to safely start the arc without damaging the tungsten.
- Filler metals are available in many of the same alloys as other processes. ER70S-2 is more readily available for TIG than for MIG and is likely what most shops will stock. Harder and softer alloys are also available, such as ER80S-D26 or 6010 and 6011.

Figure 8.18 Examples of TIG-welded steel, from top—A lap made with filler rod, a lap made without filler rod, and a square tube with fillet (welded bottom to top) and butt welds. These welds were made with a 1/8" mixed rare earth tungsten.

- Aluminum specifics—TIG welding aluminum is trickier than steel because the heat conductivity softens the area ahead of the weld. The advantage of TIG is being able to easily control the heat so that the travel speed can be consistent. Aluminum is usually welded with AC current. The weldor should be aware that even though the weld area remains small with TIG, much more surface area will be hot because of the heat conductivity of aluminum, making handling after more risky.
  - Electrode preparation involves an extra step in most cases. Aluminum was historically welded using a pure, unalloyed electrode with a rounded or balled end. Modern inverter machines work best with an alloyed tungsten (see chart). Most weldors make a dull point with a steeper bevel and wider flat end than steel. Some may still choose to heat on a scratch block to then melt the electrode end to form a radius on the tip (using DCEP speeds the process). If this option is chosen, the ball should not exceed the diameter of the electrode; many weldors prefer a slightly larger electrode that tapers to the ball. Regardless of tip choice, the electrode diameter should be slightly bigger than the thickness of the material for most projects.
  - Directly connecting the grounding cable to the work is important with aluminum. Due to being a mediocre conductor, aluminum will arc to grounded steel tables, creating carbon (resistance) and possibly pitting if not directly grounded. Some weldors opt to clamp to a steel table or lay heavy bars that ground the aluminum to the table; in this instance, contact surfaces need to be clean and oxide-free.
  - Machine settings will vary depending on the type of aluminum being welded and the weldor's preferences. In addition to using high frequency AC, newer machines offer extra features.
    - Square-wave machines modify the sine wave for longer EP and EN cycles. This improves both surface cleaning and weld penetration. Machines may offer independent controls for frequency, electrode negative current, electrode positive current and balance. The EP portion of the wave contributes to cleaning, and the EN portion is the primary welding heat (penetration). Square-wave machines also reduce frequency cycles somewhat, though frequency is still much higher than 60 cycles. Typically, frequencies between 100 and 180 Hz produce the best welds, though most adjustable machines offer outputs from 20 to 250 Hz. Increasing frequency narrows the arc, but also reduces heat at the weld. This can

be helpful for very thin sections where low penetration and fast chilling of the weld pool are advantageous. Decreasing the frequency improves the flow of the weld pool and penetration, but can cause the arc to wander if set too low. A "soft" square wave rounds off the top of the square wave slightly. This is available on most new inverter-type machines and provides a smoother arc with a more fluid weld puddle.
- A triangle wave and even trapezoidal wave outputs are available on some inverter TIG machines. These output types give the weldor further control of the heat/clean cycle and can be used in place of increasing the wave frequency for thin materials.
- Pulse settings may be an option if the welding will be out-of-position or done without a filler rod. Otherwise, pulsed welding may produce too little heat for effective penetration on thick materials.
- Cast aluminum can be welded with DCEN if pure helium is used as the shielding gas.

○ A hazy finish to the weld almost always means that it is a cold weld that will crack. A fresh weld needs to shine. Likewise, the weld pool should always have a shimmer before the filler metal is added. Shop managers should consider investing in a Brinell-style ball-indent tester for welded aluminum structures.

○ To fully reap the benefits of heat-treated base materials such as 6061-T6, the welds should also be heat-treated. This cannot be reasonably accomplished without a dedicated facility; thus, most units built for entertainment purposes will not be fully heat-treated. This should be accounted for in any engineered structures, such as truss or platform framing.

○ The filler metals for aluminum that most shops will stock are fairly narrow due to the fact that most shops use very few alloys of aluminum (6061-T6 being the most common to entertainment structures). If a unique project comes up that requires using an alloy unfamiliar to the shop, it is best to refer to the handy chart in the *Aluminum Design Manual* produced by the Aluminum Association that makes it very easy to choose the correct filler for a given combination of alloys.
- 1100 is a very soft filler rod with an 11-ksi tensile strength. It is compatible with 1000 and 3000 series alloys such as 3003. It is an appropriate choice for props such as aluminum-framed furniture and aluminum sheet projects.
- 4043 provides a stronger weld with 1000 and 3000 series and is compatible with 6061 alloys. Its tensile strength is more than double that of 1100 at 24 ksi.
- 4943 is an upgrade in tensile strength from 4043, averaging 35 ksi. It may be chosen over 5356 for its slightly lower melt temperature and better fluidity.
- 5356 has a very high tensile strength of 35 ksi and is best suited for harder 5000 series alloys and provides the strongest weld for 6061.

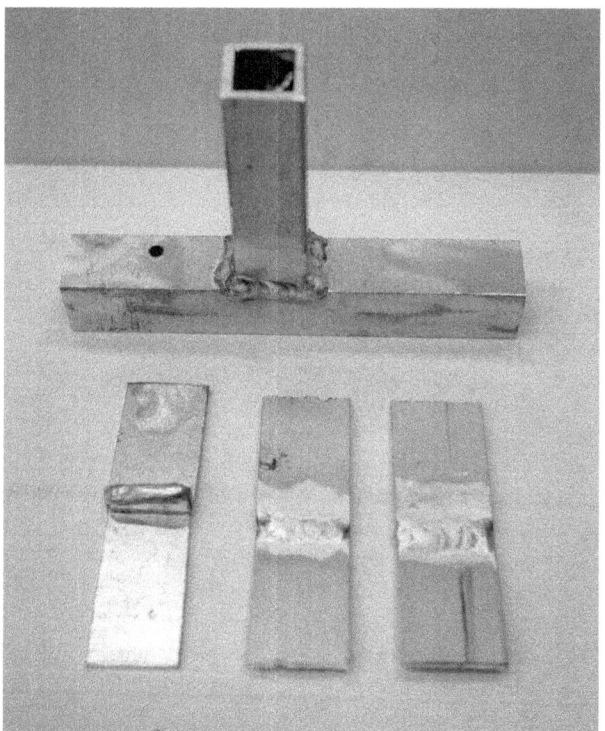

Figure 8.19a Example TIG welds in aluminum by the author (not a certified weldor). The tee joint at the top demonstrates flat and fillet welds (done with the tee vertical). The bottom row shows a 3003 sheet with flanges welded with no filler and 6061 strips lap welded without filler (middle) and with filler (right). A 3/32" mixed rare earth tungsten was used for these welds. A lanthanated tungsten would have produced better welds.

Figure 8.19b A close-up photo of a TIG weld on an aluminum truss made by a certified welder. Note the consistency of the weld bead.

Source: Photo courtesy of Jake Lacher.

- Other alloys — While semi-exotic metals such as magnesium and titanium can be TIG welded, this is unlikely to be required in an entertainment shop. Below are notes regarding alloys that may be used for decorative purposes in the industry.
  - Stainless steel can be one of the most frustrating materials to weld because there are many alloys and many need to be welded with compatible filler. Most of the stainless steel that will be encountered in the entertainment industry can likely be welded with 308 filler (316 is an exception), though the weldor should ensure compatibility before commencing with the weld. There are at least eight different filler alloys available for stainless steel. If the alloy of the source material is unknown, there is no universal filler, but an attempt with 308 may be successful. Most stainless also requires shielding gas applied to the reverse face from the weld to avoid build-up of chalky oxides. Stainless quickly distorts with heat and may not return to its original position once cooled; therefore, well-designed fixtures and distortion control techniques are crucial when welding stainless. This may need to be accounted for in design as well.
  - Cast iron can be welded using high-nickel filler rods, much like when stick welding. 55% nickel rod is also used when no machining is required, though carbide tooling will cut N55. Silicon bronze filler can also be used, but it has lower psi tensile strength (50K vs. 66K for nickel). Cast iron should be preheated and slow-cooled.
  - Bronze, copper and brass can be TIG welded with varying degrees of success. This is due to the variety of alloys each may contain. For example, aluminum bronze is much harder to TIG weld than silicon bronze and can produce noxious fumes. Copper must be oxygen-free to be TIG welded. While oxygen-free copper is readily available from suppliers, scrap copper can only be determined by trial and error: if the copper bubbles while making a pool, it is not oxygen-free and will not weld. Silicon bronze filler can be used to weld silicon bronze and oxygen-free copper and allows them to be brazed to steel.

Figure 8.20 Copper leaves TIG welded to a simple copper stem. A 1/16" 2% thoriated tungsten was used.

Copper can also be welded with copper filler. Brass can be joined with a bronze rod as well, but has a much higher zinc content, so fumes must be properly controlled. As well, brass will boil and splatter the electrode when only slightly overheated; pulsed welding and high frequency may be required.

GAS WELDING (OAF)

Oxygen/acetylene is the most common combination of gases for torch welding because acetylene provides the highest BTU per volume and hottest final temperature. This is why Oxy-Acetylene Fuel (OAF) is the standard designation. Other fuel gases such as propane (somewhat common) and MAPP gas (small kits for HVAC) may be used depending on the final required temperature, but are usually only used for heating and cutting, not welding. Oxygen is not flammable but still a hazard

Figure 8.21a The Oxy-acetylene torch set at the University of Memphis. This set uses an AC4 acetylene cylinder and a 125-CuF oxygen cylinder. Note the flash-back arrestors installed at the regulators and that the cylinders are retained with a chain.

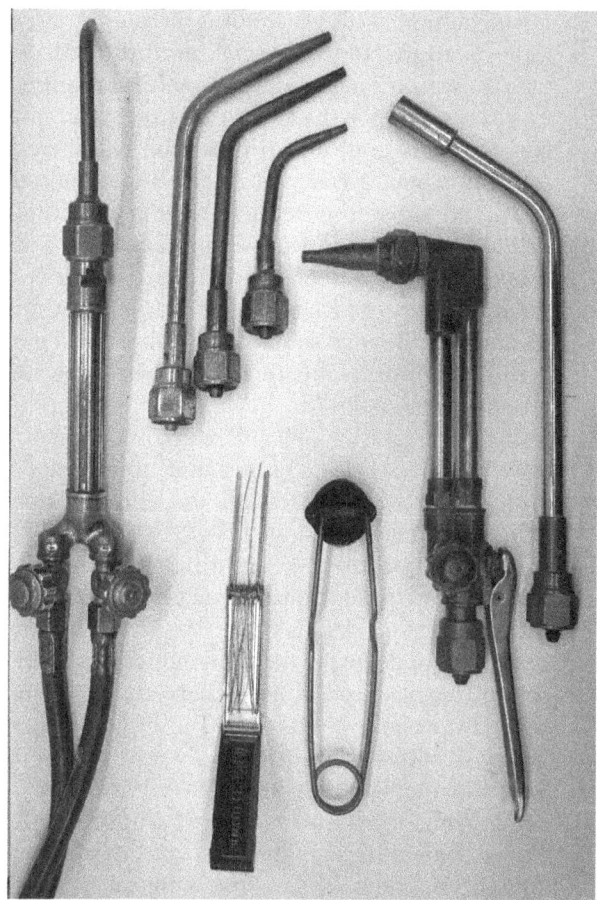

Figure 8.21b The components of an OAF torch set: On the left are the mixing handle and welding tips; on the right are the cutting head and rosebud. Also shown is a set of tip drills and a striker.

as it will certainly make an existing fire burn far faster or help a smolder become a flame. Gas torches can also be used to heat material for bending and shaping or for cutting. These processes are discussed later in this chapter.
- General considerations—While OAF welding isn't a popular method, it is an excellent way to learn to control a weld pool and is versatile enough that any shop working with steel should consider purchasing one.
  ○ Advantages—An oxy-acetylene torch will weld steel with or without filler, depending on joint type and need, much like a TIG welder. It is also great for welding bronze, though this would be a rare need in entertainment outside of repairing a prop. OAF requires no electricity, works well outdoors, is quiet and can be done at a long distance from the supply. OAF also produces far less UV than arc welding, but will still damage the weldors eyes if a proper shade glass is not used.

- Disadvantages—OAF welding creates a very large heat-affected zone, making it difficult to prevent warping in thin metal. OAF also requires more coordination than either MIG or stick, as it is a two-handed process. In addition, numbered torch tips need to be matched to the required heat, and those tips require regular cleaning. While OAF can also weld aluminum when flux is applied, it takes significant practice and is not practical for the production speed required by most shops. Beyond the normal compressed gas cylinder concerns, acetylene requires special attention (see below).
- Other considerations—Tips are not interchangeable between brands, and some brands have multiple series of torches that use different tips. When buying additional or replacement tips, care should be taken to ensure a match. Third-party tips are available for some torch styles, but the author considers it cheap insurance to buy extra tips made by the torch manufacturer. OAF sets are usually used with a dedicated cart, essentially a very large hand-truck. These can be very heavy to move when large cylinders are used. Some smaller sets may fit in a tote, but use very small cylinders and would only be appropriate for occasional use.
- Safety particulars—While all welding creates significant heat and sparks, OAF welding has a few other concerns.
  - Foremost, OAF is the only welding process with a flame that does not cease to make heat when pulled away like an arc would (e.g. if you drop the torch, it may not go out). Welding with a flame makes it quite easy to start incidental fires, so the welding area should be exceptionally clear of debris.
  - The torch should be inspected before use. O-rings on torch tips should be checked each time one is connected. A cracked O-ring could easily lead to a dangerous leak. The weldor should purge each line separately before start-up. The torch set should have flashback arrestors, either integrated into the mixing handle or as separate units. When starting up, the valve on the oxygen cylinder should be fully open; this sets the valve against an upper seat, preventing a leak. The acetylene cylinder stays at a much lower pressure, and thus, there is no need for a second seat; the valve should be open only one rotation for quicker response in an emergency.
  - The torch should always be ignited with a flint striker; a match places the weldor too close, and a butane lighter could overheat and explode in the user's hand.
  - When connecting replacement cylinders to regulators, they should always be leak tested. Most weldors use a mist of soapy water, but leak check fluid is available too. Anytime welding hoses are connected, the same procedure should be applied.
  - Acetylene is dissolved in acetone; the cylinders should never be laid on their side because the liquid acetone and acetylene gas may gather at the valve. Opening the valve would thus release the mixture into the regulator and hoses, damaging rubber components. If a weldor should encounter an acetylene cylinder that has been stored or transported on its side, the cylinder should be righted and left to settle; the safest choice is to leave the cylinder to settle overnight. Acetylene regulators should never be run above 15 psi; the carbon and hydrogen components may dissociate, creating an extreme hazard.
- Torch setup—Gas welding requires a few preparatory steps to ensure the torch will be matched to the welding requirements. Industrial-size acetylene cylinders (60 CuF+) will use either CGA510 (internal threads, shared with LP) or CGA300 (external threads) fittings.
  - Tips for welding are numbered to define the orifice diameter. Generally numbered 00–15, corresponding orifice diameter will vary somewhat by manufacturer. The most useful sizes for entertainment shops are typically 0–5; in most cases these will weld from .050″–1/4″ steel. Heating tips, often called "rosebuds" are also sized but do not use a consistently numbered system. For most shops, a "medium duty" heating tip will be sufficient. Most manufacturers offer at least two versions; some as many as six sizes. Cutting heads may also have interchangeable tips with between two and eight heating orifices; higher counts are required for thicker steels. For most shops, 4–6 orifice tips will be sufficiently versatile.
  - Regulator settings are fairly straightforward: for most shops, an equal pressure setting at about 6 psi for both oxygen and acetylene will work well for welding; the weldor may adjust up or down depending on need. When the welding is completed, the cylinder valves should be closed, the regulator screws backed off to zero and the hoses bled.
- Welding—Torch welding is fairly simple; the flame is used to melt the base material, and the filler is added to complete the weld. Torch distance is not as critical as it is for TIG.
  - Before welding, the torch tip should always be cleaned. The orifice should be reamed with the appropriate drill size, then the surface of the tip abraded to remove any buildup. A quick blast

with shop air can be used to push any detritus out of the tip. Many weldors will opt to further clean the tip with a dab of denatured alcohol.
- To light the torch, the acetylene should be turned on very slightly at the mixing handle. If the gas flow can be heard at arm's length, there is too much flow. Use a striker to ignite the acetylene, increase the flow until the carbon nearly disappears, then slowly add the oxygen. If the acetylene flame jumps from the tip, the gas flow is too high, and oxygen should not be added until the flow is reduced. There are three types of flame that may be produced with an OAF torch: oxidizing, neutral and carburizing. For welding a neutral flame is used. An oxidizing flame contains more oxygen than the acetylene can burn; conversely, a carborizing flame is short on oxygen. Either condition can create porous, brittle welds.

Oxy-Acetylene Flame Types

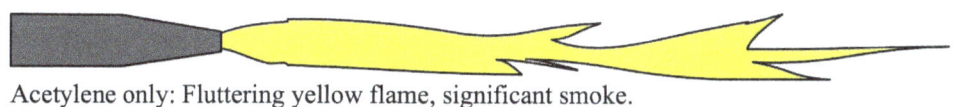

Acetylene only: Fluttering yellow flame, significant smoke.

Carborizing flame: Fluttering outer flame (smoke has subsided) changing to blue. Formation of mixing flames: outer mixed (middle of diagram) is still fluttering yellow, and the inner flame is beginning to form and changing to blueish–white.

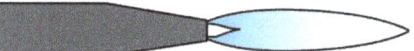

Neutral flame: Outer flame has settled to a steady shape and is light blue; middle and inner cones of mixed gas have just merged into a single nearly white cone. Should have a fairly quite medium pitch like a dull wind.

Oxidizing flame: Outer flame has reduced significantly and inner cone has become narrow and shifted back to blue coloring. Pitch is raised to whistling or hissing sound.

Figure 8.22 This diagram illustrates oxy-acetylene flame types. One note about oxidizing flames: they tend to whistle helping, identify the condition.

- Making the weld can be done forehand or backhand, like many other processes. For fusion welding, a backhand motion can help push the pool back against the chilled weld. When welding thick steel, a forehand setup will help preheat the area ahead of the weld, improving flow. With thin sections a backhand motion may be required to prevent burn-through. Heat control with OAF is achieved both by changing the distance between the flame and the material and by controlling where the flame is pointed. Like TIG, an initial pool should be established before dipping the filler rod; the weld pool should melt the rod. Having the rod directly in the flame tends to melt the rod before the pool is flowing, making a flaky weld that sits on top of the materials, not bonding them. The angles for the torch and filler rod are similar to the TIG torch.
- Popping may occur when the tip is too hot because the gas ignites inside the torch tip. This is most often caused by the tip being held too close to the weld pool or using a tip that is too small for the task. These small explosions are not only disconcerting to the weldor (and the crew) but cause molten metal to be spattered onto the tip and work area. Doing so too many times will require the torch to be shut down and the tip cleaned. The metal should be able to be heated to welding temperature from about 3/8"–1" distance, depending on thickness. If the metal does not make it to welding temperature in about 10 seconds at an appropriate distance, odds are either the flame needs to be hotter or the tip is too small for the metal thickness.

○ A gas saver is a handy device for working with an OAF torch. It is a torch rest connected to a valve that shuts off the gases with the weight of the torch. When the torch is lifted, gas flow is reestablished and a pilot flame easily relights the torch. It needs to be plumbed between the cylinders and the torch, with sufficient hose length for the gas saver to be safely away from the cylinders and enough hose to reach as far as needed with the torch. It is best used with welding and cutting tips only.

Figure 8.23 A gas saver on a custom base with the torch at rest. The weight of the torch hung from the arm closes the valve. The copper tube for the pilot flame is just behind the torch tip. The forged pedal at the bottom of the stand can raise the torch to light it before the user lifts the torch from the hanger.

- Filler metals—For mild steel and stainless steel, filler metals can be shared between TIG welding and OAF welding. Like TIG, the filler rod should be of a diameter near the thickness of the welded material.

RESISTANCE

Also called spot welding, these welders use the relatively low conductivity of steel (compared to copper) to heat the metal to its melting point and join the pieces using pressure. Welders for bandsaw blades are one example of a resistance welder, but most often tong-type welders are what are associated with "spot" welding.
- General considerations—While most projects will be better served by other methods, small projects that use thin steel can be well served by spot welding.
  ○ Advantages to spot welding include speed, a very small heat-affected area and no protruding weld. Tong-type welders work very well on thin sheets of steel and stainless steel, up to about 1/8" to 3/16" total thickness.
  ○ Disadvantages to spot welding with a tong-style machine include the types of joints that can be made (lap and flange), a limited reach (up to about 18" with auxiliary tips) and the inability to weld aluminum. The tong tips and the steel surface need to be very clean, and most machines have a fairly limited duty cycle, commonly 25%–50% depending on input voltage.
  ○ The user should be aware that spot welding creates a comparably weak joint along a seam than other processes. In the entertainment world, spot welding is best applied to smaller, decorative items.
- Welding—Making a weld with a tong-type welder is very simple. The tongs are clamped onto the material to be welded, and on most units, a lever type momentary switch is held until the weld is made (tongs should compress slightly). Most units can operate for a maximum of about 30 seconds per weld.

Figure 8.24 A 120-volt resistance spot welder with 6" tongs.

STICK (SMAW)

While stick welding, also known as Shielded Metal Arc Welding, has fallen out of favor for most shops, there are still some reasons to consider a stick welder.
- General considerations—These are low-cost machines that can often be found for even less money when purchased used. Brand name machines can last decades, requiring little to no maintenance.
  - Advantages to stick welding include the ability to work many feet (50+ ft) from the power supply with sufficient gauge cable, compatibility with a wide array of filler metals, no compressed gas is required, and there are no issues working outdoors. Stick welding is quite good for steel (especially thick sections) and cast iron. While these machines can also weld aluminum and stainless steel, the process is not practical for most shops' needs in entertainment. Another advantage of stick welding is the availability of hard-facing electrodes. This is a very good way to add a highly wear or impact-resistant surface to steel.
  - Disadvantages include significant smoke and fume generation; enough that a respirator is recommended even with dilution ventilation or a smog hog. The filler rods have a fairly short life (i.e. they get used up quickly), which requires clearing slag before welding can resume each time the electrode is replaced. As well, there is a good bit of waste since the last 1"–1 1/2" cannot be used.
  - A range of machine types makes it quite easy for a shop to find a "just right" fit.
    - Older AC-only welders may be collecting dust in a shop corner, but are still perfectly usable machines if the weldor is ok with the somewhat limited choices of compatible electrode.
    - Newer DC multi-process, AC/DC stick only or AC/DC stick/TIG machines open up the possibilities for use with a wider variety of electrodes. Many larger shops opt to purchase an AC/DC machine that will primarily be used for TIG, but offers the ability to stick weld when needed. Inverter-based machines are compact and can weigh under 15 lb while still supplying a 200-A output. Many of these are also set up to be DC TIG sources.
    - Gas engine welders offer an extra type of flexibility for on-site installation. While the reader may be familiar with truck/trailer-mounted units, smaller portable units are available. Most of these machines also provide auxiliary power for tools and thus remove the need for a

Figure 8.25a A dial-type AC or DC stick welder. This style welder allows for precise amperage settings and works with a variety of materials.

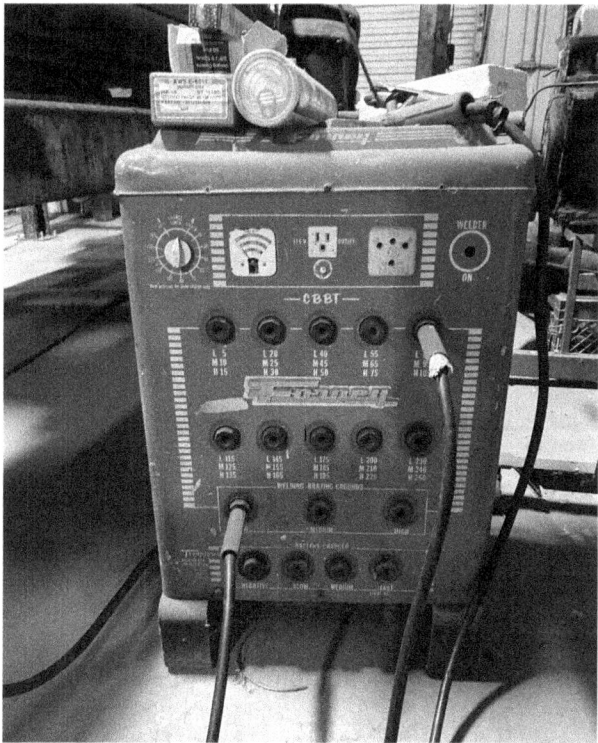

Figure 8.25b A patch panel type AC welder. Though not as precise when choosing amperage, these machines are still quite serviceable.

separate generator. Miller Electric now offers a hybrid plugin/gas engine portable unit, but it is for stick welding only. Some large engine driver units also have an integrated high-CFM air compressor. All engine-driven units have a DC output.
  - Safety considerations that differ from other processes are minimal. When using electrodes 3/16″–1/4″ in diameter (unlikely in entertainment shops), the welding helmet needs a shade 12 filter. Gloves should be heavily insulated, and the weldor must remember that the electrode is live at all times unless the machine is shut off.
- Current mode—Choosing between DCEN, DCEP and AC will depend on filler metal required, material thickness and material type, as well as the weldor's preference with some filler rods. Machines that offer a dig feature are quite helpful when using the low amperage for a given electrode; dig boosts the amperage when a voltage drop is sensed. This makes for easier starts and less tendency to stick the electrode.
- Starting—Striking the arc is usually done via two methods: gently tapping the electrode while vertical or by scratch starting, which involves making a small check-mark motion, or a slight drag and lift.
- Filler metals (sticks)—Electrodes for stick welding use a four-digit code. The first two digits indicate tensile strength in ksi, the third digit indicates weld position (1—all positions, 2—horizontal and flat, 3—flat only), and the fourth indicates the alloy and flux properties.
  - Steel welding has four commonly used electrodes. "*" denotes best performance.
    - 6011 (DCEP, AC) deep penetration with easily removed slag, tolerates poorly prepared steel (grease, dirt, paint).
    - 6013 (DCEN*, DCEP, AC) shallow penetration with slightly tougher slag, great for thin sections.
    - 7014 (DCEN*, DCEP, AC) great all-around rod, high strength, medium penetration, easy to remove slag.
    - 7018 (DCEP*, AC) low hydrogen rod particularly popular for its shallow penetration with a high deposition rate for fast travel. The drawback to 7018 is that the hygroscopic nature of the flux makes it difficult to properly store. If used for any project that must meet code, 7018 has a 4-hour exposure ceiling. They can be re-dried in a rod oven.

Figure 8.26 An example of a cast iron finial stick welded to 1/2″ steel rod.

  - Cast iron is typically welded using nickel-core or high-nickel (85%+) electrodes for machinability. These may be labeled as "soft". Nickel electrodes can be used to weld iron to iron or iron to steel. There are non-machinable electrodes for cast iron with a lower nickel content.
  - Stainless steel and aluminum can be stick-welded, but it is far less precise than using MIG or TIG. Most shops will consider it impractical.
- Techniques—Specific alloys may have unique properties that require slight adjustments to the welding process.
  - Steel is the primary metal welded with SMAW in industrial settings. The widest variety of electrodes available are for welding steel alloys. While stick welding has largely been superseded by MIG for most of the thinner materials used on entertainment fabrication, it may be the process of choice when installing units in new construction where power may not be available and/or a compressed gas bottle is impractical. With practice, even 16-ga steel can be welded quite easily. Welding with SMAW will require practice, but some tips can help.
    - The arc should be about the same length as the electrode diameter. Thin materials may be

served by "whipping". This is a technique used to control heat; the electrode is moved using a rise and fall motion because a momentary long arc reduces heat in the weld slightly. The motion is similar to the movement made with the filler rod when TIG welding.
- Sections less than 3/16″ thick usually do not need to be beveled, though a slight open root or beveling may be preferred for butt welds. Fillet welds and corner fills may be well served by a weave bead.
- When making a horizontal weld across a vertical surface, pointing the rod upward by 5°–10° helps prevent drift and undercutting. The same technique can serve overhead welds, though the angle will need to be increased to as much as 45°.
- Controlling the weight of the cable so that it does not pull on the electrode holder can make welding much easier. Some weldors lay the cable across a leg when seated or over a shoulder when welding out of position. At a welding table, the cable may be laid across an unused area, but should be protected from sparks and hot slag.
  ○ Cast iron can be stick-welded quite well. Many electrodes are DCEP only, which keeps the workpiece cooler, but AC works well with some electrodes. Grey iron is used for most decorative iron and for machined castings such as those for tool and machine bases. Malleable iron is a more durable alloyed iron that can be welded, but requires more care in regard to temperature. It is unlikely to be found in most castings needing repair in an entertainment shop.
    - The area surrounding the break or seam to be welded should be ground clean. Cast iron has surface impurities from the molding process that need to be cleaned away to prevent inclusions in the weld. If the weld is on a part being repaired, any paint or other coating should be removed.
    - The casting should be preheated to 500°–800° if the entire casting can be heated. Castings too large to heat should be stitch-welded, peened (gentle hammering of the weld to relieve stress) and allowed to cool to room temperature before any further welding. Insulating the casting after welding with kaowool or rockwool slows cooling and helps prevent cracking.
    - Unless the section is very thin, the iron should be grooved at a 60° angle (on both faces if thicker than 3/8″) to a depth of about 1/2 the section.
    - When repairing a crack, both ends should be drilled to about 1/8″ diameter to prevent the crack from traveling during the welding process. The weld should be done from about 1/3 of the way in to the crack, traveling back to the drilled hole, then repeated at the opposite end. The center part may require split travel as well, depending on the length. No single weld pass should exceed 1″–1 1/2″. The casting should be peened and allowed to cool between each welding pass.

OTHER PROCESSES

A number of other processes for shaping metal are more related to welding than to other machines used in metal fabrication. The oxy-acetylene torch, for example, is quite versatile, being able to heat and cut in addition to welding. The techniques that follow share the same safety requirements as the welding processes already discussed.

PLASMA CUTTING

Plasma cutting is one of "go-to" technologies for almost any shop that does significant fabrication work using steel sheet and plate. The process is also suited to coping pipe when a hole saw type jig is insufficient. Plasma cutters use a high-voltage arc to ionize a stream of gas (usually compressed air), which then melts and vaporizes the metal being cut. Plasma cutting is compatible with almost all electrically conductive metals. While they are fairly expensive, value is found in speed and versatility. An example of a plasma cutter in use can be seen in Figure 11.18b.
- General considerations—Like other welding products, low-cost machines may work for some period of time, but name brand machines will offer better support and higher-quality consumables that last longer.
  ○ Advantages of plasma cutting include fast, fairly clean cuts in most metals with a very small heat-affected zone. On some metals, a slight amount of slag will need to be cleaned off. New inverter-based machines are very compact while maintaining capability. The machine used in the scene shop at the University of Memphis will cleanly cut 1/2″ steel and weighs 21 lb. Plasma cutters are capable of piercing cuts; generally about 50%–75% the total cutting capacity.
  ○ Disadvantages to plasma cutting start with the cost of the machine and the consumables. Machines require VERY clean compressed air;

most users add a micron filter at or near the machine. Piercing can throw a big "splash" of molten metal until the arc completes the cut. While plasma cutters will cut aluminum, the cleanest cuts are achieved when using compressed gas on CNC machines. High amperage cutting (60 A+) may require standoff only cutting (no drag shield).
- Other considerations include differing eye protection: flat work with a drag shield can be done via shade 5, but high amperage use without a drag shield requires a shade 8 or 9. Plasma cutting will cut into/through a metal table if care is not taken to raise the intended material well above the table. CNC machines use a grid of thin strips set on edge for this reason. The same method can be used for manual cutting if the cut area is large enough to require it. Spacers outside of the cutting area are usually sufficient. Most manufacturers base the cut capacity on about 10″ per minute travel speed. When choosing a plasma cutter, the duty cycle should be similar to choosing a welder: 60% duty cycle at or a little thicker than the most often cut material. The machine should also continue gas flow (air) after the cut is made. This helps preserve the life of the consumables.
- Cutting—Using the plasma cutter is a relatively straightforward task. For the most part, the tip is either held above the materials or the drag shield is placed on the edge of the material, and the trigger is pulled, starting the cut.
  - A good machine will have a high frequency touch-less start. Some low-cost machines require contact with material to start the arc and should be avoided for anything beyond hobby use. When making a cut, a simple rule-of-thumb applies: travel speed should be as fast as possible and as slow as necessary. This may seem like a contradiction, but with practice, it will make sense. Straight line cuts allow faster travel than complex shapes. Slower travel works better with a somewhat lower amperage.
  - Piercing should usually be done at a height 1.5–2 times the recommended cut height for thick material (the arc may need to be started at cutting height, then raised). Thin sheets can be pierced while holding the torch at a slight angle away from the operator and toward the waste material.
  - Pulling the torch is usually easier than pushing; this is especially true when using a drag shield. Adding a simple rolling guide-wheel kit or a circle cutting guide can smooth out operation when using a stand-off tip.
  - Templates can be used to cut complex shapes. Templates should be cut undersized to match the offset of the drag shield. Many users make templates from MDF or similar material. While they will be charred by the arc, they are often good for many uses. Metal templates are conductive and can interfere with the arc.
- Steel—Steel is by far the easiest material to plasma cut. It cuts cleanly with well-filtered compressed air.
  - A drag shield is commonly used unless the steel is very thick and requires very high amperage. Most shops will never cut steel thick enough to require this, as it has a fairly low amp requirement per thickness.
  - Steel makes significant sparks while cutting that travel farther and faster than when using OAF, so the operator should be aware. If the operator travels too fast or jumps ahead, cutting will likely become partial and shower the user with molten dross.
  - While the cuts are fairly clean, there will be adhered dross on the back side of the cut. Most of this can often be removed with a chipping hammer, leaving only a slight burr to be ground away. The edges may have a bit of a ripple and also need to be ground smooth.
- Stainless steel—While most shops won't work with a great amount of stainless steel, thin stainless steel sheet is quite useful for many projects. As well, shops may find the need to modify existing stainless steel items like sinks and furniture for custom use. Thin stainless steel (.188″ and under) can be cut quite well with compressed air, but the edges will oxidize. If this is problematic, some single-gas machines (usually operated on shop air) can run pure nitrogen or F5 (5% hydrogen/95% nitrogen) for low to no oxidation cuts; pure nitrogen will create more dross than F5.
- Aluminum—Regular cutting of aluminum with plasma will not be practical for most shops. Cutting with shop air leaves a rough, oxidized edge that must be removed before welding. For occasional use, cutting oversize will allow grinding or milling to the finished size. Thin aluminum sheet tends to warp as well. To cleanly cut aluminum, a multi-gas plasma cutter must be used; these are designed to be used with CNC machines to cut very thick sections. Most shops will opt to either hand-cut the aluminum or use a CNC router, even if that means outsourcing.

BRAZING AND SOLDERING

Many fabricators may not be familiar with brazing but it is a very useful technique. Soldering is quite

common, and many in the industry have soldered at least with an electric iron, and some with a portable LP torch. The difference between the two is simply temperature; brazing uses filler metals with a melting point that exceeds 840°F (450°C), while solders melt below 840°F. Both can create very strong joints, for example the carbide teeth on a saw blade are brazed to the plate. While there are a variety of brazing methods used industrially, such as furnace brazing and dip brazing, only two methods are easily employed in entertainment shops: torch and TIG brazing.
- General considerations—While neither process will be a common technique used in entertainment shops, having the capability and knowledge expands the types of projects the shop can complete.
  ○ The advantages to brazing and soldering are the ability to join a wide variety of metals including dissimilar metals and even some ceramics. Both leave little to no raised bead to be ground flat, have a lower heat impact on the materials and can be a very good way to join dissimilar thicknesses. Most brazing alloys hold up to vibration very well; this is why many industrial applications use brazing over welding. Solder is light duty compared to brazing, but is very low cost and effective for non-structural applications. Both processes can be quite fast as well. Aluminum is the main alloy that likely won't be included; while it can be soldered, it is hard to do and not practical for most projects.
  ○ The disadvantages to these are that for many applications, neither provides the structural bond required for large, complex assemblies like scenery. Both can work quite well for sculptures, furniture or repairs. Brazing and soldering often require flux which will need to be cleaned off once the joint is complete. Brazing may anneal some metals, losing stiffness.
  ○ Metals likely to be brazed or soldered in the industry include mild steel, cast iron, copper, brass and stainless steel. Flux, when used, provides final cleaning of the material surface, prevents oxidation during heating and assists the flow of the filler metal. Copper is the only alloy likely to be brazed without flux unless a TIG welder is used.
  ○ Filler rods for brazing may be flux-coated or uncoated depending on the type of filler and the application.
    ▪ Bronze is available plain and flux-coated. For OAF brazing of steel, cast iron and stainless steel, coated rod is used. For nickel and copper plain rod and paste flux may be used. Bronze is a very low-cost brazing filler.
    ▪ Phos-copper is the short name for brazing alloys that contain phosphorus, copper and often some percentage of silver. These rods are uncoated and are used to braze copper to copper or brass and other dissimilar metals. Alloys with a higher percentage of phosphorus are more ductile and flow more easily. The addition of silver helps with gap filling for poorly fit joints. The advantage to phos-copper filler is the color match to brass and copper as well as better adhesion to these materials. The downside is high cost.
    ▪ High silver brazing rods are a type of phos-copper with 30% or more silver content. These are often available flux-coated and are excellent for brazing dissimilar metals and stainless steel.
    ▪ Nickel silver and other high nickel brazing alloys still contain some copper and often zinc. These have some of the highest durability applications and are used to join tungsten carbide to steel and for tooling repair. These alloys are also excellent for joining other dissimilar metals.
    ▪ Aluminum brazing rod is used with paste flux to join aluminum to aluminum, copper or brass. Unless there is a very specialized need, most shops will join aluminum using another method.
- Torch brazing (OAF)—For most shops, the oxy-acetylene torch will be the tool of choice for brazing. The same tips used for welding are used for brazing, though the user may opt to use a much smaller tip for brazing per thickness.
  ○ Technique may require a little practice, but brazing is much easier to pick up than OAF welding.
    ▪ When paste flux is used, the metal must be cleaned of any oxidation first and for steel any residual oil needs to be removed as well (carbon formed from burned oil can effect bonding).
    ▪ The joint needs a tiny bit of space for the filler to run into because brazing relies on capillary action. The space should not be such that the filler runs through. While brazed joints in industry can get very complex, most brazing for scenic and prop use will be quite simple and won't require spacing fixtures. End-to-end butt joints are the only configuration that should not be brazed because there is not enough surface area available. All brazed joints can benefit from a bit of surface texture, such as from abrasive blasting or sanding.
    ▪ One thing to be aware of is that a brazed joint may be undone by simply reheating. This can make recovery of parts easier, but can also

mean isolating the heated zone if multiple connections are to be made close together.
- To make the joint, heat the base materials to above the melting point of the filler metal but below the base material's melting point; allow the heat in the base material to melt the filler. If paste flux is used, heat the area indirectly. Flux-coated rods should not be used directly in the flame. This melts away the flux before it can enter the joint making flow more difficult, or the filler may simply sit on top. The base material should never melt.

Figure 8.27 A torch braze on scraps of 1″ square tube with fluxed bronze filler and a braze on scrap copper using phos-copper filler.

- TIG brazing—Using a TIG machine to braze is much like using one to weld. The main difference is temperature and filler metal. When brazing with TIG, a slightly longer stick out of the electrode may be used (approx. 1/2″) but the arc length should remain short. An acute grind of the tungsten will help widen the heating zone, reducing the likelihood of melting the base material.
  ○ Advantages include better heat control than OAF, especially with a pulsed TIG machine, ability to bond zinc plated and galvanized steel when care is taken and bronze rod is used because the melting point of bronze is much lower than zinc.
  ○ Disadvantages include the complexity of coordinating heat, torch movement and filler metal placement and the need for shielding gas and torch consumables.
  ○ Technique is more complex than using an OAF torch, but will be familiar to anyone with TIG welding experience. TIG brazing is a great application for learning to use the pulse function on a TIG machine if it is available. This helps control heat (avoids melting the base material) and helps the weldor build an attractive stacked braze when a very slow pulse rate is set. TIG brazing is not compatible with aluminum; thus, most operations will be done with DCEN. AC can be used and may help clear oxidation on some alloys. Once the heated zone is established, there is no need to dab filler; it can be laid along the seam and continually pushed into the pool. The base material needs to be very clean.
  ○ Filler rods should be uncoated to prevent contamination of the electrode, but otherwise the same alloys can be shared between OAF and TIG brazing. Most materials will require the use of a paste flux compatible with the chosen filler alloy.

Figure 8.28 Examples of TIG brazing using phos-copper filler. On the left copper to steel and on the right steel to steel.

- Soldering—When done with a hand-held LP or MAPP gas torch, the process of soldering is very similar to brazing. In most cases paste flux will be used to help the solder wick into the joint. Solder joints can be tighter than brazed joints.
  ○ Technique mimics brazing; the material is heated and the solder applied to the hot metal. The material needs to be free of oxidation. For copper, this is usually done with emery cloth, but a non-woven abrasive wheel or stainless steel wire brush may work as well.

- Solders may be made from various soft metal alloys. This allows them to be compatible with varying base metals and types of work.
  - Lead-free solders should be used where possible. Though they have a slightly higher melting point, they lack the dangers of working with lead. A variety of lead free alloys are available for most applications.
    - Electronics solders consist of tin and copper; tin, silver and copper; or tin, copper and nickel. These are usually flux-cored and require no additional flux.
    - Plumbing solders are the most likely lead-free types to be encountered in the entertainment shop, even if the final product will not be used to carry water. These solders are best suited to joining copper tubing and sheet and thus work extremely well for sculptural work. These are alloys of tin and copper; tin and antimony; or tin, antimony, copper and nickel or silver. They are quite strong and flow well when paste flux is used.
  - Leaded solder is almost always a blend of tin and lead. The percentage of each varies, with higher lead content comes lower melting point and better flow. These are commonly used for electrical connections via electric iron and should never be used for water supply. Care should be taken in handling and using leaded solder. It should only be used with strong ventilation that will pull fumes away from the user and should be handled with disposable gloves when possible.

OAF CUTTING

Most shops will likely only use an oxy-acetylene cutting torch to take previously welded units apart for recycling. While an OAF torch can be fairly accurate, doing so takes a very steady hand and the cut piece will require significant cleanup. Regardless, OAF cutting is still a useful tool and skill. It may be the only way to remove a corroded or cross-threaded bolt, for example. For most shops, the cutting head and tips included with a medium duty torch set will be fine. If more than one cutting tip is included, the user should be aware that the number of heating orifices determines kerf and max thickness.

- Advantages—Most shops likely have an OAF set that includes a cutting torch. Even if the shop does not have an OAF set, the buy-in is far lower than the cost of a plasma cutter and the torch is much more versatile. OAF cutting has a low operation cost as there are no consumables except the gas.
- Disadvantages—A few caveats to OAF cutting include poor cut quality compared to plasma (practice will help), only compatible with steel alloys and creating a large heat-affected zone (which can lead to distortion). As well, even the best cut will leave some dross on material and a lot on the welding floor.
- Torch set-up—Gas pressures for cutting are different than for welding and heating. Because additional oxygen will be used to blast the molten metal out of the cutting area, the oxygen pressure needs to be dialed up. For a medium duty torch, that will be 10–20 psi, while the acetylene will remain between about 4–6 psi. As well, while setting the neutral flame, depress the cutting lever valve to see how it effects the flame. Adjust as needed for the flame to remain neutral with the cutting gas included.
- Cutting—Using an OAF torch to cut is fairly simple. Using a neutral flame, hold the torch just above the material to be cut (about 3/8″) until a molten pool is formed, then use the lever to inject extra oxygen to clear the pool. With practice, the torch can be used for continuous cutting by tilting the head so that the flame heats ahead of the cut. A slight tilt toward the waste side of the cut also helps with clean up. If a cut shows excessive amounts of slag

Figure 8.29 An example of soldered copper on the left showing the contrast between the solder and the copper with a sample of copper brazed with phos-copper filler which is much closer to the copper color.

on the back side, it typically indicates the metal is being overheated; this requires either an increased travel speed or reducing the heating flame (which may require a smaller cutting tip). When piercing, ensure the metal is fully molten before adding the cutting jet flow. When cutting thin sheet metal, tilting the torch toward the waste side of the cut at a fairly acute angle (30°+) will help prevent overheating and distortion.

- Another trick when one cannot start a cut on the material edge is to drill a lead-in hole slightly away from the final cut, much like making an interior cut with a jig saw.
- Different tips will be needed for different fuels. Acetylene cutting tips are flat; propane/MAPP gas tips are concave. As well, cutting tips need to be cleaned more often than welding tips because they inherently make slag.

Figure 8.30 Sample cuts of 16-ga sheet (top) cut at a steep angle (left end) to make a clean cut and vertically (right) showing how the slag refills the kerf. Below is a sample of 1/4" plate cut with the torch near vertical while making a slight shark-fin cutting pattern for minimum slag.

OAF HEATING

Another use for an oxy-acetylene torch is for heating materials to be shaped. While very small items may be able to be heat-treated, it is rather impractical for a shop. Both welding tips and heating tips (rosebuds) may be used.

- Advantages—As mentioned in previous sections, many shops already have and oxy-acetylene set up. These are a versatile means to heat a variety of alloys for shaping (or preheating for a weld) and they are cost effective, especially when with a gas saver is used (these can feel quite aggressive with a rosebud). The only other welder that can be used for heating is a TIG welder, but it is only capable of heating a small area.
- Disadvantages—Heating tips (rosebuds) need to be matched to the flow capability of the regulators, so most users will stay with the heating tip provided in a torch set. These tips can also be quite intimidating as they create a huge flame and project heat out a great distance compared to welding tips.
- Techniques—Each type of metal will have unique characteristics to address when heated for shaping. Steel is the easiest metal to work with because the color changes are quite obvious as heat rises. Other metals may show minimal to no color change. Too much heat will create a porous, scaled surface as well. As a rule of thumb, use which ever welding tip heats the piece of steel to cherry red in about 1 minute. Faster heating tends to burn the surface (or melt it away) and slower heating simply wastes fuel. Other metals may require a Tempil stick to identify proper heating.
  - Welding tips work very well for heating a small area making tight radius bends in solid shapes. Care should be taken to heat enough area to prevent cracking on the stretched face of the bend. These can also be used to heat the end of a pin or rivet for peening or heating a small area in sheet metal for raising. Welding tips work well for annealing soft metals as well. The cutting tip can also be used for heating when a welding tip is not providing enough heat and a rosebud is too much.
  - Heating tips will likely only be used with steel and can be used for heating rivets, shaping such as forging (within reason) and bending wide or thick pieces. Wide pieces require the torch to be moved consistently over the area to avoid creating stresses when bending.
  - Annealing soft metals like copper and aluminum can be done with an OAF torch, making them

much easier to shape. Both can be annealed by covering the surface with carbon (use a 100% acetylene flame), then heating the area evenly until the carbon burns off (aluminum should be heated from the opposite side of the carbon). Cleaning the oxidation from aluminum prior to laying down the carbon also helps lower the chance of a blowout.

RESOURCES

- *Welding Essentials* (second edition) — This volume is an excellent resource for in depth information for all welding processes including soldering and brazing. It is formulated as a question and answer training guide. Though many of the processes will not be applicable to the entertainment industry, the information regarding common welding techniques, joint preparation and types and other common aspects of welding that are applicable to entertainment fabrication are discussed in depth.
  - ISBN 978-0831133016 William L. Galvery Jr and Frank Marlow, Industrial Press, Inc.
- *Welder's Handbook* — Though the author comes from an aircraft building back ground, the information included in this book is not jargon filled technical speak. It is a well rounded guide to all of the common welding processes and the equipment required for each. Many of the examples are aircraft or automotive related, but the techniques can easily be transferred to the types of fabrication done in the entertainment industry.
  - ISBN 978-1557885135 Richard Finch, HP books.
- Miller Electric — Miller is a premier manufacturer of welding equipment. The companies website offers a plethora of free articles with tip and tricks to improve welding skills as well as articles explaining the technology options available.
  - www.millerwelds.com
  - www.millerwelds.com/resources/article-library/
- National Fire Protection Agency (NFPA) — The NFPA is a robust resource for fire and life safety info. One key document that all welding shops should review is the "Hot Work Fact Sheet".
  - www.nfpa.org
- Occupational Safety and Health Administration (OSHA) — OSHA covers every area of work place safety, but section 1910.252 covers welding, cutting and brazing. It is a worthwhile read for anyone working in a welding shop.
  - www.osha.gov

Chapter 9

Fastening

This chapter is intended to introduce the reader to an array of fasteners used to attach non-metallic products to metal members, as well as common adhesives that may be used for fastening with or in place of fasteners. How a fastener is made, its shape, strength, and exposure all determine longevity and appropriate use. Similarly, every formulation of adhesive has properties that the user should be aware of before applying to a project. Choosing a fastener can be as simple as what looks the most appropriate on the finished product, to as complex as needing an engineer to sign off on the fastening choices used in a structure. This text is intended only to introduce the reader to the types of fasteners available and the features that aid in adopting them for use. No structural data is provided, and in any case where life safety is a concern, an appropriately trained person should be making the application decisions.

THREADED FASTENERS

When using metal fasteners with metal members, alloy compatibility is important when the completed units will be in service for long periods or are permanent. Galvanic response charts are readily available, thus will not be repeated here. Many readers may know that aluminum and steel tend to be incompatible but may not be aware that zinc-plated steel and aluminum fasteners do not effect stainless steel, but the stainless member accelerates the corrosion of the fasteners, whereas using a stainless fastener on cast iron or mild steel can have the opposite effect; the fastener accelerates corrosion of the base metal. What follows is not an exhaustive list, nor a complete listing of all of the features and combinations that may be available. The intent is to introduce some of the criteria that would be considered when choosing each type of fastener and an overview of some of the less common variants that can be quite useful to an experienced fabricator.

- Cap screws—What most of us refer to as bolts and machine screws are in the broader category of cap screws, i.e. those with some sort of flared top that can be engaged by a tool. These are one of the most common and strongest attachment methods available. They are easy to use and offer a wide range of sizes and styles to fit almost any application. It is also helpful to be aware that they are available with right- and left-hand threads. Bolts are also graded into strength categories that are important to application. Their downside is that they are generally hard to hide and can loosen with vibration. For situations where vibration is an issue, locking nuts or chemical thread lockers are available. Threads may be rolled, i.e. pressed as part of the manufacturing, generally making the threads a larger diameter than the shank or may be cut into the bolt shank.
  - Grades refer to design values for strength. There are multiple grading standards for bolts; if the bolts are used for structural purposes, the buyer/user must know the grade standard to identify design values. Higher grades have cap markings on hex head bolts but lower grades may not, therefore the original packaging may be required to determine bolt strength. Some grades split tensile strength depending on bolt diameter. For example, grade 2 bolts may have a minimum tensile strength (MTS) of 60,000 psi or 74,000 psi depending on diameter, whereas all grade 8 bolts have an MTS of 150,000 psi. Users should refer to supplier catalogs or manufacturer specs for structural data.
    - Inch thread bolts vary by standard. SAE standard bolts have four unmarked grades

and six marked grades. All ASTM grades have a cap marking except A574.
- Metric thread bolts all have grade marks. SAE grades are 4.6–10.9, ASTM grades are 4.6–12.9, and ISO grades are 3.6–12.9.
○ Thread contact with steel components can be problematic. Bolts with cut threads are just slightly smaller at the thread area than at the shank and will allow a tiny bit of movement between components, causing wear on the bolt and possibly on the components. The best fit will always be at the unthreaded shank.
○ Spacers between objects and sleeves inside hollow components will avoid thread contact and/or prevent bending or collapse of hollow sections. Sleeves can be welded in place or slip-fit if the area is accessible.
○ Head shapes most often used in metal fabrication are hex, flanged hex, socket, and round.
- Hex head bolts are common and most users will be familiar with standard sizes be they metric or imperial. A few useful variants are worth mentioning: flanged head help distribute load and may be serrated making them "locking" and thus useful for high vibration, self-sealing bolts include an O-ring under the head, and 12-point style (not technically a hex head) are typically flanged and add a little extra security, requiring a matching wrench or socket.
- Other cap styles such as square, round, and oval (button) heads can be decorative or replace historic hardware. These are generally not available larger than 3/8″ diameter and all but square head are not graded.
- Socket head screws all have a round head and use an inserted driver (hex key, Philips, or slotted driver) and can be set flush to or below a surface of thick material with a counterboring bit. These may have fully or partially threaded shanks depending on length and various head types: standard (cylindrical), low profile, button, flanged, and flat (with a 90° countersink). Their relatives, shoulder bolts, have a smooth shank that is larger than the threaded portion; the shank is designed to be used as a pivot point. Both are well suited to items that need to have moving parts.
- Hand screws—These are sold in a variety of styles and all are meant to be hand tightened. Threaded stud knobs have various shaped plastic or knurled metal handles, thumb screws have a simple paddle-shaped top, while wing screws have protruding "ears" for more torque than a thumb screw. All are available in an assortment of diameters and lengths.

There are excellent for repertory scenery as they require no tools when combined with a fixed nut on one side of a joint. As well, they are regularly used to make adjustable fixtures for machinery.

Figure 9.1 The left columns shows the array of shapes that are available for hand-tightened knobs including pass-through and closed-end types. On the right is a similar assortment of hand screws.

- Set screws—These screws are not necessarily a fastener as the generally do not join two components, but they are used to keep components properly aligned or in place. Set screws are available in a variety of alloys and with a range of tip types, though not every alloy offers every tip style. Some offer nylon inserts making them self-locking. Most are hex socket, but square head and slotted set screws are available as well.
  ○ Cup-point screws dig in to the surface for secure hold. These are a good option for round surfaces. Some offer a knurled cup for extra hold.
  ○ Flat tip screws have less hold than cup-points but make little to no surface damage. They are best paired with a flat area for the tip to align to.

- Oval tip screws are designed to be used as guides, fit into either V or U-shaped grooves.
- Extended tip screws fit well in a square sided guide slots or can mate with a cup to prevent rotation.
- Cone point screws are best for soft materials but can also be used as adjustable pivot points.
- Soft tip screws can be used either on soft materials to prevent damage or as guides in grooved elements.
- Hollow set screws or jam set screws can be used to lock a set screw in place below the surface, much like double nutting.

• Studs—These are threaded fasteners that either have threads on both ends or some other means of affixing them in place. They are generally used to hold replaceable components.
- Press-in studs have a round flat head with a splined shoulder above the threads. The splines are pressed into a hole to permanently mount the stud. These do not require the thickness/depth that a threaded stud does.
- Thread-in studs are similar to a hanger bolt, but are strength graded. Most often found in machinery, their advantage is being able to be used for alignment during assembly because they are held fast by the base threads. Fully threaded studs are strength-graded versions of all-thread, but these may also be available hollow to be used as pass throughs.
- Glue-on and self-adhesive studs are for use with thin materials are used to mount light objects. These can be excellent for signage as glue-on studs can be adhered to a variety of surfaces like brick or block in addition to metal faces.
- Welded studs are similar to weld nuts, but with fewer variants. These are typically L-shaped or have a round mount with either top or bottom projections depending on mounting orientation (below or above material face, respectively).

• Nuts—Nuts are usually a required element when using bolts to connect units. A wide variety of types allows matching many scenarios. Many of the most useful nuts (except for hex) are not for structural use; they merely provide a convenience.
- Hex nuts are the most common but a few variants beyond the standard version are available. Heavy hex step up wall thickness for additional strength, jam nuts are thin and designed to be used in pairs for locking installs, panel nuts are thinner than jam nuts and are meant to be used to mount items to display panels, flange nuts have a smooth flared face to act like a washer during installation, and finally acorn (or cap) nuts cover the end threads keeping them safe from damage. For structural use, graded nuts that match bolt grade should be used.
- Locking nuts prevent loosening due to vibration and use various methods to create the "lock".
  - Nylon-locking nuts have a plastic ring with no threads to add friction but should not be reused in critical applications. These are available with and without a flange.
  - Deformed nuts have some portion (top or center) that is compressed to add friction and are reusable for a few cycles.
  - Flange lock nuts are hex nuts with a one-way serrated flange; the serrations dig in to the face of the material to hold it in place. When these nuts move in a reverse direction (removed), they will damage the surface.
  - Tooth washer lock nuts have a permanently attached lock washer for quick install. These hold much like a serrated flange without the risk of surface damage.
  - Castellated nuts have slots in the top and are meant to be paired with a cross-drilled bolt and are locked in place with a cotter pin. These are easy to install and remove and can be repeatedly reused. Cotter pins should not be reused.
  - Extreme vibration locking nuts use various methods to lock the nut including compressed inserts, deformed flexible tops, and even two-piece nuts that compress an inner flange. These types of locking nuts are often used for critical applications such as rides in themed entertainment.
- Special use nuts offer a variety of types that can solve unique challenges. Though some are quite expensive compared to simple hex nuts, in the entertainment field where projects sometimes morph or need to adjust to fit a new space, these can be worth the investment.
  - Split nuts rotate along their horizontal centerline (like a snatch block) and can be added to middle of threaded rod. When combined with a slotted or hooked mounting tab, parts can easily be added to an existing threaded rod without removing any existing components. They also save the time required to thread a nut onto very long rods where multiple items might be mounted.
  - Push-button nuts have a quick release allowing them to slide along threads. Like a split nut, these can be ideal for mounting objects along a very long threaded rod. Load ratings are much lower than a similar-sized hex nut, which will need to be accounted for.
  - 12-point nuts are usually flanged and typically found in machinery but can be used to

discourage disassembly and are less prone to rounding when a proper wrench is used. They are available in similar strengths to hex nuts.
- Tamper-resistant nuts all require a matching install/removal tool and may be cone shaped with slots, spanner style, or with an a-symmetrical edge. Often these are only used on 1 or 2 bolts where multiple bolts hold a unit in place because of their high cost.
- Square nuts may not be common but can still be useful. They are easier to use with an adjustable wrench and may require no wrench when installed with one side against a perpendicular surface.
- Wing nuts are the ubiquitous hand-tightened fastener. There are at least ten varieties of wing nut beyond the standard hardware store fair. These can be cast, flanged, extra wide, and low profile and even include nylon-locking. They are a convenient, low cost means of making reliable, quick connections.
- Slotted round nuts are a solution to setting a nut flush to the surface with minimal tolerance. These use a slotted screw driver to tighten but require precise bolt length to not impede the driver slot. The drawback for U.S. users is they are only available with metric threads to the authors knowledge.
- Push nuts are thin spring steel and have teeth to prevent the nut from backing off. While quick to install, they are not easy to remove and are often used to retain a bolt in a removable unit; they are not designed to hold loads.
o Threaded knobs and machine handles are not technically nuts but make great alternatives to wing nuts because they are more comfortable to use and are harder to lose. Examples in Figure 9.1.
o Weld nuts are separated out here from constrained nuts because they do not use a mechanical means of fixture. As well, there are many styles to choose from including hex, square, round base, narrow base, and offset. It is wise to weld these nuts with a sacrificial bolt in place to protect the threads. Many have projections to hold them slightly away from the surface for good weld penetration.
o Constrained nuts are those which use some device to hold them in place permanently or semi-permanently.
- Flag nuts have an attached metal strap (usually tapered) that is meant to press against a perpendicular surface for wrench-free tightening of a bolt.

- Clip-on nuts are made from spring steel and slip over thin sheet to align with an existing hole. They do have limited reach.
- Snap-in nuts are also known as cage nuts because they are a square nut fit into a sprung cage designed to snap into a square hole. These are quite useful to a shop that has an iron worker to repeatedly punch square holes, but difficult to employ otherwise.
- Adhesive mount nuts are for very thin sheet where a rivet nut will not grab, and a clip nut will not reach. They are not self-adhesive and are typically installed with epoxy.
- Screw mount nuts are similar to T-nuts used for wood, but in place of spikes, the flange has drilled holes that can be used for screws or rivets to hold the nut in place.

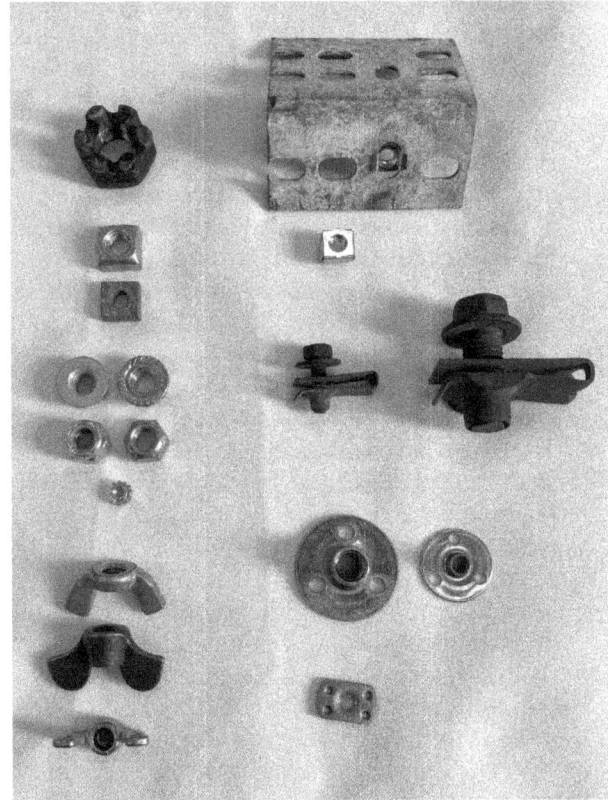

Figure 9.2 Examples of various nuts. The left column from top shows a castellated nut, square nuts, five variants of hex nut, a typical wing nut, a ductile iron wing nut, and a nylon-locking wing nut. The right column from top shows cage nuts (one mounted in slotted angle), clip nuts, screw mount nuts, and a weld nut.

o Threaded fittings are available for odd connections.
- Couplers are often used with threaded rod to connect to threaded anchors in ceilings or

other surfaces. They can also be used as spacers or stand-offs between bolted units.
- Similar and quite useful to exhibit and display fabrication are tube connecting nuts. These have spring steel flags that allow them to be pushed into round tube and retained. This can make for a quick blind connector for units that need to break apart using up to 2″ OD mechanical tubing. They should not be used for structural purposes.
- Stand-offs are large hex bushings that combine a socket and stud. They are often used for separating units while staying rigid.
- Adapters may be hex or round and are available in an array of configurations. Their overall purpose is to connect differing threads, commonly two differing bolt sizes, but can also convert from bolt to pipe thread or inch to metric for example.
  - Bolt and nut caps are available and are made from metal, plastic, or rubber to cover bolt or rod ends to prevent sharp edges from interfering with clothing or moving parts. Some are two piece requiring partial installation before the nut or bolt is in place. These are found on nearly every theatre seat to prevent fabric from snagging or scrapes to the user.
- Washers—Washers are not always required when using bolts to join metal items. In fact, a flat washer under the head of a bolt makes it more prone to rotation which may be good or bad depending on application. Washers both distribute load and may act as a thrust bearings allowing nuts or bolt heads to rotate more easily or increase friction to hold components in place.
  - Flat washers are the most common style of washer used, though many users may not be aware of how many versions exist. Each bolt size may have many different sizes of flat washer available: standard, SAE, and USS are the most common types and each may offer various outer diameters per bolt size. Outer diameters for each standard also differ from one another as do thicknesses and interior diameter tolerances. Standard washers are either ungraded or grade 2; SAE and USS offer grades 5 and 8.
  - Conical washers are dome shaped and are good for moving parts because they provide a bit of resistance but still allow smooth movement.
  - Lock washers use either spring pressure or teeth to create friction, holding nuts in place in high vibration applications. Some toothed washers are directional. In some cases, a flat washer may be used under a split washer to prevent surface damage
    - Split washers are helical spring steel and very common. They are mostly for right-hand threads since the split is designed to catch the surface when rotating to the left.
    - External tooth washers work well when a lock is needed on a slightly oversized holes where internal teeth would not touch the surface. They do need to be sized such that the teeth engage the fastener face.
    - Internal tooth washers work best with tight tolerance holes but easily engage the face of the fastener while leaving a clean perimeter.
    - Internal/external tooth washers are also quite common and hold better than spring washers, especially on small fasteners. There are also versions pre-dished for use with countersunk heads.
    - Tab-lock washers have flags that can be bent over both the nut and the edge of the component being fastened or into a slot. These only work where the flags can be fully bent over components.
  - Oversized washers were developed to distribute load on delicate material, originally sheet metal. These washers are available in many diameters for most bolt sizes starting about 50% bigger than standard flat washers and may be as large as 3″. Clipped versions may have a single or double flat "sides" cut to fit along an edge.
  - Square washers are thicker oversized washers that can be used in channels or slots to prevent rotation. They are usually available in 2–3 sizes for each bolt diameter. They are also often used with structural channel and the associated fittings.
  - Wedge washers are for bolting through the sloped flange of C-channel and I-beams, allowing the bolt head or nut to sit against a flat surface. They are available in black and galvanized iron, aluminum, and stainless steel.
  - Leveling washers are quite thick, two part washers used for mating uneven surfaces. They consist of a dome half and matching bowl half.
  - Tag holders are teardrop-shaped washers with a bolt hole at the large end, and a small hole at the narrow end to attach a split ring or hook. Excellent for labeling components.
  - Slip washers may be slotted flat washers or keyhole shaped. Either can be used to adjust fit after installation. Keyhole washers match best with round head bolts.
  - Retaining washers are similar to push-on nuts but are designed to hold fully thread bolts in place for assembly. They are generally plastic, but metal versions are available.

○ Adhesive backed washers stick very well to clean metal surfaces, allowing them to be installed prior to assembly and remain in place even for modular units. These may also help seal a hole when required.

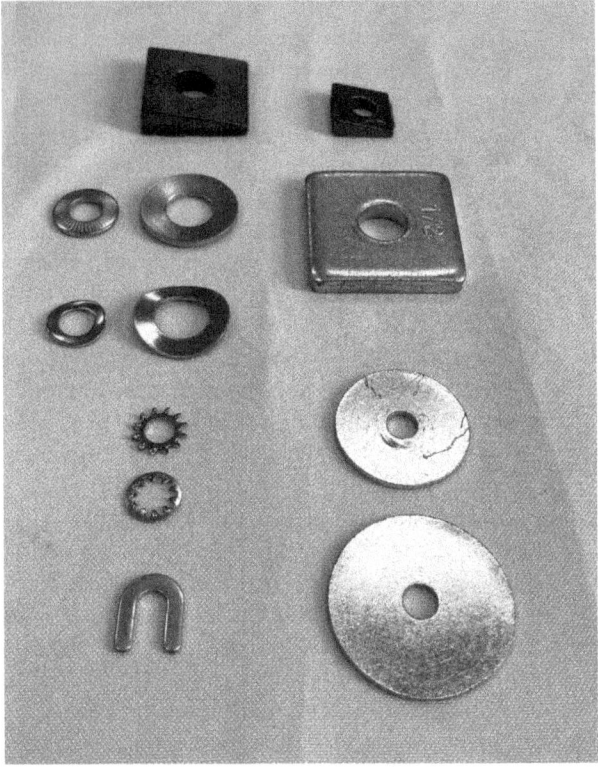

Figure 9.3 Examples of various washers. The left column from top shows a malleable wedge washer, conical washers, wave washers, toothed washers, and a slotted washer. The right column shows a square washer and two sizes of fender washer for 1/4" bolts.

- U-bolts—These are a common fastener when hanging pipe or tube. Though they are not used for many entertainment projects, one variant stands out: the square U-bolt. These are available from 2" to 8" wide and are an excellent means of mounting objects to square tube framing because the placement is readily adjustable. The most common sizes use 3/8" diameter rod. Standard round U-bolts are available in an array of sizes made from zinc-plated and stainless rod. Some are load rated, but not all. Unless the source of the U-bolt is verified, it should be assumed to be unrated.
- Rod ends—These are an excellent means of making adjustable connecting rods for mechanized projects. Ball-joint ends allow for mis-alignment of the ends without binding; solid ends need to be parallel. Ball linkages have a threaded stud on the flexible head. Clevis rod ends use a fork and pin connection designed to straddle the attaching material. Both styles of rod end are available with left or right-hand threaded studs or sockets. Most often, these will be connected by a dual thread stud allowing them to be easily adjustable, like a turn buckle. Some varieties are available with an unthreaded shank for custom threads or welding.

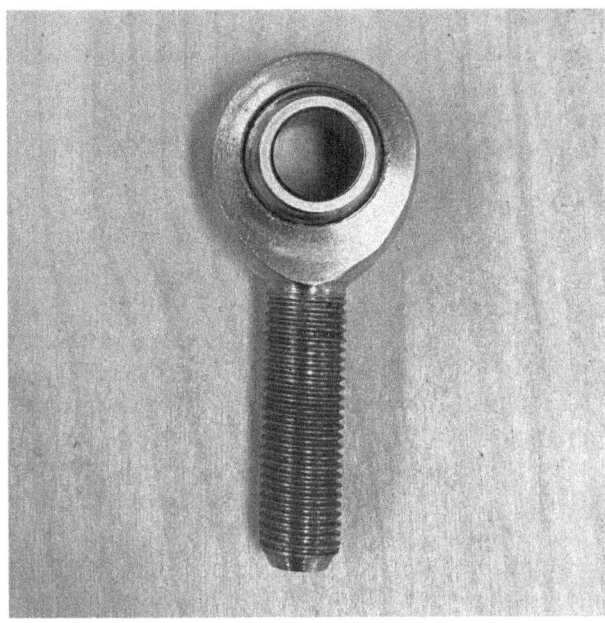

Figure 9.4 An example of a spherical rod end, also called a ball-joint end. This example is 3/8"-24 left-hand thread and about 3" in overall length.

- Threaded inserts—These are a quick means of adding threads to thin materials where tapping would not provide sufficient hold or in thicker material to repair damaged threads.
  ○ Rivet nuts are quite similar to a large blind rivet but with internal threads. These are excellent for making strong threads in thin materials. Most require a specialized tool, similar to a rivet gun to set them, but screw set varieties are available with slightly lower holding strength and fewer choices of alloy. See Figure 5.27 for examples.
  ○ Socket nuts are not technically threaded inserts, as they are not always permanently installed. They can be pressed into place or used like a socket head cap screw and set below the surface by using a counterbore. These are tightened with a hex wrench.
  ○ Press-fit nuts are splined inserts for thin sheet metal. Unlike splined inserts for thick metal, these have a thin surface profile equivalent to the thickness of a washer. Similarly, press-fit inserts

are typically splined but sit flush to or below the surface on slightly thicker sheets.
- ○ Repair inserts have threads inside and out to replace damaged threads. Damaged threads must be drilled oversize and rethread to match the insert. Locking types may use anaerobic adhesive or wedge shaped keys that are pressed in after the insert is threaded into the hole. There are also self-tapping inserts for softer metals that save the rethreading step. While many may be familiar with helical inserts for thread repair, for fabrication use they are far too time consuming to install to be valuable.

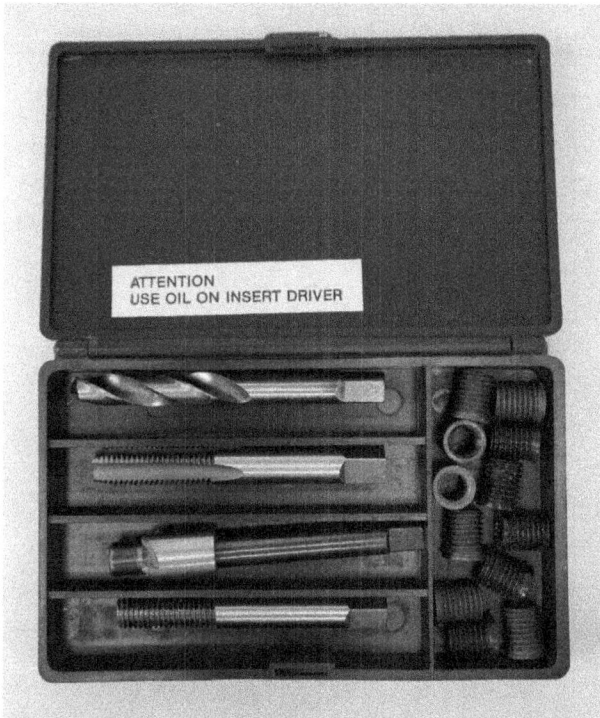

Figure 9.5 A repair insert kit including a drill matched to the plug tap (matched to the external threads of the inserts), a spotting drill to make a slight indent so that the flare at the top of the insert will sit flush, and the installation tool.

NON-THREADED FASTENERS

- Quick fasteners—There are a few ways to attach materials to metal that are fast, strong and have no threads. While this makes them harder to remove if necessary, they are often much easier to hide than bolts or screws.
  - ○ Blind rivets are also known as "pop" rivets because the draw pin breaks off when the rivet is set. These are one of the most popular quick fasteners for metal because they are low cost, relatively fast to install, strong and vibration resistant. There are also an array of options that can make choosing a bit of a quagmire. Head styles may be dome (the most common), large dome (for distributing load), and flush mount (countersunk). To make things a bit more complex there are also double dome and double flush mounts. Blind rivets may be aluminum (including painted options), steel (zinc plated), stainless steel, copper, brass, or nickel and many alloys offer high strength versions. Inch and metric shanks are both available and the ends may be open or closed. Each shank diameter will offer various grip ranges. Backing washers are available to increase pull-out resistance, but must be included in the thickness range. Supplier and manufacturer catalogs often include application charts they can help choose the best rivet for a project.
  - ○ Drive pin rivets are a type of blind rivet that require no special tools since they are installed with a hammer. Simply drill the appropriate size hole, insert, and drive in the center pin.

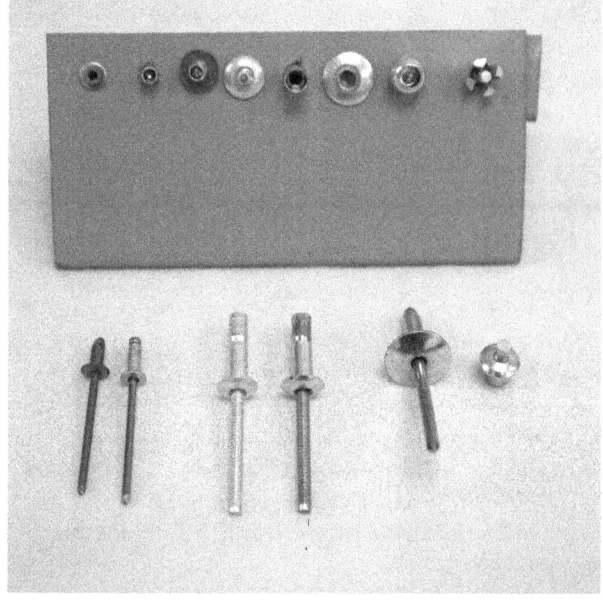

Figure 9.6 Front and rear views of blind rivets installed from left to right—three 1/8"D dome head rivets (the last has a rivet backer) with copper and aluminum examples below, a pair of 3/16"D self-locking rivets (one aluminum and one steel), a pair of 1/4"D button head rivets with a large dome below, and a drive pin rivet with an unused example below.

- Solid rivets, when used for aircraft and other industrial applications, are often cold set with a compression tool or with an air hammer and proper chisel. For the rare occasion these find decorative use in entertainment, hot setting is the easiest and most cost-effective solution. The rivet head needs to be placed in a matching cup while the pin end is either hammer peened or set with an air hammer and cupped chisel.
- Quarter turn (AKA dzus fasteners) are two part fasteners designed for easy installation and removal of panels. There are a variety of mounting styles, along with engagement methods such as screw heads or wings. These could be used for light-weight modules or to hold access panels and guards for scenic automation.
- Cleco pins are for temporary holding while a component is either bolted, riveted, or plug welded in place. A variety of styles are available: pliers operated Clecos offer expanding pins in various sizes for holes and right angle clamps for flanges on thin sheet. Larger wing nut operated pins use expanding jaws and work on thicker materials.

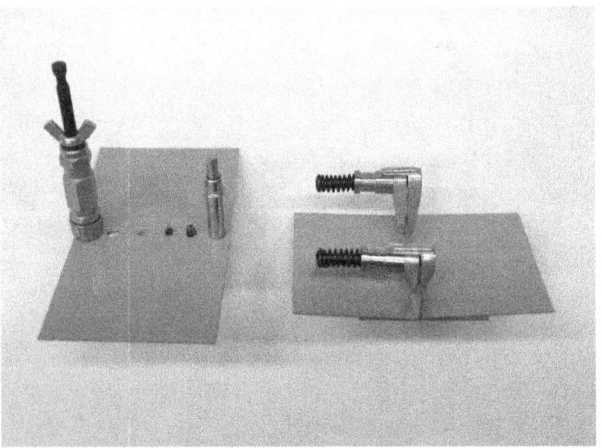

Figure 9.7 Cleco fasteners holding sample sheets in place. On the left are a wing nut draw Cleco pin and 1/8" and 3/16" spring type Cleco pins showing the body and the jaws. On the right are side-grip style Cleco clamps that also use a spring hold.

- T-nails are hardened steel nails with a T-shaped head originally developed for attaching lumber to concrete block, such as furring strips in a basement. These fasteners found their way into scenic construction because they will also pierce thin-walled steel, making it easy to attach wood members to steel frames, when used properly. Because these nailers are putting as much force as a framing nailer against a much smaller nail, they can be dangerous if used improperly. It is critical that these only be applied to thin-walled steel (up to about 16 ga) and only through the face of the member while truly vertical. Contact with a vertical element or too thick of a steel section and/or being at a slight angle can cause the nail to ricochet; no one wants a sharp projectile to rocket across the shop. 14 ga T-nails are available from 1/2" to 2 1/2" in length.

Figure 9.8 On the left is 3/4" plywood nailed with 1 3/4" T-nails and on the right lauan facing installed with 1/2" T-nails. The strips of nails below each sample show how they are packaged.

- Retaining rings—Also called snap rings, these are not technically a fastener but are often used to retain pins for moving parts. They generally fit into a slot either on a shaft or in a bore. They do require retaining ring (aka snap ring) pliers to install and remove.

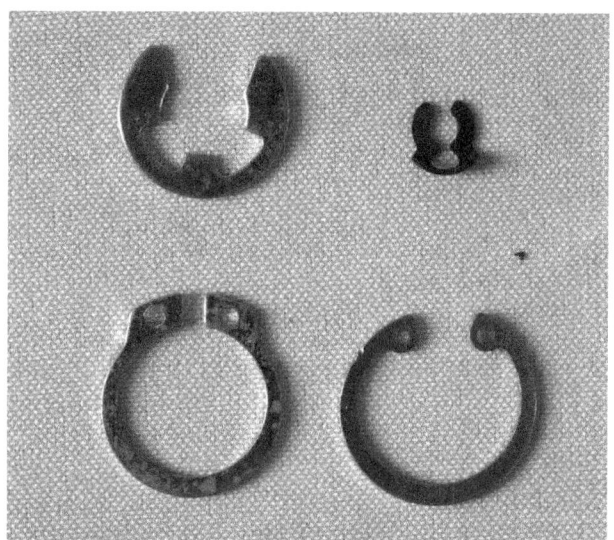

Figure 9.9 Retaining clips clockwise from upper left—An "E" clip, a push-type exterior "C" clip, an internal "C" clip, and a flush mount external "C" clip.

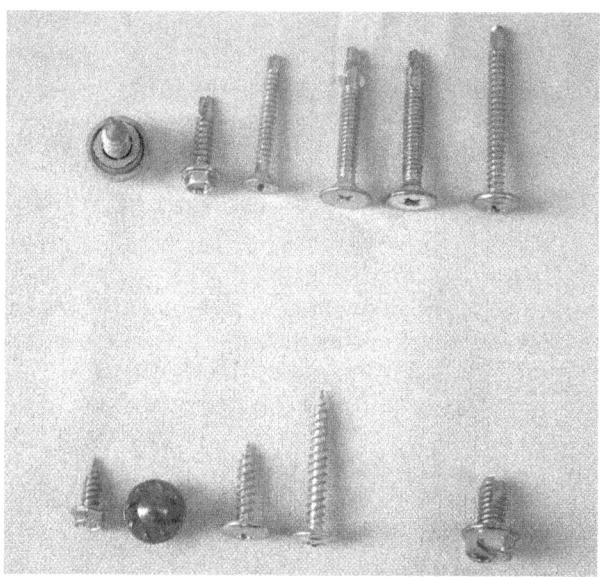

Figure 9.10 Top row from left—a self-sealing, self-drilling hex drive screw, a standard hex drive, self-drilling screw, a self-drilling drywall screw (often called a "tech" screw), a pair of self-drilling wafer head screws with pilot points (the wings at the tip of the left screw and a used version with the wings worn away on the right), and finally a truss-head self-drilling screw. Bottom row from left—self-piercing hex head screws (sometimes called "zip" screws, truss-head sheet metal screws and a self-tapping screw.

- Screws—There are a variety of screws available for fastening metal to metal and other materials to metal. Most use hardened steel except for black phosphate self-drilling drywall screws.
  - Sheet metal screws have a very sharp point designed to punch through very thin sheet and push metal away as they pull through. They are generally used to anchor sheet metal to softer materials such as wood.
  - Self-drilling screws are made from hardened steel with a drill point to create an anchor hole. Some have "wings" just above the drill point to create a pilot hole in thick materials, such as plywood, allowing easy attachment to metal. If no wings are present, pilot holes will need to be drilled in thick materials, but no drilling is required so long as the combined thickness of materials is less than the shank length of the drill point, such as when lapping metal roofing.
  - Self-tapping screws require an anchor hole to be drilled ahead of installation but are designed to cut threads as they are installed allowing the fastener to be removed and easily reinstalled later. These are commonly used in thicker metal than self-drilling screws.
  - Self-sealing screws have a gasket under the screw head (may be plastic, rubber, or urethane) to seal the screw to a surface. The most common style are self-drilling with a hex head, but round and pan head sealing screws are available as well with a variety of points. These are typically used to seal out the elements but also help reduce noise from vibration.

- Pins—These simple connectors are an excellent way to join components that need to attach and detach regularly. Readers may have encountered various types of pins in exercise equipment, equipment covers, or even to attach accessories to a riding mower. Pins have similar strength characteristics to bolts but are faster and easier. Some pins are center and cross drilled for distribution of grease within the joint, making them ideal for moving parts, such as in automated scenery.
  - Clevis pins have a flared round head on one end and are either single drilled at a specific length, or drilled with multiple holes allowing their usable length to be adjustable. These pins are most often held in place with a secondary pin called a bridge pin, but a cotter pin could be used for semi-permanent installs. These pins are often used with washers both to fine tune length and to prevent wear from the clip.
  - Quick-release pins have a ball bearing keeper near the end that is held in place by an internal rod. These pins usually have T-handles with a push-button that allows bearing to retract into the pin. Industrial suppliers also sell matching receptacles for these pins.
  - Safety pins and lynch pins are similar in that both have a permanently attached wire bail that

prevents the pin from sliding out of place. Safety pins are round with either a curved or rectangular wire bail that snaps over the end of the pin. A lynch pin is D-shaped, allowing them to mate well against a flat surface and have a sprung wire bail that flips up and down.
- Bridge pins (or hitch pins/hitch clips) look much like a larger version of a bobby-pin for hair. They are used to hold larger pins or shafts in place. They are often used for retaining receiver hitch pins for towing but can be used on any drilled shaft or pin where a quick-removal method is needed.
- Dowel pins can be used as fasteners when press-fit into a properly sized hole or used for alignment in a slightly oversized hole. These often have one rounded end and one squared end.
- Spring pins are common fasteners in many tools. They are available in two varieties: rolled or coiled. These pins are designed to be keeper pins and are not structural fasteners. While the may be used for alignment, they are easier to break than a solid pin. Spring pins require a special ball-nosed punch for removal.

- Finishing ends—These are plastic and metal plugs that fit into tube as well as metal caps that fit over tube provide a finished look and protect hands from any burrs or other injury.

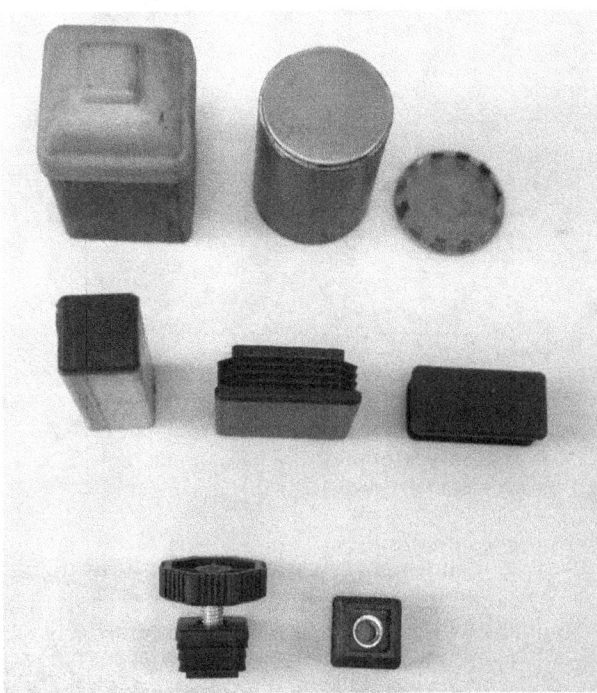

Figure 9.12a The top row shows a slip-on steel cap for 2" square tube and a steel insert cap for pipe or thick-walled tube. The middle row shows plastic inserts used to dress-up tubing and avoid injury from any internal burrs. The bottom row shows threaded inserts for 1" square tube and a threaded leveling pad.

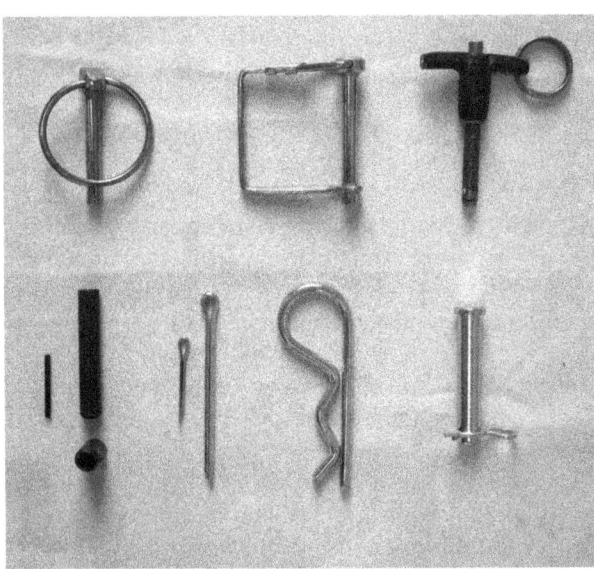

Figure 9.11 Top row from left—a lynch pin, a safety pin, and a quick-release pin. Bottom row from left—spring pins, cotter pins, a bridge pin, and a clevis pin.

HARDWARE

There are a few pieces of hardware unique to working with metal that deserve mention.
- Threaded tube inserts—Made from both plastic and metal, these end-caps push into square and round tube and provide a threaded mount for leveling feet or threaded stem casters.

Figure 9.12b Leveling insert kit for 2" square tubing. The legs shown will be used to level a project on a sloped outdoor concrete pad.

- Weld-on hinges—When working with steel, unplated hinges designed to be welded can be used in place of drilled hinges. These are available as standard barrel hinges (back flap and piano), lift off (or gravity) hinges, and self-closing (usually used for gates).

Figure 9.13 A pair of weld-on butt hinges (top) and a weld-on gravity hinge (bottom).

- Magnetic hardware—Steel also offers the ability to use magnets in unique ways. Simple magnetic hooks and clips can be used to attach set dressing or organize a machinery cart. Electro-magnets are available in various strengths at relatively low cost and can be used for quick-release effects, or to simply join a pair of steel-framed wagons.

ADHESIVES

When adhesives are used with metal, the surface needs to be exceptionally clean, especially free of oil, grease, or wax as metal essentially has no pores to absorb the adhesive. In some cases, sanding or abrasive blasting of the surface will add tooth that improves adhesion. Adhesives and tapes have two main uses in fabrication: attaching (or aiding therein) large sheets to metal frames and for small projects where welding or brazing would have too much impact or where the materials are dissimilar, such as decorative props.

GENERAL SAFETY CONSIDERATIONS

Skin contact should be avoided, as some adhesives require solvent to be removed which presents its own hazard. Disposable gloves are a cheap solution. If working with any adhesive bare-handed, hands should be washed immediately after use to avoid accidental ingestion. All solvent-based adhesives release fumes that likely contain Volatile Organic Compounds (VOCs), many of which are likely carcinogens and/or sensitizers. Generally, a respirator is not required (unless used in large quantities), but strong dilution ventilation that pulls fumes away from the user (and from other workers) should be in place. Additional concerns may be listed with each adhesive type. Users should read the label and consult the Safety Data Sheet (SDS) for any product before use.

- Epoxies—These are usually two part adhesives that react when mixed. These are not super-fast setting but are exceptionally strong when cured. Machinable and filled versions can be used for thread repair, sealing and surface repair. Epoxies are solvent, water, and acid resistant and some varieties also tolerate high heat. Overall, epoxies are best suited for use on small areas such as repairs or adding details to a metal prop.
  - Paste, gel, and putty sticks are the best formulations for metal.
    - Gel epoxies have a wide variety of set times, are typically packaged in tubes, and work well for vertical and overhead use. Most formulas use a 50/50 mix; the gel consistency makes amounts easy to gauge by eye. Gels may have a longer storage life after opened than liquids.
    - Pastes are commonly sold in plastic tubs and require measuring and mixing. These are the most common consistency to be available filled with powdered metal and are the most likely candidates for being machinable. These also tend to have the highest tack, so components may not require clamping.
    - Putties are typically sold as concentric sticks that have both components pre-measured. The stick is cut and the two components kneaded to a consistent color before application. Most putties are intended for repair and are either packed into or over a hole or break; they rarely work well for bonding two components. Many putties have a very long storage life, commonly years.

Safety Considerations
- Fumes from epoxies can trigger asthma. Smokers and others with conditions that strain the lungs are at the highest risk of irritation or reaction.
- Epoxy resins are sensitizers meaning allergic reactions can worsen with repeated exposure. Skin contact with uncured epoxy or the dust from sanding should be avoided.
- Sanding before fully cured presents a unique risk: components are still active and will continue curing after inhalation causing permanent damage to mucus cells. All epoxies should be left to fully cure before sanding.
- The hardening component can cause chemical burns if it contacts skin unmixed.

- Mastic—These adhesives are generally sold in 9–10 oz or 28 oz cartridges for use in a dispenser (caulk gun) and are available in a wide variety of formulas, both water-based and solvent-based. Most are highly water-resistant or waterproof. Designed specifically for bonding dissimilar materials, these are commonly used to attach wood facing, such as lauan, to metal frames. For large surfaces, a mechanical fastener should be combined with the adhesive, both for place holding during cure, and to avoid delamination if the frame if twisted during a move. Mastic is not well suited for metal-to-metal bonding.
  - Solvent varieties have faster cure time and are best for bonding to metal but require good ventilation. Contact with skin should be avoided.
  - Polyurethane-based mastics are the best low VOC formulas for bonding to metal. Most latex adhesives need a porous surface and do not work well with metal. Generally, water-based mastics have a lower bond strength and much longer cure time than solvent-based. These adhesives also have varying viscosities; thicker tend to have quicker tack (15 min setting/12 h cure).
  - Open time varies from 10 minutes to an hour or more.
  - Most remain fairly flexible when cured. Some varieties are formulated to do so in low-temperature environments where other adhesives would become brittle.
  - Excellent storage life when unopened but a quite short life once in use. Plugs and tip covers are available to prolong storage life. Solvent-based varieties may still cure even when the nozzle is covered.
  - Fairly high cost per area, but high strength often requires less adhesive.
- Household cement—These adhesives are solvent-based, generally a mix of nitrocellulose and other resins. These work well on a variety of materials, such as metal, glass, and ceramics, and provide a very strong bond when cured. Most have little initial tack and very long full cure times, up to 72 hours. A few do offer quick set times but still require 24 hours to full cure. They are excellent for small projects where positioning could be difficult or needs fairly precision application.
- Anaerobic—While these may be used as surface sealer in automotive applications, their application in fabrication is as thread locker. As the name suggests, they work in the absence of air, but must be in contact with clean metal to cure. There are various strengths of thread locker, but for most applications, medium strength removable will be the best option. Thread locker is available as liquid, gel, and in sticks similar to a glue stick.
- Cyanoacrylate (CA)—These glues are "instant" bonding adhesives available in a wide array of varieties. The most applicable for working with metal are high temperature (though they would not survive welding!) and toughened (with rubber). Most types are available in multiple viscosities, the thickest of which are often used to fill gaps. CAs are quite useful for bonding small pieces of metal to metal or other materials to metal.
  - Accelerants, also known as "kickers", can be used as a contact primer or to instantly cure CA glue after application.
  - Baking soda can be used as an accelerating filler.
  - Most varieties have a strong odor and should be used with ventilation.
  - High cost per area, but this is offset by the small quantities used.
  - Best storage life is attained when refrigerated.
  - Set time varies with formulation but is generally less than 30 seconds. Cure time also varies with formulations, but most require 24 hours to reach full cure.
  - Non-flexible varieties can be brittle when cured.
  - Available in colors.

Safety Considerations
- CA glues release fumes that can irritate eyes and lungs or trigger asthma, especially when heated.
- Most varieties will instantly bond skin.
- Avoid contact with cotton or leather, such as gloves, as it can cause a rapid exothermic reaction that can lead to burns and release irritating fumes.

- Polyester resin filler—Commonly referred to by the brand name Bondo, polyester resin is used as a sandable filler for metal. While it isn't used to bond metal to metal or other materials, it is one of the lowest cost options for filling imperfections in metal surfaces that will be painted, especially steel. While polyester resin alone will bond to aluminum, filled versions that incorporate aluminum powder are much more durable over time.

Safety considerations
- These resins are a likely carcinogen and proper PPE (respiratory protection, gloves, and goggles) should be in place along with ventilation.
- The chemicals contained in polyester resin, especially the hardener, are sensitizers that may do permanent damage to sensory organs (especially olfactory) and the respiratory tract with prolonged and repeat exposure. Exposure can also cause liver damage. According to SDS sheets, a single exposure could trigger these health effects.
- These resins are flammable until fully cured.

- Automotive seam sealer—These are generally mixed urethanes and are used by the automotive industry to seal body panel seams and joints. They are excellent for this as well as having adhesive properties and being compatible with both metals and plastics. Sealers are available in small handheld tubes, as well as dispenser tubes that fit in a standard caulk gun. They are paintable and remain very flexible once cured. When used with proper care, they are an excellent way to achieve a seamless look, especially on sheet metal projects.

Safety considerations
- Urethane seam sealers contain strong solvents, thus fumes have high VOC content and should be used with proper PPE and ventilation. The effects are such that some SDS sheets list auditory effects and balance loss possible from a single exposure, as well as neurological effects from prolonged exposure. Many of the solvents are list as "known animal carcinogen" thus skin contact should be avoided.

- PSA tapes—Also known as double stick or double face tapes, these are great for connecting thin metal sheets or other materials to metal frames; they work especially well with plastic and where some flexibility is needed. They are easy to use in any orientation.
  - The variety of types is extensive, from foam backed to clear films and in multiple thicknesses and widths, including small sheets. Those designed for exterior use are the most durable.
  - These offer a wide array of tensile and bond strengths, but high strength types will be more expensive.

- Adhesive transfer tape—These are sometimes called "glue on a roll" or "dry adhesive". Unlike double-sided tape, there is no substrate; these are 100% adhesive formulated to apply like tape. Some require a dispenser that applies the adhesive, while removing and retaining the backing material. For bonding to metal, acrylic-based adhesive is the most available and compatible. Some versions are available up to 48" wide (at a very high price), but narrower rolls are much more practical. The advantages to this type of adhesive is instant bonding at near full strength without the danger of bonding skin like CA, the complete lack of odor, compatibility with nearly any smooth surface, and the ability to be applied in any orientation. Some have a bond strength exceeding five pounds per square inch.

RESOURCES

- *The Prop Building Guidebook*—Although fairly narrowly focused on properties construction for TV, film, and theatre, it distills the most relevant welding skills and materials for properties fabrication into one chapter.
  - ISBN 978-1-03-215461-9, Eric Hart, Focal Press.
- *Metal Fabricators Handbook*—Though this book is aimed toward custom fabrication for automobiles and motorcycles, it is an excellent resource for learning to shape sheet metal. It also has very good information about MIG and TIG welding.
  - ISBN 978-0-89586-870-1, Ron & Sue Fornier, HP books.
- *Pocket Ref*—This super compact reference book is essentially a miniature encyclopedia for every kind of fabrication imaginable. It may not have every bit of data for every industry, but it is the perfect jumping off point for further investigation. Fabricators will find useful data on welding including compressed gases, soldering alloys, welding electrodes, and amperages, as well as welding symbology.
  - ISBN 978-1-885071-62-0, Thomas J. Glover, Sequoia Publishing.
- *Welding Essentials, Questions and Answers*, 2nd Edition—This is an extensive resource that covers nearly every aspect of industrial welding and cutting processes. Though there are no color photos, the graphics are excellent and very helpful for both learning and planning projects.
  - ISBN 978-0831133016, William Galvery and Frank Marlow, Industrial Press.
- McMaster-Carr is an industrial supplier that offers thousands of products related to metal fabrication, including raw materials in small quantities. The company offers a print catalog, app, and website.
  - www.mcmaster.com
- Grainger is an industrial supplier that offers thousands of products related to metal fabrication, including raw materials in small quantities. For those that work at a large company, state facility, or college/university, it is likely that the organization has an account with Grainger. The company offers a print catalog, app, and website.
  - www.grainger.com

Chapter 10

Blades, Bits, and Consumables

Machines and power tools all use some kind of replaceable part in order to function. All are considered wear items; some are one-time use, while others may be sharpened and reused multiple times. This chapter will help the reader determine which types of consumables best suit a project and/or material and is organized by function from cutting to finishing. The chapter discusses key features that may be available, and variants when appropriate. With the information provided, the reader should be able to discern the types of consumables that are best suited to their shop's common tasks.

BITS AND BLADES

A variety of tools exist for cutting and boring metal. Many are very similar to bits and blades for wood working, though only twist drills and hole saws are actually shared.
- Twist drills—These are the most commonly encountered bit and may be shared with wood working. Standard and split point designs are compatible with most metals and most commonly have either 118° or 135° point angles. Bits are available in inch, metric, and letter/number sizes. 135° bits are best for hard materials like steel, while 118° bits work well in tempered aluminum. Very large holes in any metal can benefit from a more obtuse drill point angle. Split point bits remove the heel of the point grind, mostly keeping the bit from wandering when starting a hole. A center punch is still helpful. Three flute bits will provide a cleaner cut and rounder hole than those with two flutes. Drilling in steel and other hard metals increases strain on bits and machines. Drill chucks should be fully tightened and all materials clamped well.

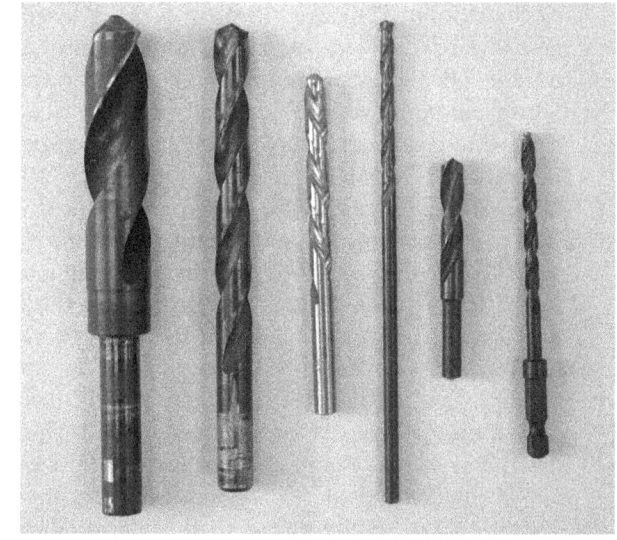

Figure 10.1 From left to right—A Silver and Deming drill, a split point bit, a titanium-coated bit with standard point, aircraft bit, a S/M (stubby) bit, and a 1/4" hex shank bit.

- ○ Twist drills are available in different types; for most, length increases with diameter.
  - S/M for screw machine (often referred to as stubby) are designed for automated drilling machinery but are also very handy for reaching into tight spaces when paired with a right angle drill.
  - Jobber bits are the most commonly available and will be the bits that most readers have used. Maintenance lengths are slightly shorter and available through commercial suppliers; these are excellent for drilling solid shapes.
  - Aircraft drills offer multiple fixed lengths (e.g. 6" and 8") for each drill size. These are very useful for setting up jigs on a drill press;

DOI: 10.4324/9781003454175-11

177

the length saves the need to reset work-table height when changing bit diameter.
- Reverse twist drills are "left handed" bits that cut via a counter-clockwise rotation and are sometimes used for screw and bolt extraction (occasionally, one is lucky enough for the friction from the bit alone to remove the remains of the fastener). They may also be used when milling to avoid changing motor direction used for other processes such as climb milling.
- Reduced shank twist drills have a smaller diameter shank than their cutting diameter. Shanks are typically reduced to either 3/8″ or 1/2″ to fit the most common chucks. One popular style of reduced shank twist drills are Silver and Deming bits. These oversized bits have a traditional grind and require a pilot hole equal to the cross section of their point. They are excellent when a large hole is needed in thick steel. These should only be used in a drill press when drilling hard materials.
- Double margin twist drills are high precision versions that reduce or remove the need to ream a hole after drilling. Though somewhat higher cost, these can save significantly on labor when precision parts are being made on a mill, for example.
- Metals and coatings on twist drills are designed for different uses. Beyond drilling holes, they may be used to remove broken fasteners or to modify hardware for installation.
  - High-Speed Steel (HSS) is likely the most common alloy used for drill bits over all. This alloy is so named because it is far more durable than carbon steel and thus improves cutting speed. Sharpening these bits will restore them to essentially new. HSS bits will dull faster in steel than other alloys but work well in soft metals.
  - Black oxide-coated bits are heat-treated HSS that are corrosion resistant and cut slightly faster than a plain finished bit. These are the most common bits used for drilling in steel because they are durable and cost-effective. Sharpening these bits will remove the oxide surface, but the effects of heat treating will remain when sharpened properly and not overheated during use.
  - Cobalt bits are not coated, but rather a HSS and cobalt alloy (typically 5%–8% cobalt). They are for exceptionally hard materials like stainless steel or other hardened steel but may be up to three times as expensive as HSS. Sharpening these bits will restore them to essentially new; using a diamond wheel is preferable.
  - Titanium nitride bits are HSS cores with an atomically bonded coating. They are exceptionally durable and will stay sharper longer than other alloys. Sharpening these bits will remove the coating making them equivalent to an HSS bit.
  - Drills for tapping are always smaller than the final fastener size. Inch-sized threads under 5/16″-18 use number-sized drills, while those 5/16″-18 and up use letter-sized drills. Some taps will work okay with standard inch or metric pilot holes. For example, a 1/4-20 tap is best matched to a #7 drill (.201″ D) but a 13/64″ drill (.203″ D) will work as well, while a 1/4″-28 tap is best matched to a #3 drill (.213″ D) and a 7/32″ drill may be substituted, but the threads may not be full depth. Metric taps are paired with metric-sized drill, but these may not be standard sizes. For example, most metric drill bits sets step up by .5 mm per drill, whereas an M8 tap would use either a 7.2 or 7.4 mm drill depending on thread count. Most drill and tap charts also list the nearest imperial tap drill size for metric threads.
- Straight flute drills—These are typically solid carbide bits that resemble a ream, but with only two flutes. They are used to drill into hardened steel alloys. The straight flute design (and short length) makes them less prone to breaking than spiral flute bits. They are expensive and thus would only be acquired for special projects.
- Step drills—These multi-diameter drills are excellent for drilling thin stock. Their advantage is the

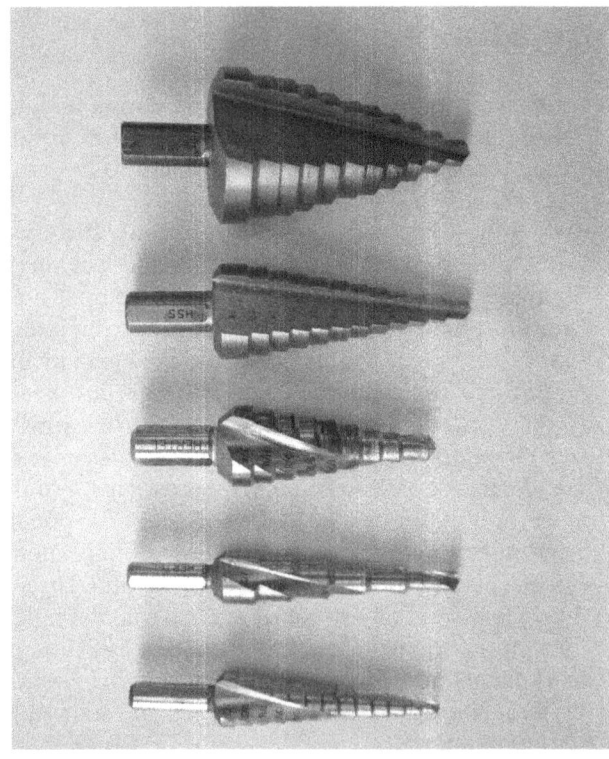

Figure 10.2 An assortment of step drills. The drills with helical flutes cut faster in the authors experience.

ability to pilot, then step up, size-by-size, to the finished required diameter. Available with varying steps (1/16″–5/32″) and diameters up to about 1 3/8″. A multi-diameter bit is a similarly cone shaped bit without the steps that will drill any diameter within its size range. This can be excellent when a hole needs to be very slightly oversized, but they only work in very thin material due to the taper.

- Hole enlarging—These bits are a type of twist drill but are unique in that they are not self-starting. These are bits have four flutes and a shallow helix to the flutes that helps prevent galling when starting a cut. Like a step drill, they can be used to enlarge a hole in stages, though each bit is a single diameter. They will cut much deeper than a step drill.
- Annular cutters—These cutters are similar to a hole saw, but much more precise. They are mostly used with magnetic base drills but can be used in a mill or metal lathe as well with a proper adapter. Annular cutters use a Weldon shank which is 3/4″ diameter and has two flat faces for it to be held in place by set screws. Like twist drills, these may be made from a variety of alloys or be coated. Like hole saws, they may also be carbide tipped. Unlike a hole saw, an annular cutter does not use a pilot bit thus the fall may be a useful disc as well. They are available from 1/2″ to 3″ diameters. These are much more expensive than hole saws but cut faster and cleaner. These cutters can be sharpened if the teeth are in good shape.
- Rotary cutters—These are similar to annular cutters and may be HSS or have tungsten carbide tips. They are intended for use in a hand-held drill or a drill press and cut a much cleaner hole than hole saws while requiring less feed pressure than twist drills. High-quality sets will have replaceable cutters; lower cost versions only have a replaceable pilot drill. A similar tool is a spot weld cutter. These are designed for removing resistance welded panels with minimal damage. They are essentially a very small rotary cutter, designed to remove an area just slightly larger than the weld made by a resistance welder.

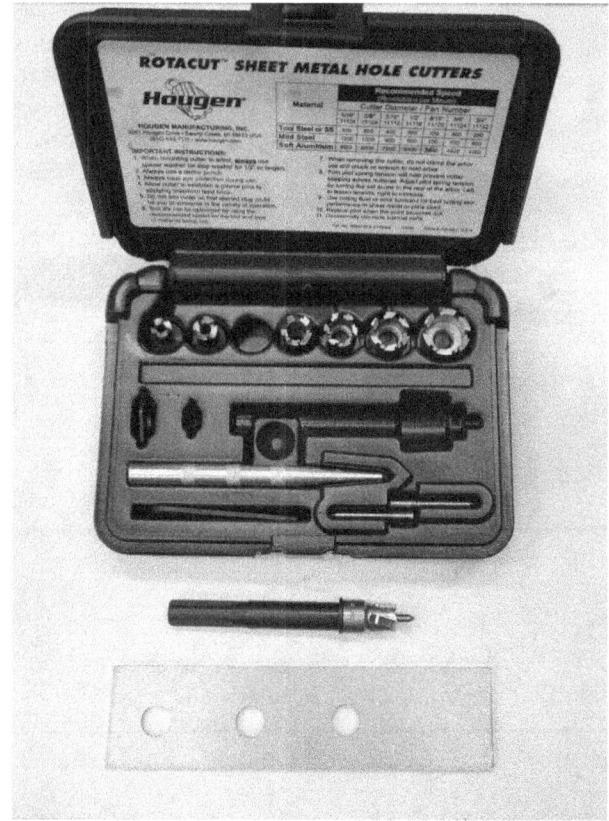

Figure 10.4 A set of rotary cutters and sample cuts in aluminum. This set has a spring-loaded center making them easy to align to a center punch mark.

- Hole saws—While these are often used in the wood shop, bi-metal saws work well in thin gauge mild steel and almost any aluminum. Carbide-tipped hole saws and carbide-tipped hole cutters are similar, but hole cutters have integral arbors. When using hole saws with metal, the RPMs need to be low (150–300) and the saw should be lubricated. Oils and cutting fluids work well in steel; dry stick lubricants

Figure 10.3 A small assortment of annular cutters showing the Weldon shank, teeth and flutes.

work best on aluminum, especially if the area will be welded. Only small hole saws should be used in hand-held drills when cutting metal. Any saw larger than about 1″ should be used with a guide, such as a tubing notcher, or in a drill press. It is very easy to bind or break saws or teeth when cutting steel; maximum useable size is about 2″. Aluminum, being softer, may allow up to a 3″ saw if the material is secured well. These cannot be sharpened effectively.

- Arbors hold the pilot drill and allow easy saw changes.
  - Standard arbors simply have threads and the saw is held in place by friction; this can make removal challenging, but for very small saws, these are the only option. Adding copper washer between the saw and the face of the arbor can make removal a good bit easier. Most have 1/2″ threads and come with a bushing to adapt to 5/8″ threads.
  - Locking arbors have a set of retractable pins (that either snap up and down or attached to a threaded collar) that prevent the saw from fully tightening to the top of the arbor threads when used properly. These allow fast and easy saw changes, but only on larger sizes.
  - Piggy-back arbors allow a larger saw to be mounted outboard of a smaller saw, turning the inner saw into a pilot. This enables enlargement of previously cut holes.

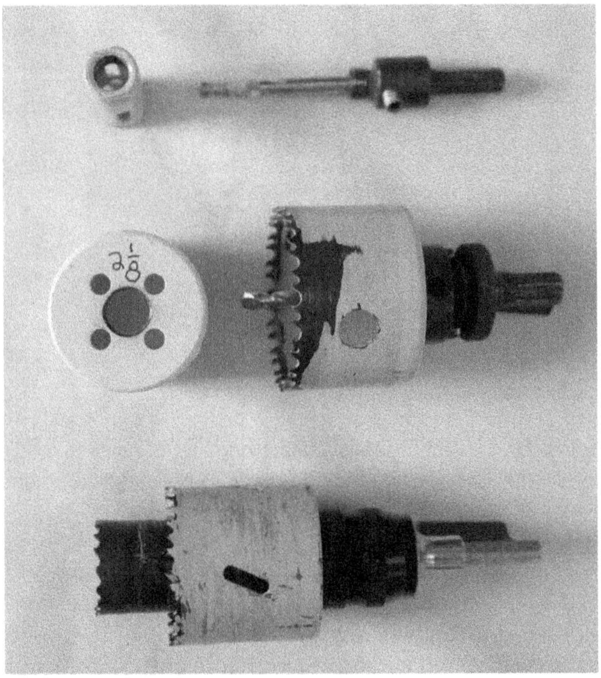

- Counter sink—There are a variety of options for these bits, but all share the same goal: to create a V-shaped recess allowing a screw head to sit flush or just below the surface. Straight flute bits are primarily used with hard metals like steel, while those for softer metals will have helical flutes.
  - These are available with various point angles from 60° to 120° with 82° and 90° being the most common because they match the taper of flat and oval head screws. 100° and 120° angles are used when setting flush rivets. Choosing the proper countersink will require having the specs for the fastener one plans to use.
  - They may be solid steel with flutes (1–6) or through drilled (less chatter) and are sized to match the diameters of screw heads. Bits for metal may have either a pointed tip or blunt tip. Some countersinks for metal may be indistinguishable from those for wood but should be made from much harder steel.
- Counter-bore—These are similar to a countersink but create a square-sided recess. They usually include either a pilot bit, for single pass drilling and boring, or a pilot stem that is sized to fit a drilled hole. They are excellent for setting the heads of socket head cap screws and small machine screws flush to or below the surface.

Figure 10.5 From top to bottom—a 1/2″ arbor, a 5/8″ arbor with locking pins, and a piggy-back (or "oops!") arbor.

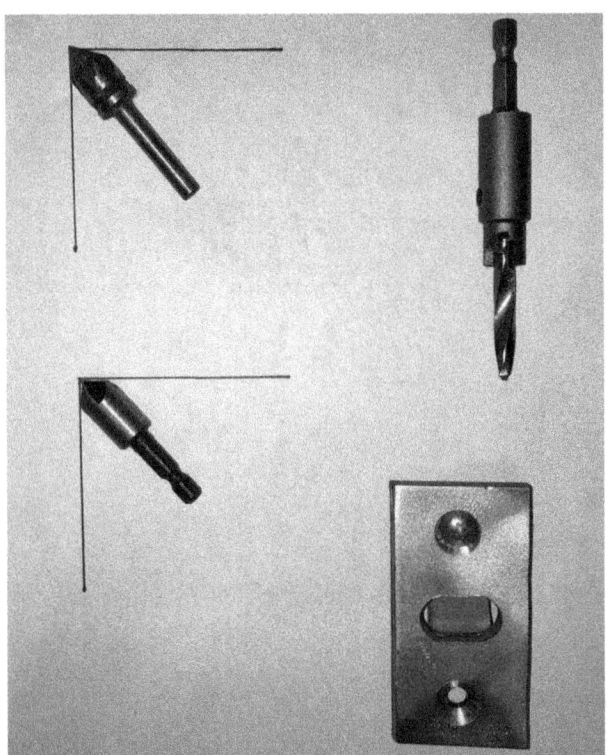

Figure 10.6 82° and 90° counter sinks with reference corners as it is often hard to discern the difference. Also shown is a counter-bore and copper mounting bracket with counter-bored holes.

- Reamer—A reamer is used to deburr a hole and/or cut to a finished size. Two flute twist drills tend to make somewhat irregular holes, especially when used in a hand-held drill. Drilling slightly under size (1/32″–1/16″), then finishing the hole with a reamer will net a far truer hole. This is a good method for projects that require movement; the truer holes will introduce less play in the mechanism and help prevent undue wear. Reamers may have straight or helical flutes. For hand work, straight flutes are best. Additionally, their slightly lower cost makes them the most common choice for powered use. Helical reamers are required for deep cuts or blind holes because of their ability to remove swarf. They are the best choice for interrupted cuts (such as a component with a keyway) and will provide a slightly smoother finish overall. They are difficult to feed by hand (even with a drill press) due to their tendency to self-feed causing galls or binding.
  - Chucking reamers are for powered use, typically in a mill or drill press. These may have a straight shank or Morse taper shank.
    - Bridge reamers are tapered and helical and are often used for mis-aligned holes. The number of flutes can vary but three and four flute are the most common.
    - Straight reamers may have slight taper at the tip in order to start easily in undersized holes. These are available with a varying number of flutes with four to six being quite common.
  - Manual reamers have square ends to match common tap handles or a tee handle. These are available as single-size straight reamers with straight

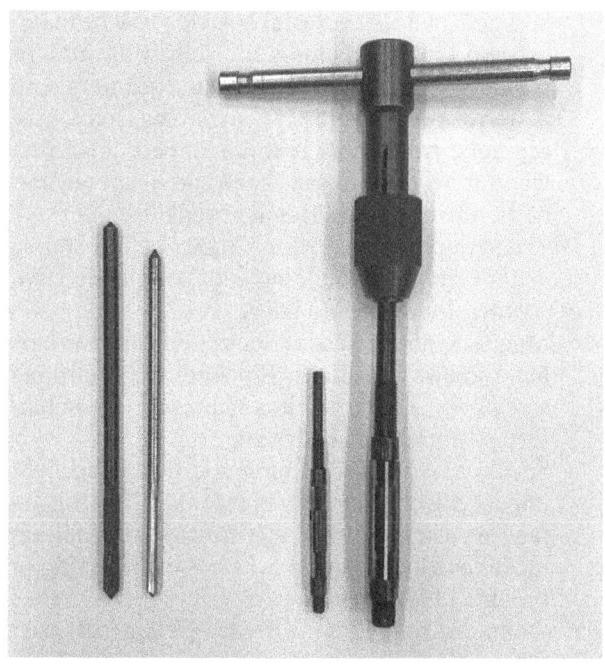

Figure 10.7b On the left are a helical flute (left) and straight flute (right) chucking reamers with straight shanks that would be typically be used on a mill or lathe; these small reamers could be used in a hand-held collet. On the right are examples of adjustable reamers that are for hand use.

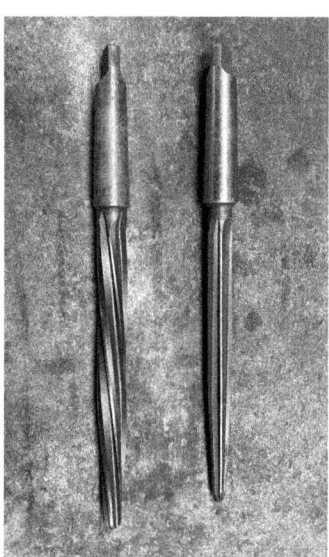

Figure 10.7a A tapered bridge reamer and a straight reamer, both with Morse taper shanks. These particular reamers are used with a large geared-head drill press.

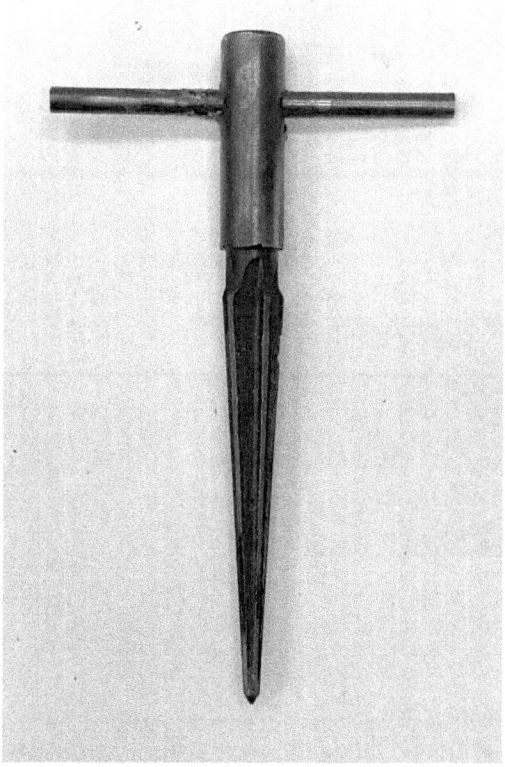

Figure 10.7c A tapered hand ream for holes in sheet metal and deburring small tube or pipe.

and helical flutes, adjustable style straight reamers and tapered reamers for deburring tube or reaming sheet metal. Helical hand reamers tend to have a less aggressive angle than chucking reamers. Adjustable reamers have blades that when moved down the shank the diameter narrows; moving up the shank widens it.

- Drill and impact accessories—There are few simple tools that can make building and fixing easier that every metal shop should have.
  - Magnetic nut drivers are designed to drive hex-head screws and are usually used on self-drilling screws. Most have 1/4" hex shanks for use in battery powered impact drivers.
  - Socket adapters are a simple addition to a drill or impact driver for driving bolts or lags. The advantage to using them with a cordless drill is that most have a clutch that prevents over-driving or breaking the fastener.
  - Damaged screw removers are great accessories for a drill or impact. These have a short drill tip on one end and a reverse threaded tip on the other. They are sold in sets to match screws sizes, usually #6, #8, and #10. These are best paired with softer machine screws; black phosphate screws are generally too hard to drill well.
- Blades—There are an array of blades for cutting metal. Only those for tools that are generally used for assembly are discussed here.
  - Abrasive metal cutting blades are fiberglass reinforced. They are used predominantly for ferrous metals, because soft metals clog the blade. Bronze and hard copper can also be cut. These are primarily used in cut-off saws, with 14" diameter being the most common. Most of these blades are 3/32" to 1/8" thick. 7" blades are also available for circular saws from .045" to 1/8" thick but should only be used on saws with metal guards. These operate between 3K and 4K RPMs.
  - Toothed radial blades can also be used for metal cutting. Most have carbide teeth but are made slightly different than wood blades.
    - Cold cutting saw blades are used with coolant and operate at very low RPMs and are often solid HSS blades with integral teeth for general metal cutting. Blades for stainless steel will usually have carbide teeth as do some blades for aluminum. These blades must only be used in a cold saw. These blades do require break in; to do so they should be fed through the material at about half the normal speed for the first three to four cuts. They can also be sharpened a few times to lower the overall cost. Steel cutting blades perform best when coated, especially when coated with black oxide. Blades generally offer one or two tooth count options per diameter, with higher counts providing a smoother finish.
    - Dry cutting blades use no coolant and make a few sparks when cutting steel. Other metals cut with no sparks. Most of these operate at lower RPMs than wood cutting blades (about half) and should not be used on a wood cutting saw but a few suppliers do offer blades that are designed for higher RPM saws. Steel cutting blades use a modified Triple Chip Grind (TCG) and lower tooth counts than blades for aluminum. Aluminum blades use TCG teeth with negative hook angle usually 5°–6° and beveled faces that help sweep chips to the side to prevent clogging. Some aluminum cutting blades are designed for high-speed saws, such as a table saw, but should be used with dry (wax) lubricant. Manufacturers often only offer one tooth count option per diameter but may offer two widths for each. While a wider blade may create a bit more waste, they tend to be more durable.

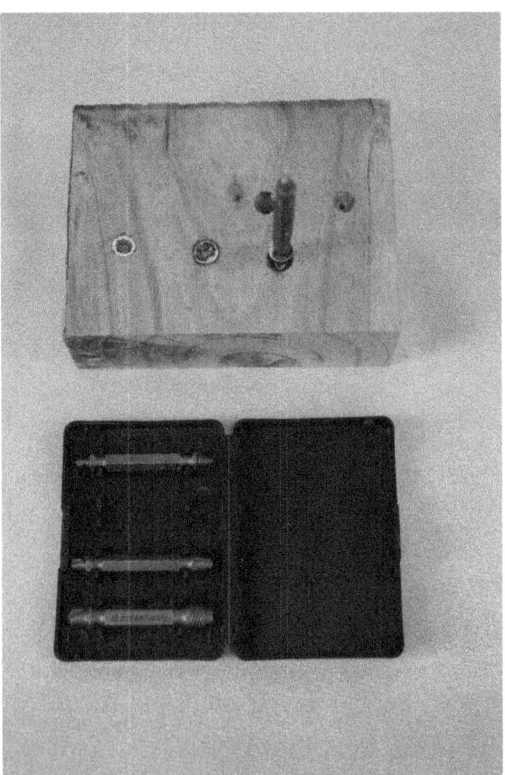

Figure 10.8 A set of damaged screw removers and the stages of removing a stripped screw: a stripped screw, the head drilled out and the screw being removed.

BLADES, BITS, AND CONSUMABLES • 183

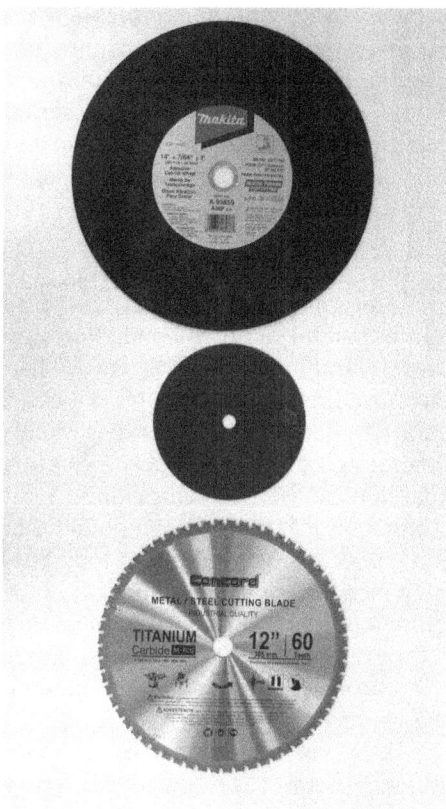

Figure 10.9 From top to bottom—a 14"×3/32" abrasive blade, a 7"×.045" abrasive that shows the fiber reinforcement quite well, and 12" dry cutting blade.

○ Bandsaw blade types will be the same whether used in a portable saw or stationary saw. Though the width and length for each machine may be different, the tooth sets are shared.

The two most common metals to cut are steel and aluminum; both cut best with a bi-metal or hard-back carbon steel blade. Mild steel tooth count requirements will vary: 20–24 tpi for thicknesses under 1/8", 14–18 tpi for sections up to 1/2" thick, and 10–14 tpi up to 3/4" thick. Some blades offer variable pitch and varying tooth size for a smoother finish (e.g. 10–14 tpi). Aluminum is better cut with a variable pitch 6–10 tpi blade for thin sections or a 4 tpi skip tooth blade for thick or heavy wall sections.

○ Jig saws are less than ideal for cutting metal, but they are a practical way to cut complex shapes when other technologies like plasma or laser cutting are unavailable. Blades for cutting steel are bi-metal or HSS composition with ground teeth. 18–24 tpi with a wavy set are used for thin steel, while 10–14 tpi or variable pitch blades with alternate set teeth are used for thicker steel. Wood blades can work well on some aluminum, but side-set blades with milled teeth are best and usually 8 tpi. Other specialized blades include tungsten carbide teeth for stainless and cast iron, progressive teeth for multipurpose cutting (for example 10/24 for cutting thin metals

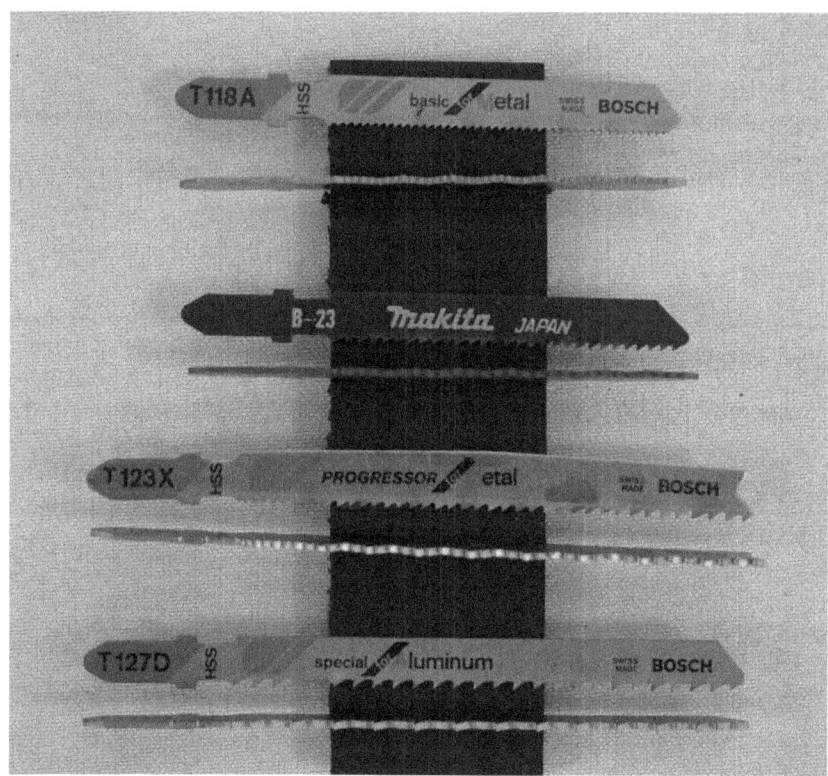

Figure 10.10 Metal cutting jig saw blades from top to bottom—24 tpi wavy set, 18 tpi raker set (left, center, right set), 18 tpi double rakers set (left, left, right, right set), and 10 tpi alternate set for aluminum.

with the upper teeth and thicker metals with the lower teeth) and extra-long blades (5″, 7″, and 10″) for cutting honeycomb and metal sandwich panels.

SANDING AND GRINDING MEDIA

While some metal products may be sanded prior to painting, sanding is usually reserved for primer coats and not metal. Grinding and polishing are the more common processes for trimming, shaping, and dressing welds. Nearly every grinding machine has a variety of types of media available from coarse for fast material removal to very fine for polishing. How the media is bonded will determine which kinds of metal the abrasive will be compatible with.

- Cloth media—When used for metal cloth backed abrasives are typically closed coat, meaning 100% of the backing material is covered, though semi-open coat (30% lower grain density) may be preferred if any coatings are being removed.
- Grit—This refers to grain size by screen (number of grains able to pass through 1″ area); lower numbers are larger grains/more coarse which leaves a rough finish, while higher numbers use smaller grains for a smoother finish. For fabrication work, 36–220 grit is likely the most useful range of coarseness. Very low grit, such as 36, would be used for removing scale, for example while a 220 grit would be used to smooth a surface enough to be ready for paint. Like sanding wood, working up from coarse to finer through multiple stages will ensure a much smoother finish with few to no residual marks.
- Compounds—Sanding and grinding media for metal are made with a narrower range of grit compounds than those for wood. Each has properties that should be matched to the task.
  - Emery is a natural mineral made up primarily of aluminum oxide, iron, and silicon. It is affordable and durable. Rarely bonded to anything other than fabric, it is readily available on narrow rolls, 1/2″ to 1″ wide. Emery is often used to prepare copper for soldering or brazing and removing light oxidation on steel. Fine emery is suitable as an initial stage for polishing.
  - Aluminum oxide is a natural mineral and the most commonly available due to its durability, fairly low-cost, and variable friability, which makes it adaptable. It is the most common mineral used to manufacture abrasives for metal working. Sanding belts and discs as well as grinding stones are most commonly made from aluminum oxide. It can be used wet or dry depending on media type and is fast cutting.
  - Silicon carbide is a very hard, man-made compound that is not noticeably friable, thus dulling as it wears. It cuts faster than aluminum oxide but does not last as long. It is best suited for grinding non-ferrous metals like bronze and copper. Bench and stationary grinder wheels may require frequent dressing to maintain cutting ability.
  - Diamond is the hardest naturally occurring mineral. Two of the most common places to find diamonds in the metal shop are bonded carving burrs for rotary and flex shaft tools and as truing tools for grinding stones. Though not common, there are bonded diamond cutting wheels for sheet metal and diamond wheels for bench grinders that may be used for sharpening.
  - Zirconia alumina is a man-made compound that is extremely durable, fast cutting, and long lasting. It is often blended with aluminum oxide. Due to its friability, it presents new sharp surfaces that work well for grinding hard metals like stainless steel or 4130 chromoly. It is most often found on cloth-backed belts and disks.
  - Ceramic alumina is the hardest man-made compound listed here. It is excellent for heavy machine use, such as belt and disc sanding, especially for hard materials. Well-made ceramic abrasive may have up to six times the life span of aluminum oxide variants. Ceramic abrasives have low heat build up and are often chosen for working thin material that may warp if overheated.

SANDING AND GRINDING CONSUMABLES

- Hand grinder wheels—Most hand-held angle grinders use wheels between 4″ and 9″ with 4 1/2″ and 5″ being the most common. Inline grinders usually use abrasives from 1″ to 3″ diameter. Stone-based abrasive wheels are available for ferrous metals, aluminum, and even ceramics. Because the wheels are not cross compatible but look nearly identical, the user must check labeling. Some wheels can be used with a variety of metals; for example, a grinding wheel for steel can work quite well with silicon bronze. Reinforced wheels should be inspected before installation and be disposed of if any chips or cracks are found.
  - Cut-off wheels are available in various thicknesses from .045″ to 3/32″. While thinner wheels cut faster and with a smaller kerf, they are more delicate. These are available in two types: type 1 are flat discs, while type 27 have a depressed center like grinding wheels.

- Grinding wheels for angle grinders are usually fiber reinforced and available in four types. Type 27 have a depressed center and a flat face; type 28 have a depressed center and are dome shaped for reach without hub interference (while available in 4 1/2", these are more common to 7" and 9" sizes); type 29 have a depressed center and an angled face (for more surface contact); and type 11 non-reinforced cup wheels designed for high contact area. Grinders that share a 5/8"-11 threaded arbor can use wheels with or without a threaded hub. Small grinders that use a 10 mm × 1.25 do not have a threaded hub option from most manufacturers.
- Combined wheels are designed for cutting and grinding with angle grinders and are usually 1/8" to 5/32" thick. These are not for extensive cutting but work well on small cross-sections. They work well for deburring but should not be used for heavy grinding.

Figure 10.11b An example of an aluminum weld ground flat with an aluminum-specific grinding wheel. These have sharper cutting grains and mostly do not load. They also create very little heat in use. The author would opt to finish the joint with a fiber disc or flap wheel.

Figure 10.11a Left column from top—a type 27 grinding wheel for ferrous metals, a type 27 grinding wheel for aluminum and a type 27 grinding wheel for concrete. It is important to note all are 1/4" thick and there is no visual difference when looking at the grinding surfaces. The right column from top—a type 29 cupped grinding wheel for ferrous metals, a type 27 cutting wheel and a type 1 cutting wheel.

- Fiber discs have grit bonded to a heavy-duty fiber backer (which may be resin-impregnated fabric) that makes them very durable. They mount to an angle grinder with a flexible backer (either plastic or stiff rubber) and retaining nut that replace the mounting components for grinding wheels. These are often used for stripping paint or grinding aluminum, but with a little practice they can also be used to make a decorative swirl pattern on metal surfaces, especially when used in a variable speed grinder.
- Flap discs consist of overlapping leaves of sanding media bonded to a backer, either fiberglass, or phenolic that will wear away with the sanding media to prevent surface damage. Most are flat or tapered (type 27 or 29), but curved discs can be very handy for working on unique shapes. The advantage over sanding discs is longevity; as the leaves wear away, new surface is exposed. These

offer a much wider array of grit choices than grinding wheels. Most metal workers will opt to have at least 60, 80, and 120 grit wheels.

Figure 10.13 On the left are a medium-coarse polishing wheel (top) and a stripping wheel (bottom) for 4 1/2" angle grinders. On the right are 2" twist-on discs for a die grinder: a medium-coarse polishing disc, a surface cleaning disc (for oxidation), and a stripping disc.

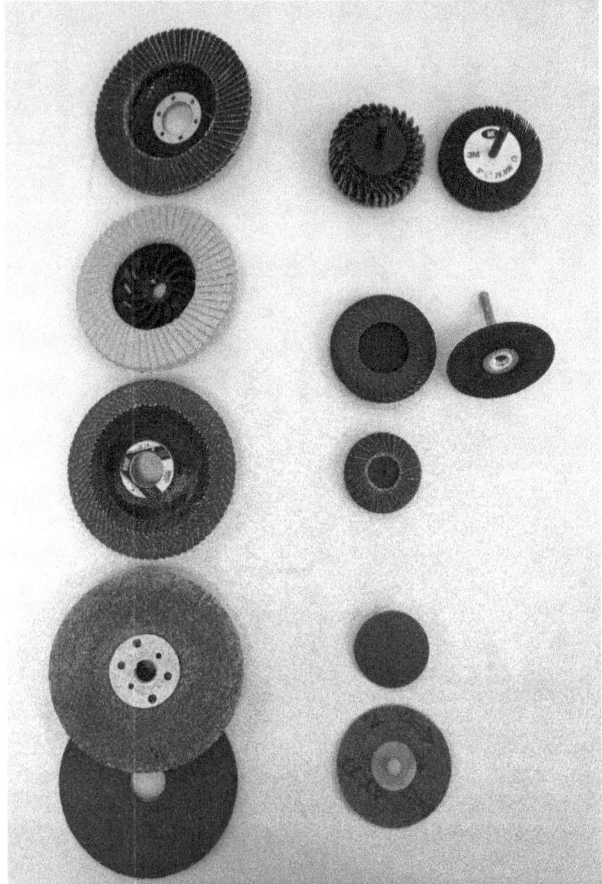

Figure 10.12 Left column from top to bottom—a type 27 flap disc with fiberglass backer, a type 29 flap disc with a phenolic plastic backer, a curved flap disc and a pair of fiber discs. Right column, wheels for die grinders from top to bottom—flap wheels, roll lock flap discs, and roll lock fiber discs.

- Stripping discs use coated non-woven abrasive to prevent clogging. They are designed to strip paint and other finishes from hard surfaces with less marring than other mechanical methods.
- Non-woven polishing discs are a great finishing tool, especially for metal that will be left bare. The fine non-woven abrasive is bonded to a fiberglass backer, so care must be used as they wear.
- Wire wheels and cup brushes are used for cleaning such as removing rust, welding slag, or paint. The bristles are most often carbon or stainless steel, though brass and brass plated bristles are options for more delicate tasks. There are three main types: light cleaning with fine, crimped wires that are not in bundles; twisted knot (or just knotted) that are good for removing paint and rust; and stringer bead wheels that are more durable and used for weld clean up (removal of slag) and may offer different face widths, but not bristle lengths. Be cautious of using wire wheels with aluminum; they can melt and gouge the surface with too much pressure and should not be used to prep for welding. Wire wheels and cup brushes have a stronger tendency to pull the grinder and shed wires; they should always be used on the leading edge while wearing a leather apron and face shield in addition to safety glasses. The addition of leather sleeves may be wise as well. Knotted and stringer bead types use approximately .020" diameter wire, while light cleaning brushes vary from .008" to .014".

Figure 10.14 On the left, a knotted wire cup brush, a stringer bead wheel, and a well-worn knotted wheel. On the right are two die grinder wire wheels (top and middle) and a low-speed wheel for drills (bottom). It is important to note that visually there is no difference between the bottom two wire brushes, yet the middle brush is rated for 20K RPM and the bottom brush 4500 RPM.

- Stationary grinder wheels—Wheels for bench and pedestal grinders are not reinforced like those for hand-held grinders. Stone wheels should be inspected for chips and cracks before each use. The simplest way to test a grinding stone before installation is to suspend it from center on a string and then tap with wood or plastic mallet at four quadrants; it should make a ringing sound. If an area has a dull thud, the wheel is cracked and cannot be used. Stone shapes are indicated by type in ().
  - Stone wheels for bench grinders will usually be straight-sided type 1 wheels made from a variety of abrasives, with aluminum oxide being the most common. Optionally a shop may choose cone type wheels: elliptical taper (16), straight taper (17&17R), or cylindrical (18&18R).
    - Grey aluminum oxide is the most common because they are low cost and work very well. They offer varying coarseness but have mixed grain and are not considered "precision" wheels. Coarseness is often simply listed as "fine" or "medium". These are general purpose wheels for heavy grinding or deburring of ferrous metal.
    - White aluminum oxide wheels have a finer, more consistent grain and vitrified bond, which runs cooler. They are well suited to basic tool sharpening and manufacturers offer them with specific grits; 60 or 120, for example.
    - Silicon carbide wheels are a grayish-green and are for grinding non-ferrous metals, though aluminum is too soft and will clog the wheel. These are offered in specific grits and are excellent for grinding bronze, brass, and similar metals. Fine silicon carbide wheels are used to sharpen carbide tooling; for most shops that will be limited to sharpening masonry bits.
    - Foundry stones may be brown aluminum oxide or zirconia. Brown aluminum oxide is a long-life variety of aluminum oxide that cuts cooler than grey or white. Zirconia wheels are for harder metals such as stainless or 4130 chromoly.
  - Flap wheels are similar to flap discs, accept the flaps are not bonded together; they only attach at the wheel hub. The density and stiffness of the flaps determine the wheel's ability to adapt to a surface. Some are available with non-woven interleaves that help reduce or eliminate the sanding lines caused by the grit. These are quite good at conforming to contours.
  - Wire wheels for bench and pedestal grinders are the larger version of those for hand-held grinders, though rated for much lower RPM. While these will still shed wires, they are less prone to doing so than those run at very high speed on angle grinders.
  - Non-woven abrasive wheels for stationary grinders are available in an assortment of "grits" from very coarse for stripping to very fine (about 320G) for polishing. Nylon fiber wheels will also specify density; lower density will conform to contours better but wear somewhat faster. They are an excellent next step after flap wheels for pieces that will remain bare metal.
  - Polyurethane abrasive polishing wheels are for final finishing of non-ferrous metals and work particularly well on aluminum. These wheels have embedded silicon carbide abrasive and are usually 2000–4000 grit and are faster than buffs and rouge.

188 • FABRICATION FOR THEATRE AND ENTERTAINMENT

Figure 10.15a A bench grinder with a flap wheel and low density non-woven wheel mounted. The tool rests have been removed for working on contoured shapes. The clear guards have also been removed as this machine is strictly used with a face shield.

Figure 10.15b A bench grinder with a wire wheel and silicon carbide wheel mounted. The tool rest has been removed from the wire wheel as these wheels tend to catch and trap items when a tool rest is present. Even with clear guards, the wire wheel is strictly used with a face shield.

Figure 10.15c A bench grinder with non-woven wheels mounted. The left-hand-wheel is a 150 grit medium density flap style wheel that conforms to detail well; the right-hand-wheel is a high density solid 180 grit wheel that is used to polish raised details. The tool rests have been removed for working on contoured shapes as have the clear guards as this machine is strictly used with a face shield.

- Grinding belts—There are a variety of styles of belt grinder, and thus an array of sizes of grinding belts. What distinguishes these from sanding belts is having a closed coat and generally harder abrasive grit than those for wood. The abrasive media will determine which alloys a belt is compatible with. Non-woven abrasive belts are also available for most machines and can be used for rust removal or polishing on flat and contoured material depending on the machine and belt size.
- Rotary tool abrasives—These are used in a variety of small grinders and are for hard-to-reach spots and for deburring.
  ○ Carbide burrs may be sized for both small rotary tools and heavy-duty die grinders. Double cut burrs are beset suited for hard metals, while single

cut burrs work well with aluminum. Adding a bit of dry lubricant can help prevent clogging when working with aluminum. These should always be used at high RPM to prevent chipping the burr.
- Stone points are mostly made from aluminum oxide, but harder and softer compounds may be available. These are available to fit both small rotary tools and full-sized die grinders. Mounted stones are slower cutting than burrs but do not chatter or grab and provide a smoother finish. Mounted stones will wear quickly on hard metals that will change their shape.

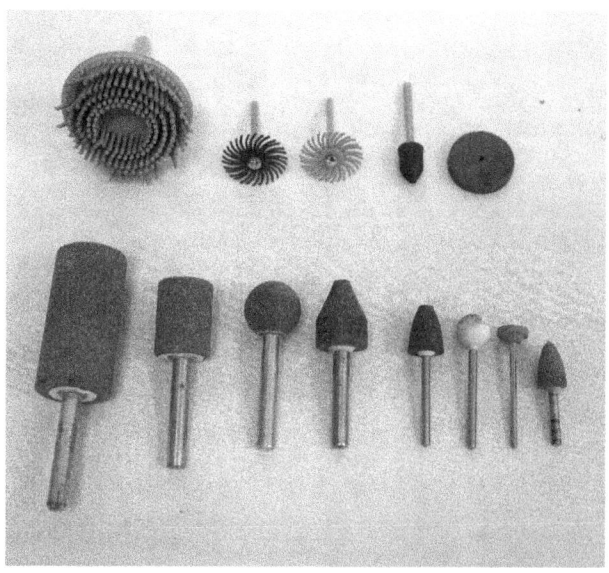

Figure 10.16b Grinding points and polishing wheels for rotary/pencil grinders and die grinders: top row—poly bristle disc, poly bristle wheels, and rubberized abrasives; bottom row—aluminum oxide mounted stone points.

- Diamond points are primarily sized to fit rotary tools and pencil grinders. These are often used for wood and plastics but work equally well on non-ferrous metals other than aluminum. They are longer lasting than stone points and will not change shape as they wear. They are available with varying coarseness but this may be hard to determine from many vendors.
- Sanding cones are another option for finishing. The advantage to these is the availability of various grits, and cylinder or cone shapes. As they wear, cloth layers can be peeled back to reveal new abrasive, or in some cases, the cloth will simply wear away to reveal a new surface.
- Flexible abrasives are used on various rotary tools. These are rubber and similar polymer compounds embedded with abrasive. They are very good at fine smoothing of small contours. The downside to these is the tendency to leave a film (melted rubbery stuff) that needs to be cleaned off after grinding/polishing.
- Stem-mounted wheels and brushes are available for drills, die grinders, and rotary tools. Brushes for rotary tools with an 1/8″ shank should not be used in heavier tools such as inline grinders. Likewise, brushes with 1/4″ shanks are available for either drills or die grinders; they cannot be interchanged. Those designed for drills have a max RPM of 3500–4500 where as those for die grinders will be rated at 20,000 RPM or more. Visually, they are nearly identical so the user must check the max RPM before installing a brush-on a die grinder. Examples are shown in Figure 10.14.

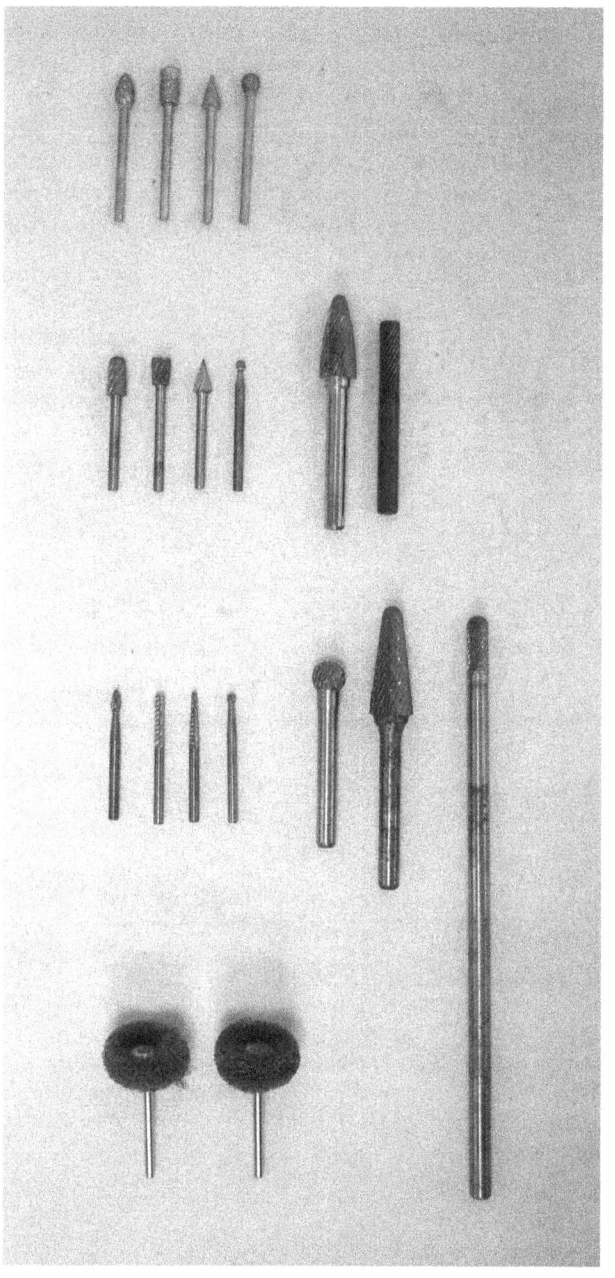

Figure 10.16a Various burrs for rotary/pencil grinders and die grinders from top to bottom—diamond burrs for iron, bronze and stone; single cut burrs for aluminum; double cut burrs for ferrous metals; and non-woven polishing buffs.

Figure 10.16c Sanding cones mounted on a die grinder being used by the author to clean up a freshly made cast-iron pan for the Metal Museum in Memphis, TN.

machine they are mounted on, the process remains the same.
  ○ Buffs are mostly made from layers of woven cotton such as muslin or felted fiber. Harder (denser) buffs are used with initial "cutting" rouge. As finer rouge is needed, lower density buffs are often used. Buffs are available for rotary tools, angle grinders (variable speed machines are the most compatible), electric buffers, and pedestal polishers.
  ○ Rouge bars are a wax base embedded with very fine grit. The rouge is applied to the polishing buff, and then the buff applied to the metal. Rouge is available in assorted coarseness much like other abrasives, but the most coarse rouge is still very fine. These typically follow a common color code from coarse to fine: black emery, brown Tripoli, white, green, red jewelers, and blue. Many users will find a set with brown Tripoli, white, and red jewelers sufficient for most projects.
  ○ Non-woven buffs for rotary tools are about 1/2"×1" and are excellent for surface prep on small items, just like their larger counterparts. These are a good choice for removing oxide from small aluminum tube before welding, for example.
- Polishing—Buffs for polishing are available for pedestal, bench, and hand-held tools. Though the shape of the buffs will vary depending on the

Figure 10.17b Stages of polishing from top—rough surface from using a non-woven stripping wheel, most of the scratches removed with a medium non-woven disc followed by three stages of buffing with white, green, and red rouge.

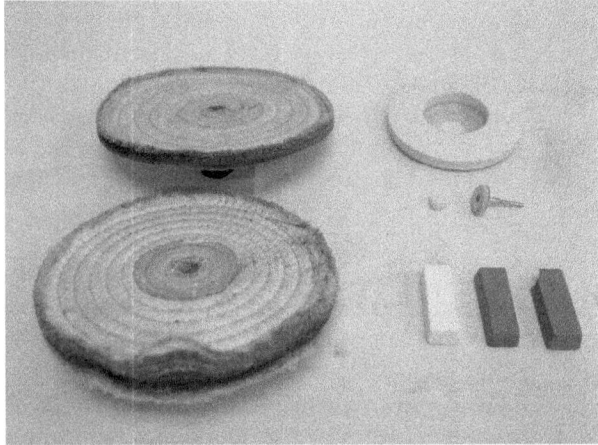

Figure 10.17a On the left are hard and soft muslin buffs for a bench grinder/polisher and on the right, from top—felt buff for 4 1/2" angle grinder, felt bobs for rotary tool, and an assortment of rouge.

Chapter 11

Techniques

This chapter is in some ways the heart of this book. It is intended to provide tips, tricks, and common techniques used in metal fabrication. Ideally, it will be beneficial to both those beginning their journey into metal fabrication, while still providing a few useful gems for long-time fabricators. The author has endeavored to provide photos that illustrate the techniques and explanations that help the reader visualize how each technique could be applied to projects.

WELDING TABLES AND SURFACES

One of the first steps when making the move toward metal fabrication will be setting up a welding area. One key need will be a (or many) welding work table. Tables should not be shared between the wood and steel shops if at all possible and should not be located within 35 ft of a wood working area. There are various options for welding work surfaces. In some cases, units may be large enough to require fabrication on a floor, but for most, smaller units will ease handling and transport and therefore can be built on a work table. Many shops choose to fabricate their own modular tables that can be joined when a larger work area is needed.

- Solid top—Wood is a common option for welding table tops because they make it easy to screw jig blocks to, and the surface is easy to replace when worn. When wood tops are used, some means of fire mitigation should be nearby. A solid steel surface

Figure 11.1 One of many 16' × 24' welding work tables at Adirondack Studios. These tables have plywood tops.

may be a good choice for shops that primarily work with steel; components can be tack welded to the surface preventing any movement during final welding. These tops need to be fairly thick to prevent warping. In addition, with an all steel table the welder's ground cable can remain attached while components come and go. In addition, solid tops allow the fabricator to draw layout lines in soap stone (easy to remove) for an entire project before placing components.

- Expanded steel—A simple work-table surface can be made by adding flattened expanded steel to a steel frame. The advantage to this is a low-cost table that can easily be built by shops new to welding that is quite light weight. If space is at a premium, a work top could have removable legs for easy storage, while still providing a large work area. In addition, they can be made very large quite easily since expanded steel sheets are available up to 12 ft long. The disadvantages to this style table included very limited means to clamp or jig to the table surface and the inability to mark placements. As well, care should be taken when fabricating the table to avoid warping the top or leaving weld bead above the surface that will interfere with layout.
- Fixture—These tables are designed to allow the fabricator to easily clamp or wedge pieces in place for welding. Older tables were often very thick steel grids (typically 2″ bars and 2″ square openings) that used tapered wedges dropped into the grid for holding. Newer tables have a grid of clipped circular openings on 2″ centers that allow 1/4 turn dogs and clamps to be dropped in. Many tables are sold as kits that also include hold down sets and clamps that are similar to those used on T-slot tables. The holes can also be used for through-bolting jigs and brackets. For smaller spaces or those that make smaller items like furniture, these tables may be ideal.

Figure 11.3 A top view of a fixture-type welding table with the included hold down kit.

- Bar type—These tables consist of a grid of welded rectangular bar (vertical) similar to the cutting surfaces on CNC plasma machines, sometimes placed over a catch pan. These are often fairly compact tables but have a much higher load capacity than other small tables and may include tool drawers.

Figure 11.2 The expanded steel 4′ × 8′ welding table at the University of Memphis.

These are excellent for maintenance areas, or shops that fabricate automation equipment where the weight of a large electric motor or hydraulics being fitted may be too much for a lighter duty table. In addition, they can be used as cutting tables for plasma work without much worry.

- Portable—These tables are fairly small and intended for site use. They typically have a through-slotted top, much like a drill press table. The large slots allow the head of an F-clamp or C-clamp to pass through for clamping items to the surface. They often have adjustable fence guides along at least two edges that can be used as clamping faces for true 90° corners. Some include tool racks in the base for MIG pliers, magnets, and clamps.

STORAGE

Another key element that all shops will share is safely storing material. Because metal is often much heavier and usually much longer than lumber, it is difficult to move into storage racks and those racks must be much stronger than those designed for lumber. The wide variety of commonly used metals also presents its own challenge: having enough room for each shape and/or size needed. Like other storage, access is a concern for both crew safety and ensuring the right material is used for a project. Another consideration is storage of useable offcuts. Essentially all projects will require components that are cut to length, and some material will always be left over. For many shops, these will have value and need to be stored in a sorted manner as well.

Figure 11.4a Some steel storage at Adirondack Studios. Many shops opt to store materials above a cutting area for convenience. Note chains on upper level to prevent accidents and a steel order on carts ready to be hand sorted or moved to the rack with a small forklift.

Figure 11.4b For an academic program, scrap material still has value. At the University of Memphis, the author has built storage bins under the main cutting table to sort scrap by length and type.

MAKING COMPONENTS

What follows are a few tips and tricks that will give the less experienced fabricator some insight into how to best approach making scenery, props, and other projects from metal.
- Welding—A few tips and tricks for those new to welding will be helpful as they experiment with new materials. Some may be good refreshers for experienced fabricators too.
  - Stick welding is not the most popular method used in shops, but the machines are prevalent, fairly cheap to acquire and still work quite well for those who wish to work with steel. As noted in Chapter 8, it can be more difficult to learn and to apply.
    - When learning to stick weld starting a new electrode can be difficult. For the first few, start with the stick almost flat (10°–15° angle) and drag-tap on a scrap block to establish the arc then quickly tilt the electrode up to the proper welding angle. This will create a small hollow on the end making it easier to restart.
    - A similar technique and be used to fix an electrode that has had the flux broken off from being stuck in a weld. The stick will be much harder to start and the very shallow angle will need to be held longer to burn the stick back to the in-tact flux. If the welder is fairly new, it may have a dig function that can help prevent sticking.
    - Backhand (pulling) welding is often a much easier way to learn to stick weld than forehand. Starting with flat butt welds, then moving to horizontal fillets followed by vertical welds is the best way to build skill without getting frustrated too quickly.
  - When TIG and OAF welding, some choose to bend the filler rod leaving about a 4″ long leg that can be dipped in and out of the weld pool by rotating the rod.
  - Testing welds when learning is wise. The very simple test is using a hammer with a fairly hefty swing from multiple directions. This will provide a sense of how strong a test weld is. Cutting through the length of the weld with a bandsaw is a good method for observing how well a weld penetrated the base material. These methods are not a substitute for having welds tested by a certified facility, nor hiring a certified weldor for projects where life safety is a concern! Examples of "hammer tested" welds can be seen in Figure 8.13b.
  - Sheet metal can be particularly frustrating to weld because it warps much easier than shapes and thicker sections. Resistance welding is the best option because it reduces warping, but many shops will need one so rarely that the investment is not a good value. There are a few techniques that will help make fabricating sheet metal objects easier.
    - Welding spoons (copper backers) are often used to repair a hole, but they are also excellent to use as backers while butt-welding sheets with a root gap, such as that created by butt-welding clamps. This open root technique also reduces heat in the panel, helping keep distortion at bay while the spoon keeps the weld flush to the back face, reducing dressing time.
    - Stitch welding is a technique that moves the heat around on the panel to keep any single area from overheating. A common method is to tack weld the seam in a few places, then weld a short distance at each end followed by a similar length weld on center dividing the seam into two equal sections. The process is then repeated, continually dividing the remaining sections until the weld is complete.

Figure 11.5a An example of 16 ga sheet metal panels held in place with butt-welding clamps that are tack being welded with the aid of a welding spoon.

TECHNIQUES • 195

Figure 11.5b A hole (made intentionally) has been repaired using the welding spoon. Carbon is visible on the spoon from direct contact with the welding wire.

Figure 11.5c The sample is fully stitch welded. The overlapping welds are not the most attractive but will be ground flat for a finished surface.

Figure 11.5d The stitch welded seam after careful grinding with a flap disc. The finish is not perfect but would usually get a thin layer of body filler (sanded) before painting.

- A lapped seam is made by creating an offset with a joggler tool then joined by rosette welding the back of the seam. These small welds mimic those made by a resistance spot welder and minimize distortion and surface impact. These seams should be welded in the same order used when stitch welding a full seam. The jog tool may be a pneumatic tool that also has a punch used for making holes for plug welding the seam, or an insert tool for an air hammer that requires plug welding holes be punched separately.

Figure 11.6a An example of a lapped 18ga steel sheet with examples of plug welds completing the joint made in a pair of welding coupons.

Figure 11.6b The front surface of the complete lap-welded seam. Good weld penetration is evident and the surface can be quickly smoothed with a flap disc.

- A flanged seam on the back of the panels is one trick that can save some frustration. The flanges adds stiffness to the panel, which helps reduce warping and any weld that burns a little too deep will be much less likely to burn through. The seam can be welded with a MIG, TIG, or OAF welder; when using TIG or OAF, this can also be done with no additional filler metal. Even if a shop does not own a brake, one can be made fairly easily from angle iron that will be sufficient for bending a small flange; for thin sheets a brake bar for HVAC work can be well suited to making a short flange. The shortest flange possible will make the best looking and strongest seam. While this tends to leave a valley on the face, it can be filled with body filler or brazed.

Figure 11.8a An obtuse (60°) mitered corner held by a flexible magnet and ready for tack welding.

Figure 11.7 Examples of flanged seams in 16 ga steel sheet welded with MIG (L), TIG (C) fusion (no filler), and OAF (R) fusion. Note the MIG weld is a bit harder to make as clean with the addition of filler metal. The author also clearly slowed down a bit at the end of the weld.

- Joints—Most structures fabricated from metal will have welded joints. How the technical designer chooses to make the joint will depend on a few factors: speed of assembly, required final finish, and the material shape being joined. What follows are examples of a few somewhat complex joints and the steps for preparing the materials.
  ○ Angle iron corners can be mitered (best for obtuse angles) or have one flange trimmed to make a butted corner (best for 90°). Thick angle may require one or both faces to be grooved for proper weld penetration. Welds may be on the inner face only, or on both faces when required. Face welds may need to be ground flat for aesthetic reasons.

Figure 11.8b Angle iron sample trimmed to make a 90° corner and ready for welding.

- Notch and bend is a great way to create obtuse to 90° corners. In thin-walled square or rectangular tube this creates a corner with no open ends to be capped. The process does require careful cutting to avoid damage to the outer face; this cut is often made with a portable bandsaw; other options include using a vertical bandsaw or a dry cut circular saw set to the proper depth and angle. A cutting wheel in an angle grinder can be used as well but is more difficult to control. This technique can also be used with angle sections; thick material will require either heating the bent face or grooving the inside slightly to accommodate a tight bend. If the inner face is grooved it will need to be welded. An example of notched angle is shown in Figure 11.50a.

Figure 11.9 Samples showing a prepared 1″ square tube and a finished corner that has been fillet welded.

- Coped joints are used when welding to round tube. The cope may be cut in nearly any shape, but most often it will be cut in either round or square tube of similar size. Pipe is often coped to make welded joints as well. Coping tube can be done with any tubing notcher, but hole saw types are most common. Pipe is easiest to cope with a plasma cutter due to the thicker wall, though a hole saw can work if run slow and kept well lubricated. There are also dedicated machines for notching pipe for shops that do so regularly. Measuring for coped tube can be tricky, but starting by measuring from the center of member that the cope will abut will yield a very close length that can be trimmed if needed.

Figure 11.10a A tube coping jig halfway through cutting a cope in 1″ round HREW. It is best to have the end of the tube extend past the vertical centerline of the hole saw, otherwise the teeth may catch and break off as they reach a lip.

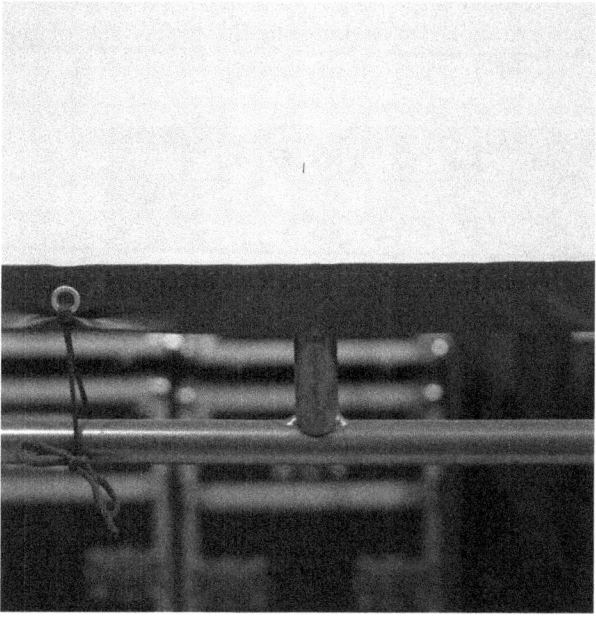

Figure 11.10b A 1″ round tube frame for a 16′ diagonal screen using coped joints.

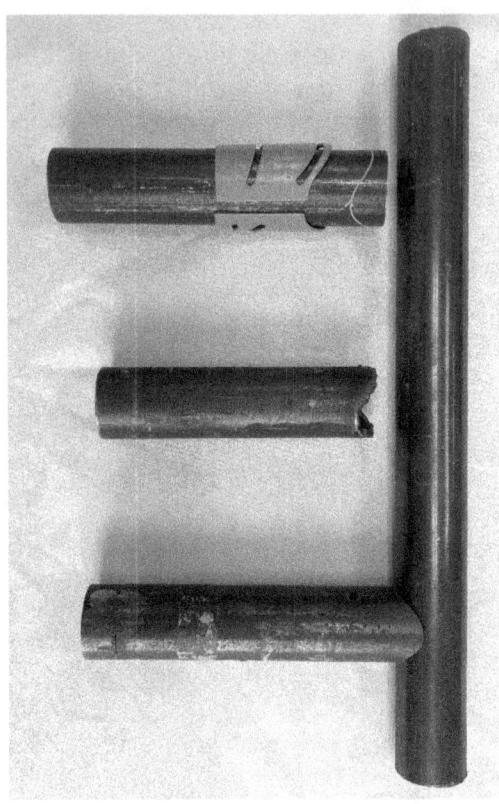

Figure 11.10c Samples of pipe with layout lines, plasma cut cope, and sample joint after clean up. An example of a coped pipe scenic unit can be seen in Figure 3.6a, the forced perspective ceiling grid.

- Tees adjoined to angle should be made in a manner similar to a trimmed joint in angle by removing the flange while leaving a tang of web available for welding to the inner face of the angle.

Figure 11.11 An example of a trimmed tee section fitted to an angle. The pieces have only been tack welded at this stage.

- Butt-welding thick steel sections requires either a groove on each piece and/or an open root. The depth of the groove should be 1/2 the thickness for single-sided welds and 1/3 the thickness for double sided welds. This is usually combined with a root "gap" to ensure the weld bead fully engages the material. This gap will usually equal about 1/2 of the thickness of the un-grooved material.

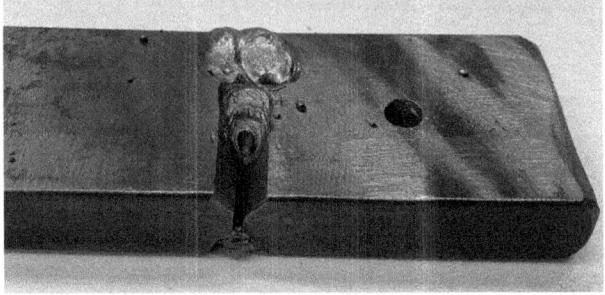

Figure 11.12 A section of 3/8" steel bar showing the prepared groove, root gap, and partial weld.

- Pass-through bushings are often welded into square or rectangular tubing to prevent collapsing the walls when bolting. This is most often

Figure 11.13a A pass-through bushing fitted to 2" square tube. The images show the beveled edge of the pipe for good weld penetration. The hole was cut with a hole saw that matches the OD of the pipe.

Figure 11.13b A cut-away section of the bushing insert shows the final product. The weld on the face would be ground flat upon completion and the bore cleaned up with a die grinder.

can be done fairly quickly with an angle grinder and the tab bent with pliers or a hammer.
- A V-notch cut to fit the joint is the most elegant solution, but also the most time consuming. It is tricky to not over cut the notch as well as keep it square and parallel across both vertical faces.

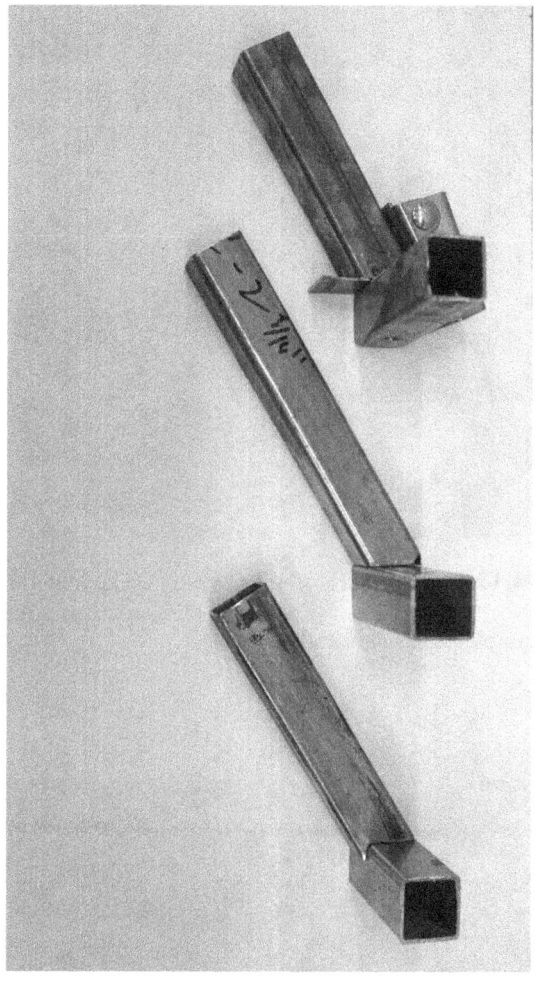

Figure 11.14 Examples of mitered transitions from top—an underhung miter with filler tab (it is easiest to weld the tab in place, then trim), a transition with the top of the tube notched and bent, and finally a V-notched transition.

done for large bolts in thick-wall tube. These are made from tubing with an ID similar to the bolt that will be used. To do so, a hole that matches the OD of the insert must be cut in both faces. This is often done with a hole saw because it ensures good alignment on both faces and is a relatively easy method for creating large accurate holes.
- Miters in square or rectangular tubing can present a conundrum when they need to be joined to the face of another component of the same size. The extra length of the hypotenuse requires special attention. There are three main choices.
  - Under-hanging the excess material is great for speed but leaves a spot that must be burr free to prevent injury, and it exposes the interior of the angled member to the elements if the unit will be used outdoors. It is the least desirable finish. One can weld a small cap in place but this is awkward.
  - A somewhat more complex solution is to cut a small notch at the top of the miter and fold the excess material down to form a transition that in essence bisects the angle. With practice this
- Notching bar stock for butt or tee joints is an excellent trick that makes a clean joint with quick easy clean up. It is similar to making a plug weld. One tip if many joints need to be made is to install an 1/8" × 7 1/4" cutting wheel on an 8" bench grinder; this will make keeping the notches perpendicular to the bar face much easier than using a hand-held grinder. Setting this up will require spacers to center the balance plates on the arbor.

Figure 11.15a An 8" bench grinder with a cutting wheel installed for notching bar. The shield has been flipped up only for photo purposes.

Figure 11.15c The finished sample joint; it will be easy to make the weld bead flush to the face.

Welding carts for MIG welders are often one of the first welding projects a shop completes when starting into steel fabrication. While very nice carts can be purchased, one good reason to make a cart for a compact welder is the ability to design one that can navigate obstacles such as hoses and cables or that can also roll over rough terrain on job sites. As well, many commercial carts have a fairly high center of gravity.

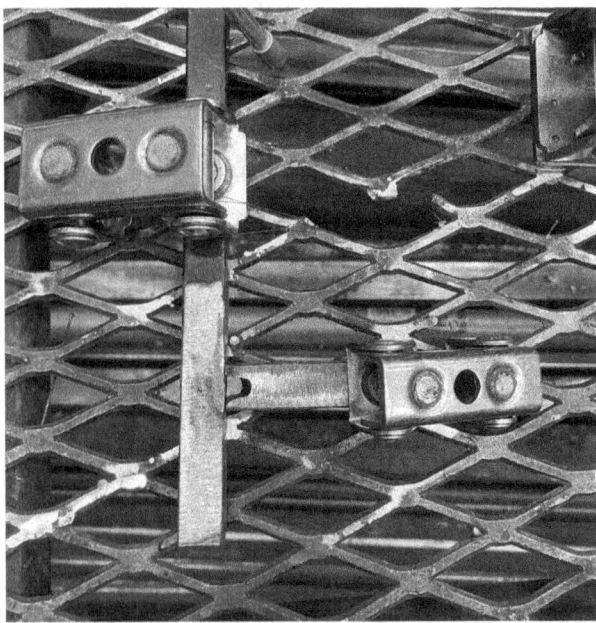

Figure 11.15b A sample of notched bar held in place, ready for welding.

Figure 11.16 The welding cart for a compact welder at the University of Memphis. This cart hops over not only cables but tube steel when large units are laid out on the floor and the welder needs to be in the center. The large rear wheels allow it to be tipped up and moved like a hand truck.

- Plasma cutting—Though using a plasma cutter is quite easy, a few tips can aid in making more precise cuts.
  - Some machines will allow direct tip to metal contact at low amperage, but most work best with a small gap between the tip and the metal. This can be achieved three ways: a steady hand, a stand-off, or with a drag shield. Using a drag shield is the most popular choice. A shielding cup with two grooves in an X-shape replaces the standard cup. This provides a flat face to drag along the metal surface while providing venting for the cutting tip and is usually rated up to 40 amps; enough to cut approximately 3/8" thick steel. A stand-off simply clips to the standard shielding cup. It will increase the gap between the cutting tip and the metal and is usually recommended for high amperage cutting. Some companies offer universal stand-offs with height-adjustable wheels; these can be used to cut beveled edges. Short, simple cuts may be done free-hand, but it is difficult to make precise cuts. Free-hand work is generally best for plasma gouging, used to remove large welds.
  - Many companies sell a circle cutting accessory for plasma cutters. When cutting a circle, a small hole is drilled at the center to anchor the pin end of the jig; the other end should have an adjustable height wheel (or two) attached to a sliding grip for the shield. This allows adjustment of both radius and cutting height. If a solid disc is needed, the center point could be anchored in a donut-shaped magnet with an appropriate diameter center hole.

Figure 11.18a A plasma cutter set up with a circle cutting jig. The jig is adapted from a rolling stand-off; the torch is using a drag shield. The photo also shows the center hole required to index the guide.

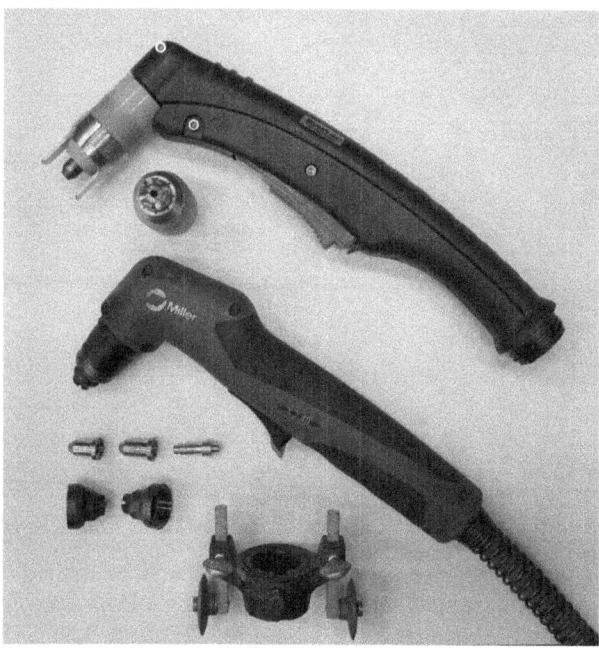

Figure 11.17 At the top is a 60 amp quick connect plasma torch with a stand-off for cutting (rotated for photo clarity) and a drag shield below. Below is a 40 amp plasma torch with 30 amp and 40 amp tips and drag shields (the electrode does not change) and a universal stand-off at the bottom.

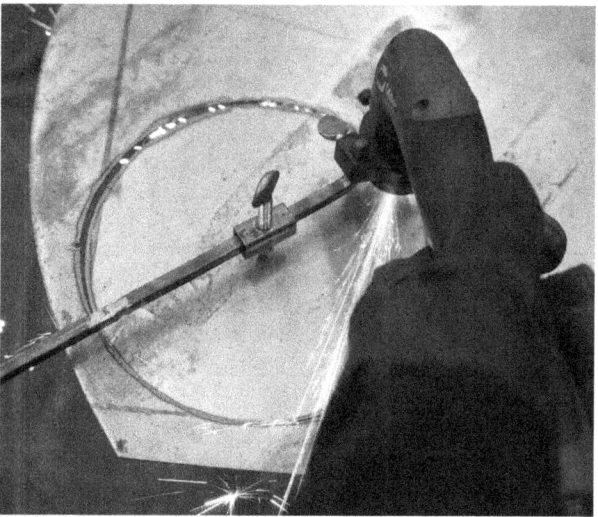

Figure 11.18b The circle cutting guide in the process of cutting.

- MDF templates are an excellent way to cleanly cut complex shapes when CNC technology is not available. This is best done with a drag shield as it has the least impact on the MDF. One key when making the template is to under-size it by the distance from the center of the cutting tip to the point the MDF will make contact with the drag shield. The author has found that 1/8″ MDF is a better fit to most drag shields than 1/4″ thick material. In a pinch, thick chipboard can be used as well, but it will likely not survive more than one or two uses.

Figure 11.19 Cutting the side plates for a roll bender built by the author using an MDF template as a guide.

- Threading—For those unfamiliar with cutting threads, taps are used to cut internal threads while dies are used to cut external threads. When a custom mounting point or threaded fastener is needed, having a tap and die set is important. This is one place where investing in a well-known brand name set will be worthwhile. Cheap sets tend to be made from softer metal; dies will dull or chip, causing tearouts in the threads and taps are much more likely to break leaving the user to either try to remove the broken tap or start over. See examples of taps and dies in Figures 5.31 and 5.32. Soft alloys of aluminum such as 1100 or 3003 are slightly more prone to clogging tools, but the most commonly encountered 6061 and 6063 thread well. 2024 and 7075 are the alloys best suited to making hardware requiring threads when they can be attained and machined to shape.
  - Tapping is fairly straight forward, but there are a few tricks. It is critical to keep the tap vertical; some shops use a tap guide or self-aligning tap holder to keep the tap vertical. A drop or two of cutting fluid not only eases the process, it helps keep swarf from clogging the tap. In addition, after the tap has caught and made a revolution or two, it should be backed out 1/4 turn or so to clear any burrs. If it binds sooner, reverse direction sooner. This should be repeated every 1/2 to full turn as the tap advances until the tap spins freely. A hand tapper is handy tool that ensures the tap is vertical if this is a regular process for a shop. For threads that do not pass completely through thick metal, a set of taps that include plug and bottoming taps will be needed.

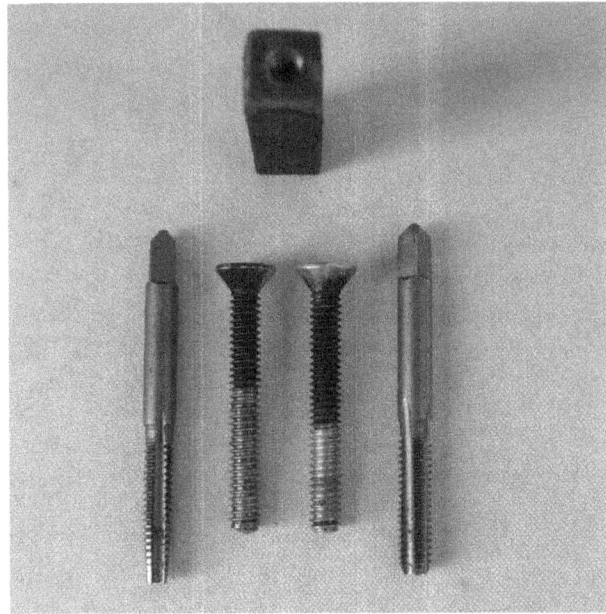

Figure 11.20 An example of how bottoming threads increases thread contact. The bolt on the left was inserted to its stopping point after the standard tapered tap was used and then marked with paint. The bolt on the right was inserted after bottoming the threads and marked with paint showing the approximately 1/4″ difference in thread depth.

  - Dies can be much trickier to align than taps. To solve that problem, self-centering dies are a great investment. Threads are often cut on round bar, but a die can be used to extend the threads on a bolt with a plain shank and even on a square bar with a little preparation. The same rotate and reverse system used with taps also applies to cutting with dies.

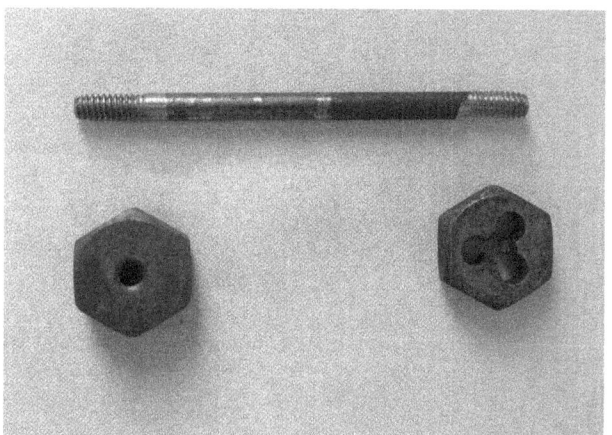

Figure 11.21 On the left are threads cut with a self-aligning die that are nicely centered and on the right an example of mis-cut threads (intentionally exaggerated) cut with a standard die.

Pipe threads, when cut manually, use the same process as those for bolts but using larger tools. Handles for pipe threading are ratcheting to save room during use. If a significant amount of pipe needs to be threaded, either a portable powered threader or a stationary threader will be a much better choice.

SHAPING COMPONENTS

There are a variety of tools and machines that can be used to shape metal. This section is intended to explain many of them as they apply to projects that may be encountered in entertainment.
- Cold bending solids—As metal bends, a fabricator with a little practice can learn to recognize the feel of the metal releasing into the bend and to know how much it will spring back. Gaining this will make it faster and easier to achieve the desired finished product.
  - A bending fork can be used to easily make tight bends or it can also be used for long radius bends by making a series of slight bends at regular intervals. Care must be taken to not make the intervals too far apart; this will make a faceted "curve" as opposed to a smooth curve. Ascending/descending radius curves can be made by changing the bend interval proportionally. The trick to bending this way is to develop a feel for pulling the lever end an equal amount with each pass.

Figure 11.22 An example of using a fork bending jig made from 1/2" round bar welded into holes through 3/8" bar. The sample bend was done by moving the rod about 1/2" into the jig for each bend.

- Hammer forming an arc between two stationary surfaces can sometimes be a good solution for moderately small arcs. Welding two sections of pipe to a mountable base is the best solution, but if care is used, any two parallel bars at a fixed distance will suffice. Much like bending with a fork, the material is placed, struck, moved, and struck again until an arc or circle is formed.

Figure 11.23a The start of a ring being hammer formed using the jaws of a large utility vise. While not ideal, the pliability of the hot-rolled steel makes damage to the jaws unlikely.

Figure 11.23b The hammer formed ring completed. The material was moved about 3/8″ before each strike to aid in creating a fairly round final product.

- Hossfeld benders will make a variety of smooth and sharp bends in solid sections. Most of the dies are for fairly large dimension pieces, but cold bending 1/2″ cold-rolled round bar any other way is quite difficult for example. The

Figure 11.24b Using the Hossfeld like a brake to bend a 90° angle in 1 1/4″×1/8″ strap steel. The bending die (left) will allow acute bending to about 45°.

Figure 11.24a Finalizing an eye bend in 3/8″ cold-rolled rod. The eye diameter is determined by the diameter of the center pin; here using the full 1″ diameter. Supplied are two center pins netting five eye diameters from 3/8″ to 1″.

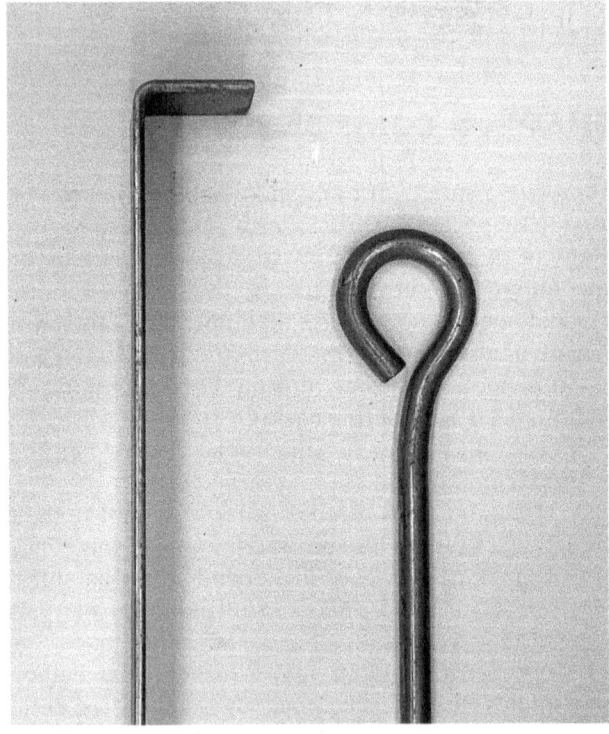

Figure 11.24c The completed example shapes made with the bender. The eye has been touched up in a vise.

Hossfeld manual provides an incredible number of die combinations to make almost any shape. It will make eyes from round bar, bend angle iron, and fold strap steel. Many shops have one purchased in the 1960s or 1970s that works like new.
- Scroll benders are generally bench mounted tools for shaping smaller solid sections. They use a lever with a pivoting die to pull the material around the shaping die mounted on center. These are often used for small radius bends but can also make sharp bends up to 90°.

Figure 11.26 A roll bender built by the author with a test sample of 1" square tube (front) and a test rolling 1"×1"×1/8" aluminum angle. The bender has interchangeable rollers that can be spaced to accept the flange of the angle or support wider material. The rollers can also be repositioned to allow for tighter radius bends on thin material such as strap steel. The roller was made mostly from scrap materials with the exception of the rollers, drive wheel, and ACME thread.

- Kerf cutting is an excellent way to make radius bends in angle sections relatively easily with minimal equipment. It is unlikely to be used for other solid shapes, though could be used with tees if the web is cut. To make the final product

Figure 11.25 The authors scroll bender being used to make a long radius bend (for the size of the machine) using a "custom" die made from a large metal spacer.

- A roll bender can bend strap or bar stock with the same dies used for square or rectangular tube. For angle iron, the machine needs to have split bending dies that make space for one leg of the angle iron. The process is simple: once the material in engaged by all three wheels, increase pressure on the center die and roll the material though, then increase the pressure and run the material in reverse. This is continued in stages until the desired bend is created. One important note is that extra material is needed for this process; the first and last bit of material between the pressure roller and the in-feed/out-feed rollers will remain straight.

Figure 11.27a Cutting kerfs in angle requires care; the blade needs to avoid the flange surface while still making a full depth of cut. This setup uses a fence spacer so that the web of the angle meets the blade very near center for a flat-bottomed cut. The additional square tube is to ensure the angle is clamped tight and flat to the table.

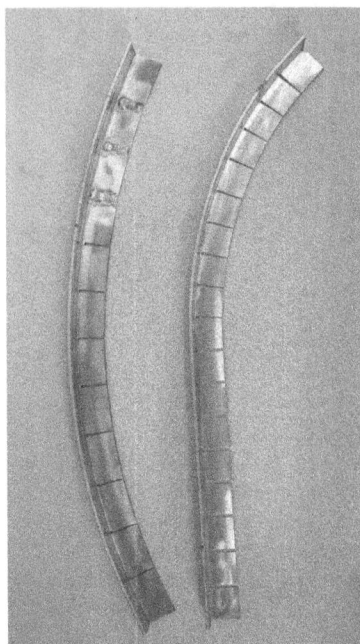

Figure 11.27b Samples of 1" angle with different kerf distances demonstrating the change in radius. One sample has been partially welded. (The author is aware that his TIG welds on aluminum are tolerable at best.)

accurate it is often easiest to use an online calculator designed for this task to determine the number of cuts and distance between cuts. This can also be done by trial and error, but it is far less accurate. The advantage to kerfing is that it prevents the web from bowing, which is likely if roll bent without compensating dies. The process is straight forward once cutting placement is determined: mark the metal, cut only the flange taking care not to mar the inner face of the web. The next steps are to bend the section to fit a template or drawn pattern and weld all of the kerf cuts. While this can be a tedious process and a bit slow, it is easy to accomplish smooth curves with minimal tooling.

- Shaping tube — Bending is the most common way to shape hollow sections, but tubing can also be sectioned to make other shapes.
    - Benders are available in a variety of sizes and many can bend pipe and thin-wall tubing; most are designed to bend round sections. One key skill related to bending tube is marking tubing for proper placement of the bend(s) and aligning these in a bending tool. One of the trickiest bends to make is a U-bend that needs to have an accurate outside-to-outside distance.
        - Conduit benders are designed for thin wall (EMT) but can bend rigid if the bender is rated for it (not all are). This can also be used to bend thin-wall HREW up to about 16 ga. They are affordable and relatively easy to use, though rigid conduit or HREW will take extra oomph. In a pinch, these can also be used to bend thin-wall square tubing if only the outside of the curve will be visible.

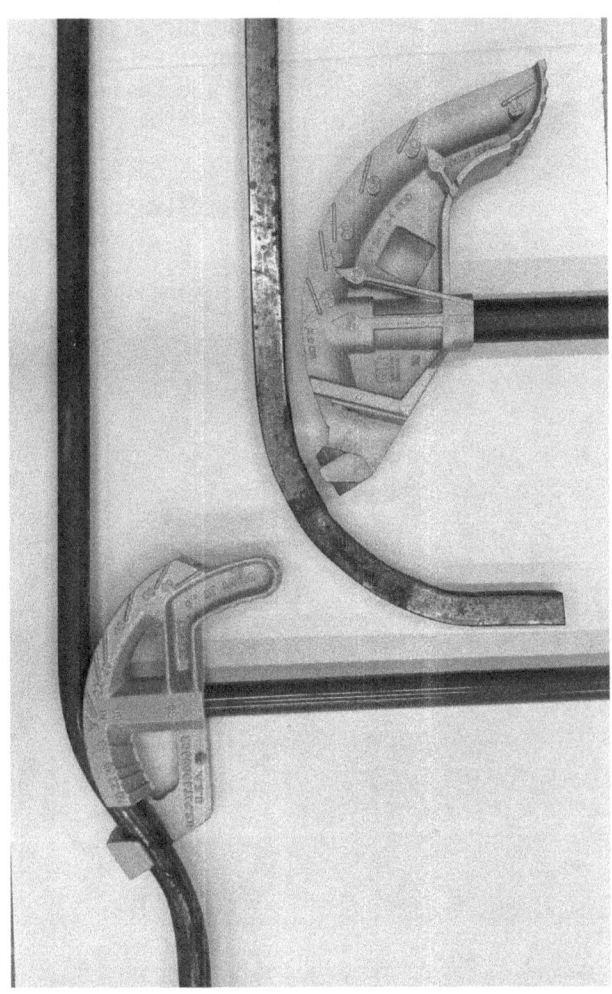

Figure 11.28 Examples of 16ga 3/4" HREW round tube bent to an offset and 16 ga 1" square tube to 90° with a large bender rated for rigid conduit. Though it is not the cleanest bend, it would suffice if only a few parts were required.

- Draw benders are one of the best ways to produce tight radius bends in hollow tubing because they support multiple faces while bending and the interchangeable dies offer an array of options for both shape/size and the Center Line Radius (CLR) of the completed bend. When making bends, it is best to keep the weld seam to the inside of the bend. If an S-shaped bend is needed, the seam should be perpendicular to the bends. One of the keys to planning the required length and shape of the final product is to include any extra material needed to engage the clamping block and to base all measurements on the centerline of the tube. While they are much easier to use than other benders, they are not necessarily as fast to use as one might imagine. Each bend takes a bit of time to get material set properly in the dies and may take a bit of prying to remove them since the tubing does deform just slightly.

- Hossfeld benders can bend hollow shapes such as square tubing and pipe. Square tubing can be bent with either compensating dies or standard dies that indent the inner face to prevent deformation of the sides. Most shops purchased their bender many years ago and do not have compensating dies. When bending pipe, these machines are best suited for bending a fairly long radius. Much like the fork bending of small solids shown in Figure 11.22, pipe is bent in evenly spaced stages.

Figure 11.29a 1" round HREW being bent in a vertical draw bender. This shows action of the machine quite well. Visible on the left is the clamp block that holds the tubing tight enough to be pulled through and around the bending die. Note the use of a magnetic angle gauge to determine the proper bend.

Figure 11.30a A Hossfeld bender set up to bend 1" square tubing. The bending die has a wedge-shaped face that creates an indent on the inner face of the tube. As the tube stretches, the outer face will bend inward somewhat as well.

Figure 11.29b Examples of the dies used in the bender shown in Figure 11.29a. The 1" round dies on the left show the arrangement of the dies when installed. On the right are the pressure die, clamp block, and 4 1/2" CLR bending die for 1" square tube and an example bend.

Figure 11.30b A completed 90° bend in 1" Square tube. This view shows how the compensating die has lifted off the completed bend.

Figure 11.30d The completed 90° bend. This was done in four stages as the bending die is not intended for CLR bending. Note the follower die has been moved toward the handle for increased leverage when bending.

- Roll bending hollow sections follows the same process as that described for solid sections. One important note is that adding too much pressure at once can kink thin-walled tube.

Figure 11.30c A Hossfeld bender set up to bend 1 1/4" HREW. This view how shows how the inner die and the follower need to align. Behind the follower die is a retaining block holding the end of the tube in place.

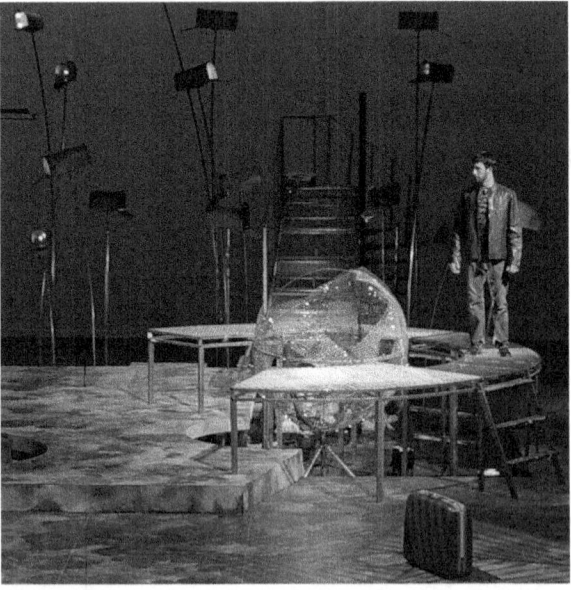

Figure 11.31 The set for *Eurydice* at the University of Memphis made extensive use of roll-bent square tubing for platforms and round tubing for the sculptural mailboxes.

- Hand bending can be done with thin-walled tubing if a durable material, such as plywood, is used for the template and the radius is not too tight. This requires material to be quite a bit longer than the needed final product in order to have the leverage needed to make the bend. This is quite similar to using a bending fork for solid materials as cold bent steel will always spring back somewhat when bending.

○ Rounded corners can be made in square or rectangular tube by cutting out a curved slice leaving one wall untouched that is then bent to fit the inner radius cut. It is easiest to use a template for this. This will not be a common method, but with practice it makes very attractive corners for projects where the frame will be exposed. It is most suitable for aluminum as it is easy to cut. The best solution for steel is to purchase weld-in corners or elbows.

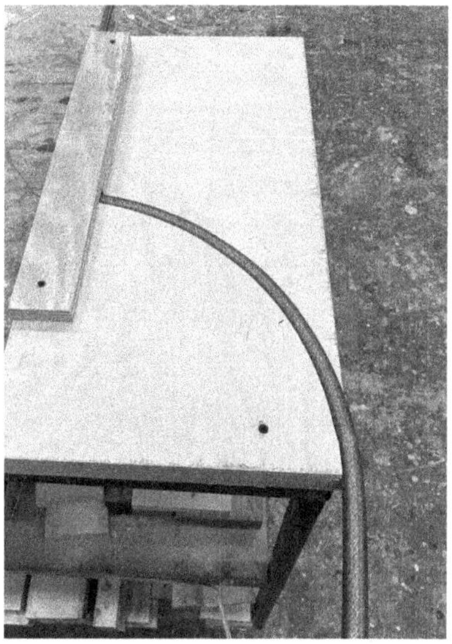

Figure 11.33a An example of a rounded corner in 1" aluminum square tube showing the template, cut (done with a jig saw) and a completed (welded and ground) corner.

Figure 11.32a An example of a plywood template used to bend 1/2" EMT conduit to a smooth curve.

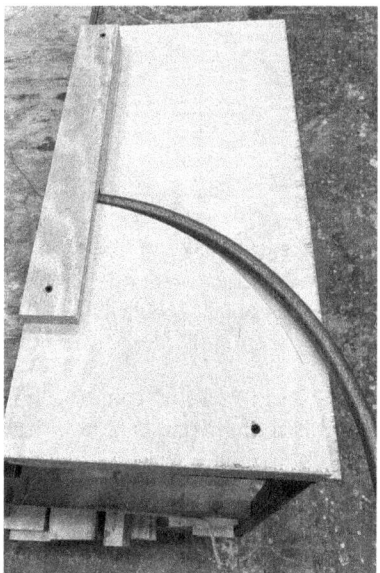

Figure 11.32b An example of spring back from bending with a plywood jig. It takes a little trial and error to find the right pattern size that will make the proper final bend radius.

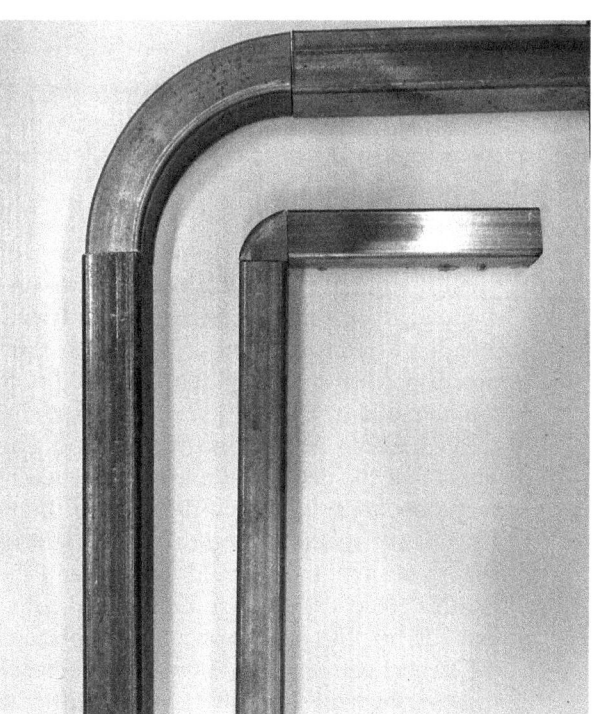

Figure 11.33b Examples of a tubing corner for 1" square tubing and a 2 1/2" CLR elbow for 1 1/4" square tubing.

- Kerf cutting can be used to make bends in tubing much as they can in angle sections. This would only be done when other bending methods are unavailable and only used for non-load bearing applications. Another interesting application of kerf cutting is to create tapers in tubing and pipe.
  - Making tapers in square or rectangular tube can be done three ways: a single taper to one face, a single taper to a midpoint, or double taper to center. Tapering only one face will require accounting for the length needed for the hypotenuse. With any taper, the finished tube will be shorter than the original piece; this will need to be accounted for in the length of the final piece and will vary depending on the length/steepness of the taper. It is possible also to taper two faces to center making a stake point.

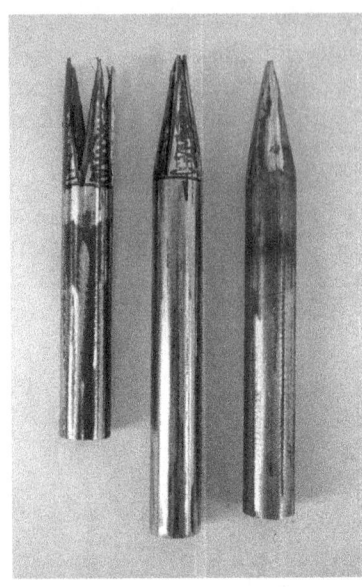

Figure 11.35a Samples showing the process of cutting wedges in tube to produce a relatively smooth point.

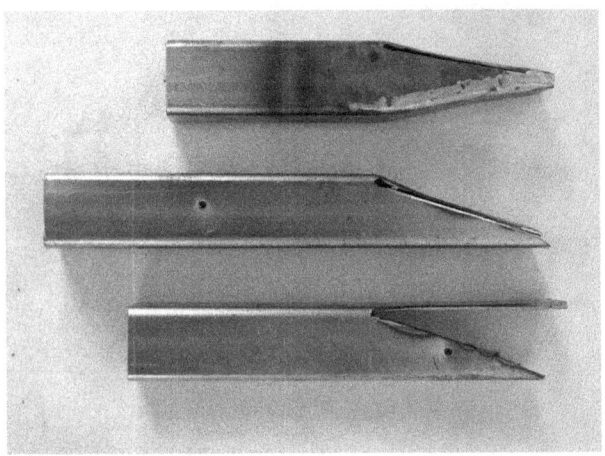

Figure 11.34 From left to right—A 1″ square tube tapered to center, a taper to one face that did not account for the hypotenuse length and a sample of a taper to face properly cut in order to fully cap the hypotenuse.

  - Round tapers require four cuts or more. For small diameter, thin-wall tube, four wedge-shaped cuts will make a fairly smooth transition; larger diameters may need six to eight cuts. Sharp transitions similar to a bell fitting can be made by cutting a series of short slits with a cutting wheel. The thickness of the wheel and the depth of the cuts will need to vary depending on the difference in diameters. If the sections need to hold weight or will be masted, they should overlap and the smaller piece should have an internal collar that can be plug welded once it is in place in the larger tube/pipe. As above, the taper will shorten the piece somewhat so beginning with an extra-long piece is wise.

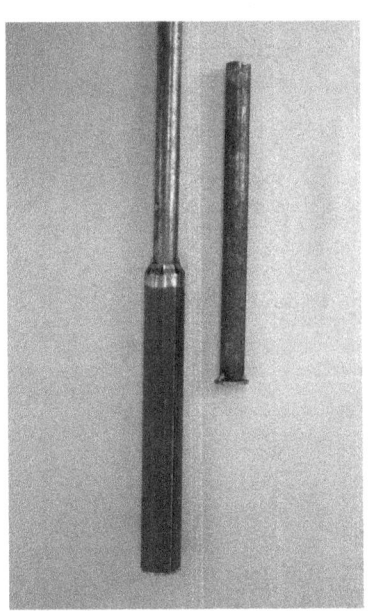

Figure 11.35b A transition joint cut in 1 1/4″ tube to fit 3/4″ tube. The sample to the right also shows the internal cap that braces the extension, keeping it parallel.

- Sheet metal—Because sheet metal is thin and pliable, many shapes can be made with it that no other material can successfully achieve. Sheet metal can be formed into domes, arcs, channels, boxes, and other shapes fairly easily with the right tools and techniques. What follows is merely a primer to shaping sheet metal.
  - Brakes are used for making clean straight bends. While seaming pliers are excellent for small tabs, a

brake is usually required to make bends of any significant length. As well, thicker materials require the extra leverage that a brake provides. Large brakes have counterweights to assist with the bend.

- Setting a brake for the thickness of the material being used is important. Setting the depth too shallow can cause the die to cut into soft material or even cut though, while setting too large of a distance can lead to a bend with a radius or to having the material slip while bending.

Figure 11.37a A tabbed sheet metal pan layout on 16 ga steel along with the test pattern in chip board.

Figure 11.36 Setting a finger brake to match the material. The fingers should be set slightly farther back from the bending face than the thickness of the material to be bent.

- Box (or pan) brakes are used to make objects with multiple sides that cannot be made on a straight brake. Even overlapping tabs can be made with proper planning. One of the best methods for planning a box is to make chip board pattern of similar thickness to the sheet that will be used for the final product and use it to plan the steps in the brake. Each bend can be easily numbered and the pattern folded and unfolded for use by any member of the crew.

Figure 11.37b The ends of the pan are too narrow for a larger finger, thus the end is bent in stages moving the finger from left to right to achieve a clean bend. The connecting tabs were hand bent with seaming pliers.

Figure 11.37c Bending the sides of the pan is relatively easy. They are placed to not interfere with the ends. This view shows the punched ends where the pan will be welded.

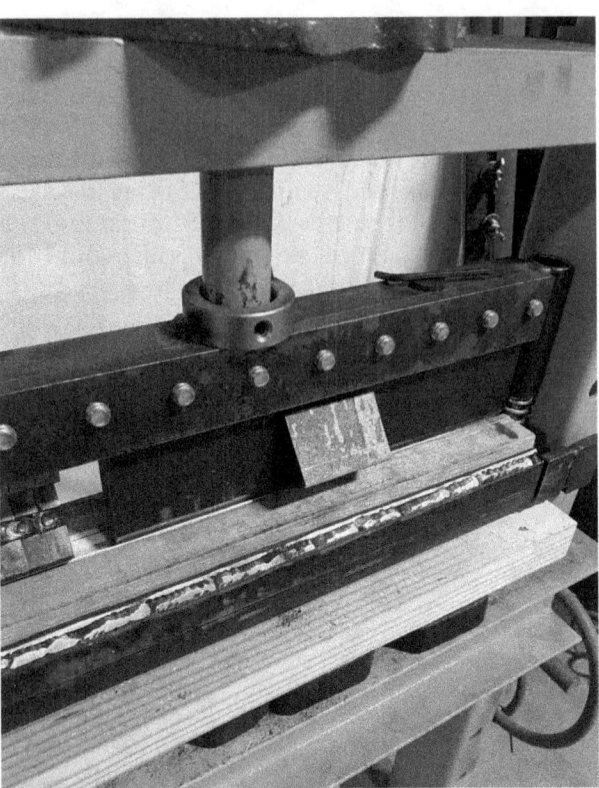

Figure 11.38a Making the second bend using standard dies on the press brake shows the interference they present due to the existing first bend.

Figure 11.37d The completed pan with the tabs plug welded and ground flat.

- Gooseneck dies are V-shaped dies that are used in a press brake for making bends that double back such as for brackets and hangers. Standard flat dies interfere with the material from the first bend unless the area is very small. A similar interference happens under the dies on a traditional brake.

Figure 11.38b Making the second bend with a set of gooseneck dies shows how the tab made in the first pass can tuck in.

Figure 11.38c A comparison of the two second bends with the dies used to make them. Note the inability to make a second 90° bend using standard dies.

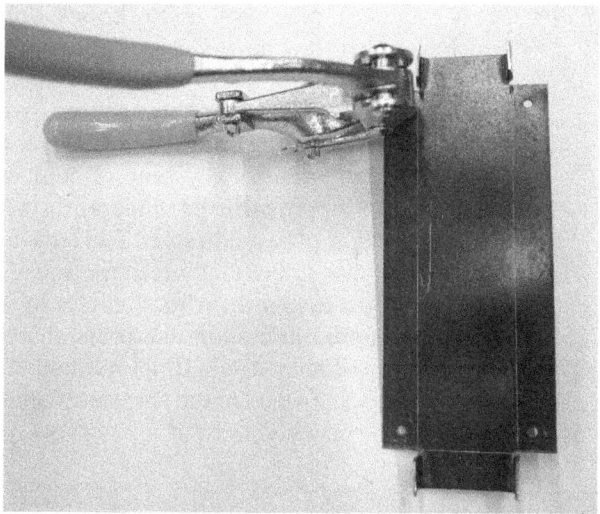

Figure 11.39 An example of a swing-arm punch being used to make holes that will be used for plug welding a steel pan after it is formed.

- Punching is a better choice than drilling when a very clean and precise hole in thin material is required. Twist drills with two flutes (the most common) tend to make somewhat triangular holes in thin sheet, especially if they are slightly dull or have points that are not ground perfectly even. Larger hole saws tend to be unwieldy in thin sheet, especially as they break through the surface and leave very sharp edges and burrs. Small saws used for pilot holes need to be used with care.
  - Hand punches, sometimes called a "Whitney" punch, use a manual lever to push the head of the punch though the die. These are available as both hand-held and bench mount versions. Most punches have a starting dimple that helps with centering. These are used along the edge of very thin sheet, usually 18 ga and under, to make holes for Cleco pins, welding or holes for switches and indicators in a control panel. They typically have a depth stop that makes aligning holes along an edge easier.
  - Knock-out punches use a threaded stem to draw the head through the backing die. This requires a pilot hole slightly larger than the drawbar be made first. Due to the large size of most drawbars, the pilot hole is often made with a hole saw or step drill. These punches should be operated using a box wrench or socket; using power tools, such as an impact, tends to strip the threads of the drawbar easily. If more power is required, hydraulic versions are available. The advantage to a knock-out punch is the ability to be used anywhere in the face of a sheet and their ability to punch through thicker material than other through punches, up to 10 ga mild steel.

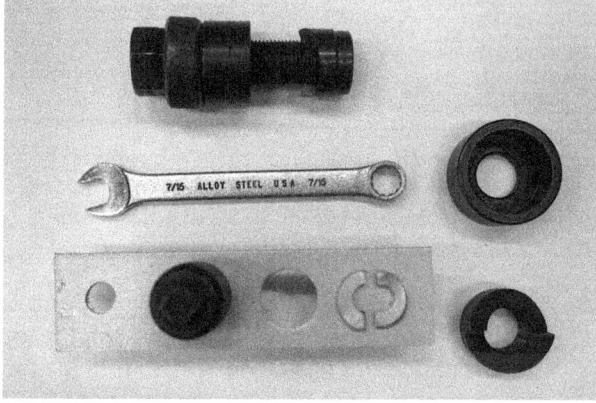

Figure 11.40 A sample showing the stages of using a knock-out punch in aluminum. From left to right—a pilot hole for the arbor, the punch set (larger punch above shows the stacking order), and a completed hole with the waste material.

- Press punches are similar to knock-out punches in that they have a center guide pin that requires a pilot hole to align the punch and die. Instead of a drawbar, these are pressed through the sheet using either an arbor press or hydraulic press. One key requirement is being able to support the die while ensuring a pass through for the guide stem. The advantage to these over knock-out punches is speed, especially when used in an arbor press for thin sheet. When used in a hydraulic press, these may have a capacity up to 10 ga mild steel. Placement is somewhat limited since any panel needing to be punched must fit in the press.

Figure 11.41 Punching steel sheet on an arbor press with a completed hole and second punch set shown. The bottom plate of the press has four sizes of pass-through slots to support different-sized dies.

  ○ Using a slip roll to make a cylinder or cone is fairly straight forward. Using the formula for the circumference of a circle πD will provide the net length required. This will be sufficient for a butt-welded seam; a lapped seam will require additional material. The material is then sent through the roll in a series of passes, increasing the elevator roll with each pass, until the desired diameter is acquired. Cones move through the machine much the same way, though only one end of the elevator roll is adjusted and the operated must rotate the material as is slips through. One important note: The minor diameter needs to have an arc length that is slightly longer than the circumference of the drive rolls if the cone is to be completed on the machine. For example, a cone made from a 90° sweep would need a minor arc length 4x the circumference of the drive roll. Many sheet metal supplier websites offer calculators to aid in laying out a cone pattern.

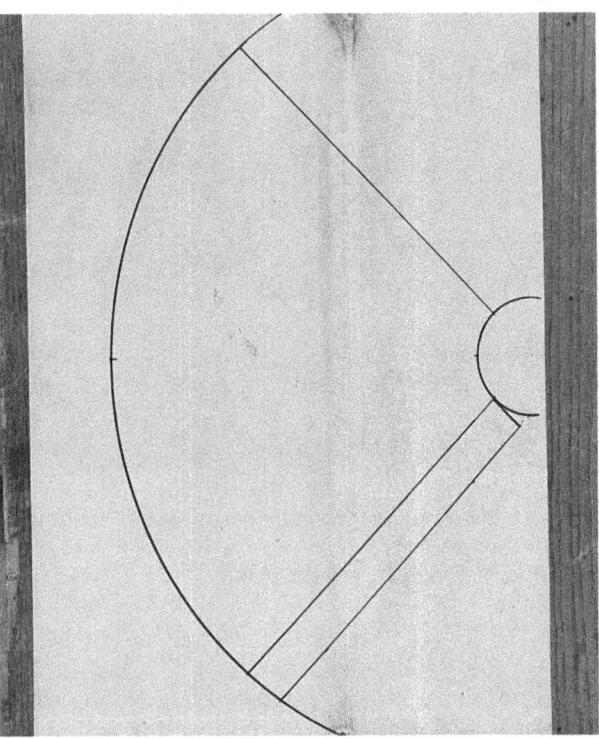

Figure 11.42a The flat pattern for a cone on sheet aluminum. The extra rectangular area will be a lapped joint.

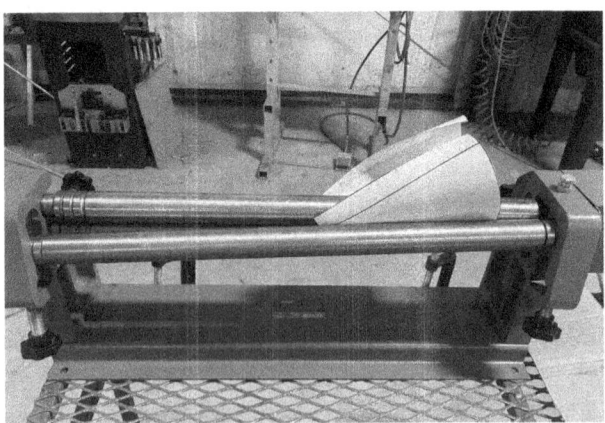

Figure 11.42b Rolling the cone on the slip roll. Note the angle of the elevator roll. In addition, the pressure rolls have been set with high pressure on the narrow end only allowing slip at the large end of the cone, as the large end needs to be kept nearly perpendicular to the drive rolls.

shrinkers/stretchers are designed for quite thin sheet (usually 18 ga or less) and are for long gentle bends or shallow domes.
- Ring rolling—Creating metal loops with rod is quite easy. Either a stand-alone ring roller or the rod grooves in a slip roll can be used. The operation is essentially identical to using a slip roll for sheet: the rod is fed into the appropriately sized groove with the elevator roll raised slightly, then the rod is passed through and back until the desired diameter is achieved.

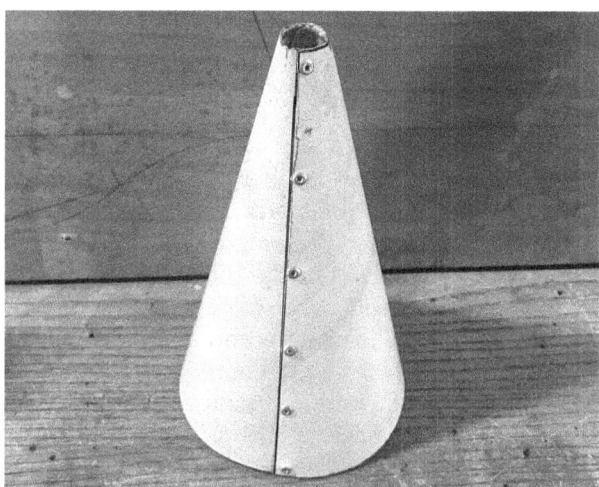

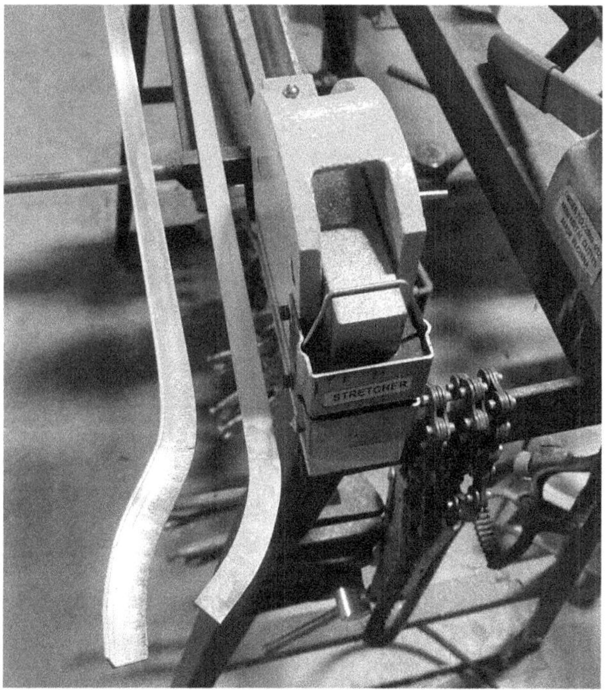

Figure 11.42c The completed cone. The author made one semi-critical error: the minor diameter of the cone is far smaller than the drive rolls, requiring the final bending to be completed by hand.

○ Shrinking and stretching sheet metal and thin metal trim pieces to make curved components to size requires patience and a bit of practice. The full length of the bend, or perimeter of the dome, should be crimped slightly, then repeated until the desired result is achieved. Note that

Figure 11.44a Starting the process of making a ring using the wire grooves on a slip roll.

Figure 11.44b Completing a 6" diameter ring from 1/8" hot finish steel rod.

STEEL

There are only a few techniques unique to working with steel. Steel and aluminum can both be cut in similar ways, welded with essentially identical processes,

Figure 11.43 A section of 16ga aluminum angle trim demonstrating both shrinking (flange on outside of bend) and stretching (flange on inside of bend) and a piece of 16ga aluminum strap showing the jaw marks removed with a flap wheel.

and cold formed to many of the same shapes. The primary shaping method that will be unique to steel for most shops is hot forming. Heating before shaping is common with steel because it is the ideal metal for this; it has an easy to see and learn color change across a broad temperature range, becomes quite soft when properly heated, and retains its strength and stiffness once cooled. Aluminum is much more difficult to hot form because of the lack of a color change. Thick copper and copper alloys such as bronze also hot form well but are less likely to be used. What follows is a short introduction to common hot forming techniques that can be handy to learn.

- Bending—Hot steel is relatively easy to bend so long as it is at proper heat. Steel should be a bright orange-red, not cherry or dark cherry when bending. Bending steel at too low of a temperature makes it more likely to create surface cracks, especially on tight bends. Using steel patterns or jigs that the hot steel can be wrapped around or pressed into is the best way to make repeatable, accurate shapes. Rings, twisted square bar and strap, offsets and S-hooks are common shapes that can be made quickly. Most shops will use an OAF torch to heat the steel, but a small propane furnace is another good option for shops that make larger batches of parts.
  - Twisting bar can be done by placing one end in a vise, heating the area that needs to be bent, then twisting the free end with pliers, tongs, or a wrench. Blacksmiths tend to make twisting wrenches. One important note: the entire area of the twist needs to be heated at once to produce a consistent helix.
  - Rings can be easily be made by clamping one end to an appropriate diameter pipe (slightly smaller than the required ID as the steel will spring back a bit), then heating the bar or rod as it is pulled around the pipe. This can be heated as progress is made; no need to heat the entire bar at once. The author prefers to use the non-heated section of bar as a handle until it conducts too much heat, then switch to locking pliers for the remainder since they do not slip.

Figure 11.46a A section of 1 1/2" pipe has been drilled as an anchor for bending a section of 3/8" cold-rolled bar into rings.

Figure 11.46b The rings completed fully wrapping the pipe. The anchor end will not be used.

Figure 11.45 1/2" square bar twisted using a 12" adjustable wrench as a lever. The bar will only twist where heated, in this case a 1 1/2" long section. Some of the soap stone marking is still visible, even after heating.

Figure 11.46c The rings cut free with a cutting wheel. The anchor needs to be cut as well to free all material.

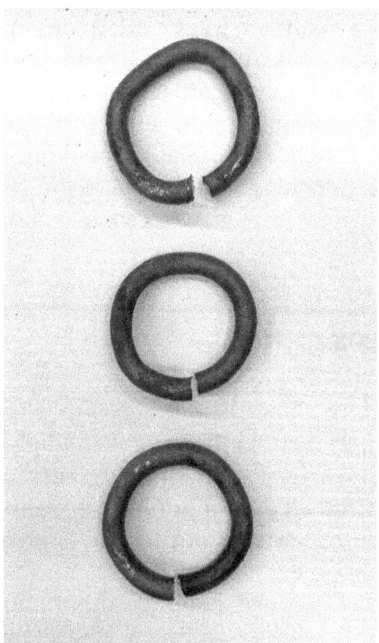

Figure 11.46d The rings for comparison; the top "ring" is waste material. Though wound in a spiral on the pipe, they are fairly easy to straighten in a vise. The rings can be welded shut if needed.

- S-hooks and offsets are made with similar jigs. One end is placed in a keeper, then the heated bar is woven through the forming pins.

Figure 11.47 Examples of S-hooks formed using a shop-made jig. The bends are started on the bottom pin with material against the keeper (left) then around the upper pin. The upper pin is shorter, making the first bend much easier. The upper-most S-hook was cold-bent.

- Upsetting—This is a technique most often applied to square bar but works well on round bar as well. The process is simple: clamp the bar tightly in a vise (wider jaws hold best), heat the end, and then strike it squarely with a hammer. This will create a nicely flared end that makes a very nice furniture foot. Some adjustment may be needed between passes to keep the end inline with the center axis of the bar. Blacksmiths often use an upsetting block, which is simply a very large piece of steel on the floor, to upset bar up to 2" square by dropping the bar on the block once heated.

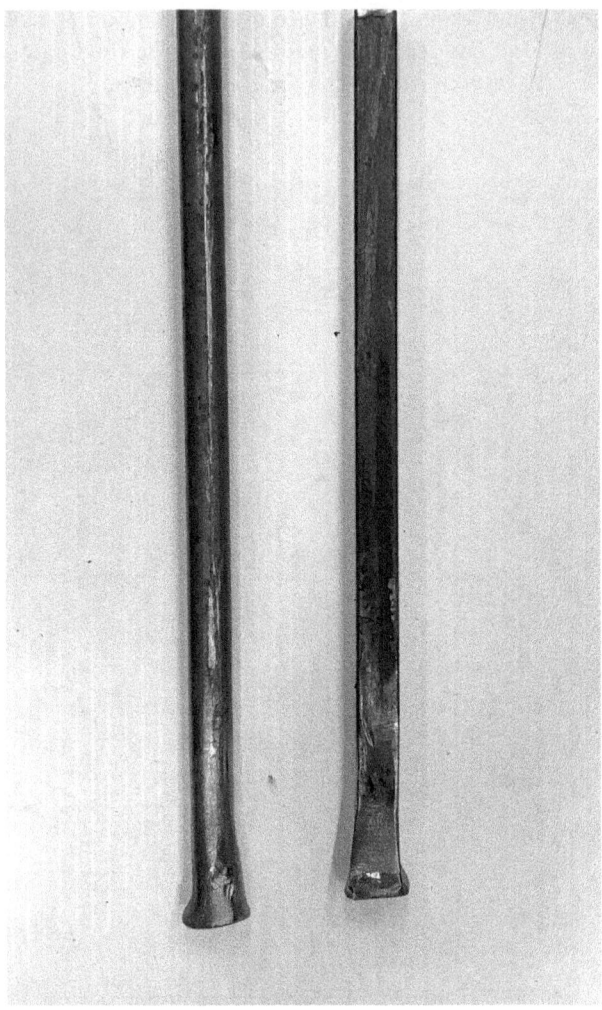

Figure 11.48 Examples of 1/2" square bar and 1/2" round bar upset for a unique end flare.

- Peening—The rounded end of a ball peen hammer is an often misunderstood tool. One of the best uses for one is to finish a hot rivet. Though often done with the head set in a rivet buck, this really can be done on any solid steel surface. The whole rivet should be heated before insertion, then placed on the backer. The ball end of the hammer is used to set the rivet by striking the rivet on center to expand it into the hole, then strike off center working around the perimeter to finish "heading-off" the rivet. While not often done, a hot rivet will hold very tightly and looks like no other fastener. It would not be useful for large scenery but can make an excellent detail on a film prop that will see action for example.
- Anvils—The classic multi-use tool for shaping steel is an anvil. One requirement is a proper set of hammers. Having a pair of ball peen hammers (10–12 and 16–18 oz) as well as a pair of cross peen hammers (1 lb and a 1 1/2 lb or 2 lb) will make most shapes a shop would ever need to make. Though most shops do not have an anvil, for prop and craft shops even a small (55 lb) anvil can be a very valuable tool. A few basic skills that may be handy are explained below. For those interested in more information, a selection of books on blacksmithing are listed in Chapter 15.
  - The horn of the anvil is for bending hooks and loops, stretching or widening when combined with a cross peen, and for opening or straightening rings. These tasks can be completed with the flat face of either a ball- or cross peen hammer.
  - The face is used for squaring up bar after bending, tapering (the steel is held to the face at a slight angle while struck with a hammer at double the angle), and for many other shaping tasks such as stretching and flattening using a cross- or straight peen hammer. The direction the peen intersects the hot metal will determine whether the metal gets stretched length- or width-wise.
  - The Hardie hole (square) in the tail of the anvil is designed to hold tools such as a hot cut (strike hot metal with a hammer to cut off, avoiding the tool), a shaping stake or "fuller" (Strike hot metal to press it into the negative shape of the stake) or a veining tool used to make grooves in flat steel. The Pritchel hole (small round one) is mostly for hot punching (strike a sharp punch directly over the hole), though some tooling may also fit.

ALUMINUM SPECIFICS

One important reminder about building with aluminum regarding material strength: while it is a light and strong material, it is critically important to ensure the design takes the reduced strength of the weld-affected area and pull-out strength of fasteners into account.

- Bending—Using a brake for bending aluminum sheet is very similar to working with steel with a few additional requirements. Only very thin sheet can be bent in a single pass to sharp angles. Any sheet over about .040" will need to be bent using either die with a slight radius or use a two-stage bend (or more for very thick sheets). Another trick that can work well on thick sheets is to cut a groove on the interior of the bend to a depth of about half the thickness, then weld it once the bend is complete. Press brakes often have blunt dies that work quite well with aluminum.

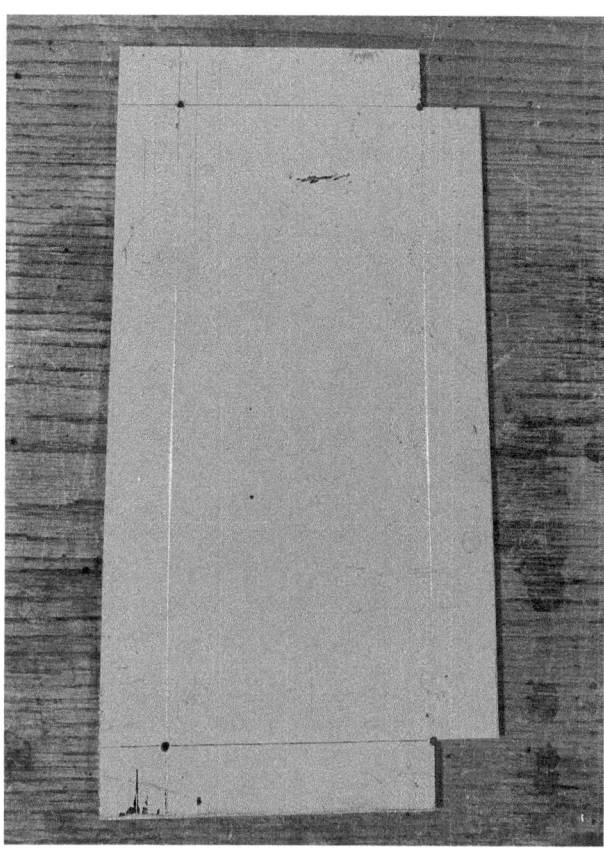

Figure 11.49a Preparing a sheet of aluminum to make a small tray using a press brake. The holes drilled at each corner relieve stress when bending; these would be hidden if the tray corners were welded.

Figure 11.49c The complete tray, upside down, showing how the drilled corners aid in avoiding cracks.

- Notched corners—Cutting a 90° notch in aluminum angle is an excellent way to make a very clean corner for projects like a sign frame. This provides a clean reveal and a flat surface to easily mount sheet materials.

Figure 11.49b Bending aluminum in a press brake to form a small tray. The dies in this brake have a slight radius making them a good match to bending aluminum.

Figure 11.50a Aluminum angle trim with 90° V-notch cuts that, when bent, will frame the advertisement.

Figure 11.50b Checking the fitment of the frame, showing how the completed frame would protect the sheet material. Corner joints have been welded on the back to maintain a flat mounting surface.

ASSEMBLIES

Many of the techniques and finished products included in this section could present serious life-safety risks in application. It is of the utmost importance than completed units that will support people or be suspended over them be made by a competent weldor. The author has endeavored to suggest techniques that can be made by many shops that have a trained weldor in house, but the author and publisher take no responsibility for the misapplication of the information contained herein. The reader must determine how applicable the techniques presented are to their individual process or shop and how to implement them safely.

- Flats—Metal-framed flats assemble in much the same way as wood flats but lack the ability to be racked square after assembly. This means the layout of the components must be quite accurate and true in order to produce a well-made flat. Using a layout table for smaller flats, or possibly the floor for larger flats, can ensure repeatable accuracy.
  - The first step after cutting components is to lay them out and hold them in place in a manner that will not interfere with welding (often with wood blocks). A 3-4-5 triangle is an excellent means of ensuring that components that need to be perpendicular are. When using a layout table, a fence for two sides can aid in setting up one-off units.
  - Tack welding the entire frame (using opposing tacks at each joint to equalize stress) will ensure the ability to make changes after final measuring if needed. Diagonal measurements should be used to check rectilinear units.
  - Final welding should also be done in an order that helps equalize stress. For many applications only two or three sides of components will require welds. When faces that will be covered are welded, some grinding may be required for material to set flush.

Figure 11.51a A wall section made from 1 1/4" square steel tubing laid out and ready for welding. The wood blocking will help maintain squareness. Though a 3-4-5 triangle was used to establish baselines, the diagonals were still compared prior to tack welding.

Figure 11.51b A segment of a similar wall as above tack welded at opposing corners to help relieve stress. The diagonal measurements are compared once more before final welding.

Figure 11.51c Multiple sections of wall framing laid out to ensure bolt pattern alignment. All units have been welded on three sides, leaving one face with no welds to impede the installation of facing.

Figure 11.51d The walls from above being installed for a production of *The Most Happy Fella* at the University of Memphis.

- Platforms—Metal-framed platforms will often be assembled in much the same way as those made from wood. In some cases, such as using extruded aluminum or spaced-frame steel, the toggles may not need to be the full depth of the perimeter as they are on wood-framed units.
  ○ Rectangular tubing is an excellent material to replace wood framing on modular platforms. Assembling a platform should follow the same process as building flats (shown in Figures 11.51a–d). Increasing the depth of the rectangle adds significantly more bending strength per pound of material than increasing wall thickness. This is an example of where varying sized components may be used based on their role (such as span length) in the structure. Examples of rectangular tube-framed platforms are shown in Figure 3.2.
  ○ Spaced-frame platforms are a simple way to add significant strength to the framing without adding too much weight. This design offers increased resistance to deflection over 2″ rectangular tube and allows for lower visual impact than rectangular tube. In many cases toggles will only be required on the top to support the surface material. Examples in Figures 3.1 (frame has been faced) and 3.6a (right hand, upper level).
  ○ Bar truss platforms are spaces-frame style with bent round bar filling the space between the top and bottom tube chords, like bar truss. These are exceptionally strong; one manufacture has regularly displayed their version with a tractor parked on top.
  ○ Extruded aluminum platforms made with custom extrusions can allow platforms to be hybrids. These can be designed to sit directly on a deck,

Figure 11.52a In the image many components of the modular decking at Accurate Staging, Nashville are visible: in the foreground, a modular platform converted for use as a wagon; behind it a mobile storage rack holding individual legs in the upper basket and platforms with legging pockets below; behind and to the left are modular stairs with hand rails and scaffold-like "walls" that are used to support the platforms on more decks converted to wagons by making use of the legging pockets.

Figure 11.52b A detail view of the modular platform and custom extrusions: the perimeter frame, toggles (T-braces), and legging pockets are custom extrusions while the bolt-on low-profile caster plates are house fabricated.

- Square tube is one of the most common materials for a shop to stock and may be used solo to frame stairs so long as sufficient legging is used. Like other methods, the treads will need to be made from other materials.
  - Stair units that need to be uniquely shaped may be built from welded "cube" frames for each tread with sufficient depth to overlap 1/3–1/2 of the face of the tread frame above/below. Though this method uses more material, only straight cuts are required and many short pieces of reclaimed material can be used. This design also allows each tread to be a unique size and shape as long as the back of each tread is flat. There are a variety of ways to add facings that match the tread contours such as filling below the tread with carved foam, or cutting a matching contour (likely from plywood) to attach to either the bottom of the cube or to the floor depending on need.

be elevated on independent legs or scaffolding, and/or have bolt-on accessories like casters or hand railings.

- Stairs—There are a multitude of ways metal shapes can be combined to make stair units. Most units will likely be a mix of materials. A few examples that are fairly easy to build follow.
  - Rectangular tube used for carriages is common. Most often the treads will be framed with square tube and covered with plywood or tread plate. Increasing the depth of the rectangular tube will increase its capable span. It also provides a flat continuous surface making weld-up easier. Large rectangular tube can also be seen in Figure 3.2 used as the supports for the upstage stair unit.

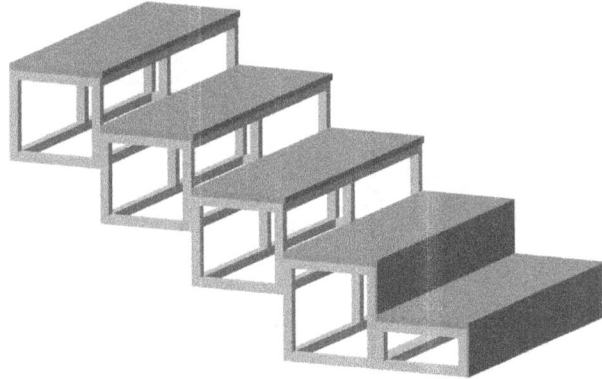

Figure 11.54 A CAD drawing of a cube-based stair unit. In this example the rise is 6", with an overlap of 4", making each cube 10" overall except the bottom two steps which have been sized to provide a sturdy base. The facing is removed from upper stairs to better show the structure.

Figure 11.53 Stairs constructed with 2"×4" rectangular tube carriages and 1" square tube-framed treads. It is part of the inventory at the University of Memphis having been saved from a previous production; they can be modified for future use as needed.

  - Square tubing can be used as a spaced-frame carriage, much the same way it can be done for a platform. When treads are welded in place, they become the toggles and increase resistance to bending. A surprisingly long span can be made this way, even with thin-walled tubes such as 16 ga.
  - Combining rectangular tubing for the base of the run (much like the bottom chord of a truss) with square tubing above for the rise and run also makes a fairly strong set of stairs, though strength will depend on the depth of the rectangular tube used.

Figure 11.55a A set of space frame steel stairs made from 1″ 16 ga steel tube and 3/16″ tread plate. These too are in the inventory at the University of Memphis and can be adapted as needed.

Figure 11.55b Descent to the "lair" stairs for *Phantom of the Opera* in progress at the University of Memphis. These units were constructed from 2″×1″ rectangular and 1″ square tubing. They were supported by legs and anchors in the block wall.

- Channel and angle can be used for both carriages and treads, though channel is a simpler solution for carriages. Angle as tread framing can be excellent for wood treads; when the flange faces up it will protect the face of the wood tread from wear and chipping. Angle can also be a simple way to add a mounting surface for a riser when the flange is pointing down. When combined with tread plate, this saves the need to bend the tread plate to provide enough stiffness.

Figure 11.56 Stairs fabricated to match the modular platforming at Accurate Staging, Nashville. The stairs are standardized with 6″x3.63plf channel, accommodating their longest required rise.

- Contoured—These surfaces can be difficult to make with metal. Sculptural shapes often need to be a hybrid of materials to achieve the desired look, with metal making up the understructure and an array of materials used to make the surface.
  - Rod and mesh combine to make an excellent understructure for rock- and tree-like textures. Hot-rolled rod is easiest to bend. Long arcs may be bent by hand, while tight bends may require tools such as a bending fork or template. Depending on the needs of the project the bar stock may be welded together to form a solid armature or bound with tie-wire. Light gauge mesh can be manipulated by hand (gloves should be worn) and attached to the bar with wire or even zip ties. Top coatings will need to be applied by some means that pushes the material through the mesh to adhere well.
  - Flat bar is also quite useful for scroll shapes. Hot-rolled steel is readily available and will make fairly tight bends without heat if not too thick. Aluminum flat bar is also easy to source and roll bends quite well. Other benders, like a Hossfeld or scroll bender also work well with both metals,

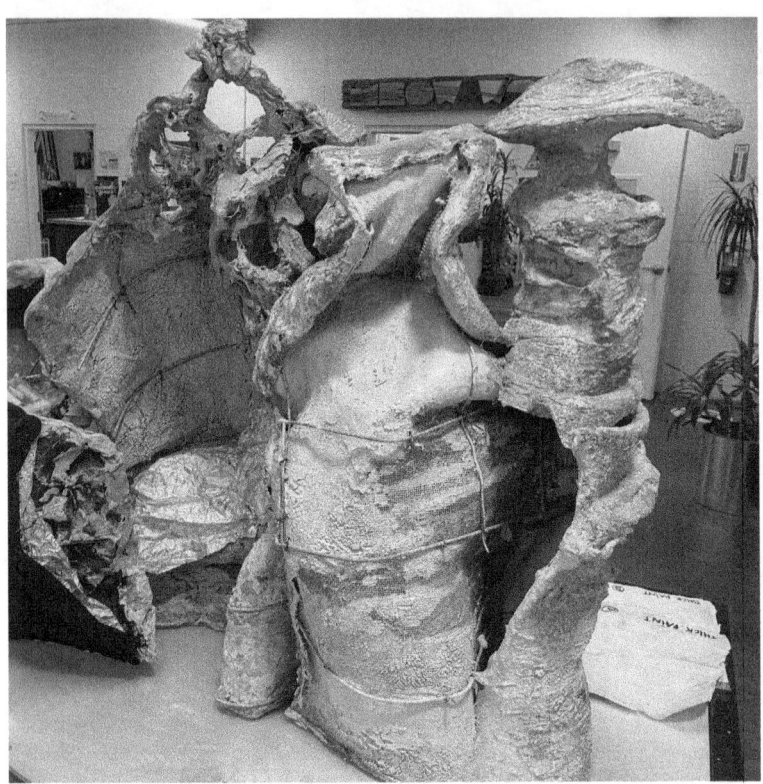

Figure 11.57a The back of a sample stone wall in the shop at Meow Wolf. Note the rod is connected with tie-wire and the mesh attached with simple zip ties. The images is an excellent example of the texturing material coming through the mesh.

Figure 11.57b A chandelier built by the author for *Cyrano DeBergerac*; the perimeter of each arm and upper scroll is steel flat bar reinforced internally with 1/2" square tube. The top cap is also steel. This combination allowed the chandelier to be climbed on.

but care should be used to not stretch aluminum when bending.
- Other small metal shapes such as thin-walled tube can be formed with hand tools as shown elsewhere in this chapter. Expanded sheet can be used similar to mesh to make a much more durable surface or left in view. It is harder to shape than mesh, but the open area allows for the metal to move in multiple axes without too much trouble. Solid sheet, even when light gauge, will complicate the process since equipment specific to shrinking or stretching will be needed.

Figure 11.58a The back for a compound curve chair being fabricated from 1/2" square tube and 3/4" flattened, expanded steel by graduate student Jay Deen.

Figure 11.58b The same chair on stage for the internal "opera" *Don Juan* for University of Memphis production of *Phantom of the Opera*.

- Spans—There are a number of ways to use metal for spans and they often achieve this easier than lumber or with a smaller section size.
  - Steel bar truss, sometimes called "wiggle wire" trusses, can be purchased from manufacturers of metal buildings and can often be ordered through steel supply warehouses. These are one of the strongest options and are often much lighter than the required I-beam for the same span would be for the loads common to the industry. This is due to the truss having a higher resistance to bending than an I-beam. An example of a span supported by bar truss can be seen in Figure 3.6a.
  - Rectangular tubing is an excellent solution for short to medium spans. Much more compact sections are available than those for I-beams and tube resists twisting better than channel. Examples of rectangular tubing being used for different spans can be seen in Figure 3.2.
  - Trusses are always great for long spans; square and rectangular tubes are another option for fabricating trusses when flat faces are needed to mount other material, such as plywood or grating.

Figure 11.59 Trusses fabricated from 2" square tubing for the chords, and 2"×1" tubing for the internal members. The span is 34'. These are used to extend the stage over an orchestra pit by 48".

- I-beams and channels are the traditional sections used for spans in building construction. Channels are often preferred over I-beams in entertainment structures due to relatively light loads and the large flat surface of the web that allows for easy attachment of materials used for decoration or masking. While a channel needs more bracing than an I-beam, they are available in smaller sizes and are not generally used for very long spans. Aluminum channels are a more common choice than steel.

ASSEMBLY TIPS

- Keeping units true—When welding, the heat distorts materials to some extent. One of the best ways to ensure welding has the lowest impact on the trueness of the unit is to do so in stages. Most weldors will lay out the entire unit or at least the perimeter then tack one face on all joints. The next step is to make any needed adjustments, then tack weld an opposing face at each joint. One last check for squareness and then the rest of the welds are made. How the framing is held in place can also help or hinder
  - To check for squareness on large units, the best methods is to compare the diagonal measurements of the longest hypotenuses. For smaller units checking inside and outside with a speed

Figure 11.60 An aluminum speed square and a steel framing square, each with the outer vertex cut off. This creates space for a weld, making it easy to check interior 90° corners as shown on the samples.

or framing square may be sufficient. One trick is to remove the exterior vertex of the square to avoid weld interference.
- Holding components in place for welding can be done with a fixture, magnets, or clamps. Each tool has its place.
  - Fixtures may be wood or metal templates that hold components in place for repeatable shapes. Most often these hold the parts accurately while offering enough flexibility to prevent tension build up in the unit. These take time to build and are thus only valuable when multiple identical units are required. When wood is used, it is best to create holes or spaces under the weld area. This will prevent charring which can impart impurities in the weld, especially when welding aluminum.
  - Magnets are the fastest way to hold parts in place, but they can be tricky to place accurately when they are strong permanent magnets but could move during welding if they are low-cost magnets with minimal hold. These should always be removed before final welding to avoid overheating the magnet. A number of unique magnetic tools are shown in Figures 5.24 and 5.25.
  - Clamps provide the best hold, so components are less likely to shift as the weld starts, but they may hide tension created by heat causing parts to spring into the wrong shape or place when released. This is less likely to happen with a tack weld than a full weld. An assortment of welding clamps is shown in Figure 5.18. Most clamps will withstand some heat from welding, but overheating can affect the metallurgy of the clamp.
- Attachment—Shops often need to attach non-metallic materials to metal. There are a variety of ways to do so and most are discussed in Chapter 9. What follows are a few tips regarding fastener use.
  - Self-drilling screws are an excellent way to attach materials to metal frames when the appearance of the fastener is not a concern. When attaching thick material, screws with a drill point and pilot wings prevent the material from being caught on the threads of the screw. The trick to these is using an RPM similar to the same-size twist drill and keeping the fastener perpendicular to the metal face. A good rule of thumb is 1000–1400 RPM for most screws. These are also not reusable; the drill points will be too dull to start a new hole but can be carefully reinserted into the original hole in some cases.

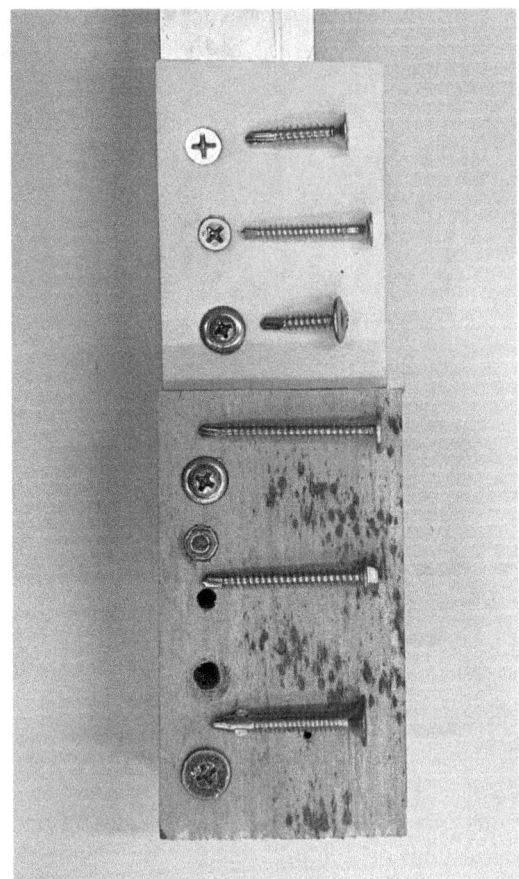

Figure 11.61 Examples of various styles of self-drilling screws. The screws in the soft, thin cellular PVC (top) do not require pilot holes, but the thicker denser plywood does for many screws. The example shows a wafer head screw with piloting "wings", which is the only screw shown that does not require piloting before installation.

- T-nails are another common way to attach material to metal frames because the small head makes them easy to hide with a bit of filler. They are also very fast and easy to install. These were designed for attaching to concrete block but work well on aluminum and thin-wall steel tube. The nail gun has a drive mechanism similar in size to a framing nailer but is putting that force against a much smaller nail. The nails need to be driven in while perpendicular; they can ricochet off the surface of steel even at a slight angle. Holding the nail gun tightly with a second hand on top of the air chamber to steady it helps ensure proper installation. Though the nails hold well, the addition of a bit of mastic adhesive will prevent the facing material from working loose during transport or other movement.

Figure 11.62 A steel-framed wall in process for the Phantom's "lair" in the University of Memphis production of *Phantom of the Opera*. All facing was attached with T-nails and construction adhesive. The vertical edges of each sheet were additionally attached with a few self-drilling screws.

- Double stick tape is an excellent way to mount materials to metal frames. Many types of these tapes are available, but one with some thickness will be usually be required. Adhesive films generally do not have enough bite to connect different surface types, though they can work well for attaching aluminum foils to other materials or aluminum sheet to aluminum framing. For steel, the surface must be exceptionally clean. An extra pass with denatured alcohol after degreasing will improve adhesion. Aluminum simply needs to be free of dust or other shop contaminants.

Figure 11.63 Acrylic sheet attached to steel frames for the set of *Empire of Eternal Void* at the University of Memphis using exterior grade, double-sided foam tape; this avoided the risk of cracking from drilling and/or screwing.

- Metal-filled epoxy can be a great choice for repairs where light machining is needed or to repair internal threads for non-critical applications. One popular brand is JB weld, but there are many companies that make filled epoxies in varying consistencies from gels to putties. They are quite strong but are not used to join metal to metal in most cases. They work quite well to add small metal parts to props when close-up details are needed.

WORKING WITH COPPER

While working with steel and aluminum may be familiar to many fabricators, copper is less often used in the industry but has many properties that make it excellent for certain applications.

- Annealing—Hand shaping of copper is best done after the material has been annealed (some copper is available as dead soft, but most will be tempered). This is easy to do with an OAF torch. Passing over the surface of the copper with an acetylene only flame will cover the surface with a layer of carbon. Heating the material with a neutral flame until the carbon burns off will heat it to dead soft. A propane torch produces plenty of heat to anneal cooper as well but will not produce carbon that can be used as a heat indicator. A Tempil stick between 800° and 1000° can be used. In a pinch, work in a dimly lit space and stop heating the copper the moment it shows a bit of red heat.

Figure 11.64b An example of a copper sculpture (about 5" high) with leaves made from annealed copper.

- Soldering—Soldering copper is similar to any other soldering but is most often done on plumbing joints. It is just as viable for sculpture as long as the color mis-match is acceptable. To make a joint, the copper must be very clean (usually done with fine emory

Figure 11.64a An example of annealing copper. The surface has been covered in carbon and is in the process of being heated just to point of the carbon burning off. This results in nearly lead soft copper that can be easily worked.

Figure 11.65 A found object lamp that uses copper tube as the primary structure. The joints and formed hardware have been joined with propane and silver solder. Non-copper components are either bolted or epoxied in place.

cloth) and get a dab of flux. Heat should be applied away from the joint until the flux bubbles (cleaning away any remaining oxide) and the solder applied at that moment; the flux will help draw the molten solder into the joint. Once heat is removed, the parts will need to be held in place for a minute or two (or sprayed with cold water) to ensure they set.

- Brazing—For copper joints that require a color match, brazing with phos-copper will be the best solution. This will require the additional heat of an OAF torch or jewelers acetylene torch. The process is essentially identical to brazing steel with bronze rod, though no flux is required when the copper is clean. Care should be taken to not overheat the copper; it is fairly easy to melt with an OAF torch.

Figure 11.67a A veining stake and hammer pair—note the shape of the hammer head fits into the center gap of the stake.

Figure 11.66 An example of a phos-copper braze (OAF torch) on a sculptural copper leaf where color match and the ability to patina the components was required.

- Shaping—Copper can pick up very fine detail and can be manipulated into more shapes than other metals. Copper will harden as it is worked (especially when hammering) but it is easy to re-anneal for continuing work. It can also be pressed into wax (medium density micro-crystalline wax works best), hammered against a shot bag for larger shapes (such as the altar seen in Figure 5.46b which was hammer formed before being smoothed in the English wheel), dapping blocks, and shop-made sinking and

Figure 11.67b An example of using a shop-made chisel to vein a simple leaf. The chisel is aligned with the center of the stake to make the groove in the copper.

232 • FABRICATION FOR THEATRE AND ENTERTAINMENT

Figure 11.67c Using the shaping hammer on the back of the leaf to smooth and extend the veining texture.

Figure 11.67d The completed leaf. The stem has a reverse curve making it easier to attach.

raising stakes. These techniques can also be used on steel sheet, but it is best to heat the steel first, which requires a forge of some type.
- Spinning—This is a unique technique for shaping soft metals such as copper and brass. This is a traditional method for making parts for lighting fixtures and a very few, high-end manufacturers still use this process. It is actually relatively easy: a form (often turned hardwood) is placed in a lathe chuck with a disk of metal bolted to it on center or held in place by a blunt tailstock to apply pressure. Spinning tools that are either metal rods or hardwood dowels with rounded ends are then placed in a forked tool rest that provides the leverage needed to press the spinning metal disk into the grooves of the pattern. While shops are unlikely to do this in house, it can be outsourced to decorative metal working shops.

FINISHING AND PRESERVATION

In most cases, steel will be the only metal used in a shop that needs a preservative coating for long-term use. While paint is likely the most familiar to most readers, there are various other finishes for metals to consider.
- Painting—This is a very common way to prevent oxidation or corrosion of metals, especially steel, and most importantly to provide color. Though aluminum oxide is self-bonding and essential perpetually preserves it, it does tend to be a dull gray. Clear protective coatings are often preferred to maintain any sheen that the raw aluminum may have. Paints for metal differ from those for wood. Oil-based paint used to be the standard for metal, but modern Direct To Metal (DTM) paints can also be water-based, usually acrylic. Oil-based alkyds tend to be better for rusty surfaces (with lose rust removed) and acrylics best for new metal (with scale removed). These use various additives that help the paint adhere to non-porous surfaces and often have a somewhat higher VOC content than those for wood. There are also formulations specifically for aluminum that adhere far better than those generally formulated for all metals.
  ○ Surface prep is important when painting. All paints, primers, and colorants need a very clean surface to work properly. Oil is usually the biggest enemy of any coatings and can be hard to remove. Using metal prep (usually phosphoric acid-based), denatured alcohol, and occasionally acetone (though this is quite volatile and needs to be used with care) are the best ways to thoroughly clean a surface to prepare for coating.
    ▪ Filling deep irregularities and sometimes seams is often done by applying catalyzed

polyester auto-body filler that is then sanded flush to the surrounding metal. Spot glaze putty is a similar filler for small imperfections that needs no mixing.
- Most paint, even those specially formulated for metal, need some "tooth" on the surface to bind well. Abrasive blasting is a great way to provide a high-bond paint surface but may read through the final surface if not filled. One excellent way to both paint and fill any small irregularities is to use a high-build polyester primer. These are akin to body filler that has been thinned to a sprayable consistency. They require very good ventilation combined with an appropriate respirator. Other priming options include rust converting primer (usually phosphoric acid-based), sandable alkyd resin primers, and self-etching primers that have an acidic base (especially useful for painting aluminum).
○ Clear "paints" aren't really paint as there is no pigment. These are long-lasting top coats that offer various finishes from matte to gloss, though gloss finishes are the most common.
- Lacquer is traditionally a type of clear coating made from tree resins and wax, such as shellac. Synthetic lacquer is a modern take usually based on a nitrocellulose compound. While these are more durable, they aren't always more desirable. Shellac is durable, easy to thin with denatured alcohol and easy to color with solvent dyes. It can be removed/reconstituted by applying fresh denatured alcohol. These are available in quarts and gallons and thus can be applied over large areas.
- Acrylic is a plastic monomer that is a common binder in a variety of paint types. Acrylic urethanes (a.k.a. acrylic lacquer) are the most applicable to metal products as they are durable, UV stable, and chemical resistant. Acrylic urethanes may be moisture cured (which works well in high humidity climates) or activated by a catalyst. These are usually high-gloss finishes as they are most commonly used for automotive applications and are available in clear and opaque colors. These are sold both in bulk containers and aerosol cans. One advantage to acrylic urethanes is the easy of adding tint or metal powder to create custom translucent coatings. For small projects, auto-body supply shops will often mix custom colors into aerosol cans, which is very convenient.
- Enamel is a broad category of paint and originally applied to oil-based paints that used an alkyd resin. These are still available and provide a durable glossy finish but are not available as a clear coat. Clear "enamels" are mostly available in aerosol cans and are blends of resins. Unfortunately, this makes them best for small projects. They are excellent for encapsulating physical color as well as dyes and patinas. Spray enamel offers matte, satin, and gloss finishes and is more durable than lacquer. These should be fully cured before being placed outdoors or exposed to moisture.
○ Application methods for paint are shared with other materials and generally will be familiar to most readers, thus they are not discussed in depth here.
- Sprayers are a common method of application because they provide the smoothest final finish when used properly. All paint spraying presents an inhalation risk, thus proper PPE and ventilation need to be in place.
  □ "Cup guns" are nearly synonymous with spraying paint for moderately large surfaces. A few common versions are readily available and all work well with both water-based and solvent-based paints. Care should be used with any catalyzed paints because these can cure in the sprayer and cannot be removed if this happens. All versions have adjustable air flow surrounding the nozzle that controls the shape of the "fan".
    - Capillary sprayers are low cost and work well with thin finishes, especially solvent-based ones. These usually have a fairly small orifice and do not work well with high-solids paints. These use significant CFMs to create the vacuum that pulls paint from the tank into the air stream; this tends to create a good bit of over-spray.
    - HVLP (High Volume, Low Pressure) sprayers divert some of the supply air to the paint container. This pushes far more paint into the air stream than a capillary gun, thus covering area faster while creating much less over-spray. The pressurized tank also helps move paints with medium solids content through the gun.
    - Gravity fed sprayers move the paint tank to the top of the gun directly feeding the paint into the air stream. These are compatible with high-solids paints and produce low over-spray but the additional weight above the center-of-gravity can make them somewhat awkward to use.

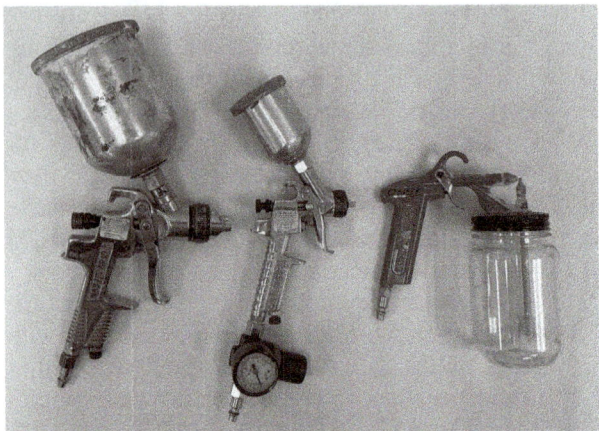

Figure 11.68 Examples of gravity fed cup sprayers, including a detail sprayer with an attached regulator (saves adjusting shop air) and a capillary sprayer (called a "Critter") that shows how a capillary sprayer works: the nozzle directs air across the dip-tube creating a venturi effect that pulls the fluid up into the air stream.

- User fillable aerosol options include pressure canisters that can be filled and then pressurized with shop air like filling a tire. These often do not provide as fine of a mist as commercial aerosol cans but still offer a suitable finish for many projects. Small aerosol sprayers made by Preval have a small glass jar and disposable aerosol sprayer. These create a very fine finish and work best with very thin liquids. The author regularly uses them with various darkening agents.
- HVLP stand-alone systems use a small compressor to create two air circuits: one to pressurize the paint tank and one to aerosolize the paint as it leaves the nozzle. These systems are fairly expensive, but are readily portable, fairly easy to clean and provide a very fine finish with most paints.
- Airless sprayers use a pump to draw in paint and pressurize a hose that feeds the hand-held spray gun. These are best for very large areas, or very large projects due to the significant amount of cleaning time required after use.

- Aerosol cans are readily available from paint stores, hardware stores, and home centers. Companies offer a wide array of colors and finishes, but the cost per area is quite expensive, making them best for small projects. With care, these will provide an excellent finish; too often users do not follow the instructions and keep the can far too close to the surface, making ripples, and overdo each coat, leading to drips. The majority of these are solvent-based paints that need to be used with appropriate PPE and/or dilution ventilation.
- Brushes and rollers can be used to paint metal just as they can for wood. Since metal is not absorbent, the risk of ridges or brush strokes increases with a brush and the risk of bubbles increases with a roller since most often a foam cover is used for painting metal (a napped roller will always create texture). Maintaining wet edges while applying paint with either method is important; abutting new paint against dried paint creates ridges. Additives are available for both oil- and water-based paints to improve wetting action.
- Faux finishing may seem unusual for metal but can be used for aging, such as simulated rust or imitating texture such as wood graining (which was common on vehicles built in the 1920s and 1930s) that can make a metal object fit into a historic setting. Other techniques include using water droplets to suspend paint, oil-based paint floated on water for dipped marble finishes and aged metals. A few companies offer "paints" that combine powdered metal at a high enough concentration that when applied (to metal or other

Figure 11.69 Examples of pressure canister sprayer (left) and Preval aerosol sprayer (right) as well as samples of their respective spray patterns. The pressure canister does offer a variety of nozzles, but all have a much higher flow then the aerosol sprayer.

surfaces) the object takes on the appearance of authentic metal. These are an excellent solution when working with aluminum as this combines light-weight and stable properties with the coloration of heavier or more costly metals such as brass, bronze, or stainless steel. These metal coatings can be patina'd much like solid metal.
- Colorants—These are different than paint in that they use a chemical reaction to color the metal. That may sound complex, but these are finishes that can be applied in any shop. Other complex processes such as anodizing aluminum or chrome/nickel plating steel offer increased durability but will need to be outsourced due to the dangerous chemicals involved, high cost of equipment, and environmental licensing most require. Sprayable cold-chrome may be another option available at auto-body shops; this simulates chrome very well and is much safer and lower cost.
  ○ Reactive colorants are formulated for specific metal types. Many of these will react faster on warm to semi-hot metal than on cold metal. Many can also be applied in stages to add to the darkening effect, though the piece needs to be rinsed and dried between applications. All will need to be rinsed with fresh water to stop the reaction.
    ▪ Bluing is used by gun smiths as a colorant for barrels and it is usually oil preserved. It is a very quick way to create a dark translucent finish on steel. It can also be used on cast iron, but it tends to make a bit more of a dark, rusty finish. It is available in various concentrations (traditional blue, super blue, and others) and forms (gel, paste, and liquid). It can be preserved with oil, wax, or sprayable clear coats.
    ▪ Brass dark is formulated to darken copper and copper alloys. Most products sold with an "oil-rubbed bronze" finish have been treated with brass darkening solution. It top coats the same as bluing.
    ▪ Alumi-black is "bluing" formulated for aluminum. It will not darken as significantly in one treatment as other metals. It is also fairly difficult to get a consistent color. Buffing aluminum with a clean non-woven abrasive pad by hand, then wiping with denatured alcohol yields the best consistency.
    ▪ Plumb brown is intended to create a rust-like finish on steel and cast iron, though a single treatment leans much more toward tan than brown. It must be clear coated or it will transfer to other surfaces; oil and wax are the most compatible. A similar chemical, Japanese brown, makes a somewhat darker finish. Both work best when applied to warm steel, up to about 200°F.
    ▪ Copper and bronze patinas for steel are usually applied with a sprayer and create translucent finishes on steel without creating rust. They will rust fairly quickly if not clear coated.
    ▪ Liver of sulfur is a simple chemical that is dissolved in water to make a reactive colorant. The concentration of the mix and water temperature will affect how fast it reacts and how deep the color develops. Adding about 10% ammonia to the solution will dramatically accelerate the reaction. This mixture can be used on copper and its alloys as well as silver (for example aging a prop that has been silver leafed). The solution smells bad (especially with ammonia) and wanes when exposed to air over time so small batches should be mixed only when needed. The chemical is available in gel and dry forms. The dry form is the most shelf stable, while the gel is the easiest to dissolve. Examples of the effect of liver of sulfur on copper can be seen in Figures 11.64b and 11.70.

Figure 11.70a Examples of darkening chemicals on various metals. From the top—textured steel with Birchwood-Casey plum brown gun barrel finish (left) and traditional gun blue (right); Steel F/X Bronze patina on steel; Japanese brown from Sculpt Nouveau on steel; Steel F/X Red Copper patina on steel; copper with color from heat (left), Birchwood-Casey brass dark (center) and liver of sulfur (right); and aluminum treated with Birchwood-Casey alumi-black.

Figure 11.70b
An oak leaf sculpted and cast in bronze by the author that has a liver of sulfur patina. The raised veins have been buffed to remove the patina, creating highlights.

- Dyes and patinas are used to add pastel and bright colors to metal surfaces or metal bearing paints.
  - Dyes are usually acid- or solvent-based when used on metals and are fairly transparent. Many can be mixed with lacquer, shellac, and various epoxies to make durable coatings. When not mixed with a carrier, clear coat will be required to preserve and prevent fading.
  - Patinas have a flat finish and may provide a hint of texture. Many do not need a top coat and will continue to develop over time. They are reactive and most often used on copper and its alloys. Some may be used on steel; those for copper only will induce rust on steel.
- Physical techniques—Color can come from physical techniques as well.
  - Abrading hot steel with a brass brush (usually a wire wheel in a drill) will create a bright gold finish. The pressure wears away the brass while the heat bonds the brass to the surface.
  - Heating alone can develop color in metal. This is easiest and most obvious when applied to copper, but it can work well on steel as well. For copper this can be done with a propane, MAPP, or OAF torch. Each will create color variations at different rates and produce slighting different coloring. Copper can attain reds, blues, and purples while steel will show ambers and blues.

Figure 11.71 From top—copper treated with ferric nitrate (left), mahogany patina (center), and powder blue patina (right); steel with green patina and green dye; steel with red patina and purple dye. The dyes were disbursed in shellac.

Figure 11.72 On the left is a steel leaf colored by heating it with a propane torch just until color change (navy blue) then brushed with the solid brass wire wheel shown. On the right from top—steel spot heated with a slightly carborizing flame, steel heated with a propane torch from the reverse face, and a sample of copper spot heated with a carborizing flame.

- Aging—On the opposite end of the scale is the need to age metal rapidly. Props artisans often need to distress newly made items to make them fit into a historic era. There are a few ways to induce rust on steel which can then be neutralized before encapsulating. Often drying oils or waxes are the best way to "preserve" the rust. Tung oil, bees wax, and furniture wax (which may be tinted to add depth) are good choices.
  - Salt and vinegar is the simplest and safest solution to inducing rust on steel. The process will be slow and may take 8–24 hours to create noticeable rust. The steel or iron can be dipped, sprayed with a hand sprayer, or coated with a brush. As the solution dries, it will need to be rewetted with water to continue the aging process. The solution should use about one tablespoon of salt per ounce of vinegar. Any vinegar will work, but 5% white vinegar is the most common choice.
  - Hydrogen peroxide works well to rust steel slightly faster than salt and vinegar, has virtually no smell, and is quite safe to handle. It can also be mixed with salt and vinegar to increase its reactivity. It can be applied by submersion, brush, or with a hand sprayer. A good recipe is 16 oz peroxide, 2 oz vinegar, and 1/2–1 tablespoon of salt. Peroxide will require multiple applications to achieve dense rust and works best when using a newly opened bottle.
  - Bleach is another chemical that will induce rust on steel and will actually cause stainless steel to rust if exposed for long periods. Bleach is somewhat dangerous to handle and will create noxious fumes when left to evaporate. At a minimum appropriate glove and goggles should be worn. Any bleach that gets on skin should be rinsed off immediately and thoroughly. Bleach should only be applied with a brush (sponge brushes work well) and left to evaporate in a well-ventilated space, paint booth, or simply set outside away from the public and crew.
  - Muratic acid can be diluted with water (dependent on the concentration of the source acid) and then applied to clean steel with a pump sprayer or brush. This will produce rust in minutes. It can then be neutralized by sprinkling it with baking soda. Let the soda sit for a few minutes and then rinse. Muratic acid should only be stored in plastic and all parts of a sprayer, if used, should be plastic as well. The user must wear protective clothing (like a Tyvek® jacket or jump suit), appropriate gloves with long cuffs, and lab style protective goggles, not safety glasses. Care should be taken to limit contact time with the steel; muratic acid will create rust flakes that

Figure 11.73a Samples of rusted steel from top to bottom—vinegar and salt, bleach (with added salt on the right-hand portion), and salt water.

Figure 11.73b A tool cart made to look like an antique by inducing rust on the steel with muratic acid. The wood slats are sawn from an authentically aged oak 4×4. The acid has also etched the paint on the large wheels supporting the antique look.

come off, defeating the purpose, if left too long. Muratic acid from a hardware supply is prone to weaken over time when stored.
- Clear coats (non-paint)—While paint is a common way to protect metal objects from oxidation, there are traditional methods that also work very well to protect metal from the elements.
  - Waxes such as bees wax or petroleum-based waxes (most furniture wax), which may be sold tinted, are often applied directly to unpainted metal or reactive colorants. Other waxes, such as carnauba, are excellent as protective coatings for paint or clear coats. All waxes will require occasional re-coating. These can work well outdoors but will require more frequent re-coating.

Figure 11.74 A cast-iron coffee table base designed and cast by the author rusted with blueing and finished with furniture wax.

Figure 11.75 A cast-iron and bronze hand rail designed and cast by the author. The bronze bases and caps were colored with brass dark, buffed then coated with clear satin enamel, while the iron panels were colored and sealed with dark tinted tung oil.

  - Drying oils can be used as a sealer. These are best for porous metal like castings. Tung oil (100% pure tung is generally not available in hardware stores; many of those labeled tung oil are tung, linseed, and petroleum blends), mineral oil, and linseed oil are best. Tinted oils like dark tung oil can be used to color and seal simultaneously. These will usually take 1–3 coats to fully protect the metal. Tung oil is often combined with melted bees wax and applied to less porous metals (especially steel) and provides a finish that can be buffed to a satin sheen. Bees wax and mineral oil blends can be purchased commercially as butcher-block sealer.

RESOURCES

- Steel F/X—This company supplies a variety of reactive colorants, dyes, and patinas. One unique offering is patinas in gel form that make them easy to use on vertical surfaces. They also offer a PDF guide to patinas as a free download.
  - www.steelfxpatinas.com
- Sculpt Nouveau—This supplier offers patinas and dyes for steel, copper and copper alloys, waxes (protective and tinted), and protective clear coats. An example of a unique coating offered is Ever Clear Black, a translucent black acrylic urethane that can be thinned with additional un-pigmented Ever Clear for a custom finish. Many of their patinas and reactive colorants are available in aerosol cans, hand sprayers, and bulk containers. They mostly do direct sales but their products can be ordered from Sherwin-Williams and are stocked by some local art supply stores in many states.
  - www.sculptnouveau.com

- Birchwood Casey — This is one of the oldest suppliers of gun blue and related products. They offer bluing in more formulas and consistencies than any other company including a felt-tipped pen for touch up. They also offer plum brown, darkener for aluminum and copper alloys, and protective oil (drying) that buffs to a satin finish.
  - www.birchwoodcasey.com
- Jax Chemical Company — Another supplier that offers blackener for an array of metals including stainless steel (possibly the only company that offers this option), darkeners for copper alloys, patinas for copper alloys, a variety of metal prep and cleaning chemicals, and plating and polishing solutions.
  - www.jaxchemical.com
- Van's Gun Blue — This is a small company that offers both an excellent gun blue for iron and steel and a low VOC cleaner degreaser that is much safer to use than solvents or acids.
  - www.vansgunblue.com

Chapter 12

Machining

Much like welding, machining is a skill that is fairly easy to learn the basics of and takes significant experience to master. When starting down the road to machining, like other skills, time will be needed to develop a "feel" for cutting various materials. When beginning, a good rule of thumb is to take shallow cuts and feed material slowly. With experience (and maybe a broken cutter or two), the operator can develop a sense of when increased feed and/or a deeper cut is ok. While most projects in entertainment will not require a machinist, having some machining skills can offer excellent solutions that other methods cannot supply. Any scenery that needs to move in some way, by simple means such as a lever or crank or by complex systems such as variable speed motors or hydraulics, will require customized parts. Something as simple as a slot that allows a bolted junction to be adjustable can be quite difficult to make without a mill (Figures 12.4–12.7 show examples of this in application). For most shops, a metal lathe will have far fewer uses than a mill, but they can cross over to working with high-density plastics and may then be worth the investment, at least for a small bench-top model. Outside of manufacturing parts for automation, the level of precision required may not be that high. Many entertainment projects will only require a tolerance in hundredths or even tenths of an inch, whereas machinists tend to work to thousandths of an inch or fractions of a millimeter (which may be required for automation systems). This means that the machining techniques below are fairly easy to learn and apply. When ultra-precision is required, a project can be outsourced to a machine shop.

MANUAL TASKS

Some shaping tasks can either only be completed by hand work or are best done by hand. For example, when a very smooth surface is required, a machine shop will likely use a very specialized grinder that is well beyond the scope (or cost/value ratio) of most scenic shops. Hand filing, when done with care, can produce an equally smooth finish on small projects without the cost. Measuring and layout are additional skills that are generally done by hand unless Computer Numeric Control (CNC) equipment is available.

Layout and Measuring

While marking on metal can be more difficult than on other materials, there are a number of tools that ease the process. Many of these could also work quite well on high-density plastics. Many measuring tools are covered in Chapter 5, but a few specific to machining are covered here.

- Dividers—These tools may seem too simple to be effective in machining, which tends to be precision based, but they are fast to set and apply. The human eye and sense of touch are quite accurate; thus, setting dividers is actually quite accurate and a good way to transfer a dimension from one place to another, mark centers along a line or the center of a circle, or mark an inset from an edge. When used for layout, they are often combined with layout fluid, making them as easy to use as a compass is for wood work. Their other advantage is ease of use while an item is mounted on a machine; other tools are often difficult to fit or lose a setting.
- Jenny calipers—These can be used either for scribing a linear offset, much like a marking vernier caliper, or for finding the center of round or square bar. Marking an offset is easiest with a set of calipers that has a ledge on the odd leg, instead of a hooked end. To find the center of a round bar or disks, the

Figure 12.1a Using a divider to set the maximum cutting distance for a section of round bar. This mill is fitted with table stops that were set to limit travel to this point.

caliper is set to slightly longer than half the center distance, then used to strike a series of arcs (usually four, as near to every 90° as possible); these can then be connected to find center.

- Spring calipers—Both inside and outside versions will mostly be used on a lathe to compare diameters but may rarely be used on a mill, for example milling a flat area into a rod to a specific thickness or comparing an inside bore. Again, the sensitivity of fingers can tell when calipers just slip past. Inside spring calipers can be seen in use in Figure 12.32.
- Sliding calipers—These are usually used on materials to determine initial size or check final size. It is

Figure 12.2a Using dial calipers to check the internal diameter of a steel disc that will be fitted with an oil-impregnated bronze bearing.

Figure 12.1b A set of jenny calipers and two layout samples. By striking four arcs on the steel disc and connecting the intersects, the center can be accurately marked. The author ground a small notch into the odd leg, making them easy to use to mark an offset on thin material.

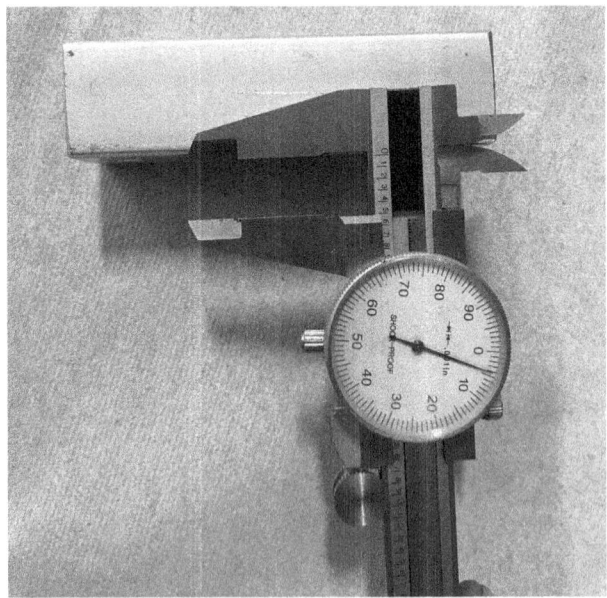

Figure 12.2b Having measured the thickness of the aluminum block, the caliper has been set to the 1/2" distance and is being used to mark center.

very important to ensure the jaws are plumb and/or square to the material for accurate reading. This is trickier for inside measurements since the tool is not clamping itself to the material and for depth there is little surface area for the reference face. These are often too cumbersome to fit on a mill but may be easily used on a lathe. Sliding calipers can also be used to transfer a measured distance.
- Scribes—Marking is best done with scribes because they are more precise (fine line) than ink markers or wax pencils. For example, if a marker were to be used to mark a stopping point, which side of the line does the operator machine go to? Hand-held scribes work well with a straight edge or square. Marking fluid can enhance contrast, making the marks easy to see. Guided scribes, such as a marking vernier caliper, require the user to carefully maintain orientation during use for accurate marking.

Figure 12.3 Using a marking caliper to lay out a small aluminum tray that will be bent on a press brake.

- Punches—Marking nodes or centers with a punch is quick and makes less surface impact than lines. This is the purpose of a prick punch, as they make a very tiny mark; the mark can be expanded with center punch for centering a drill if needed.
- Setup blocks—These are precision-ground solid or punched blocks that sometimes have threaded holes for mounting. The most common are imperial 1–2–3 blocks (1″ × 2″ × 3″) or metric 25–50–75 (millimeters). They can be used to set up materials and machine accessories for many tasks.
- Feeler gauges—These are calibrated stainless steel leaves that are slipped into gaps to determine an offset. They are available in either imperial or metric thicknesses. Many sets have dual thickness leaves, with the tip being ground thinner than the main body.
- Machinist angle blocks—These are often sold in sets of two (45°–45°–90° and 30°–60°–90°) or sets of 12 (1/4°–30°). Much like a machinist square, they are used to set up tooling or components to be machined accurately. They are sometimes used in combination with feeler gauges to ensure there are no gaps between the block and the component being aligned.

Hand Work and Tools

- Bench block—This is a very simple and useful tool for punching (driving out pins) and filing round material. They are best for small items when filing, such as bolts when using a thread file for repair.

Figure 12.4 Using a bench block as a brace while dressing freshly ground flats on a drill bit with a file. This also works well to remove burrs from bits that have spun in the chuck.

- Bench vise—This is one of the most versatile hand tools in a shop. They can be used to hold almost any sensibly sized project for hand work and most can be rotated around the base, making it easy to reposition work without reindexing the work in the jaws. A vise that rotates parallel to the drawbar further increases this capability. There are various considerations to keep in mind while using one.
  - Any play in the jaws of a vise can allow them to rise or twist. While this may not be an issue for some hand work, it can be dangerous on a machine. Jaw rise (moving jaw lifts) can introduce error when filing a surface (out of level); jaw twist can leave one end of material loose in the jaws, allowing the material to move during a cut or while filing. All material should be placed on center as often as possible. Any inserts, such as magnetic soft jaws, increase the likelihood of jaw drift.
  - V-blocks are a handy way to hold round material. Many utility vises have jaws for pipe that will not hold small rods. Adding V-blocks (or making them) can add versatility to a utility vise.
  - Soft jaws made from copper or aluminum sheet to fit a vise can reduce lift and/or twist issues that arise from magnetic add-ons. Using these soft materials also improves the vise's ability to grip the rough surface of castings.
- Filing—Files only cut on the push stroke and should be matched to the final shape needed. They should also be as small as needed but as big as possible for speed. Filing may be done in stages, coarse to fine. Files are most often used for final dressing material after a power tool has removed the majority of the required material. Filing guides can be used along an edge to ensure an even depth of cut. This is often done with hard sheet metal, such as shim stock, but can be card stock or styrene sheet as long as the cuts are very even. The advantage to these is the soft material won't damage the file if contact is made.

Figure 12.5 An aluminum V-block with a 1/4" deep groove made by the author combined with a soft-face jaw cover to hold threaded rod for cutting without damage. Behind the saw is another shop-made V-block (1/8" deep) and an example of the block both were machined from.

Figure 12.6 One of the biggest problems with milling is that the cutters are round; thus, the end-stops will always have a radius. A square file (especially if sized to match the slot width) can make fairly quick work of squaring the end of a slot. The example shows squaring a groove half completed.

- Drilling—Some projects are too big to place on a drill press or mill. Using a guide block with a hand-held drill can greatly increase accuracy. To do so, set a relatively deep mark with a center punch, then drill just enough to align the bit. Place the drill block using bit as centering device, clamp the block in place (when appropriate), and finish drilling. This is especially helpful when drilling hollow shapes that need the holes to align on both faces.

Figure 12.7 Using a drill block on round tube to guide a 1/4" bit. The cantilever clamp was chosen because the jaw pads are grooved to grip the tubing quite well.

- Reaming—Finishing a hole made by a twist drill with a hand reamer will produce a far more accurate diameter, especially in thin material. Fixed-diameter reams are the most common, but adjustable reams can be used as well. Rotary cutters are often used for this reason but may not be readily available in the range of sizes that twist drills are. Adjustable reams allow the user to oversize the hole by a varying degree to match a required tolerance.

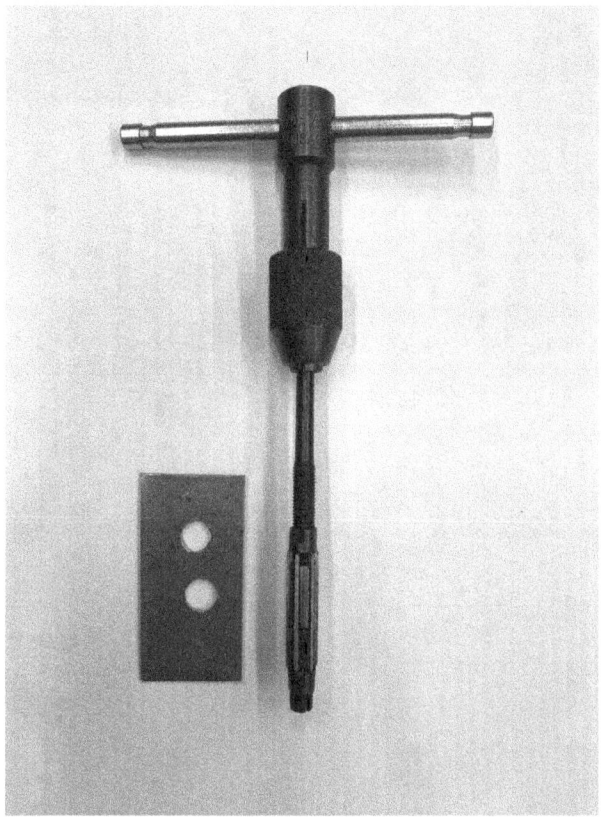

Figure 12.8 On the top of the 16 ga steel sample is a hole drilled with a twist drill; on the bottom is the same-size hole after reaming with the adjustable ream shown.

- Broaching—One of the few machining skills that is almost always done by hand is using a broach to cut a key slot in an inside diameter. The sizes needed for most industry projects will work quite well in an arbor press. The manual feed allows the operator to feel how well the broach is cutting. A hydraulic press may be needed for very large broaches or in very hard material, but any deviation from truly vertical could lead to a shattered tool before the user has an inkling of a problem. Broaches come in sets that include guide bushings for various bores, the cutters, and sets of shims. Many cuts can be made in a single pass, but those that require an extra deep keyway will be cut in multiple passes by adding shims behind the broach. Broaches are also available square with four cutting edges and hexagonal (six edges) to shape drilled or punched holes.

246 • FABRICATION FOR THEATRE AND ENTERTAINMENT

Figure 12.9a Using a manual broach in an arbor press to add a keyway to shaft collar.

Figure 12.9b The collar after broaching, showing how clean these tools cut.

MILLING

Milling metal is very similar to using a router on wood: a rotating cutter cuts and shapes the material. Many of the cutters for a mill are quite similar to a router bit as well. There are major differences though. A mill is a stationary machine and the metal is moved through the cutter. Even the smallest mill is much larger than a router and operates at much lower speed; top speed for a mill is likely 2500 RPM or less, whereas a router generally operates at 10K–20K RPMs. Mills are versatile machines and even a small machine can be quite useful for an array of projects, some of which are demonstrated at the end of this section.

Machines

There are a variety of options when choosing a mill. For many shops a simple bench-top mill/drill will be sufficient. Because these machines are expensive, a purchase should be carefully considered and account for growth. Mills (and lathes) tend to be used with care; thus, purchasing a preowned machine can save a good bit of money and still net a quality machine. There are some advantages to a turret mill such as a multi-position head and vertical movement of the work table that are a better choice for shops that produce mechanized or automated projects. The ability to cut and drill precisely provides a significant advantage over even a high-quality drill press.

- Machine types—There are two common types of mill that will be encountered in most shops, the mill/drill and the turret mill. Other milling machines, such as a horizontal mill, may be encountered in dedicated machine shops as well as a variety of finishing machines that operate much like mills. Mills of any type are usually specified by horsepower or wattage and the size of the work table.
  - Mill/drill style machines are "entry level", but likely sufficient for most shops, unless that shop focuses on many projects that involve movement or automation. The big advantage to this style machine is the array of sizes available with the biggest machines still being bench (or stand) mounted and thus easier to find space for.
    - Square column/dovetail column machines offer a very rigid head and ensure that the quill maintains indexing even when raised. Many of these allow the head to be tilted up to 45° (though tramming the head may be a very good idea after doing so depending on the machine or mechanism that allows this). Lower cost machines may not be reversible (less important on a mill than lathe) unless

they use a DC motor. An example can be seen in Figure 7.8a.
- Round column mill/drills are most often belt driven and the head can rotate about the column to reach the extremes of material but not tilted. This does reduce rigidity somewhat and means the head will need to be aligned and thoroughly clamped in place for each setup. When the head must be raised because the stroke of the quill is insufficient, indexing to the worked material will be lost. A fairly large mill/drill is likely to be a lower cost option than a turret mill while still providing most of the same capability. Most machines have limited RPM options when compared to a variable speed compact mill, but this is generally not an issue unless working with more exotic materials such as stainless steel. Figure 7.8b shows an example of a fairly large round column mill/drill.
  - Turret mills (aka Bridgeport or knee mills) offer the most features and versatility, but even the smallest of these takes up significant floor space and weighs upwards of 1000 lb. Most are belt driven and offer similar HP and speeds to large mill/drills. The two primary upgrades are a head that is mounted on a ram (allowing it to move in and out, rotate left and right when viewed from front, and tilt front to back) and that the Z-axis movement is done by moving the X-Y bed or the "knee". The moving knee allows a quick change of cutting depth while maintaining indexing. These machines usually have a two-speed gearbox (lower gearing offers increased torque for large cutters), are the only type likely to have a mechanized quill feed which is great for repeated drilling or boring, and have a spindle brake, making it easy to change collets. Many machines will be set up with fluid cooling, three axes of Digital Read-Outs (DROs), and powered X-axis feed from the factory. The features can be added to other machines.
    - A subset of turret mills are the "universal" type (or horizontal/vertical). These have a drive just below the turret that can be used for horizontal milling, a much more rigid connection than the turret. This may be an advantage for a machine shop that needs to cut a unique shape over a fairly long piece but is unlikely to be worth the extra cost for an entertainment shop unless it is acquired used for a good price.
- Mill parts—While mills are similar to a drill press, there are a number of differences that make them more versatile and accurate. Understanding the available features can aid in deciding which type of mill may be best suited to a given shop.
  - The head consists of the motor, speed and directional control mechanism, and the spindle. On some machines the head may be rotated and/or tilted.
    - Tool holding on a mill is done via collets or tool holders. R8 collets are the most common in the U.S., while ER collets are more common internationally. Tool holders use the same taper as a collet but hold the cutter in place using a set screw. This saves the need to release the drawbar for each tool change when they share a common shank diameter.
    - The drawbar passes through the quill from above and threads into the collet to pull it into the spindle. A drawbar hammer is a combination tool with a socket on one end and a brass head on the other used to loosen and then tap the collet free. There are kits to adapt a butterfly air ratchet to speed up this process, but you would have to change tooling a lot to need this.
    - The spindle should have quick feed (like a drill press), a fine feed (usually a hand-wheel), and a means to lock it at depth for horizontal

Figure 12.10 Visible in this image is the spindle lock (silver lever on the left) to lock the spindle at a fixed height during milling, the hand-wheel for fine down feed and the depth stop nuts (center) for the quill.

cutting. Either a lever or hand knob will lock out the quick feed engaging the fine hand-wheel. This can be seen in Figure 7.8b; the hand-wheel is in the center of the three-spoke quick feed. Many mills offer a depth stop rod similar to those on a drill press; this makes drilling/cutting depths easily repeatable.
- The bed moves on both the X and Y axes and has T-slots for material holding. High-quality machines will have lash adjustments on the lead screws; lower cost machines will not and lash (amount of handle rotation before movement, especially when changing direction) will increase over time due to wear. The bed should have locks for each axis for when single axis movement is used, which is most of the time. Some beds offer adjustable stops for the X-axis, which is quite convenient for repeated cuts.
- DROs are a fairly common add-on to any axis of many machines, though the X-axis is the most common since the Y-axis travel is limited. Some machines may be ordered from the manufacturer with them. Some bench-top machines include a DRO for the Z-axis since that is the hardest to see where to stop when used for a blind cut.
- Power feeds are common in machine shops where the machines are running nearly constantly. They are a time saver and can improve the finished cut because they provide a more consistent feed rate than a human, especially when surfacing with a fly cutter or facing mill. Combining power feeds with DROs is almost as good as having a CNC machine at a much lower cost, with no external computer required.
- Lubrication is an important part of usage and maintenance. Higher-end turret mills often have a "one-shot" oiler that uses a central pump to push a tiny bit of oil through plumbing to each of the ways, saving a great deal of time for the operator. Other machines require manual oiling. This should be done by moving an axis fully to one end, adding oil on the movement side, then running the axis fully to the other end to spread the oil. The operator should ensure both extremes get oil. The same should happen for the quill, though these often have a cup oiler or can be oiled from the top.
- Material holding—It is vitally important that materials be completely secured before milling operations commence. Both the material and the cutter in use could become dangerous projectiles if the material should come loose from its anchor(s). It is important to remember that end mills in particular have up-cutting helical flutes that in many instances are pulling up on the material.

- A hold down set is one of the most common and versatile methods for holding material to the bed of the mill. These consist of a variety of parts that work together to hold materials in place. The components are shown in Figure 12.11.
- Self-positioning hold downs can be added to a hold down set or purchased with studs and T-nuts as a set. Though expensive, they are often much easier to use than three-piece strap configurations.
- Many shops and/or machinists opt to make custom hold downs. These are often made to supplement a hold down set with features or sizes the set does not offer. Examples can be seen in Figure 12.14.

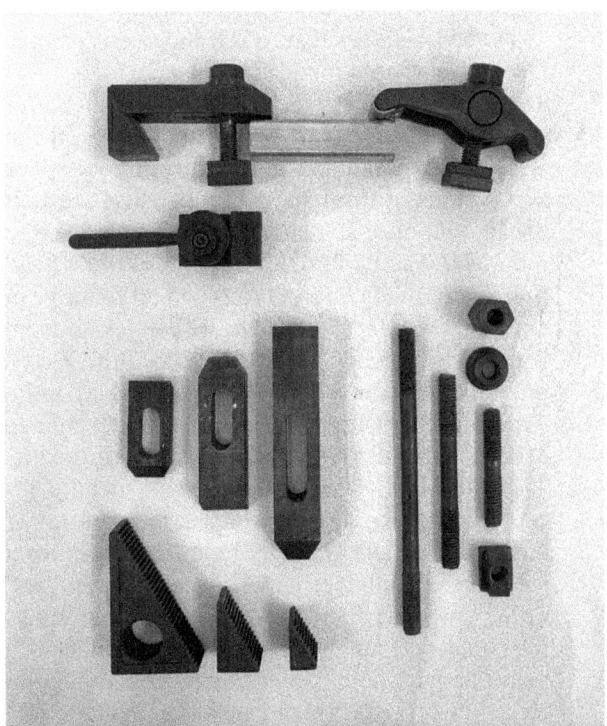

Figure 12.11 Shown are components used for holding material to the T-slot bed of a mill. Along the top is a standard bridge set with step block, strap, and stud on the left and a self-positioning clamp on the right. Immediately below is a low-profile cam clamp the author modified for use on a mill. Along the bottom are examples of differing sizes of step blocks, straps, studs, and nuts.

- Machinist vises are another common means for holding material, but they are limited to fairly small items unless a two-piece vise is used. That said, they are still a very good addition to even the most basic mill and should be given real consideration for purchase. There are a few downsides to working with a vise. In a pinch, a quality

drill press vise may make a suitable substitute as long as its lack of rigidity is accounted for.
- Jaw rise and twist happens to a tiny degree even on very good vises. This means that the material in the vise is not being held by as much surface area as it may appear. Counterintuitively, the error tends to increase with additional pressure. If working with a small piece of material that needs to overhang the end of the jaws, a spacer of equal thickness placed at the opposite end can counter twist. Rise is more pronounced when parallels are used and it is very difficult to fill the space at the bottom to prevent rise. Any work that needs to be done with parallels should be done with a very solid vise.

Figure 12.12 An example of preventing jaw twist. Since both clamps needed to be milled to the same length, clamping one at each edge of the vise jaws will hold the jaws parallel with no need for spacers.

- Alignment of the vise to the bed can be a challenge since many do not have a square base. Machined dowel pins in the T-slots are one option for alignment of a fixed vice. Otherwise, a depth gauge can be used on two identical reference points. Indexing a vise that can be rotated about its center axis can be another challenge. A reference edge clamped in the vice and set equidistant from the front edge of the work table is the best method for alignment. Many machinists choose to calibrate vise rotation using setup blocks, then carefully scribe a mark on the base and head. Rarely should the user trust the degree index included on the vise for accuracy.

Figure 12.13 With a machinist's straight edge gently clamped in the vise, a right angle block and depth gauge are being used to compare left and right sides to ensure the vise jaws are parallel to the bed. The pivot mechanism on the vise has been tightened slightly and the brass end of the drawbar hammer is used to tap the vice into adjustment.

- To ensure material is level in the vise, it should be placed flush to the bottom, or on parallels. If material needs to be worked at an angle, it should be placed against an angle block in the vise or an angle vise can be used.
  ○ Angle vises are useful for odd projects but tend to be less robust than horizontal ones. The best option for rigidity is a vice that rotates left and right instead of lifting front to rear but lift vises are more common. Because of their nature, light cuts are best.
  ○ Accessories are available that make using a vise preferable for some projects.
    - Parallels are metal strips (usually fairly thin) paired by width that are used to elevate material above the base of the vise while keeping it level. This is especially useful for through milling, such as when making a slot, to avoid

a collision with (and damage to) the vise. Sets vary from 1/8"-thick bars to 1/2"-thick bars. Thicker bars stand up easily in the vise but limit jaw closure.

- V-blocks are often used in a vise to hold round objects securely in a vertical orientation. One block may be sufficient, but two blocks are often preferred. These may also be a good option for holding a square bar for end milling as they increase the surface area in contact with the vise and hold the bar on four sides instead of two.
- Custom blocks are sometimes necessary to hold unique shapes in a vise (unless one is lucky enough to own a fractal vise). While this is often better done with hold downs, even if a sacrificial plate needs to be placed underneath to protect the bed, there are occasions such as the need to hold a casting when it is necessary. In these instances, the holding block may need to be fabricated or machined before work on the final product can begin.

○ Shop-made hold downs are an excellent first milling project. The advantage to making strap-style hold downs is that they can be made to fit smaller projects than typical commercial sets, and they are easy to use with slotted angle blocks. In addition, low-profile clamps can be made fairly easily that hold material from the edges, making surfacing easier in many cases. Another good first project is to make a set of T-slot nuts; this allows the operator to choose the diameter of the threaded stud to best suit their needs.

○ Right angle blocks (sometimes called angle irons) are used to hold material on a vertical plane, such as to mill the edge or end of a bar. These provide a much more solid anchor than a vise and can hold much longer or larger material if multiple blocks are used.

○ Rotary tables are very useful accessories that can cut circles and arcs; many offer the ability to mount dividing wheels for indexing. Some can be used horizontally or vertically and are great for things like squaring the end of a round rod, or adding flats to match a drill chuck.

- Cutters—For milling these are offered as standard length and long. Overall length may vary by cutter diameter. Installing a cutter into a collet is nearly identical to installing a router bit. Unlike a router, R8 collets are closed by pulling the collet into the spindle via the drawbar. ER collets use a closer similar to the nut on a router collet, only much larger. Some machines may use a tool holder that uses a set screw to hold the cutter; these require a flat in the cutter body to seat the set screw.

○ When using a cutter, especially an end mill, one needs to understand climb milling vs. conventional milling. Conventional milling is feeding the mill into the material from the leading edge; another way to visualize this is the curvature of the flutes should pull the cutter toward the material during the feed. Climb milling is rarely used and only for very shallow cuts because the flutes are pushing the cutter away from the material. This can easily allow swarf to build up between the bit and material, leading to a broken cutter.

○ End mills are the most common cutter used in the mill and the term usually refers to high-speed steel (HSS), solid carbide, or cobalt steel helical cutters. HSS cutters are also available with a titanium nitride coating like twist drills. For single-ended cutters, shanks may be the same size as the cutting face, larger than the cutting face or for some larger cutters smaller than the cutting face. Double-ended cutters are usually a single diameter along their full length. Beyond diameter, there are many features to be aware of though features may not be available in all possible combinations.

- The number of flutes effects the type of material the mill will be most compatible with, feed rate, and finish quality. End mills are available with 2, 3, 4, 6, or 8 flutes. Higher flute counts are best for harder metals (such as alloy steel and cast iron) and produce a smoother finish. They may also allow faster feed rates due to taking smaller "bites". Cutters with fewer flutes are

Figure 12.14 A set of strap-style hold downs with riser bolt, a pair of low-profile, edge-holding clamps, and a cylindrical square made by the author. The strap clamps were made to fit a set of right angle blocks for which the hold downs used on the mill are far too large.

best suited to softer metals and deep cuts; they provide better chip clearing and avoid clogging. This is also a common option for initial passes in mild steel that may be fairly deep.
- The helix angle is most often 30° which works for an array of hard to very hard materials. When cutting soft metals, such as aluminum, an increase to 37° helps clear chips faster, reducing the likelihood of a clog.
- Roughing mills have serrated flutes and don't make a smooth face; they allow feed rates up to 3 times those of a finishing mill. Finishing mills are less dependent on feed rate than depth of cut. These may be used at higher RPM and take a very shallow cut.
- Mill ends may be square bottom or have a slight radius at the outer corner. The rounded corner can reduce stress points, especially when notching thin materials which are more prone to fracturing at sharp cut areas.
- End geometry determines how an end mill can be used. Standard end mills have no cutting area at their center and are designed to be moved into the material laterally, or via drilled access. Center cutting end mills do have the capability to plunge cut but should be reserved for shallow cuts, or for flat bottoming a pilot hole.
- Sizes typically range from 1/8" to 1 1/2" in diameter with a cutting depth ranging from 3/8" to 2" relative to the size of the cutter for single-ended cutters and up to 1" for double ended. Most cutters will offer 2–4 cutting depths per diameter.
○ Slot drills, or "drill mills", are similar to end mills in that they will cut a horizontal path, but only after they have drilled through the material. They are worth the investment when multiple slotted parts are required because the single step saves a good bit of time.
○ Carbide insert end mills provide a shallower cut than helical mills and operate at higher RPMs. Plain-side mills are similar but have inserts that cut along the vertical edge like a helical end mill and can make deeper passes. Both add pressure on the mill and should be reserved for milling castings.
○ Facing mills are cutters used for surfacing large areas. These are mounted to a dedicated tool holder and may be HSS or use carbide inserts. These need to be used with care because the high amount of surface contact requires additional torque. Carbide inserts tend to be slightly less sharp than HSS (to prevent chipping); this combined with the large cutting area puts significant strain on the mill. A facing mill can be seen in use in Figure 12.27a.
○ Fly cutters are the better option for surfacing in smaller mills. These use a head with a small HSS cutting bar that extends out at a shallow angle. They cut similarly to the tooling on a lathe, removing a very small amount of metal across a large area. These too should be used only to make shallow finishing cuts. They also pair well with soft materials that are likely to clog a facing mill.
○ Key-seat or woodruff cutters are T-shaped and are used to cut both woodruff slots and keyways. These are not exorbitantly expensive and are handy to keep in inventory for any shop that either repairs equipment or makes mechanized or automated scenery and props. A woodruff cutter can be seen in use in Figure 12.29a.
○ Angle cutters are, as you would expect, tools with a tapered face(s) for beveling in some fashion.
- Tapered end mills are helical and offer a range of cutting angles from .5° to 45°. These are typically center cutting (for plunge cuts) though as the angle approaches 45° depth of cut in a single pass will decrease.
- Chamfer cutters most often have a 45° cutting angle and are used to relieve square edges. These are offered in three forms: larger diameter cutters with teeth similar to those on a key-seat cutter, smaller diameter cutters similar to a countersink with the flutes cut into a solid shank and those that use a carbide insert (or multiple inserts). It is not unusual to use these to cut to the center of a bar edge (or the flange of a tee or angle iron) to make guides for V-groove wheels. Chamfer cutters can be seen in use in Figures 12.23b and 12.28.

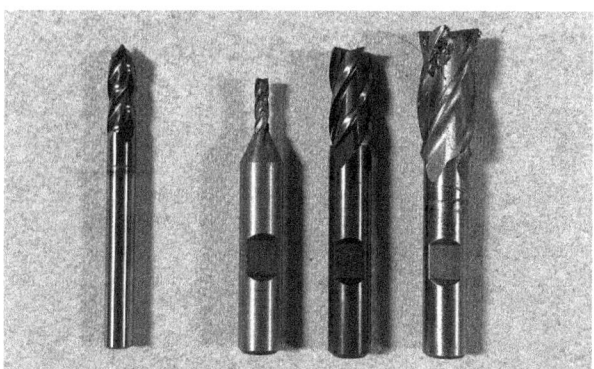

Figure 12.15 On the left is a 1/4" slot drill. On the right are examples of three sizes of four-flute end mills, all with a 3/8" shank diameter. These all have a flat for use in a tool holder.

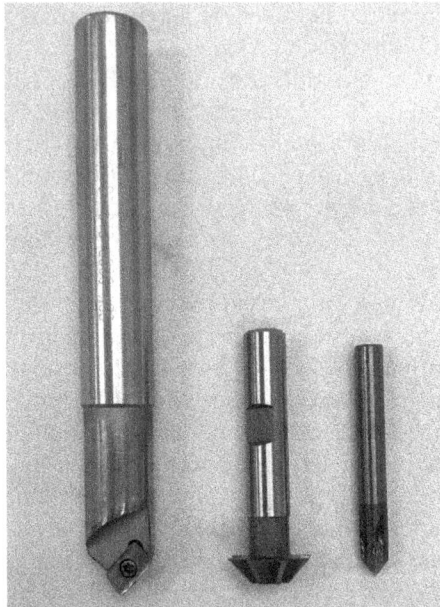

Figure 12.16a Examples of chamfer (or bevel) cutters: a cutter with a carbide insert (left), a 3/4" HSS bevel cutter (center), and a 1/4" HSS chamfer cutter that will cut on center (right).

Figure 12.16b An example of steel angle milled to a center bevel used as guides for the carriage on a CNC router.

- Gear tooth cutters are also as one would expect, for cutting teeth in gears. This is a complex process that requires additional fixtures and won't be discussed here.
  ○ Slotting and/or sawing is sometimes best done on a mill because it can be done with a significantly smaller kerf than other cutting methods. Slitting saws can be as thin as 1/32" (or smaller for jewelry work). The most likely need for this in an entertainment shop would be to cut delicate tubing, such as 1/4" OD aluminum, which would otherwise be damaged by larger saws or crushed by a tubing cutter. Turret mills with a horizontal drive are very effective for this.
  ○ Ball mills are similar to end mills but are for cutting 1/2 round grooves. This is a specialized task unlikely to be encountered often, though it could be very useful for making linear bearings from plastic.
  ○ Forming cutters such as an outside radius and custom shapes are occasional use items and unlikely to find many uses in entertainment. Like ball mills, they can be very useful for making guides by milling high-density plastics.
- Machine setup—There are some key techniques used to prepare a mill for cutting. Setting the machine up for a specific task will help ensure a better finished product.
  ○ Aligning the spindle to the center of the material is a common task when accurate drilling is

- Dovetail cutters are not used as a stand-alone cutter but follow an end mill to add the undercuts to a groove. These are used by machinists to make ways for custom guides, jigs, and machinery. They are unlikely to be found in an entertainment shop.

Figure 12.17a Setting a wiggler in the mill. The needle was canted to an angle and then gently pressed to center with the pencil until vibrations ceased.

required. This is often done with a "wiggler", a simple mechanical device inserted into a collet. This also allows the operator to zero handwheels for any milling that needs to start at and cut away from center.

Figure 12.17b Centering a steel disc on the wiggler needle to prepare for drilling.

Figure 12.18a An edge finder placed and ready to use. Note the eccentric end offset from the shank.

○ Finding the edge of the material is another common task. An edge finder is a simple tool that consists of a sprung disc with either a round or pointed indicator tip attached to a shank. To use one, the disc is rotated off center (a spring will hold it in place), then the machine is started. Once spinning, the material is pressed into the indicator until the offset and the shank align. With a pointed tip, the micrometer wheel on the chosen axis can be set to zero; with a round indicator, the micrometer wheel should be set to half the diameter of the tip. It is important to note the direction of travel to ensure the micrometer ring is set to the correct side of zero. This can also be used to reset a DRO.

Figure 12.18b With the mill running, the material is moved against the indicator point on the edge finder until the eccentric is aligned to the shank.

Figure 12.18c Setting the micrometer wheel on the X-axis to .1″ matching the offset (from center) of the center finder.

- Setting tool depth is important for non-through cuts. Cutting T-slot nuts from bar stock would be a good example of this as the depth of cut needs to be fairly accurate to ensure fitment with room to move easily.
    - Zeroing the depth indicator or DRO on the Z-axis by setting the cutter flush to the material is simplest method. A feeler gauge can be placed between the material and the cutter if needed. This is likely to be the best method when material is held in a vise since the total height of the vise and material is unlikely to be a simple measurement.
    - Gauge blocks are a precise means of setting up tooling. Two styles are common: sets of precision blocks in an array of thicknesses and widths and step blocks which are simple aluminum blocks made like a small staircase. Adjustable blocks use a pair of wedges to change height and have a toe that is placed under the cutter. These tools offer easy-to-use methods to set cutter depth for projects that are held directly to the bed.

Techniques

There are some basic milling techniques to learn that will serve many projects. These are the simple things that are most likely to be useful to scenic and props fabrication. Projects requiring more extensive machining are likely to be jobbed out to a machine shop as they will be faster, more accurate, and thus more cost-effective.

- Material setup—The key to any milling project is ensuring the material is aligned precisely.
    - Square to the table is the most common position for material. The T-slots in the table should be ground true (unless damaged) and can be used as guides. Precision steel dowel pins that fit tightly in the T-slot are a handy way to align simple shapes such as rectangles or to place a vise. Some operators make a fence that will drop into the T-slots to align materials. In addition, an engineer's square, 1-2-3 blocks, and/or a cylindrical square that can be secured to the bed can all help align materials vertically ensuring they are perpendicular to the bed.
    - Hold downs and clamps are used in unison with alignment tools. Adding just a bit of pressure from clamps helps keep the material in place as adjustments are made. One trick that may not be obvious is the ability to stack the step blocks from the hold down kit when mounting tall materials. When using a simple spacer that matches the material thickness, it is wise to add a section of shim stock to increase pressure on the material to be machined.
- Drilling—While most drilling tasks will be completed on a drill press, a mill is the machine of choice when the placement of the hole needs to be precise, and larger mills usually have more torque to drive large bits. Rotational speed for a bit should always match the bit diameter and material. A good rule of thumb is based on a 1/2″ bit. For mild steel, 500 RPM is the maximum; the RPM can be doubled for a 1/4″ bit or halved for a 3/4″ bit. Speeds can be doubled when drilling aluminum and halved for cast iron. As a reminder, the cutting angle of the bit point should also be considered by material type. Other alloys will use different parameters.
    - Piloting for large twist drills is common since most do not have a split point. The pilot bit should be the same diameter or just slightly larger than the web of the larger bit. This ensures even wear on the cutting edge of the large bit; an oversized pilot hole can wear a groove into the cutting edge if done repeatedly.

Figure 12.19 This image clearly shows the pilot hole (3/16″) drilled to match the web of the larger 3/4″ bit. This keeps the full length of the cutting edge engaged.

- Tapping—A mill can be used under power for tapping, but it takes special taps and great care to not break a tap. An easy work around is using the mill to guide a tap and handle for manual threading. If the drill bit is replaced with a centering cone, this can be gently pressed into the recess of the tapping handle to hold it plumb while the tapping process is started. The fine feed wheel of the Z-axis makes it fairly easy to maintain consistent pressure as the tap is fed (though not so much pressure as to not be able to reverse the cutting action to break swarf free).

Figure 12.20 Using a small live center from a micro-lathe to vertically align a tap handle while threading the jack screw holes on a set of hold downs.

  ○ Countersinks and counterbores may be integral to the drilling process or done as an additional step. Twist drills are available to do this as a single step, but the diameter of the counterbore or chamfer is limited. Doing either process as an additional step adds time but increases the options of final product. Counterbores are additionally available with a pilot bit (twist drill) or pilot point. Those with a pilot bit are usually matched to the sizes of common socket head screws.
  ○ Reams may be fitted to a mill, but the disadvantage to this is the need to do so immediately after drilling so as to not lose the material's index on the spindle. If many holes needed to be drilled and reamed, this would be very time consuming. The better option is to invest in a double margin twist drill (or set) for precision diameters. Reams may be well suited to enlarging a hole to match an existing piece of hardware, and the rigidity of mounting work on the mill would improve success.
  ○ Spot drilling is a technique used when a smooth surface is required around a hole through a casting. It is essentially very shallow counterboring, but the cutting area is larger, often sized to match a flat washer.

- End mills—These are the most common cutters to use in a mill and can complete many tasks. Most mill owners will opt to have a set with a shared shank diameter to save changing collets with each tool change. Sets with either 3/8″ or 1/2″ shanks are the most common choice.
  ○ Slotting is one of the easiest tasks to complete and can be a game changer for some shops as they

grow into fabricating projects for motion. A slot allows parts to be adjusted when necessary. If a standard end mill is used, a pilot hole of at least the diameter of the end mill should be drilled near the start of the slot; the mill can then cut to the end point. When a slight tolerance is needed (say a 13/32" slot for a 3/8" bolt), then the pilot should match the final slot width. A 3/8" end mill should be set to cut along one edge, then moved to the other edge of the slot on the return pass. This is best done by feeding the cutter as a conventional cut. Center cutting end mills eliminate the need for a pilot hole in thin materials; a slot drill further simplifies this process by allowing the same cutter to both drill the pilot and cut the slot even in fairly thick material (though the drill point must be fully below the bottom face). A second pass can be made to increase tolerance if needed.

Figure 12.22a Milling a section of 1/4" × 4" steel to width. This also removes the rough edge as this section was plasma cut from a wider piece. The cutting dross was ground away prior to milling.

Figure 12.21 Starting a 1/4" slot with a slot drill (or drill/mill) cutter. Note the drill point that transitions into the helical cutter.

- Straight cuts done with an end mill can be side and end cutting, grooving, or surfacing of small areas. Feed rate for these cuts will depend on the material, depth of cut, and percentage of the cutting face that is engaging the material. For example, if a 1/4"-wide cut is needed along the edge of the material, a 1/2" end mill can be fed faster than a 1/4" end mill at the same depth.

Figure 12.22b An end mill being used for an odd project: the finished end of the gearbox shaft needed to be extended to fully seat a V-belt pulley. The box is being modified in order to convert a wood-cutting bandsaw for cutting steel.

- Right angle blocks are an excellent addition to the work holding arsenal for a mill. Most thin, wide bar stock has a slightly rounded edge. When a square edge is needed, it can easily be milled. This is a task best completed with angle blocks as they will hold the material much more rigidly than a vise (or even a pair of vises) will because they support much more of the material face. They can also be used to hold material at odd angles when a vise cannot.

Figure 12.23b A section of 1/4" × 4" plate being chamfered to fit the base of a press brake. This material will be the top surface of an insert designed to adapt the brake for thin sheets. Due to the material length, additional support is being provided by a shimmed fence and steel dowel pins. Ideally this would have been braced with an additional angle block on center if one had been available.

Figure 12.23a Using a machinist's straight edge to ensure the material is flat before milling. This is especially important for chamfering; otherwise the depth of cut would be irregular.

- V-blocks in a vise are the best way to hold short pieces of round stock for end milling, center drilling, or boring using a boring head. This is a common way to prepare a bore for bearings for example. Boring deeper than the quill travel is best done with a horizontal boring machine but can be done on a knee mill with care. V-blocks provide additional surface area for a better hold but do not ensure the material will be vertical; that will need to be checked with a square or angle block.

Figure 12.24 Center drilling a short section of 3/4" round bar using a V-block in a machinist's vise.

- V-blocks can also be used to hold round material to the bed for milling tasks such as adding a flat area for a set screw or cutting a keyway. While standard hold down clamps can be used for this task, the clamp bars should straddle the shaft at the V-blocks and be supported at both ends when possible. Some V-blocks include clamps for the material and only require the block to be clamped to the bed.

Figure 12.25 Squaring the end of a short piece of ACME thread using V-blocks and hold downs to anchor the material with copper tabs added to prevent damage. This can be done without a divider head; once the first plane is established, the bar can be rotated and placed using a square.

- Parallels are the best way to prevent damage to a vise when drilling through material or when the edge of the material to be worked would set below the vise jaws. Parallels are generally purchased in sets that match the width of the vise and in a range of heights compatible with the vise depth.

Figure 12.26 Using parallels to hold material in the vise while making a set of T-slot nuts. In this case, none of the parallels in the set were tall enough for the material, so two have been used face down acting as shims.

- Surfacing—Smoothing the surface of a section of steel can be done with either a facing mill or a fly cutter. The multiple cutters of a facing mill make arriving at a smooth finish easier than using a fly

Figure 12.27a Surfacing a section of 1/4" × 4" mild steel with a 1 1/2" diameter facing mill to make an insert for a press brake. The hold downs were moved as needed to allow for clearance of the cutter.

Figure 12.27b A fly cutter being used to surface a block of 3003 aluminum. This cutter is set for about a 2" diameter cut and is operating at 1000 RPM.

cutter with its very small contact area. Choice mostly depends on the machine available. While the mill shown in Figure 7.8a uses the same R8 collets as the larger 2HP drill mill shown in Figure 12.27a, a facing mill would quickly overload the smaller mill, but a fly cutter would work quite well.

- Chamfering—Chamfering is usually reserved for the edges of a bar, either to make guides or relieve the corner slightly. Various cutters are available to do so and the type of material being worked as well as the required depth of cut will determine which version is best. Solid chamfer bits have the advantage of being able to cut grooves.

Figure 12.28 Grooving an aluminum block to make it into a V-block. The finished product can be seen in Figure 12.5.

- Keyways—Any project that is powered by a person or a motor will likely use shafts as a means of power transmission. While some parts may be held in place by set screws (aligned to flats on the shaft are ideal), a keyway and square key stock will provide far more surface area to translate the force applied. A keyway is relatively easy to add to a shaft, even in the center of the length. Most often this would be done by mounting the shaft to the bed via V-blocks and the cutter aligned to the vertical center of the shaft. Like other cuts, the size and depth required will determine the number of passes required to safely cut the keyway.

Figure 12.29a Using a woodruff cutter to add a keyway to the shaft of a gearbox to make it compatible with a V-belt pulley. Because this is the output shaft of a worm-driven gearbox, the shaft was easily fixed in position by clamping the input shaft.

Figure 12.29b The gearbox from Figure 12.29a mounted to the motor with the required pulley installed.

- Rotary table—This is a fantastic accessory for a mill. For those who may be put off by the expense, a combination table that can be used horizontally or vertically and has the option to add dividing plates may offer the best value. For horizontal use, the table can be used to cut a rounded end, create an area clearance around center, such as for setting mounting hardware flush, or increase the accuracy of drilling a series of holes evenly spaced around the perimeter of a disc. When used in a vertical application, it can be used to cut drive flats on a round bar for a custom drive shaft or cut a pair of keyways at 90° for example. Any section longer than a few inches will require an additional tailstock for support. Rotary tables are available in various diameters and gear ratios. The gear ratio will determine the number of revolutions of the hand-wheel per degree. It is important to always rotate the table the same direction during a series of cuts; all tables have some lash that will introduce inaccuracy if the direction is reversed during use.
    - A tailstock is required for longer sections of material. Setup and alignment of the tailstock can be quite involved, especially if a "universal" tailstock is used. These are variable height units that can be set to match multiple table diameters. These will require vertical centering to the table, then lateral alignment when placed at the opposite end of the work table. Figures 12.30c and 12.30d shows this fairly well.
    - Dividing plates are an accessory for some tables that make angular indexing far easier and more precise than simply using the degree scale fitted to the table. When an odd number of points are required, such as 17, the number of hand-wheel rotations becomes problematic without the dividing plates (e.g. on the table in Figures 12.30a–d, this would require 5 5/17 rotations). These plates replace the hand-wheel with the appropriate numbered plate, a spring-pin indexing crank, and a sector arm set that help the user identify the required division. After the first process is complete (often drilling), the table is rotated to the next sector point and held fast by a pin.

Figure 12.30a Centering the chuck on the rotary table using a dial indicator in a magnetic base. This is the easiest method with the table in the horizontal position.

Figure 12.30b Using a rotary table to drill six evenly spaced holes along the perimeter of a steel disc (angular indexing). This rotary table has 90:1 gearing, making determining hand-wheel rotations required fairly easy: 90/N. For the six holes required on the piece shown, 90/6=15. The hand-wheel was rotated 15 revolutions per hole (60°).

Figure 12.30c Preparing the rotary table for vertical use. The tailstock must be vertically aligned to the center of the chuck before placing it on the table. Squaring the rotary table to the mill with the tailstock connected makes it easy to measure the position of the tailstock for placement at the opposite end. For this project, the material did not need to be centered under the quill; for cutting on center an edge finder would be used to set the Y-axis position to zero.

Figure 12.30d Using the rotary table and tailstock to mill a 1/2" × 1" hex drive onto the end of a section of 3/4" steel bar. Like the drilling example, the table was rotated 60° between cutting passes.

LATHE WORK

Much like a wood lathe, a metal lathe is designed to shape round stock or to make some portion of non-round shapes round. Unlike a wood lathe, materials are not cut free-hand; thus, complex shapes are much harder to make. This is generally not an issue since the materials that require machining are rarely used for decorative projects as those turned from wood are. Metal lathes are for precision work, much like a mill, and though the range of end product is more limited than a mill, many tasks can only be effectively completed on a lathe. While many shops will not find value in owning a lathe, knowing the various tasks that can be completed on a lathe adds solutions to a project manager's bag of tricks since they can be outsourced when needed. Metal lathes excel at turning plastics as well, which may help them find a place in shops that work with a broad spectrum of materials.

Machines

There are a variety of options when choosing a lathe. For many shops a simple bench-top model will be sufficient. Because these machines are expensive, a purchase should be carefully considered and account for growth. How the mandrel is powered will be the biggest option choice outside of size. Though very large machines are available, most shops will find 7 × 19–10 × 24 machines adequate for most projects.

- Types—There are various types of lathes for metal working but the two most common are bench lathes with belt-driven mandrels (or "tool room" lathes indicating higher tolerance) and engine lathes, which are designed to mechanize the tool feed; these tend to have gear-driven mandrels. Most modern bench lathes have a lead screw to feed tooling so the terms have become somewhat interchangeable. Lathes are intended to cut fairly long material of relatively small diameter (as compared to length). There are three common drive types:
  ○ Belt-driven lathes are by far the most common among bench-top lathes and older lathes. While these do not offer the infinite array of speeds that electronic controls may provide, they are simple, reliable, and have been making quality parts for decades. Most use (and supply) "change gears" that are fitted to the lead screw to change its speed; this is quite important when used for threading. For longevity, purchase a lathe that is supplied with steel change gears (not nylon).
  ○ Electronic variable speed (VS or EVS) units often use a DC motor paired to a rectifier and speed controller. High-quality machines will employ a gearbox to offer two-speed ranges (the lower range offering more torque at lower RPMs). This is commonly available for small bench lathes up to about 8" × 22", though larger machines may offer this feature.
  ○ Geared head lathes have two transmissions: one to drive the mandrel and one to drive the lead

screw. These are much faster to set up for new materials as there are no belts to reposition or gears to replace. They also tend to be large and expensive.
- Sizes—Naming conventions for lathes are listed as swing by length between centers. Swing is the maximum material diameter, which may be specified based on a removable section of the bed. For example, a 7 × 19 (or 7–19) lathe should clear a 7″ diameter section of material above the bed. A metal lathe is not capable of working solid material of maximum diameter for the full length between centers because it must clear the carriage. Manufacturers should also specify swing over carriage, which may be the better defining measurement when choosing a machine.
- Lathe parts—There is a good bit of jargon related to the parts of a lathe. Understanding these helps the buyer both with purchasing a machine and accessories.
  - The head stock houses the mandrel, where material drive components connect, the gears driving the lead screw, the drive mechanisms (belts, gears, etc.), and the engagement lever for belt-driven machines.
  - The lead screw is used both for mechanizing the cutting process and for threading. Many belt-driven machines do have a gearbox in addition to change gears used to set the RPMs of the lead screw. The carriage will also have a thread count dial that engages the lead screw via lever engagement.
  - Drive mechanisms are required to solidly connect the material to be turned. Most machines will supply at least a three-jaw chuck, and often an independent four-jaw chuck and a face plate.
    - Chucks are the most common means of holding material on a lathe because they are fast and convenient. They are not always the most accurate method. Chucks often have or will introduce a tiny bit of run out but it is usually not enough to impact the final project if care is taken during material setup. Some shops will opt to have multiple chuck diameters for larger machines.
      - Self-centering chucks may have three or four jaws, with three-jaw chucks being the most common. These chucks will have two sets of jaws—inside jaws for smaller bars and outside jaws for larger material. The jaws will be stamped with a position number and must be placed in the proper slot in the chuck. Three-jaw chucks work well for round and hexagonal materials. Four-jaw chucks are used for squares and octagonal shapes.
      - Independent chucks are mostly four-jaw, with each jaw being moved by its own lead screw. These jaws are reversible, negating the need for extras. Independent chucks are used to avoid run out or for materials that need to be offset while turning. Taking the extra time to set up an independent chuck using a dial indicator can eliminate any error that could be presented by a self-centering chuck. For many machines, the supplied four-jaw chuck will also have a much larger capacity than the provided three-jaw.
      - A drill chuck is usually used in the tailstock for spot-drilling center holes or boring but can be used on the drive mandrel. If the tailstock and mandrel share a common MT size, then this is quite simple. If the mandrel and tailstock have differing tapers, it is simplest to buy an additional chuck and Morse Taper adapter. This is a very good solution for holding small material and much lower in cost than adding a collet set. High-quality drill chucks usually have less run out than self-centering chucks, but with a much smaller capacity (usually no larger than 1″).
- Collets offer higher precision than jawed chucks and are fast to set up if a collet chuck is in place. The most common collet option will be 5C style, but ER collets can be used as well (though with a different chuck). Using collets will require one collet per diameter of material; 5C collets additionally offer square and hex sizes as well as inside hold style. 5C collets are available in 1/64″ increments, but for most shops a set that ranges from 1/16″ to 1″ by 1/16″ increments would be sufficient. If small bar of any shape is the most common material being turned, collets are a good investment.
- Face plates are a useful method for driving either odd shapes or shapes that are too large to fit a chuck. These use bolts or hold down plates similar to those used on a mill to mount material. An example would be a sheave that needs the center bore either repaired or enlarged (such as for placing a sleeve bearing). Since the center of the casting would be tapered, it could not be held safely in a chuck but could be held to the face plate by its spokes. This would be a rarely encountered project, but setup is much the same as with a four-jaw chuck or may be done off the machine.
- A lathe dog is an option, but it is quite unusual to encounter a need. A shaft (or bar) is center drilled at both ends and placed via centers in the mandrel and tailstock. It is then driven by a "dog" clamped to the shaft that is in turn

engaged by a drive plate on the mandrel. This could be used for eccentric work.
- The bed is the main structure of the lathe and holds the tailstock, includes the ways and rack gear for manual movement of the carriage, supports the lead screw at each end, and sometimes has a removable section near the head stock to increase swing. (This section is usually a very small portion of the bed.) The center is open to allow attachment of accessories such as a steady rest. Some larger lathes have a sliding bed; moving it away from the mandrel increases swing and/or maximum material length.
- The carriage is the workhorse for the operator and moves along the length of the bed between centers. It may be driven by a hand-wheel or the lead screw. Its other components not only hold the tools but control how those tools engage the material.
  - The cross slide moves perpendicular to the bed and is how the operator moves tooling into the material. The cross slide on most machines will be fitted with a top slide that can rotate about a center axis and holds the tool post. When cutting, the slides and cutter should be set for as little overhang as possible, while still providing the necessary movement for the depth of cut. This may require repositioning the top slide on the cross slide since many machines offer multiple mounts for the top slide. If possible, eliminating the top slide from the equation will provide a much more rigid mount for the cutter and make finishing an easier task. Unfortunately, most machines require an adapter to do this.
  - A follow rest is not commonly included with small (especially imported) lathes, but they are very useful for small diameter cutting and should be given serious consideration as an add-on. These mount to the carriage and support the material on two axes, opposing the pressure of the cutter. They work well to prevent bending of small diameter material. They can be fabricated fairly easily if the shop already has a mill.
- A steady rest for metal is similar to one that would be used on a wood lathe, but they mostly have solid bar stabilizers (usually brass) with no wheels so they need some lubrication to not mar the surface. These are needed when working with long material or for horizontal boring. They do need to be installed with the required travel of the carriage in mind. One can be seen in use in Figure 12.36a.
- The tailstock is the unit at the opposite end from the mandrel. It will mount centers or other tooling such as a drill chuck in a moveable ram, most often via Morse taper. Centers are the most common item to mount in a tailstock and may be either live, with bearings for reduced friction, or dead, which are solid. Live centers are generally preferred but older lathes may only have a dead center; these may work fine with lubrication (or if turning plastic). A variety of centers are available to fit a multitude of projects. The most common is a pointed end (different angles from 60° to 90° are available) but other styles such as a bull nose center (conical) to fit inside tube or pipe are available. Some companies offer kits with interchangeable ends. Another add-on for a tailstock is an adjustable mount for the center that allows for cutting tapers.

- Cutters—Like a wood lathe, various shapes of cutting tools are available; unlike wood lathes, it is not unusual for a machinist to make a custom-shaped cutter. Similar to a mill, both HSS and carbide tools are available. Unlike milling cutters, carbide cutters are the most common but are not solid carbide. Instead they have a carbide tooth bonded to a steel shank or a replaceable carbide insert mounted to a steel shank. Bonded tools can be professionally sharpened but are more often simply replaced when dull or chipped.
  - There are three basic types of external cutter regardless of materials: general turning (various shapes), thread cutting, and parting.
    - General turning cutters are available in standard shapes, many of which offer both left-hand and right-hand versions. Tools that use carbide inserts are specified by the shape of the insert, clearance angle (similar to the letter codes used for brazed carbide), rake angle, hand, and shank size. Many manufacturers offer comprehensive charts of insert and shank options. Tool part codes will be simple for bonded carbide tools. Both types of carbide offer different cutters optimized for soft materials, steel, or alloys such as stainless. Figure 12.31a outlines applications for common brazed carbide tools; tools using inserts follow similar usage.
    - Parting tools, like general turning cutters, may have bonded carbide or a carbide insert; these have a limited depth of cut. Tool holders that use a depth-adjustable HSS blade are a better option when deeper parting cuts are required. Figure 12.37 shows such a tool in use.
    - Thread cutting tools offer two basic shapes: straight shank tools and cranked-neck tools. Straight shank tools are ground to the thread face angle and require the top slide to be set to the proper intersecting angle when cutting threads. Cranked-neck cutters can be fed

directly by the cross slide but are less versatile as they will cut only one pitch per tool.
- Boring bars are another type of cutter but these only serve one purpose: smoothing the interior of hollow material after drilling. While a cranked-head cutting tool can be used for boring, boring bars allow for a much deeper reach. As reach increases, the depth of cut and feed rate have to be reduced accordingly.
- Knurling tools cut either straight single ridges or cross-hatched ridges onto the circumference of materials. This is a common finish for hand-wheels and knobs or threaded caps. It is also an excellent way to secure insert bushings into a bore.

Cutter Diagram	Letter Designation	Handed	Usage
 AR	A	Right & Left	General turning, facing, finishing and boring.
 BR	B	Right & Left	Interrupted cuts, roughing, cutting to shoulder without a square face.
 C	C	Neutral	Grooving and chamfering
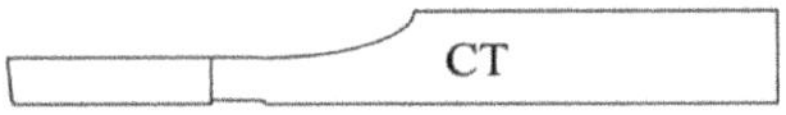 CT	CT, CTL	Handed	Shallow parting; relief angle to left (CT) or right (CTL).
 D	D	Neutral	General turning, facing, undercutting. Can be distinguished from E type cutters by the slight radius at the tip.
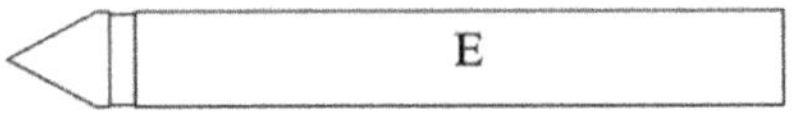 E	E	Neutral	Thread cutting (with angled top slide)
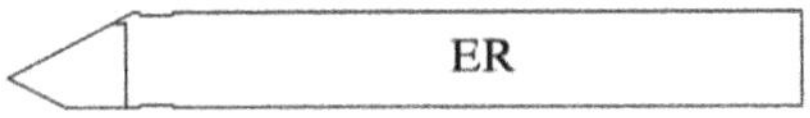 ER	ER, EL	Handed	Thread cutting; cutter is ground to thread angle.
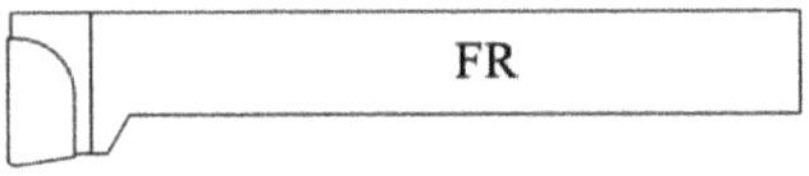 FR	F	Right & Left	Facing to a 90° shoulder, turning close to the chuck, boring to a 90° shoulder.
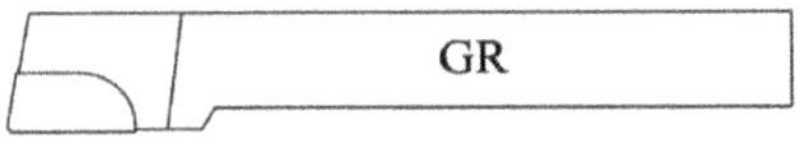 GR	G	Right & Left	Turning, boring and facing; 90° shoulder not required.

Right hand bits cut toward the mandrel; Left hand cut away from the mandrel.

Figure 12.31a The chart outlines the most common shapes for brazed carbide lathe cutters. Cutters labeled C-2 are for soft materials; C-6 cutters are for steel and cast iron. Insert tools of similar shape will have similar cutting properties.

Techniques

- Measuring and marking—Scribing layout lines on a work piece is often as important for turning as it is for milling. With round material this can be difficult. Measuring as work progresses is fairly easy.
  - Transferring marks made on a work bench to the circumference of the material can be done either by holding a scribe along the edge of the tool post or by clamping a scribe in a tool holder. It can then be aligned to the mark by moving the carriage. The circumferential mark should be made by rotating the mandrel by hand; doing so under power could be dangerous.
  - Calipers are usually used as the work progresses. Spring calipers are sufficient for most work, but if higher precision is required, these should be set slightly oversized for outside roughing or undersized for inside cuts. A diameter can then be measured with sliding calipers or a micrometer, allowing the operator to zero the micrometer wheel on the cross slide and use it for the final pass(es).

Figure 12.31b Examples of brazed carbide cutters in the top row and insert cutters along the bottom row. In this image the variety of shank sizes available is clear.

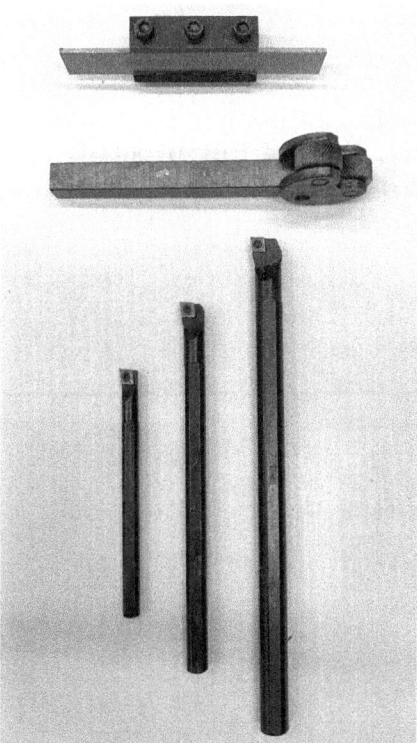

Figure 12.31c From top—a parting tool, a knurling tool, and a set of boring bars.

Figure 12.32 Using spring calipers to compare the internal bore being cut through a nylon roller turned to replace a broken roller from a panel saw.

- Mounting material—Lathes offer a few options for mounting material but a three-jaw, self-centering chuck is the most common choice.
  - A three-jaw chuck is a fast and common method for driving material. It does require changing the jaws for inside or outside hold. Material mounted with inside jaws should be inserted to at or near the full depth of the jaws; smaller material may pass through the mandrel increasing rigidity. The overhang (or stick-out) of materials held only with a chuck should not exceed 3 times × their diameter. An overhanging section of 1 1/8" bar held with inside jaws can be seen in Figure 12.36a. Some sets of inside jaws are stepped on the outside surface to hold hollow rounds internally. When using jaws for an outside hold, the material should be fully seated to the face of the appropriate step. All material held in a chuck should not be assumed to be held true. For accuracy, material should be checked for run out with a dial indicator. Figure 12.39 shows material being held in outside jaws for boring.
  - Collets are a much more precise means of mounting small sections of round, square, or hex bar. The only downside is the diameter limit. For outside holding collets the maximum diameter is 1 1/8" for 5C and 3/4" for ER32. 5C collets additionally offer inside expanding collets up to a 2 1/2" maximum diameter. ER series collets offer tapping collets designed to securely hold taps for internal threading as well as versions for square and hex bars.
  - The tailstock will be required for anything longer than a few inches. This requires drilling a dimple for the center on solid sections; a cone center can be used on hollow sections. This is done by carefully marking the center of a rod or bar, then center punching to ensure alignment of the center drill. Center drills are short, doubled-ended step bits used only for shallow drilling. Like other drills, they are available in HSS, cobalt, and carbide for compatibility with an array of materials. The small point at the tip creates a pocket for lubricant to prevent overheating dead centers. Diameters are specified by numbered sizes 00000–1 (1/8" body with increasing point diameter) and 2–5 (3/16"–7/16" body diameter and 3/64"–3/16" point diameter). A set that contains 1–5 or 2–5 will be well suited to most projects. Center drills are available in three styles.
    - Plain center drills have a simple chamfer leading to the point. A 60° angle is most common and these are used for most tasks.
    - Radius type drills create a convex surface between the face and the point. These are reserved for tapered cuts when the tail center will be off axis from the drive end.
    - Bell type drills are chamfered but have a slight perpendicular edge designed to cut a shallow counterbore, making it easy to spot a consistent depth of cut.

Figure 12.33 A 5C collet with a section of 3/8" square bar. Alongside is an example of a 5C collet for round bar that shows the external threads used by the closer. The closer on this machine uses a large hand-wheel (black ring) which is common.

Figure 12.34a A section of 1 1/8" bar marked, punched, and ready for center drilling.

MACHINING • **267**

Figure 12.34b A shorter piece of the same 1 1/8" bar being surfaced for use as a cylindrical square. The complete square can be seen in Figure 12.14.

- Straight cuts—Cutting along the length of material is the main reason to have a lathe. Even if this is only for part of the length of the material, such as turning down the end of a shaft for threading to add a keeper nut or to fit into a bearing such as for making rollers.

- Facing—This is a good skill to acquire and it is especially important when making a flanged bushing. The trick is to leave just a tiny (but even) amount

Figure 12.36a A facing cut on a section 1 1/8" bar stock that will become a cylindrical square.

Figure 12.35 Cutting the outer face of a flanged bushing that will pass through a 1/4" plate and provide support for a shaft.

Figure 12.36b Flanged bushings made by the author. Though the tooling setup on the lathe is not shown, the result of facing the shoulder is clear in this image.

of material when cutting along the length that will then be removed in one or two passes to make the face. Care needs to be taken to not over travel and gouge the final diameter of the body.
- Parting off—This is a skill that needs to be done with care, as it tends to generate more heat than other cuts and it is essential that the tool has necessary clearance in the material. Many tasks will not require parting; it is most common when multiple pieces are being made from the same bar. Shallow cuts may be done with a CT type tool; deeper cuts will require a dedicated parting tool with an adjustable blade.

Figure 12.37 An example of parting off a knurled section of 3/4" rod. This is being cut at 120 RPM with a good bit of oil.

- Threading—This is a common task in machine shops but less likely to be done in an entertainment shop. Regardless, the ability to either custom thread or add powered threading to projects has value.
  ○ Die heads are expensive (though used heads can be a significant savings) but are a very fast way to use a lathe for threading. "Self-opening" heads hold the dies on a spring-loaded mechanism that releases from cutting at maximum depth. These are ideal if a series of parts with partial threads is needed and an off-the-shelf part does not exist. Manually opening dies are available for continuous threading on long parts. These usually have an adjustable cutting depth so that threads may be cut in multiple passes and be set to cut slightly under- or oversized threads.
  ○ Tailstock die holders are a fairly low-cost accessory that will hold up to 1 1/2" dies; this achieves a capacity of about 3/4" diameter rod. This size will also support up to 1/2" National Standard Pipe Thread (NPT) dies for shops that use small pipe a lot. These are typically used with adjustable round dies, but fixed dies work as well. They are available in two styles: manual sets that include a "tommy bar" for added leverage when turning the die by hand (with the mandrel locked) or floating holders that are designed to be used under power. These require very low speed and a good bit of cutting fluid. Both styles have a limited cutting depth of about 2".
  ○ Manually cutting threads with a cutting tool on the cross slide is done using the lead screw. The angle of the top slide is usually set to 30° to cut common 60° threads. Change gears (or transmission) in the head will determine lead screw rpms which will set the Threads Per Inch (TPI) or thread distance by millimeter (may require additional change gears) being cut. This requires experience on the operators' part as it is a multiple-pass technique wherein the operator must advance the tooling the appropriate amount each time and synchronize the manual engagement of the lead screw by observing the thread dial indicator. The advantage is the ability to cut custom threads and cut threads on much larger material than most manual dies can easily cut.
  ○ Internal threading can be done under power using a floating tap holder, but it is not easy since it is a blind cut, making it easy to break the tap by bottoming it. Being hardened steel, these are very difficult to remove. Tap holders that will mount in the tailstock are available for manual threading. Using a tap mounted in a standard tap holder is a good solution too. If the tap holder has a dimple at end, it can be aligned using a live

end in the tailstock. It does take a bit of practice to feed the tap, then adjust the tailstock to maintain pressure until the tap is adequately seated and the tailstock can be moved away. This process is quite similar to tapping on a mill, as shown in Figure 12.20.
- Drilling—While drilling is more often done on a mill, boring is common practice on a lathe, but boring bars require adequate space. If the plan is to bore solid material, it will need to be drilled first. For short sections this is fairly easy: the material is aligned in a chuck or on a face plate, the tailstock is replaced with a drill chuck with an MT mount and the drill bit fed into the material. Care should be taken to ensure the drill will not collide with the chuck, face plate, or spindle when (if) it breaks through. Being mounted in the tailstock does help prevent the bit being pulled into the material on breakthrough as it can be in a drill press.

Figure 12.38 Drilling the initial bore for a flanged bushing.

- Boring—This is a common practice on a lathe. Any item that needs a precise fit on a shaft or bearing is better bored than drilled. Standard twist drills inherently make a hole slightly bigger than their actual diameter and may be inconsistent depending on the point grind. Finishing a bore on a lathe ensures a smoother and more accurate size. Boring bars are designed for this task.

Figure 12.39 Boring a short section of 2" diameter nylon rod. Though this is not a metal example, the setup of the boring bar is the same and the author needed a replacement roller for a panel saw.

- Knurling—This is another task that is best performed on a lathe. Knurling is a common finish for hand knobs and studs. As the knurls are pressed into the material, some material will be raised; thus, it is the depth of cut that creates an even knurled pattern. Knurling should be done at a slow speed with cutting fluid, especially on harder metals. Knurls need to maintain engagement until the process is complete; otherwise, the tool will cut overlaps.

Figure 12.40 Attempting to knurl 3/4" steel bar. Unfortunately the top slide on this lathe has too much play to cut evenly on such hard material.

Threads

Cutting and repairing threads is not always an efficient means to solving a problem for many shops. Buying a replacement is often more time and cost-effective when you factor in shop labor costs. There are situations such as repairing machines, making custom props, and building effects where threading may be the only solution. In addition, custom-cut threads have some advantages: oversized (by diameter) threads increase friction and are less likely to loosen due to vibration; undersized threads reduce friction which can increase speed of operation. Understanding thread types helps make these tasks easier.

- Thread types—There are three types of thread that will be commonly encountered in entertainment shops: bolt threads, machine threads, and pipe threads.
  o Bolt threads are the most commonly encountered thread type and there are two systems of measurement likely to be encountered: inch threads and metric threads. These share a 60° cutting angle and both have standardized pitches that vary by bolt diameter. Coarse thread bolts are the most common as they tighten much faster. Fine threads take more revolutions to tighten but have a slightly higher maximum torque value than coarse threads. Most shops will cut threads by hand, but taps for mills and drill presses are an option when many holes need threading. Taps for machines will either be helical to pull away chips or be designed to push chips ahead of the tap on through drilled, thin materials.
    - Most bolts will have standard "right-hand" thread (turn clockwise to tighten), but in some applications left-hand threads have an advantage such as on saws where they counter the direction of revolution or in turn buckles. Left-hand threads may have no indicator markings beyond grade except on some power tools and machines where a counter-clockwise arrow may be present.
    - American Standard threads are defined by diameter and TPI. This system offers one fine thread (NF) and one coarse thread (NC) per diameter (e.g. 1/4"–20 vs. 1/4"–28).
    - Metric threads are defined by diameter and distance between threads (e.g. 1.75 mm peak to peak). This system may offer two to three pitches per diameter for fine threads and one coarse pitch per diameter.
  o Machine threads are used for the moving parts of many machines, such as for moving the bed on a mill. In addition they are often used in linear actuators. These are not likely to be made or repaired in the shop but may need to be specified for projects that require motion.
    - ACME thread is a common hybrid machine thread that has a square top and bottom with tapered sides. This design is a good compromise between strength and speed of travel and is much easier to machine than square threads, reducing cost. Availability of components makes them a good choice for shop-made movement mechanisms.
    - Square threads offer fast travel and efficient power transfer but are not the strongest design and have a very coarse pitch. These are good for slow-speed operations such as vises but will mostly be encountered as manual lead screws on machinery.
  o Pipe threads are another type of thread that will often be encountered and may need to be cut when custom lengths of pipe are needed. In the U.S., tapered NPT will be the most often encountered type. When cutting these threads it is important to not over travel the cut. The taper of the thread is a component of the ability of these to seal; over cutting can prevent the threads from fully seating. The other styles of pipe thread that may be encountered are British Standard. These are the international standard and are not compatible with NPT threads. British Standard offers both tapered and non-tapered versions.

Chapter 13

Employee Safety

TOOL OPERATION AND TRAINING

The first line of defense against injury and accident is proper training for all employees covering safety policies, proper tool operation and guarding, Safety Data Sheets, and workplace Right-To-Know. Training procedures need to be documented and kept on file. Training procedures should be reviewed regularly, and after any workplace incident, they should be immediately updated anytime a change is warranted. The primary source of safe use information for all tools and machinery should be gathered directly from the manufacturer. Only qualified personnel who have been identified in the training plan should teach operational techniques commonly used in the shop. A qualified person is defined by the Occupational Safety and Health Administration (OSHA) as person with a recognized degree, certificate, or extensive experience and ability.

PERSONAL PROTECTIVE EQUIPMENT (PPE)

Employers are required to provide appropriate Personal Protective Equipment (PPE) to employees at no cost to the employee (with some exceptions; refer to OSHA 1910.132). Every shop should have a written safety policy developed by competent personnel that identifies required PPE and where employees can both acquire PPE and be trained in its proper use when needed. OSHA defines a competent person as one who has the authority to take prompt actions to eliminate or mitigate hazards in the workplace. This may be an employee or a consultant during development, but the execution of the safety plan requires a competent employee on site. It is good policy to have PPE available for visitors or observers as well. Qualified personnel should oversee all training. The competent and qualified personnel may be the same or different employee(s). For any employer who is unsure of what kinds of safe operating procedures they should adhere to, the National Institute for Occupational Safety and Health (NIOSH) offers a multitude of resources and can even help find a certified professional, such as an industrial hygienist. NIOSH is a division of the U.S. Centers for Disease Control (CDC) and does not inspect nor enforce workplace regulations; that is the purview of OSHA, a division of the Department of Labor. NIOSH offers hundreds of publications regarding training, offers information on a range of materials used in industry, and has training centers.

*(A note of caution for freelance and contract workers: independent contractors are not considered employees and therefore must provide their own PPE. This can be an expensive but necessary cost that should be part of a contractor's fee negotiations.)

Bodily Protection

- Gloves—A caveat to gloves: they should not be worn in any situation where they could get caught in a moving apparatus. Drill press quills and stationary grinders are particularly dangerous in this regard. Though a wide range of gloves are available, two types stand out for working with metal.
  - Fabric gloves are available in a wide variety of styles, but many technicians prefer "mechanics"

style gloves. These synthetic fabric gloves have leather or simulated leather palms that improve grip and resist mild abrasion while maintaining dexterity. Other popular options are cotton or cotton/poly blend gloves that have a rubberized palm and fingers. These provide excellent grip and breathe well. Fabric gloves are only effective for handling materials or finished units and should never be worn while welding (especially those made with synthetic fabric that could melt).
  - Leather gloves can improve grip, protect against heat and ultraviolet (UV) rays, and are very resistant to abrasion. The thickness and flexibility of the leather will determine dexterity. Gloves with a gauntlet cuff are usually preferred for welding (see welding PPE below).
- Footwear—Footwear requirements will vary with shop usage; in a metal shop, all-leather boots are a must, even for crew who will not be welding. They may be in proximity to welding sparks and sharp edges. For larger shops moving heavier materials or assembling large units, safety-toe footwear may be necessary. This is one of the few items of PPE that the employer is not required to provide.
  - Safety footwear standards fall under OSHA-recognized American Society for Testing and Materials standards, ASTM F-2412-05 and F-2413-05. The first of these standards dictates the test methods used to verify the performance requirement of the shoe and the second indicates which tests a particular shoe qualifies for. Label data on a work shoe should be read as consisting of four parts:
    - Part #1 reads, ASTM F2413-05, and identifies that the shoes meet parts of this standard.
    - Part #2 identifies the gender (M=male or F=female) of the user. This part also identifies the impact resistance with an "I" along with the compression resistance of the toe designated by a "C", e.g. A C/50 means it is rated to resist a drop of a 50 lb object.
    - Part #3 will provide a rating for metatarsal arch compression—if the shoe has this feature. The ratings are for 50 and 75 pounds, identified by Mt/50 or Mt/75.
    - Part #4 identifies several other types of protection offered. Most relevant to a wood working shop would be a "PR" identification for puncture resistance.
- Head protection—Hard hats and bump helmets are another item that may not be required in a metal shop but could be needed at times and should be made available by the employer. Impact rated, hard hat welding helmets are available but are usually only found on industrial work sites. Head protection must comply with the American National Standards Institute (ANSI) Standard for Industrial Head Protection, ANSI Z89.1. In terms of impact protection, the revision subdivides hard hats into two types:
  - Type I hard hats are designed to reduce the force of impact from a blow to the top of the head. For most shops, a type I hard hat is sufficient. Consult an expert if you are unsure as to what classification is best for your facility.
  - Type II hard hats are designed to reduce the force of a blow to the front, back, and sides, as well as the top of the head. These are commonly required on active construction sites with various pieces of moving equipment and materials.
- Clothing—In some instances protective clothing must also be provided by an employer either by supplying the clothing directly or through a monetary allowance. For welding, a monetary allowance gives the employee the opportunity to purchase items with the best fit and mobility. The choice of clothing items and materials will vary with the material, process, and welding position. Work clothing worn under PPE should always be natural fiber in the metal shop. Cotton is the best choice, but avoid brushed cotton fabrics like flannel; the fuzzy surface can catch fire easily.
- Eye protection—Eye protection should be worn anytime a striking tool (hammer, chisel, etc.) or tool that creates flying debris (saw, grinder, etc.) is used. In addition, protective eye wear is required when handling dangerous liquids such as solvents. There are many choices for eye protection and most of them are very affordable. The purchaser should ensure that the items comply with ANSI Z87.1. All eyewear designed to resist impact will be marked with a + sign. Users should ensure that they are not scratched (badly) or fogged. Shop areas where eye protection is required should be conspicuously labeled (which may be the entire shop). One thing to be aware of regarding eye protection for metal working: metal particles are often much smaller than saw dust, and unlike fine saw dust, these may be needle sharp. As a result, fine metal particles are a much higher risk than fine wood particulate; thus, it may be more challenging to keep dust out. It is also wise to remember that a doctor can often remove ferrous metal particles with a magnet, whereas non-ferrous metal will require tweezers. Eye injury from metal particles almost always requires a trip to the

doctor; they often cannot be rinsed away with eye wash like wood dust can.
- Glasses and goggles are the most comfortable option for most workers. Safety glasses are a low-cost and effective means of protection but may not work well over prescription glasses. Goggles are not only more comfortable over existing glasses, they also are more effective at keeping dust and other small debris out of the eyes. As well, ANSI-rated prescription safety glasses are readily available. Clear safety glasses should always be worn under welding helmets. Non-prescription, shaded glasses are available for use with oxy-acetylene torches and plasma cutters. In many cases, a face shield should be worn in addition to the shaded glasses.
- Face shields are sometimes more cumbersome but they have distinct advantages: they can be worn with prescription glasses; they protect the user's entire face and can be combined with safety glasses for extra protection. The only downside is that they are not compatible with earmuffs. A face shield is a must anytime a wire wheel is being used on a grinder and should be worn during any grinding or cutting with an abrasive wheel. Shaded versions are available for OAF welding and plasma cutting; again clear safety glasses should be worn under the face shield.
- Hearing protection—The Noise Reduction Rating (NRR) is the minimum reduction of sound level (in dB) when worn properly. This is an important rating and should be matched to the machinery being operated. For most machinery, a 22 dB reduction is likely a bare minimum. The author does not stock any units rated below 26 dB. There are also many choices for hearing protection.
  - For multiple users, in-ear, disposable plugs are most hygienically friendly, but less ecological, and may not be cost-effective. They are available as corded or un-corded pairs and in bulk for dispensers. Some plugs can be disinfected or otherwise cleaned for multi-day use. This is easiest with corded pairs.
  - Banded in-ear "plugs" usually have replaceable tips, making them easy to reuse by one employee or re-tipped for a new user. Some are designed for the band to rest on the nape of the neck or under the chin to be compatible with a face shield.
  - Over-the-ear muffs are excellent as they often provide the highest NRR and are very durable. They can be sanitized for reuse but are best assigned to one user when possible. The main drawback is their incompatibility with face shields and similar PPE.

Respiratory Protection

- Respirators—These may be a necessity depending on the welding processes and the materials used by the shop. The use of respirators involves two parts: development and implementation of a written respiratory protection program with required worksite-specific procedures and elements for required respirator use, and the selection of the respirators themselves. This is an excellent reason to consult an industrial hygienist; it will ensure the program appropriately matches shop practices. Integrating respirators into the welding process may require specialized welding helmets, but most welding half-mask respirators are small enough to fit under a standard helmet.
  - OSHA provides extensive guidance regarding implementation of respirators on its website: https://www.osha.gov/laws-regs/regulations/standardnumber/1910/1910.134.
    - A written plan should follow OSHA guidelines—"...the employer must establish and implement those elements of a written respiratory protection program necessary to ensure that any employee using a respirator voluntarily is medically able to use that respirator, and that the respirator is cleaned, stored, and maintained so that its use does not present a health hazard to the user. Exception: Employers are not required to include in a written respiratory protection program for those employees whose only use of respirators involves the voluntary use of filtering facepieces (dust masks)". https://www.osha.gov/laws-regs/interlinking/standards/1910.134(c)(2)(ii)
    - OSHA requires the employer to provide respirators, training, fitting, and testing as well as medical evaluations at no cost to the employee. https://www.osha.gov/laws-regs/interlinking/standards/1910.134(c)(4)
    - OSHA also requires the employer to evaluate respiratory hazards unique to a workplace and its users, and base respirator selection on these factors. https://www.osha.gov/laws-regs/interlinking/standards/1910.134(d)
  - Respirators may be of three primary types. The selection of filters, devices, and device features

is much narrower for welding than for general applications. NIOSH provides excellent charts to aid the user in determining the proper mask for any application.
- Face-piece masks are some of the most common respirators available. To use all but filtering face-piece respirators (FFR) masks, users should be fit-tested and need to be clean shaven for them to work properly.
  - Filtering Face-piece Respirators (FFR) are the basic disposable masks that most users are familiar with. They are available in a variety of types and styles, such as nuisance masks for non-harmful dust to rated versions (such as N95) that indicate level of filtration. While these masks are common in wood shops and sufficient for most grinding tasks, they have little value in welding due to their inability to filter gases or vapors.
  - Air-Purifying Respirators (APRs) have a soft rubber face-piece attached to a frame that holds interchangeable, disposable filters. The most common are half-mask types that cover the mouth and nose, but full-face versions are an option. These must be fit to the user by a qualified person to function properly (usually sized small to extra large). Many of those designed for welding have a single filter integrated into the face-piece in order for the mask to fit under a welding hood. These are necessary when fume extraction is unavailable or insufficient, such as when welding with flux-cored wire or MIG welding aluminum indoors.
  - Welding helmets are available that integrate full-face APRs. Though more expensive than separate units, they are generally more comfortable. They may be worth the investment when MIG welding aluminum or flux-cored welding steel are the most common processes for a shop.
- Powered Air-Purifying Respirators (PAPRs) are the best choice for anyone who requires a low-resistance apparatus (such as those with asthma or other conditions) because they have a small fan unit that pushes air through the filter to the user. These are available as full-face units integrated into a welding helmet. These helmets can be used with facial hair because they use an additional bib that creates a light seal at the neck and shoulders.
- Supplied-air respirators are essentially the same as PAPR units but require a remote, purified air-source and are tethered, thus reducing the area in which they can be used.

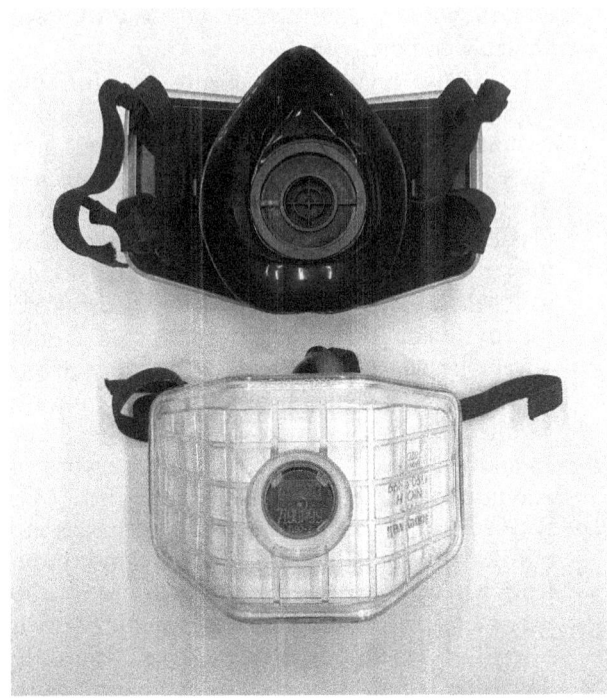

Figure 13.1 A half-mask respirator designed specifically for welding. The low profile fits well under most welding helmets.

- Environmental protection—While shop operations likely will not require the entire crew to wear respirators, air quality and other exposure can still be a concern. General protection via filtering and ventilation is an important factor.
  - Lead presents a hazard to any crew member (and those in the vicinity) that may be sanding old, painted metal (such as a park bench) since lead was a prominent component of paints until the 1970s. Shops need to be aware of the risks of lead paint. If the origin of a piece is unknown, lead test kits are readily available. If any paint tests positive for lead, it should only be removed by a professional. In large metropolitan areas the opportunity to use a commercial restorer who can either chemical dip or abrasive blast the piece in an enclosed environment could be an option. Otherwise, the object should be labeled and the paint safely encapsulated if the piece is to be used. Do not weld any painted piece, especially if lead paint is a possibility. Weldors should also be aware that some currently available primers for metal and automotive paints may be exempt from lead paint laws.
  - Welding fumes can be controlled with dilution ventilation or with fume extraction equipment. An example of a portable fume extractor can

be seen in Figure 7.22. If proper ventilation is insufficient or unavailable, respirators will be required. Weldors should always avoid welding zinc-coated steel; the fumes can cause temporary illness as well as creating voids or soft spots in the weld. Chrome, nickel, and cadmium coatings are especially dangerous because they are known to cause lung and respiratory cancer. Grinding the surface of these coated metals DOES NOT protect the weldor from exposure.

Welding PPE

The primary function of the PPE associated with welding is to protect the user from UV light; in addition it is flame retardant and usually abrasion resistant. Wearing synthetic fabrics while welding is strongly discouraged, even when covered with proper welding attire.

- Helmet—This is an absolute necessity for any welding and the shade glass should always be matched to the welding process undertaken. Many welder manuals and welding books provide charts and OSHA provides a downloadable Fact Sheet (see Chapter 8). The larger the viewing area, the better. Most helmets are a solid plastic or fiberglass shell, but fabric and leather welding hoods are available and are excellent for tight quarters. Some helmets can be attached to a hard hat as well. Look for ANSI Z87.1 or Z87+ certification on any helmet.
  - Fixed shade helmets are low cost and very close to fail-proof (unless the glass is broken or removed) but either the glass or the helmet needs to be traded out when a different shade is required. These do take some practice to learn to drop the helmet and not lose the alignment of the welding torch.
  - Auto-darkening helmets have become very popular. Brand names can be quite expensive but offer the most adjustability, longevity, and clarity. These are very versatile because many have three modes: clear viewing, grinding (shade 2), and welding (variable shade). These helmets don't need to be lifted between welds.
  - Face shields, when properly shaded, are excellent for any OAF process or for plasma cutting. The user should ensure they have Z87.1+ if one is used while hot shaping with a hammer. They should not be used for arc welding.
  - Welding goggles are usually shaded for OAF processes and are not appropriate for arc welding but may be suitable for plasma cutting. Styles with a flip-up shade glass also ease weld/braze inspection or for grinding while still providing eye protection.
  - Shaded safety glasses (not the outdoor sunglasses type) are another option for OAF processes where the weldor is above the work. They should not be worn when any slag or sparks could fall toward the wearer. They also do not protect the face from heat and may not be suitable for hot forming; a clear face shield should be worn over these. These are typically too dark to be worn while grinding and need to be traded for clear protection.

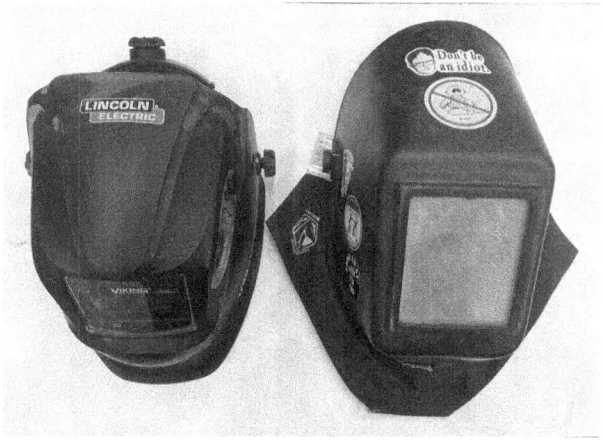

Figure 13.2a On the left is an auto-darkening helmet and on the right a fixed shade helmet with a clip-on bib.

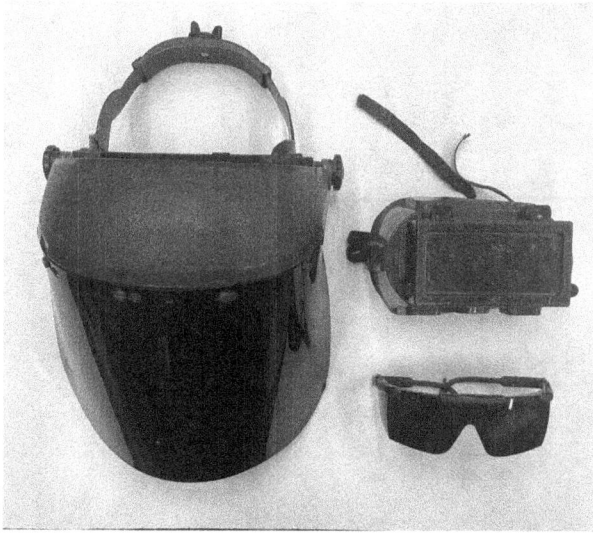

Figure 13.2b Examples of shade 5 eye protection: a face shield (left), traditional flip-up goggles (right, top), and shaded safety glasses (right, bottom).

- Helmet accessories—Welding creates heat, sparks, and intense UV. In many instances a helmet alone does not provide adequate protection.
    ○ A welding "beanie" is not part of the helmet, but rather a hat that fits under a helmet to protect the top of the head from sparks, or sunburn if working outdoors. They also help absorb sweat (and are washable!), helping keep the head-gear on the helmet dry. Some have a "cape" to cover the nape of the wearer's neck for further protection.
    ○ A helmet bib covers the gap between the chin of the helmet and the jacket, helping prevent sunburn to the sensitive skin of the neck. Otherwise, the top button of the jacket should always be closed.
    ○ A glare guard can be attached to the back of a helmet for a better view when welding outdoors. These also protect the top of the head from sparks.
    ○ Magnifier lenses (sometimes called cheaters) can help when working on detailed items. They are especially popular with TIG weldors.
- Jacket—A welding jacket is the next most important piece of welding gear. They are flame retardant and UV protective. Jackets may be leather coats, leather cape and bib (open back), treated cloth, or

Figure 13.3 Examples of welding jackets: a hybrid jacket with cloth body and leather arms on the left, an all-treated cloth jacket in the middle, and a leather cape and bib on the right. Special thanks to my students Joshua Rickard, Holly Ferguson, and Julia Kowalski for modeling.

cloth and leather hybrids. Another option is a flame retardant work shirt and welding sleeves (cloth or leather) that are worn over the work shirt sleeves. This can work well for hot days, but care should be taken to prevent exposure elsewhere on the body.
  ○ High-visibility clothing of some nature is almost always required when working on sites with material handling equipment such as forklifts, skid steers, or drivable personnel lifts. Flame retardant, high-visibility welding jackets and flame retardant shirts are available from welding suppliers.
- Aprons—For some activities, an apron is a wise addition to work-wear in the metal shop. This is especially true for grinding, where sparks will eventually erode a work shirt, and when using a mounted wire brush on a grinder. Fabric (natural fiber) and leather aprons each have their place, but leather is best when wire wheels are used.
- Gloves—These are another essential item for weldors. They protect the hands from heat, sparks, and UV. Gloves with gauntlets should be worn when welding. Depending on welding position, jacket sleeves may need to be inside the gauntlet (such as when working overhead) or outside the gauntlet, so sparks cannot roll into the glove. There are essentially three types of welding glove that can be matched to the task.
  ○ TIG welding gloves usually have no insulation and fairly thin leather that is very pliable, allowing for excellent dexterity. Since TIG welding tends to produce few sparks and uses concentrated heat, these gloves are a good match. Some weldors may opt to use these for OAF welding as well when working with thin materials and small welding tips. These are available from S to XXL sizes.
  ○ MIG gloves are relatively new to the market and are mid-weight gloves. Most use slightly thicker leather than TIG gloves and have a thin layer of insulation. MIG welding tends to make more sparks and radiate more heat than TIG welding. These gloves maintain good dexterity while offering more protection. These are available from S to XXL sizes.
  ○ Stick welding gloves (or just welding gloves historically) use heavy leather and thick insulation and are the most common gloves available. While they provide little dexterity, they are ideal for high amperage welding and the significant sparks and slag produced by stick welding. They are also a good match for flux-cored wire welding which also produces significant sparks. These are most available as XL and XXL, but large and medium sizes can be found.

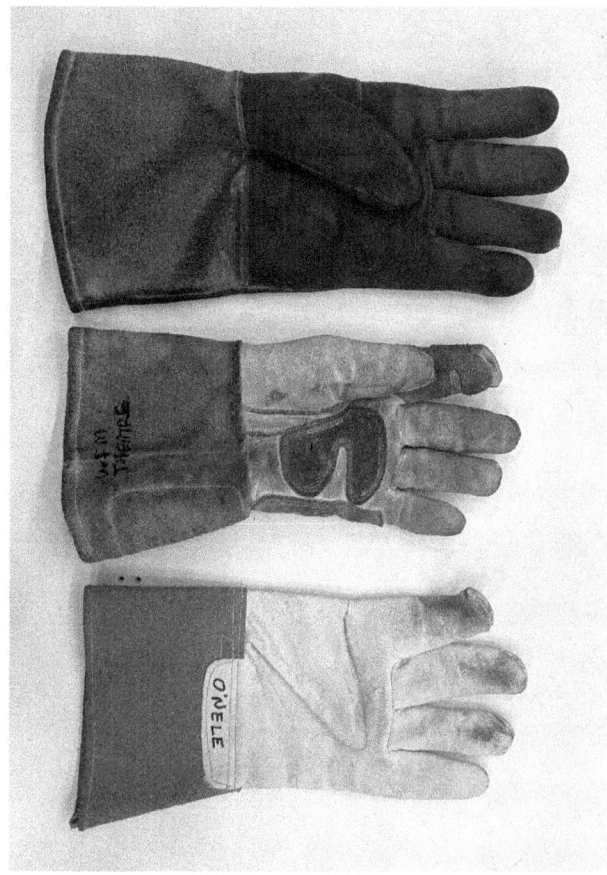

Figure 13.4 Welding gloves from top to bottom—stick welding glove, MIG glove, and TIG glove.

- Boots—Leather boots should be the standard in any welding shop. Uppers should be tall enough to tuck under the pant leg. A steel toe is not required specifically for welding, but many shops will require them since most of the materials and finished products will be heavy. Boots with metatarsal protection are an excellent choice for metal shops, but they are heavy.
- Spats—If lighter duty boots are being worn or when extra protection is required (such as when cutting with an OAF torch), leather spats that cover the boot or boot and shin are a great addition. These usually have a strap that passes under the boot and work best on boots that have a heel.
- Pants—Flame retardant pants are available to go over regular pants. This is an excellent way to stay clean and protect the weldors' legs when welding in odd positions. Welding chaps are another option that protects the wearer from heat and sparks but offer better ventilation by being open on the back.

Figure 13.5 Further examples of protective clothing. On the left is Joshua with a leather apron and tall spats, in center is Holly with leather chaps and short spats, and on the right is Julia modeling treated cloth pants. All of these examples should be worn in addition to a welding jacket and gloves; they have been removed for clarity.

FIRE SAFETY

The best plan for dealing with fire is to prevent one. Every shop should have a prevention plan that includes having appropriate equipment on hand and accounts for emergency evacuation and egress. Prevention should focus primarily on keeping heat sources such as tools that generate sparks and open flames away from combustibles (by 35 ft), especially wood dust. Proper storage of flammables (such as paints and thinners) as well as timely and proper disposal of flammables are also important elements of fire prevention. Any shop facility should comply with all local codes that may apply such as fire suppression systems or smoke ventilation.

- Extinguishers—A fire extinguisher can save lives and property by putting out a small fire or containing it until the fire department arrives; but remember, portable extinguishers have limitations. Fire grows and spreads rapidly, so the best bet may be to evacuate. Your safety and that of everyone else in your building is much more important than objects. There is no substitute for having a certified instructor teach your crew to use fire extinguishers. Local fire departments or fire equipment distributors often offer hands-on fire extinguisher training.
  ○ As a refresher of their safe use, a few tips are included below:
    - Use a portable fire extinguisher only when the fire is confined to a small area, such as a wastebasket, and is not growing; everyone has exited (or is exiting) the building; the fire department has been called or is being called; and the room is not filled with smoke.
    - To operate a fire extinguisher, remember the word PASS:

(Read the instructions that come with the fire extinguisher and become familiar with its parts and operation before a fire breaks out.)
- **P**ull the pin. Hold the extinguisher with the nozzle pointing away from you, and release the locking mechanism.
- **A**im low. Point the extinguisher at the base of the fire.
- **S**queeze the lever slowly and evenly.
- **S**weep the nozzle from side to side.

○ Extinguisher types are identified by class. Metal shops should select multipurpose extinguishers (most often a Type AB or ABC dry chemical) or CO_2 extinguishers that are large enough to put out a small fire, but not so heavy as to be difficult to handle. The fire extinguisher should be approved by an independent testing laboratory. While there are various chemicals used for extinguishers, including water and CO_2, standard dry chemical units are the most common because of their broad compatibility. For spaces where residue from dry chemicals could be problematic, halogenated-type extinguishers are used. The most applicable classes for a metal shop are as follows:
- Class A are for common combustibles such as wood, paper, rubber, and cloth.
- Class B are for flammable liquids such as paint thinner and gasoline.
- Class C may be used on electrical fires.

○ Location of extinguishers is important; they should be close to exits so the user can keep their back toward a clear exit when in use. Extinguishers should never be covered or blocked by clutter. The user should always have an easy escape if the fire cannot be controlled. If the room fills with smoke, evacuate immediately. When welding near flammable material, such as under a "hot work" permit, a portable extinguisher should be stationed near the work area, but not exposed to sparks and heat.

○ Evacuation must be part of the plan. Every employee should "know when to go." Fire extinguishers are one element of a fire response plan, but the primary element is safe escape. Every shop should have a fire escape plan and working smoke and/or heat alarms that meet local code. Many buildings also have automatic sprinkler systems that will activate when fire and/or smoke are present.

• Flammable storage—It is relatively easy to safely store flammable chemicals in the metal shop: purchase a certified storage cabinet, locate it a minimum of 30 ft from any welding or other heat source, and keep the cabinet doors closed. Some additional information that many users are unaware of is as follows:
○ If the cabinet is in a confined space such as a closet, it needs to be vented to the outside of the building (local codes will apply).
○ All containers need to be effectively sealed within the cabinet. If there are strong fumes when the door(s) is opened, the culprit container needs to be found and resealed or safely disposed of.
○ Flammable cabinets are not fire safes; the contents are not insulated from heat. The cabinet's purpose is to contain any reaction from the chemicals stored inside.

SHOP SAFETY

There are a few general safety items shop managers need to provide that are shared across various areas of the shop.

Hazardous Waste

While this book does not provide extensive coverage of paints and finishes, it does discuss the use of solvents and some flammable coatings. Rags used with non-water-based solvent(s) for cleaning metal and/or any applicators used with flammable finishes can spontaneously combust and need to be disposed of in a proper container. Solvents used to clean applicators

Figure 13.6 An example of a proper disposal bin for flammable cleaning materials across from a welding station at ATOMIC (www.atomicdesign.tv).

need to be stored in a flammable cabinet and properly disposed of as well. Solvent and solvent-based finishes should never be poured into a waste water system nor should full containers be sent to a land fill. All hazardous materials should be handled and disposed of according to the information provided in the product SDS and local code. Many companies have a contract with a hazardous waste disposal firm and some counties and other jurisdictions have drop-off sites for small quantities.

First Aid

This section is not intended to be a first aid reference guide. It is intended to provide the reader with an overview of the types of first aid training available and the common items to have on site.

- Training—Whether in a shop or at an installation site, having at least one supervisor with some level of first aid training is good insurance. At a large organization, such as a school, the campus may have trained professionals that can respond much faster than municipal providers.
  - The Red Cross offers both online and in-person training. While online classes provide familiarity, a hands-on course is especially important for Cardio-Pulmonary Resuscitation (CPR) training to be the most effective.
    - First aid basic response covers common first aid emergencies such as choking, bleeding, and overdose. First aid for severe trauma focuses on techniques to stem life-threatening bleeding.
    - CPR is taught as combined adult/pediatric or adult-only class and teaches resuscitation techniques used to aid a patient until medical personnel arrive.
    - AED (Automated External Defibrillator) training is usually combined with CPR but may be offered as a stand-alone session. This training provides an opportunity to get hands-on practice with an AED.
    - Workplace training combines the above three options into workplace safety courses that can be customized to a given industry or workplace.
  - 911 in North America connects to all emergency services and should be used anytime an injury could be life threatening. When unsure, call anyway; dispatchers are trained to determine the level of response needed and to talk callers through some first response techniques when required. When working outside of North America, it is wise to find the local 911 equivalent. In many countries in the EU, 112 will connect to at least ambulance and fire but it is not a universal number. In the U.K. 999 connects to all emergency services.
- Equipment—All shops should have the OSHA-required first aid equipment on hand but should consider additions to the basics.
  - OSHA-approved first aid kits will include the following: gauze pads of various sizes, adhesive bandages, triangle bandages, scissors, wound cleaning, foil blanket, tweezers, tape, gloves, resuscitation kit (pocket mask or other device), and a small splint (see OSHA 1910.266).
  - Burn treatment is a wise addition for any welding shop since minor burns are fairly likely. Burn gel and burn spray both contain lidocaine (2%–4%) and many add aloe and vitamin E. The gel can ease the pain and itch from minor burns. Any burn that causes bleeding should be assessed by medical personnel. Never put ice on a burn; it can reduce blood flow, impacting healing, and if held in place too long cause further damage to the tissue, resulting in increased risk of infection.
  - Blood-borne pathogen kits should be available in case of a large wound. Having a clean up kit designed to safely neutralize blood-borne pathogens and contain them as a biohazard should be kept on hand. One hopes it is never needed.
  - Quick clotting powder is available from a variety of brands. This powder is designed to be poured directly into an open wound to stop bleeding almost immediately. It is far safer than using a tourniquet.
  - Wound closures are another item to keep in the first aid cabinet that one hopes to never use. "Zip closures" are essentially temporary replacements for stitches. These consist of large adhesive pads that can be drawn together by zip-tie-like tabs. Smaller butterfly closures that have an aluminum backer on an adhesive pad that can be placed and then pinched shut to pull skin together work well for small incisions. Any wound requiring a closure device needs medical intervention as soon as possible.
  - Ice packs for sprains and strains may be instant (chemical) or reusable ice packs can be kept in a freezer. Instant packs have the advantage of simple storage but are less effective. They are excellent for job sites. Neither should be used to treat burns nor should they be placed directly on bare skin.

- AEDs are a wise investment for employers with a significant number of employees to keep on site. Some of these life-saving devices require no medical training to use (the machine will talk the user through the steps) and will not activate unless required. Most AEDs designed for consumers come with a set of training pads so that the owner can familiarize themselves with its operation.
- Eye wash should be available in any shop that produces particulates. Even while wearing safety glasses, it is still possible to have debris end up in someone's eye. In this case it should be flushed out; rubbing one's eye can lead to injury.
  - Bottles are portable, cost-effective, and available in various sizes. They can also be taken to remote job sites. These need to be replaced when expired.
  - Wash stations are units that are plumbed into a building's plumbing, usually near an existing sink. Some units may be combined with an emergency shower. These require regular testing and must be kept clean.

PPE and Oversight in the European Union and the United Kingdom

Most of North America and the European continent share similar approaches to workplace safety. Each has guiding organizations whose standards and procedures are quite similar and enforcement is handled by some division of the government. EU-OSHA is the European equivalent to NIOSH. EU-OSHA is not a governing body, rather the goal is to provide member countries with research and analysis, encourage risk prevention, and raise awareness of issues. Each member country has its own enforcement mechanism, for example the Ministry of Labor in Germany and the Health Services Executive (HSE) in the U.K. EU member countries agree to adhere to a "harmonized standard" and each country has representation on the Management Board where locally adopted policy is offered for full adoption by the organization.

Resources

- OHSA—OHSA is the U.S. regulator of job site safety. This is both a standard-developing and enforcement organization. They have an easily accessible store of references that are available to keep your job site safe.
  - www.osha.gov
- NIOSH—NIOSH is part of the CDC and Prevention and is a research agency established to research workplace safety and health and provide the resources for employers and employees to develop safe practices. NIOSH offers thousands of free articles, apps for smart phones, and a number of training resources.
  - www.cdc.gov/niosh
- HSE—HSE is the regulatory body for workplace health and safety in the U.K. The website is an excellent resource for anyone working in our tour to the U.K. The site is easy to navigate and offers relevant information to many industries, including tools to assess workplace stress. They even offer a free safety app for smart phones.
  - www.hse.gov.uk
- EU-OSHA—This is an extensive website with both online risk assessment tools and a vast set of publicly available articles. EU-OSHA also hosts additional websites and an online interactive risk assessment (OiRA) site designed for small- to medium-sized businesses.
  - www.osha.europa.eu
- European Committee for Standardization (CEN)—This organization is a consortium of representative for 34 EU countries that sets standards much the same way that ANSI does in North America. In fact, ANSI has committed to partnering with CEN (as well as CENELEC and ETSI) to better communicate how each set of standards mirror or overlap. Two useful documents have come from this partnership, both of which available at share.ansi.org:
  - Questions and Answers Regarding the European Standardization System
  - European Questions About the U.S. Standardization System

Chapter 14

Physical Safety

In addition to environmental and employee safety, fabrication shops and fabricators need to consider the physical environment in which the work takes place. Some hazards are obvious, such as moving blades on saws, but others may not be as obvious, or one may not be aware that they are a hazard until it is too late. This chapter is intended to make the reader aware of how the physical work environment can be safer. While this chapter may not cover every scenario, it should provide a good overview of general practices that can be implemented in any shop.

GENERAL SHOP PRACTICES

There are a number of general considerations that all fabrication shops should include in their safety planning.
- Slips—While slips may lead to a fall, there are other possible injuries. A pulled muscle may not require emergency care but could certainly affect work output. Far worse is a slip that leads to contact with moving machinery. Humans instinctively try to catch themselves if they slip; such a move could lead to serious injury if done while operating shop machinery. Keeping work areas, especially operator stations, around machinery free of clutter is crucial. Shop floors and other work surfaces should be chosen carefully to reduce this risk. Requiring employees to have appropriate footwear can prevent both drop injuries and slip injuries. Round stock of any kind (rod, tube, pipe) on the floor present the highest risk of slips.
- Trips—Tripping hazards may be unavoidable in a fabrication shop because humans are imperfect, but they can be kept to a minimum. Attention to the routing of cords and hoses, properly storing left-over material upon completion of a project or at least at the end of each work day, and ensuring materials laid out for assembly are not set up in egress pathways help prevent injury.
- Sanitation—Beyond keeping floors clear of dust and debris, there are other tidying tasks that will lead to a safer shop. Chemical disposal is not addressed here but should be done according to local regulations.
   - Foremost in this area is keeping food and drink out of the shop. If the work area doesn't have an attached break room, a clean zone where crew can keep water bottles with a cap should be provided.
   - Unique to metal fabrication are the sharp edges on cut materials when abrasive blades are used and the chips produced by saws with carbide blades. Care needs to be taken when cleaning chips and storing or moving cut material.
   - Grinding sparks and dust present a unique hazard as well; there is a risk of fire from hot sparks and they remain an inhalation hazard when cool. Off-cast from grinders should be aimed away from the user and other crew members as well as away from flammable materials. If possible, grinding should happen on a down draft table or near other ventilation.
   - Many shops opt to keep off-cuts as well as reusing some material after strike (for resident companies anyway). When this is the case, scrap and reuse storage needs to be accessible in a way that prevents injury from sharp edges. Off-cuts and used material that will be recycled should be in containers that ease transport.
- Material storage—Items for immediate use need to be within easy reach and the storage system strong

enough to ensure they are stored safely. How the materials are stacked can be just as important: pipe and round tube can be especially difficult to store safely. In addition, metals can be longer and heavier than lumber thus storage racking needs to be robust.

- Materials are best stored near to the cutting tools they will be used with. It is not only efficient but prevents damage from incompatibility. When possible, heavy items should be stored on lower levels. Tall slender items should not be stored on end unless racking is design to do so safely.
- Separating and sorting of materials by type and by size increases productivity. If any material is reused from previous projects, it should be stored separately from new material when possible.
- Movement for materials should also be planned. Using skates or carts reduces work load, but the layout of projects and machinery must allow space for these.

• Lighting—Shops where tools are being used need to be well lit. Both general illumination and task-specific lighting contribute to a safe work environment and accurate execution of work. Other work spaces such as venues and warehouses need to have appropriate lighting for the work being done. Where general overhead lights create shadows, task lighting should be added to machinery. This helps with both accuracy and safety.
• Ergonomics—The height of work tables and other supports is an important consideration. Tables could be height-adjustable (which can be expensive or a hassle) or a shop may have tables and work stands made at two heights–this works well to account for both varying height of the crew and the varying thickness of projects being built on the tables. Machinery is where the limit often is, as most do not allow the working height to be varied.
• Music—Many shops have music playing because it boosts morale and can set a tempo for work. This needs to be kept to a volume that allows for easy communication between crew members and needs

Figure 14.1 The aluminum cutting area at ATOMIC (www.atomicdesign.tv). The highest areas may be accessed with a forklift while lower areas provide easy access to ready to use material. Note how clean the area is kept.

to be off when critical communication is happening, such as when operating rigging during load in. On a related note, ear buds are not hearing protection and should not be worn in the shop as such. As well, they interfere with communication. While both ear muffs and ear buds that provide music and hearing protection are available, they can easily interfere with crew communication and increase risk.
- Maintenance—Ensuring all equipment and the associated consumables are in good working order is a big part of keeping the crew safe.
  - Worn or inappropriate blades in a shop are just as dangerous as dull blades in a kitchen. The operator may feel the need to apply too much pressure that may jam a machine causing kickback or damage the blade. This also causes undo wear on the machinery (such as belts and internal bearings) which will be much more expensive than replacing the blades. Worn parts on tools such as guards that are in place but maybe not work properly or bearings that allow run out present a risk that may be hard to see. These should be repaired as soon as they are recognized. Replacing parts may need to be done by a qualified technician, especially if a tool is under warranty. A monthly inspection of the functioning of safety items on machines can head off issues before they become a problem.
  - Uneven or out-of-square work surfaces on tools could jam materials in saws leading to injury. Beyond the direct risk of injury, poor quality work areas around tools will frustrate users and lead to poor working practices which introduces further risk.
- Guests—Non-employees in shops should follow safety protocols, such as having closed toed shoes, eye and hearing protection if needed, and be made aware of no-go zones, such as those around in-use machinery. Crew should be made aware of these guests as well to prevent distractions or other interactions that could cause risk to either party. Signage on shop entrances should establish these protocols as well.

CREW TRAINING AND AWARENESS

The crew is the first line of defense against risk. Proper training, attire, and communication are the best methods for establishing safe shop practices.
- Occupational Safety and Health Administration (OSHA) training—The OSHA does not directly offer certifications for work place safety; a network of certified training and testing companies offer classes based on OSHA guidelines both as in-person classes (some companies will even come on site for large groups) and online self-paced classes. These classes are commonly referred to as OHSA 10 and OSHA 30, but there are variants of each. OSHA also has guidelines for an array of training course that go well beyond the scope of the entertainment industry.
  - General industry courses are the most relevant to the entertainment industry. The 10 hour course introduces the key elements of workplace safety and health as well as employee rights. Common topics include reducing accidents and injuries, fall protection, emergency evacuation plans, and Personal Protection Equipment (PPE). Many shops require (and provide) OSHA 10 for all employees. Shop and site managers should consider the 30 hour general industry course that covers the basics of managing workplace safety and health. The course explains the employer's responsibilities, as well as employee rights. Topics cover the hazards across different industries (such as ladders/scaffolding, bloodborne pathogens, and electrical safety) and procedures (e.g. lockout/tagout protocols, machine guards, and industrial hygiene) to prevent accidents or injury.
  - Construction courses would be relevant for those in entertainment who may do on-site installation during new construction. Topics include identifying common causes of fatalities and accidents in construction such as slips/trips, electrocution, an entrapment between machinery and/or objects. The 30 hour courses are for construction site managers and focus on identifying major hazards (flammables, chemical and electrical hazards, etc.) and how to control and/or prevent accidents or injuries from them.
- Crew responsibilities—There are a number of ways the crew's behavior and communication can contribute to the overall safe operation of a shop.
  - Haste is a hidden danger that is often overlooked. Project managers need to schedule adequate time, assign sufficient staff, and ensure timely delivery of materials. This reduces the likelihood of last minute build pressure that leads to poor choices.
  - Solo work presents unique risks. Employers should avoid this whenever possible and set limits to acceptable/non-acceptable work for when this is necessary. (e.g. grinding should be fine vs. welding). Freelance contractors who predominantly work solo should develop not only a safety plan for themselves but consider having a check-in system with a trusted person. Beyond

the risks of working with machinery, moving materials and finished product need to be undertaken with extra care.
- Communication is a key skill. Too often in entertainment, workers have been expected to "tough it out" when it comes to long hours, shops without climate control or working outdoors, and the speed at which product is expected. This attitude is changing in many facets of the industry, but crew members must speak up if actions seem unsafe, or if they cannot do the task at hand for health or capability reasons.
- Impairment: alcohol and illicit drugs should be strictly forbidden on premises and prior to work. Some prescription drugs can present risks such as dizziness or drowsiness. Crew should be encouraged to inform supervisors if they have a prescription (or condition) that could put them at risk but not be required to disclose the reason or any other private medical data.
- Attire is an important consideration for the crew. Most shops do not have a dress code per se but should have conspicuous expectations of appropriate work wear. Footwear should always be sturdy, closed toe, and offer good traction. Some situations may require safety toe boots. Other clothing, hair, and jewelry should not be loose enough to get caught in any machinery. This includes significant fraying. Workers should also be aware that stains and tears inevitably happen. Those working in the welding area may need different attire than those working on forming tools. In addition, proper safety clothing should be available.
- No smoking or vaping should be the rule in any shop; these present a significant hazard to co-workers' health and are a fire hazard. Though vape devices present a much lower chance of igniting a fire, batteries have been known to do so and the unknown health effects present an unfair risk to other workers.
- Interactions between workers are not just a shop culture component but are part of safe practices. A sense of humor certainly makes the work place more enjoyable, but pranks and horseplay are problematic. It is a little too easy for pranks to escalate and rise to the point of danger.
- Lifting and carrying—Moving material and completed projects by hand is unavoidable in all parts of the entertainment industry. It can be especially difficult with metal that is delivered in sections of 20 ft or more.
  - Carts and dollies save effort and generally reduce stress on the body, but they need to be appropriate to the task. Often, steel is moved by placing small carts near each end of a bundle.
  - When carts will not suffice, managers need to ensure adequate crew is available and they are trained to properly lift and carry these items. A clearly articulated plan of the lift, repositioning, and final placement should be in place before the move begins. The old adage of lift with your knees not your back is completely true, but in addition, lift with enough people. Find lifting points that balance the load; awkward lifts happen, but they significantly increase the risk of injury.
- Machine function—With practice operators should be able to hear and/or feel when a tool is operating properly and when it is not.
  - Any tool or machine that seems to be making new noises should be inspected. This is often from something working loose or improperly installed.
  - Learning to hear the screech of trapped fall (waste material), the whine from worn bearings or rattles that may indicate run out or lose items that could come off (or not: some guards rattle and are perfectly fine) saves machinery downtime and increases safety.
  - Developing a "feel" for when a tool is operating properly is another important skill. The number one thing to learn to feel is when a blade is dull and needs to be replaced. This usually much sooner than the operator wants to admit.
  - When hand-wheels, levelers, and other moving parts become stiff or otherwise hard to adjust, it is time for maintenance. The need to force a machine into position leads to broken tools and increases the likelihood of an operator being injured.

TOOL USAGE AND MAINTENANCE

Understanding some general operating principles for machinery and ergonomics of tool use is a primary method for keeping the crew safe. As well, shop managers need to ensure all machinery is working properly. All maintenance should be performed with the power disconnected from the tool or machine.
- Safety mechanisms—This may seem obvious, but tools and machinery are sold with various safety mechanisms for good reason: they prevent substantial numbers of injuries. All should be in place and in proper working order, otherwise the tool should be removed from service. Older machinery may not have adequate safety mechanisms to meet modern standards, and though expensive to replace, the cost is still substantially lower than a workplace injury. Guards should be kept in place on tools and machines and operate as designed. This extends

beyond blade guards to dust housings and motor guards to electrical interlocks.
- Hand/body placement—When using power tools and machinery both ergonomics and keeping the operators body out of the debris path are important.
  ○ When using power tools, hands should be away from operating zones. Using clamps in place of holding material helps too. Most tasks involving cutting or drilling of metals require the material to be clamped in place, not held by hand. Grinding (such as with a bench grinder) and other finishing tasks often require the material to be hand-held; voiding the path of the sparks will keep hands and body safe. There are some circumstances when a guard or similar needs to be removed for a certain task, such as when using a fiber disc on an angle grinder. Immediately following such use, the guard needs to be replaced.
  ○ Each machine has unique operating procedures but there are general rules of safety that apply to all.
    ▪ The operator should always ensure solid footing in an area clear of detritus.
    ▪ Saws usually have an obvious path for the blade. This is an absolute no-go zone for anything other than the material to be cut; some require a larger area.
    ▪ Measuring material in the cutting zone is also not wise; many a tape measure has been lost to forgetfulness in front of a saw.
    ▪ The user should never reach over or in front of moving parts while running or during wind down unless it is part of the operation of the machine.
    ▪ Unfortunately, most machines are not designed for left-handed users. The majority of operating controls and guides are set up for right-hand use. Left-handed users should avoid "cross-over" such as reaching across to the quill of a drill press to the hand-wheel.
- Motion injuries—How a fabricator uses tools and for how long can have significant impact on their health. Users should be aware of risks, especially from portable power tools.
  ○ A study by the National Institute for Safety and Health (NIOSH) concluded that extended exposure to vibration from power tools can lead to nerve damage called Vibration Syndrome. High vibration tools such as chainsaws are major culprits, but over time even smaller power tools, such as hand-held grinders can cause injury. Workers who must use these tools for extended periods should take breaks, trade hands, and wear vibration reducing work gloves. Choosing quality tools designed to reduce vibration and replacing damaged or worn parts can also help reduce the risk of injury.
  ○ Wrist injuries can be caused by drills that jam when they break through steel, especially with corded drills that rarely have a clutch. Battery-powered drills usually have a clutch and if used properly can prevent this. Side-mounted handles on large drills provide extra leverage but do not prevent binding. Using a drill press whenever possible will help prevent these injuries.
- Team operation—Often heavy or very long materials require an operator to ask for assistance. This is fairly common with long, heavy gauge sections of steel that are too long for a cutting table. In these circumstances, it is critical that the aide understand their role which is to support the excess material while allowing the operator full control of its placement to avoid both a miscut or binding.
- Control of materials—Many materials that fabricators use are heavy, awkward, or both. Implementing in-feed and out-feed tables, rollers stands, and other material supports help prevent injury and improve accuracy. Ease of adjusting material at the machine to accurately align it leads to a better finished product and reduces the risk of awkward or frustrated moves. Nearly all cutting or drilling operations require material to be clamped or otherwise held firmly in place. This is especially true for saws using toothed blades such as a horizontal bandsaw or dry cutting saw.
- Power cords and air hoses—Beyond awareness of keeping these from being trip hazards, users need to match extension cord gauge and grounding to the tool to prevent overheating and tool damage. Both hoses and cables should be inspected for damage and repaired or discarded. Damage is often caused by misuse such as disconnecting an electrical cord by pulling on the wire jacket instead of the connector. They should also be coiled and stored properly to avoid damage. Self-retracting reels need to be used with care; they need to be locked in place during use and the recoil done in a controlled manner when finished.

Welding Area Specifics

There are some safe practices that are unique to welding areas that may not apply to other areas of metal fabrication shops. In fact, it can be much easier to mitigate risks if the metal prep area(s) and welding area(s) are separated by distance, or better, a barrier of some nature.
- Electrical safety—While the risks from the output of a welder are far less than those for anyone

who works with electrical wiring, they are not to be ignored. Electricity follows the path of least resistance and the water in the human body can be that path if care is not taken to avoid it. One simple, but important consideration is to ensure that all welding equipment is properly grounded (to earth). Welding areas need to be kept clean and dry. Grounding cables in the welding circuit need to have clean contacts and material should be cleaned where a ground clamp is attached.

- Sparks—Welding sparks are much hotter than grinding sparks; they are often liquid steel after all. Any welding sparks need to be contained to an area with no flammable materials and OSHA requires a 30 ft boundary between welding work and such materials whenever possible. When welding must be performed in an area where flammable material is present, hot work protocols need to be followed: protect as much material with flame retardant coverings as possible and maintain a fire watch during and beyond the welding activity. On some sites, any welding will require a Hot Work Permit from the overseeing authority. Sparks from welding are also proficient at finding their way into the smallest gaps in clothing. A change of position while welding can open gaps in clothing so it is wise to check before proceeding with a weld. One common mistake is wearing hybrid work boots while welding–the sparks will melt through synthetic materials on boots; grinder sparks will not unless they are held in close proximity for a long period.
- Heat—This is another rather obvious risk to welding: molten metal is hot! One strategy to mitigate injury risk (beyond wearing proper gear when welding) is to assume everything is hot until proven otherwise in the welding area. Checking for hot metal can be done by waving an ungloved hand above the material; if no heat can be felt, a quick touch with a damp rag can be a good indicator of residual heat (avoid any steam making contact with bare skin). The last step is a quick tap away from any welds before picking up the project. When in doubt, use pliers or tongs to move material.
- Compressed gases—The shielding and flammable gases used in welding are stored in high pressure steel cylinders or "bottles". These have specific handling procedures.
  - They should always stored and transported upright with valve cover caps in place.
  - Keep these away from heat, flame, and sparks regardless of content.
  - Cylinders need to be restrained (kept from falling) at all times unless moving to a new location. Cylinder mounting brackets are best, but cages and chains can be used as alternatives.
  - Always have the valve cover cap on unless in use on equipment.
  - Avoid impacts from dropping, and especially do not use one as a tool for bending.

Figure 14.2 A welding screen (framed) with a treated canvas blanket (left) and a woven high temperature welding blanket draped over (right).

- Flash protection—The intense ultraviolet (UV) light emitted by arc welding is a hazard that can cause permanent vision damage. Welding screens should be used as visual protection for non-welding areas of the shop, egress spaces, and passers-by. They can be translucent or opaque but must be rated for welding use. The same UV can cause "sun burns" on any exposed skin, leading to skin cancer with on-going exposure. Both the weldor and any other crew near the welding process need appropriate protective clothing.
- Welding blankets—To protect surfaces and flammable materials, flame retardant "blankets" can be used. These are primarily woven synthetic material that will resist very high temperatures and can be used near active welding. Treated canvas may be used to block errant sparks but should not be used close to active welding.

Chapter 15

Reference Sources

PUBLICATIONS

A wide variety of books are available that make excellent references and additional reading for fabricators and project managers in the entertainment industry. As well, a number of resources are available on the internet, although users should ensure they are consulting reputable sources. The books and websites below represent a selection of references that apply most directly to the information contained in this volume.

- *Metal Fabricators Handbook*—For readers interested in complex shaping of metal, this is an ideal reference. It includes excellent information for flat patterning, construction of modeling bucks and some information about welding.
  - ISBN 978-0-89586-870-1 Ron and Sue Fornier, HPbooks
- *Performance Welding Handbook*—While this book is focused on welding techniques for racing and aircraft, the information is still quite useful for any shop working with metal beyond steel.
  - ISBN 978-0-7603-2172-0 Richard Finch, Motorbooks
- *The Health and Safety Guide for Theatre Film and Television*—This is an excellent reference guide that is primarily focused on environmental health and safety. It has thorough coverage of laws and regulations; the effects of exposure; proper labeling of chemicals and materials; and the information contained in the Safety Data Sheets that are available for all chemicals. It also instructs managers, supervisors and teachers on how to plan and implement safe practices, including the use of respirators and ventilation systems, safe use of shops and equipment as well as areas outside of the fabrication part of the entertainment industry, such as stage make-up and dye in the costume shop.
  - ISBN 1-58115-071-7 Monona Rossol, Allworth Press
- *Structural Design for the Stage*—This volume is used to teach statical design of beams and columns in many theatrical graduate programs across the U.S. It contains necessary data to learn the basics of designing structures for the entertainment industry but stops well short of all of the information that would be provided by a structural engineer and should not be used as a replacement for consulting or hiring the appropriate consultant when necessary. Any user should be trained and only use this text when confident that it is the appropriate solution.
  - ISBN 978-0240818269 (2nd Edition) Holden, Sammler, Powers and Schmidt, Focal Press
- *Manual of Steel Construction*—This engineering reference manual provides design values for allowable stress design of steel members. It is quite comprehensive and likely to be used only by engineers and structural designers. It is the reference from which the design values provided in *Structural Design for the Stage* were derived.
  - ISBN N/A, Published by the American Institute of Steel Construction
- *Handbook of Welded Carbon Steel Mechanical Tubing*—Steel Institute of North America. This volume provides all the specification data for manufacturing as well as the engineering data necessary for use in structures. It is available for download from the Steel Institute.
  - www.steeltubeinstitute.org
- *Pocket Ref*—This handy book is also available in the large format, *Desk Ref.* It is a super compact

reference book that is essentially a miniature encyclopedia for every kind of fabrication imaginable. It may not have every bit of data for every industry, but it is the perfect jumping-off point for further investigation. Fabricators will find useful data on fasteners, area and volume formulas and data for common steel sections.
  - ISBN 978-1-885071-62-0 Thomas J. Glover, Sequoia Publishing
- *Machine Shop Essentials* — This is a Q-and-A-style book that provides excellent information regarding handwork, lathe work and milling. It also discusses fasteners, threads and metallurgy. It is well-illustrated and easy to understand.
  - ISBN 978-0-9759963-3-1 Frank Marlow, MetalArts Press
- *The Colouring, Bronzing and Patination of Metals* — This is advanced reading for anyone interested in traditional methods of coloring various metals. Some of the information is easy to apply, and some would require some experience in a chemistry lab. This text is out of print but available used. Regardless, it is an excellent reference.
  - ISBN 978-0-8230-0762-2 Richard Hughes and Michael Rowe, Watson-Guptill Publications
- *The Milling Machine* — This small but comprehensive book is an excellent reference for those new to milling. It covers a variety of machine types available and tools used for clamping, measuring and cutting. It also suggests a few excellent starter projects to orient the user to milling.
  - ISBN 978-1-56523-769-8 Harold Hall, Fox Chapel Publishing
- *Basic Lathework* — A great reference for those new to turning metal on a lathe. It is a small but comprehensive book that covers types of machines available, cutting tools and the variety of accessories that aid in setting up and driving material.
  - ISBN 978-1-56523-696-7 Stan Bray, Fox Chapel Publishing
- King Architectural Metals — This supplier offers numerous decorative and structural metal products. Cast panels, handrail components, decorative forgings and hardware are just a few of the options. When decorative metals are required, this is one of the few comprehensive suppliers in the U.S.
  - www.kingmetals.com
- National Fire Protection Association (NFPA) — The NFPA is a robust resource for fire and life safety info. One key document that all welding shops should review is the "Hot Work Fact Sheet". NFPA also has resources regarding fire extinguishers and suppression systems, emergency planning and egress requirements for buildings.
  - www.nfpa.org
- Occupational Safety and Health Administration (OSHA) — This is the U.S. regulator of job site safety. This is both a standards developing and enforcement organization. They have an easily accessible store of references that are available to keep your job site safe. OSHA 10 and 30 training courses are not offered directly by OSHA, but the curriculum used will always follow OSHA specifications. In addition, it is worth searching and downloading OSHA 1910.252 that covers safety information for welding, cutting and brazing.
  - www.OSHA.gov
- National Institute of Occupational Safety and Health (NIOSH) — This is a not-for-profit organization dedicated to providing individuals, organizations and businesses with health and safety information. It is NOT an enforcement organization. Contacting them will not lead to an OSHA investigation.
  - www.NIOSH.org

BLACKSMITHING

Although most shops will not do extensive shaping of steel, for those interested in these skills, what follows are a few key reads. Some basic classes at the various smithies around the country make a huge difference in understanding how to apply the information.
- *New Edge of the Anvil* — This book is an excellent primer on blacksmithing. It thoroughly covers shop setup, blacksmith-specific tools and their usage, and many common techniques used by smiths. It also includes sample portfolios of well-known blacksmiths that can be excellent research and inspiration for props artisans, decorators and designers.
  - ISBN 978-1-879353-09-2 Jack Andrews, Skip Jack Press
- *The Skills of the Blacksmith Vol I-III* — This series is essentially a full blacksmithing school in book form. Though not a substitute for actual training, it is both an in-depth resource for those merely interested in smithing as a hobby and for long-time professionals looking for inspiration or skill honing. All are fairly advanced but offer many useful tutorials for anyone who shapes metal in unique ways. These are available directly from the author at www.markaspery.com
  - ISBN 978-0981548-00-5 (Vol I) Mark Aspery, Self-Published
- *The Artist Blacksmith* — This book is both instructional and inspirational. Like many books on smithing, it covers workshops and equipment, tool making and anvil techniques. It is unique in that it

presents suggested projects that use the demonstrated techniques in addition to many examples of the author's work. Much of the work is architectural and therefore closely related to much of the work done in the entertainment world.
  - ISBN 978-1-861264-28-2 Peter Parkinson, The Crowood Press

- *Contemporary Blacksmith*—This is an inspirational text with beautiful photos of architecture, furniture and decor. It is excellent research for artisans and demonstrates design ideas that can be executed in materials other than steel with some creative adaptation.
  - ISBN 978-0-764311-06-2 Dona Z. Meilach, Schiffer Craft

Index

Note: Italicized page numbers refer to figures.

abrasive blast cabinets 122–123, *123*
abrasive blasting 122–123, *122–123*, 128–130; abrasive media 129; advantages of 130; machines for 128–129; sponge blasting 130
accessories (machining) 249–250; custom blocks 250; parallels 249–250; V-blocks 250
adhesives 173
aging *237*, 237–238; bleach 237; hydrogen peroxide 237; muratic acid 237; salt and vinegar 237
aircraft drills 177–178
airless sprayers 234
aluminum 2, 16–17; alloys 16–17; commercial forms and processes of steel and 13–14; I-beams 54; surfaces 17
Aluminum Association (AA) Standard beams 54
aluminum bronze 23; *see also* marine bronze
Aluminum Design Manual 49
aluminum honeycomb 61, *61*
aluminum, material prep for 128
aluminum pipe fittings 52; slip fittings 52; threaded fittings 52; welded fittings 52
aluminum shapes and applications 49–61; angles 53; bars 52–53; channels 54, *55*; extrusions 60, *60*; foils 58; grating 58–60, *59*; hollow sections 49–52; honeycomb 61, *61*; laminate 58, *58*; plate and sheet 55–58, *56–58*; punched sheets 57; rectangle and square bars 52–53; round bars 53, *53*; solid sections 52–55; tees 55; textured sheets 57; track 60–61, *61*; trim 53, *53*; zees 55

aluminum specifics (shaping) 218–219, *219–220*; bending aluminum sheet 218, *219*; notched corners 219, *219–220*
aluminum tubing 49–50, *51*; rectangular tube 50; round tube 50; square tube 50, *50*
aluminum wire cloth 59–60
American cut files 82, *82*
American Standard beams 54
American Standard threads 270
angles 36; aluminum 53
annular cutters 179, *179*
application methods for paint 233–234, *234*; aerosol cans 234; brushes 234; faux finishing 234–235; sprayers 233–234, *234*
arbor press 91
assemblies 220–227, *220–227*; contoured surfaces 223–225, *224–226*; flats 220–221, *220–221*; platforms 221–222, *221–222*; spans 226–227, *227*; stairs 222–223, *222–223*
assembly tips 227–230, *228–229*; attachment *228–229*, 228–230; holding components in place for welding 228; keeping units true 227–228
auto-darkening helmets 275
auxiliary machines: dust collection 124; fume extraction 124, *124*
aviation snips 63, *64*

ball peen hammers 66
bandsaw blade types 183
bar grating 43, 58
bars: aluminum 52–53; steel 35
bar truss platforms 221
bead blasting 130; ceramic beads 130; glass beads 130; plastic bead 130
bearing bronze 23
benders 69–70, *69–70*, 206–209, *206–209*; conduit 70, 206,

206; draw 206–207, *207*; hand bending 209, *209*; Hossfeld 207, *207–208*; kerf cutting 210, *210*; roll bending 208, *208*; rounded corners 209, *209*; round tapers 210; scroll 70; shop-made bending jigs 70; wire bending jigs 70, *70*
bending and shaping machine 117–120, *117–120*; bead roller 118, *118*; die bender 119, *119*; hydraulic press 119, *119*; planishing hammer 119; powered brake 120, *120*; power slip roll 118, *118*; roll bender 117, *117*
bending techniques 216–217, *216–217*; rings 216, *216–217*; S-hooks 217, *217*; twisting bar 216, *216*
bits and blades *177–183*, 177–184; annular cutters 179, *179*; arbors 180; blades 182–184, *183*; counter-bore 180; counter sink 180, *180*; drill and impact accessories 182, *182*; hole enlarging 179; hole saws 179–180; reamer *181*, 181–182; rotary cutters 179, *179*; step drills *178*, 178–179; straight flute drills 178; twist drills *177*, 177–178
blacksmithing tools 70–71, *71*; anvils 70; swage blocks 70; tongs 70
bodily protection 271–273; clothing 272; eye protection 272–273; footwear 272; gloves 271–272; head protection 272; hearing protection 273
brakes 210–212, *211–213*; box (or pan) brakes 211, *211–212*; gooseneck dies 212, *212–213*
brazing and soldering 156–159; advantages 157;

disadvantages 157; filler rods for 157; metals for 157; soldering 158–159, *159*; technique 157–158; TIG 158, *158*; torch brazing (OAF) 157–158, *158*
bronze 23
butt-welding: clamps 72; thick steel sections 198, *198*

capillary sprayers 233
cap screws 163–164
carbide burrs 188–189
carbide scribes 7
cast iron 19–20, *20*; ductile 20; gray 20; malleable 20
center finder 9
chain 46–47, *47*; flat link chains 47; graded chain 46; jack chain 47; lamp chain 47; utility chain 46–47; welded link 46; wire chain 47
channels: aluminum 54, *55*; bar-size channels 37; junior channels 37; standard channels 37, *37*; steel 37–38
chemical removal: of oxidation 128; of rust 128
chisels 68, *68*; cape 68; cold 68; diamond point 68; round nose and cross cut 68
chucks (lathe) 262
clamping 133–134
clamps *72–73*, 72–74; butt-welding clamps 72; cantilever 72; C-clamps 72; F-style clamps 72; quick locking 72; rack 74; Strong Hand Tools 72; toggle 72, *73*, 74
clear coats (non-paint) 238, *238*; drying oils 238; waxes 238
cold bending solids 203–206, *203–206*; bending fork 203, *203*; hammer forming 203, *204*; Hossfeld benders *204*, 204–205; kerf cutting 205–206, *205–206*; roll bender 205, *205*; scroll benders 205,

295

205; shaping tube 206–210, *206–210*
cold cutting saw *106*, 106–107; blades 182
colorants 235–236, *235–236*; dyes and patinas 236, *236*; reactive 235
commercial forms and processes of steel and aluminum: casting 13; drawing 14; extruding 14; forging 13–14; rolling 14
commonalities of welding processes: compressed gas cylinders 132–133; controlling heat 131, *131*; edge preparation 130; ergonomics 132; filler metals 133; joint types 132; position of weld 132, *132*; techniques 133–136, *134–135*; tips for perfect welding 131; visual properties of the finished weld 131–132; welding circuits 132; weld properties 130–132, *131*
compressed gas cylinders 132–133
contoured surfaces 223–225, *224–226*; flat bar 223, 225; rod and mesh 223; small metal shapes 225
controlling heat 131, *131*
coped joints 197, *197–198*
coping template 7, *7*
copper and copper alloys 20–24, *22–24*
copper, working with: annealing 230, *230*; shaping 231–232, *231–232*; soldering 230–231, *230–231*; spinning 232
corrugated sheets *40*, 40–41
counter-bore 180
counter sink 180, *180*
crew responsibilities 285–286; attire 286; communication 286; haste 285; impairment 286; interactions between workers 286; no smoking or vaping 286; solo work 285–286
crew training and awareness 285–286; crew responsibilities 285–286; lifting and carrying 286; machine function 286; Occupational Safety and Health Administration (OSHA) training 285
cross peen and straight peen hammers 66
cutters 250–252, *251–252*; angle cutters 251–252, *252*; ball mills 252; carbide insert end mills 251; dovetail cutters 252; end mills 250–251; facing mills 251; fly cutters 251; forming cutters 252; gear tooth cutters 252; keyseat/woodruff cutters 251; slot drills 251, *251*; slotting and/or sawing 252

cutters, lathe work 263–264, *264–265*; boring bars 264; general turning cutters 263; knurling tools 264; parting tools 263; thread cutting tools 263–264
cutting, manual machines 85–87, *85–87*; bench shears 85, *85*; corner notcher 87, *87*; iron worker 87; shears 85; slotted angle shears 86, *86*; stomp shears 86, *86*; throatless shears 85, *85*; tubing notcher 87
cutting, shearing and punching in power tools: abrasive saw 94, *94*; air saw 97, *97*; cut-off tool 96, *96*; drills 98; dry cut saw 93, *94*; magnetic drill press 98, *98*; metal cutting circular saw 94, *94*; miter saw 95, *95*; nibbler 96, *96*; portable bandsaw 95, *95*; power tools 93–98; throatless single cut shear 97, *97*; tubing notcher 97, *98*
cutting, shearing and punching machinery 105–117; cold cutting saw *106*, 106–107; drill press *112–113*, 112–114; horizontal bandsaw 107–108, *107–108*; iron worker 111–112, *112*; lathe 115–116, *115–116*; mill 114–115, *114–115*; semi-synthetic fluid 106; shears 110–111, *111*; soluble oil 106; stationary abrasive saw 107, *107*; synthetic fluid 106; vertical bandsaw 108–110, *109–110*
cutting tools (hand) 63–64, *63–64*

damaged fastener removers 78, *78*; broken bolt removers 78, *78*; pipe wrenches 78, *78*; screw extractors 78, *78*
dead-blow hammers 66, 66–67
depth gauge 4, *4*
dial indicator 5
die bender 119, *119*
dies 80, *80*; pipe 80; split 80; standard 80
dimple dies 65
divider 5, *6*
drill and impact accessories 182, *182*; damaged screw removers 182; magnetic nut drivers 182; socket adapters 182
drill chucks 262
drilling 254–255, *255*; countersinks and counterbores 255; piloting 254; reams 255; spot 255
drill press *112–113*, 112–114
drills for tapping 178
durability of metal 1–2

electrical pliers 81, *81*
electrical safety 125–126

employee safety 271–281; fire safety 278–279; Personal Protective Equipment (PPE) 274–278, 271–277; shop safety 279, 279–281; tool operation and safety 271
end mill notchers 116, *117*
end mills 255–258; parallels 258, *258*; right angle blocks 257, *257*; slotting 255–256, *256*; straight cuts 256, *256*; V-blocks 257–258, *257–258*
environmental protection 274–275; lead 274; welding fumes 274–275
equipment, first aid 280–281; AEDs 281; burn treatment 280; eye wash 281; ice packs 280; OSHA-approved first aid kits 280; quick clotting powder 280; wound closures 280
expanded aluminum sheet 59
expanded steel 41, *42*, 192, *192*
extruded aluminum platforms 221–222
eye protection 272–273; face shields 273; glasses and goggles 273; welding face shields 275

fasteners: adhesives 173; general safety considerations 173–175; hardware 172–173; non-threaded fasteners 169–172, *169–172*; threaded fasteners 163–169, *164*, *166*, *168–169*
fastening 77–78; damaged fastener removers 78, *78*; rivet buck 77; rivet gun 77, *77*; rivet nut gun 77, *77*; steel stud tools 77–78
files 81–82; file cards 82; file handles 82
filler metals (general properties) 133; FCAW (steel) 141; MIG (steel) 139; other alloys 148; SMAW (steel) 154; TIG (aluminum) 147; TIG (steel) 146
finishing and preservation techniques 232–238, *234–238*; aging 237, 237–238; clear coats (non-paint) 238, *238*; colorants 235–236, *235–236*; painting 232–235; physical techniques 236, *236*
finishing power tools 99–104; air file 101, *102*; angle grinder 101, *101*; bench grinder 99, *100*; die grinder 102, *102*; drill sharpener 104, *104*; flex-shaft tool 103, *103*; pencil grinder 102, *103*; pipe finisher 101; rotary tool 102; surfacing drum 104
finishing tool (hand) 81–82, *82*

fire safety 126, 278–279; extinguishers 278–279; extinguisher types 279; flammable storage 279; location of extinguishers 279
first aid 280–281; equipment 280–281; training 280
flap wheels 187
forming dies 68–69, *69*; dapping punch and block sets 69; dollies 68, *69*; shot bags 69

Gas Tungsten Arc Welding (GTAW) 142–149, *143*, *144*, *146–148*; advantages 142; aluminum specifics 146–148, *147–148*; bronze, copper and brass 148, *148*; cast iron 148; disadvantages 142; stainless steel 148; steel specifics 145–146, *146*; techniques 143–145, *144*; torch type 142, *143*; ventilation for 145
gas welding (OAF) *149*, 149–152, *151–152*; advantages 149; disadvantages 150; gas saver 152, *152*; safety particulars 150; torch setup 150; torch welding 150–151; types of flame 151, *151*
general safety considerations 173–175; adhesive transfer tape 175; anaerobic 174; automotive seam sealer 175; cyanoacrylate (CA) 174; epoxies 173–174; household cement 174; mastic 174; polyester resin filler 174–175; PSA tapes 175
general shop practices 283–285, *284*; ergonomics 284; guests 285; lighting 284; maintenance 285; material storage 283–284; music 284–285; sanitation 283; slips 283; trips 283
gloves 271–272, 276, *276*; fabric 271–272; leather 272; MIG welding 276; stick welding 276; TIG welding 276
grating *42*, 42–43; aluminum 58–60, *59*
gravity fed sprayers 233, *234*
grinders 120–122, *120–122*; belt grinders 121, *121*; disc grinders 121, *122*; horizontal belt grinders 121, *121*; pedestal grinder 120, *120*; stationary grinders 120; vertical belt grinders 121, *121*
grinding and finishing machine 120–123, *120–123*; abrasive blasting 122–123, *122–123*; grinders 120–122, *120–122*; polishers 122, *122*

hammers 65–67; ball peen 66; cross peen and straight peen 66; dead-blow 66,

66–67; shaping 67, 67; texturing 67, 67
hand grinder wheels 184–187, *185–187*; combined wheels 185; cut-off wheels 184; fiber discs 185–186, *186*; grinding wheels 185, *185*; non-woven polishing discs 186; stripping discs 186, *186*; wire wheels and cup brushes 186, *187*
hand work and tools (machining) 243–246, *243–246*; bench block 243, *243*; bench vise 244, *244*; broaching 245, *246*; cutting tools 63–64, *63–64*; drilling 245, *245*; filing 244, *244*; reaming 245, *245*; shaping tools 64–71
hardware 172–173; finishing ends 172; magnetic hardware 173; threaded tube inserts 172, *172*; weld-on hinges 173, *173*
head protection 272
heat safety 126
High-Speed Steel (HSS): drill bits 178; scribes 7, *8*
holders for taps 79; dual handle tap holders 79; hand tappers 79; self-aligning tap holders 79; sets of socket adapters 79; sliding T-handle holders 79; twist drills 79
hollow sections of aluminum 49–52; pipe 51; pipe clamps 51, *52*; pipe fittings 52; tubing 49–50, *51*
hollow sections of steel 25–35; square and rectangular 25–27, *26*, *27*
horizontal bandsaw 107–108, *107–108*
horizontal belt grinders 121, *121*
HVLP (High Volume, Low Pressure) sprayers 233
hydraulic press 91, *91*, 119, *119*

I-beams 36–37; aluminum 54; and channels 226
internal threading 268–269
iron worker 111–112, *112*

jig saws 183–184
joints 196–200, *196–200*; angle iron corners 196; coped 197, *197–198*; dies 202–203, *203*; notch and bend 197; plasma cutting 201–202, *201–202*; threading 202–203, *202–203*; welding carts for MIG welders 200, *200*

knock-out punches 64–65, *65*

lathe 115–116, *115–116*
lathe parts 262–263; bed 263; carriage 263; chucks 262; collets 262; drive mechanisms 262; face plates 262; head stock

houses 262; lathe dog 262–263; lead screw 262; steady rest for metal 263; tailstock 263
lathe work 261–270; cutters (*see* cutters, lathe work); machines (*see* lathe work machines); techniques (*see* lathe work techniques); threads (*see* lathe work threads)
lathe work machines 261–264, *261–265*; belt-driven lathes 261; cutters 263–264, *264–265*; electronic variable speed units 261; geared head lathes 261–262; lathe parts 262–263; sizes 262; types 261–262
lathe work techniques 265–270, *265–270*; boring 269, *269*; drilling 269, *269*; facing 267, 267–268; knurling 269, *270*; measuring and marking 265, *265*; mounting material 266, *266–267*; parting off 268, *268*; straight cuts 267, *267*; threading 268–269, *269–270*
lathe work threads 270, *270*; bolt threads 270; cutting and repairing thread 270; machine threads 270; pipe threads 270; thread types 270
letter/number stamps 68
locking nuts 165; castellated 165; deformed 165; extreme vibration 165; flange lock 165; nylon- 165; tooth washer 165
lock washers 167

machine setup (milling) 252–254, *253–254*; finding the edge of the material 253, *253–254*; setting tool depth 254
machining: dividers 241, *242*; feeler gauges 243; hand work and tools 243–246, *243–246*; Jenny calipers 241–242, *242*; lathe work 261–270; layout and measuring 241–243, *242–243*; machinist angle blocks 243; manual tasks 241; milling metal 246–261; punches 243; scribes 243; setup blocks 243; sliding calipers 242–243; spring calipers 242
machinist vises 248–249, *249*; alignment of the vise 249; jaw rise and twist 249
magnetic tools 76, 76–77; magnetic angles 76, *76*; magnetic grounding devices 76; magnetic torch rests 76–77; spring finger 76; tab holders 76; tubing holders 76; wooden jigs 77

making components 194–203, *194–203*; flanged seam 196, *196*; joints 196–200, *196–200*; lapped seam 194, *195*; sheet metal 194, 210–215, *211–215*; stick welding 194; testing welds 194; TIG and OAF welding 194; welding spoons 194, *195*; welding techniques *194–195*, 194–196
manually cutting threads 268
manual machines: cutting 85–87, *85–87*; presses 91; shaping 87–90, *87–90*
manual reamers 181–182
manual tap and die 79; bolt tap 79; bottoming taps 79; lamp tube taps 79; pipe taps 79; plug taps 79; taper taps 79
marking and layout tools 6–11, *6–11*
material holding 248–250, *248–250*; accessories 249–250; angle vises 249; hold down set 248; machinist vises 248–249, *249*; right angle blocks 250; rotary tables 250; self-positioning hold downs 248; shop-made hold downs 250, *250*
material prep for welding 127–130; abrasive blasting 128–130; aluminum 128; steel 127–128, *127–128*
measuring for metal working 2–6, *2–6*
metal alloys 13–24; aluminum 16–17; commercial forms and processes of steel aluminum and steel 13–24; copper and copper alloys 20–24, *22–24*; ordering metal 24; stainless steel 18, *18–19*; steel 14–16; weathering steel 19
metal-framed flats 220–221, *220–221*
metal-framed platforms 221–222, *221–222*
metal inert gas (MIG) welding *136–141*, 136–142; advantages 137; aluminum specifics 139–140, *140*; drawbacks 137; features 137–138; flux-cored specifics (FCAW) 141, *141*; other considerations 137; stainless steel 140–141, *141*; steel specifics 139, *139*; techniques 138–139, *138–139*
metric thread bolts 164
MIG welding gloves 276, *276*
mild steel 15–16; 1018 15; 1045 15; A15 16; A36 15; A53 16; A500 15; M1020 15; MT 1010 and 1020 15
mill 114–115, *114–115*
mill/drill style machines 246–247
milling metal 246–261; cutters 250–252, *251–252*; machines

246–254, *247–254*; machine setup 252–254; machine types 246–247; material holding 248–250, *248–250*; mill parts *247*, 247–248; techniques 254–261, *255–264*
milling techniques 254–261, *255–264*; chamfering 259, *259*; drilling 254–255, *255*; end mills 255–258; keyways 260; material setup 254; rotary table 260–261, *260–261*; surfacing *258*, 258–259; tapping 255, *255*
mill parts *247*, 247–248; bed 248; drawbar 247; DROs 248; head 247–248; lubrication 248; spindle *247*, 247–248; tool holding 247
mounting material 266, *266–267*; center drills 266; collets 266; tailstock 266; three-jaw chuck 266

National Institute for Safety and Health (NIOSH) 287
National Pipe Thread (NPT) 80
Noise Reduction Rating (NRR) 273
non-threaded fasteners 169–172, *169–172*; pins 171–172, *172*; quick fasteners 169–170, *169–170*; retaining rings 170, *171*; screws 171, *171*
nuts 165–167, *166*; bolt and nut caps 167; constrained 166; hex 165; locking 165; special use 165–166; threaded fittings 166–167; threaded knobs and machine handles 166; weld 166

OAF cutting 159–160, *160*
OAF heating 160–161
Occupational Safety and Health Administration (OSHA) training 285

painting 232–235; application methods 233–234, *234*; clear "paints" 233; surface prep 232–233
pedestal grinder 120, *120*
Personal Protective Equipment (PPE) *274–278*, 271–277; bodily protection 271–273; in EU and UK 281; respiratory protection 273–275, *274*; welding 275–277, *275–278*
physical removal: of oxidation 128; of rust 128, *128*
physical safety 283–289; crew training and awareness 285–286; general shop practices 283–285, *284*; tool usage and maintenance 286–289, *288*; welding area specifics 287–289, *288*

pins 171–172, *172*; bridge 172; clevis 171; dowel 172; lynch 171–172; quick-release 171
pipe: aluminum 51; clamps 51, *52*; fittings 52; steel 30–31, *31*
pipe and tubing cutters 64, *64*
pipe fittings: aluminum 52; steel 31–34, *32–34*
pipe notchers 116–117, *117*
plasma cutting 155–156, 201–202, *201–202*; advantages 155; aluminum 156; disadvantages 155–156; MDF templates 202, *202*; stainless steel 156; steel 156; techniques 156
plate and sheet: aluminum 55–58, *56–58*; sheet metal 40–41; steel 39–41, *39–41*; thin plate *39*, 39–40
pliers 71, *71*; flanging 71; glass 71; seaming 71; wire forming 71
polishers 122, *122*
polishing 190, *190*; buffs for 190, *190*; rouge bars 190, *190*
power tools: cutting, shearing and punching 93–98; finishing tools 99–104; shaping 98–99
proprietary shapes of steel alloys 44–46, *44–46*; slotted angle 46, *46*; steel track 45; strut channel 44–45, *45*; telescopic tube 46
punches 67, *68*; center and prick 67; drift 67; pin 67; rolled pin 67
punching 213–215, *213–215*; hand punches 213, *213*; knock-out punches 213, *213*; press punches 214, *214*; ring rolling 215, *215*; shrinking and stretching sheet metal 215, *215*; using slip roll to make a cylinder or cone 214, *214–215*

quick fasteners 169–170, *169–170*; blind rivets 169, *169*; cleco pins 170; drive pin rivets 169; pins 171–172, *172*; quarter turn (AKA dzus fasteners) 170; retaining rings 170, *171*; screws 171, *171*; solid rivets 170; T-nails 170, *170*

reactive colorants 235; alumi-black 235; bluing 235; brass dark 235; copper and bronze patinas for steel 235; liver of sulfur 235; plumb brown 235
reamer *181*, 181–182
rectangular bar 35–36
rectangular mechanical tubing 26
rectangular structural tubing 27, 221, 226
reference sources 291–293

respiratory protection 273–275, *274*; environmental protection 274–275; face-piece masks 274; powered Air-Purifying Respirators (PAPRs) 274; supplied-air respirators 274
reverse twist drills 178
rod ends 168
roll bender 117, *117*
rotary cutters 179, *179*
rotary table 260–261, *260–261*; dividing plates 260; tailstock 260
rotary tool abrasives 188–190, *189–190*; carbide burrs 188–189; diamond points 189; flexible abrasives 189; non-woven buffs for rotary tools 190; sanding cones 189; stem-mounted wheels and brushes 189; stone points 189
round bar 35
round tube: aluminum 50; steel 27–28, *28*
rust 128

safety footwear standards 272
sanding and grinding: aluminum oxide 184; ceramic alumina 184; cloth media 184; consumables 184–190; diamond 184; emery 184; grinding belts 188; grit 184; hand grinder wheels 184–187, *185–187*; media 184; polishing 190, *190*; rotary tool abrasives 188–190, *189–190*; silicon carbide 184; stationary grinder wheels 187, *188*; zirconia alumina 184
screws 171, *171*; self-drilling 171; self-sealing 171; self-tapping 171; sheet metal 171
scribe 7
shaded safety glasses 275, *275*
shaping components 203–215, *203–215*; cold bending solids 203–206, *203–206*
shaping hand tools 64–71; benders 69–70, *69–70*; blacksmithing tools 70–71, *71*; chisels 68, *68*; forming dies 68–69, *69*; hammers 65–67; letter/number stamps 68; punches 64–65, *65*, *67*, *68*; stakes 69, *69*
shaping manual machines 87–90, *87–90*; bead roller 90; brake 88, *89*; English wheel 90, *90*; Hossfeld 87; manual tubing roller 88; pipe bender 87, *87*; shrinker and stretcher 90, *90*; slip roll 88, *88*
shaping power tools 98–99; air hammer 98–99, *99*; flanger 98; needle scaler 99, *99*; planisher 99; pneumatic riveter 99

shaping tube 206–210, *206–210*; benders 206–209, *206–209*
shears 110–111, *111*; bar and rod 110, *111*; sheet 110, *111*
sheet metal 40–41, 210–215, *211–215*; brakes 210–212, *211–213*; hammers 67; screws 171
Shielded Metal Arc Welding (SMAW) 153–154, 153–155
shop safety 279, 279–281; first aid 280–281; hazardous waste 279, 279–280
soldering 158–159, *159*
solid sections of aluminum 52–55
solid sections of steel alloys 35–47; angles 36; bars 35; chain 46–47; channels 37–38; plate and sheet 39–41, *39–41*; proprietary shapes 44–46, *44–46*; special sheets and similar products 41–43; tees 38–39
spaced-frame platforms 221
spans 226–227, *227*; I-beams and channels 226; rectangular tubing 226; steel bar truss 226; trusses 226
special use nuts 165–166; 12-point nuts 165–166; push-button nuts 165; push nuts 166; slotted round nuts 166; split nuts 165; square nuts 166; tamper-resistant nuts 166; wing nuts 166
spot welding 152, *152*; advantages 152; disadvantages 152
sprayers 233–234, *234*; airless 234; capillary 233; gravity fed 233, *234*; HVLP 233; HVLP stand-alone systems 234; user fillable aerosol 234
square bar 35–36
square mechanical tubing 25–26
square structural tubing 27
S-shapes 37
stainless steel 18, *18–19*; 304 18; 316 18; 321 18; 416 18
stairs 222–223, *222–223*; channel and angle 223, *223*; combining rectangular tubing 222, *223*; rectangular tube 222, *222*; square tube 222, *222*
stair units 222, *222*
stationary abrasive saw 107, *107*
stationary grinders 120
stationary grinder wheels 187, *188*; flap wheels 187; non-woven abrasive wheels 187; polyurethane abrasive polishing w 187; stone wheels for bench grinders 187, *188*; wire wheels 187
steel 14–16; alloy selection aids 14–15; alloy steel 16; finishes 16; mild steel 15–16
steel alloys 14–15; carbon 14; chromium 15; copper 15;

lead 15; manganese 14–15; nickel 15
steel bar truss 226; *see also* wiggle wire
steel, material prep for 127–128, *127–128*; degreasing 127; descaling 127; rust 128
steel shapes and applications: conduit 28–29, *29*; ducting 35; hollow sections 25–35; pipe 30–31, *31*; pipe fittings 31–34, *32–34*; round tube 27–28, *28*; solid sections 35–47; steel studs 35
steel techniques 215–218, *216–218*; anvils 218; bending 216–217, *216–217*; peening 218; upsetting 217, *218*
stick welding (SMAW) 153–154, 153–155, 194; advantages 153; cast iron 154, *154*, 155; current mode 154; disadvantages 153; filler metals (sticks) 154; gloves 276, *276*; range of machine types *153*, 153–154; safety considerations 154; stainless steel and aluminum 154; steel welding 154; striking the arc 154; techniques 154–155
stitch welding 134, 194, *195*
structural angles 36

techniques: aluminum specifics 218–219, *219–220*; assemblies 220–227, *220–227*; assembly tips 227–230, *228–229*; finishing and preservation 232–238, *234–238*; making components 194–203, *194–203*; shaping components 203–215, *203–215*; steel 215–218, *216–218*; storage 193, *193*; welding tables and surfaces *191–192*, 191–193; working with copper 230–232, *230–232*
tees: aluminum 55; MT-types 39; steel 38–39; ST-types 39; WT-types 39
tees adjoined to angle 198, *198*
threaded fasteners 163–169; cap screws 163–164; hand screws 164, *164*; nuts 165–167, *166*; rod ends 168; set screws 164–165; studs 165; threaded inserts 168–169, *169*; U-bolts 168; washers 167–168, *168*
threaded inserts 168–169, *169*; press-fit nuts 168–169; repair inserts 169, *169*; rivet nuts 168; socket nuts 168
threaded knobs and machine handles 166
threading 202–203, *202–203*
threading tools 78–81, *80–81*; manual tap and die 79; thread gauges 78, *79*
thread repair 80–81; thread files 80–81; thread restorers 80,

INDEX • 299

81; universal thread repair tools 81
TIG brazing 158, *158*; advantages 158; disadvantages 158; techniques 158
tool usage and maintenance 286–289, *288*; control of materials 287; hand/body placement 287; motion injuries 287; power cords and air hoses 287; safety mechanisms 286–287; team operation 287
trim, aluminum 53, *53*
trusses 226
T-slot framing 60, *60*
Tungsten inert gas (TIG) welding *see* Gas Tungsten Arc Welding (GTAW)
twist drills *177*, 177–178

ultraviolet (UV) safety 126

vernier (sliding) caliper 5, *5*
vertical bandsaw 108–110, *109–110*
vertical belt grinders 121, *121*
vises 74–75, *74–76*; accessories for 75; bench 74; brakes 75; fractal 75; machinist 75; pipe 74; post-style 75; soft jaws 75, *76*; standard machinist 75; tilting and rotating 75, *75*

washers 167–168, *168*; adhesive backed 168; conical 167; flat 167; leveling 167; lock 167; oversized 167; retaining 167; slip 167; square 167; tag holders 167; wedge 167
weathering steel 19; A242 19; A588 19
welders and welding processes 136
welding and related processes: brazing and soldering 156–159; commonalities of 130–136; Gas Tungsten Arc Welding (GTAW) 142–149, *143*, *144*, *146–148*; gas welding (OAF) 149, 149–152, *151–152*; general welding safety 125–126, *126*; material prep for welding 127–130; metal inert gas (MIG) welding 136–141, 136–142; OAF cutting 159–160, *160*; OAF heating 160–161; plasma cutting 155–156; resistance 152, *152*; stick welding (SMAW) 153–*154*, 153–155; welders 136
welding area specifics (safety) 287–289, *288*; compressed gases 288; electrical safety 287–288; flash protection 289; heat 288; sparks 288; welding blankets 289
welding PPE 275–277, *275–278*; aprons 276; boots 276, *277*; gloves 276, *276*; goggles 275; helmet 275, *275*; helmet accessories 276; jacket *276*, 276–277; pants 276, *277*; spats 276, *277*
welding safety 125–126, *126*; electrical safety 125–126; fire safety 126; heat safety 126; ultraviolet (UV) safety 126
welding tables and surfaces: bar type 192–193; expanded steel 192, *192*; fixture 192, *192*; portable 193; solid top 191–192; techniques *191–192*, 191–193
welding techniques 133–136, *134–135*; coupons and scrap material 134, *134*; direction of travel 135; distortion 133–134; grounding 133; joining dissimilar thicknesses 135; position of weld 134, *135*; repairing cracks 135–136; venting 135
welding tools 83, *84*; bottle wrench 83; chipping hammer 83; MIG pliers 83, *84*; plug welding pliers 83; spoon 83, 194, *195*; tip cleaners 83; welding guides 83; wire brush 83
weld sequencing 134
wide flange Army/Navy (AN) 54
wide flange beams 54
wiggle wire (truss) 226
wire mesh 43, *44*; decorative patterns 43; poultry mesh 43; rectangular mesh 43; square opening 43
work holding 71–77; clamps 72–73, 72–74; magnetic tools 76, 76–77; pliers 71, *71*; vises 74–75, *74–76*
W-shapes 37

zees, aluminum 55

For Product Safety Concerns and Information please contact our EU
representative GPSR@taylorandfrancis.com
Taylor & Francis Verlag GmbH, Kaufingerstraße 24, 80331 München, Germany

www.ingramcontent.com/pod-product-compliance
Lightning Source LLC
Chambersburg PA
CBHW081800300426
44116CB00014B/2191